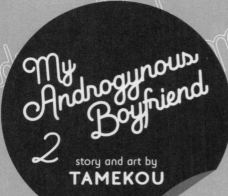

My Androgynous Boyfriend

2

story and art by

TAMEKOU

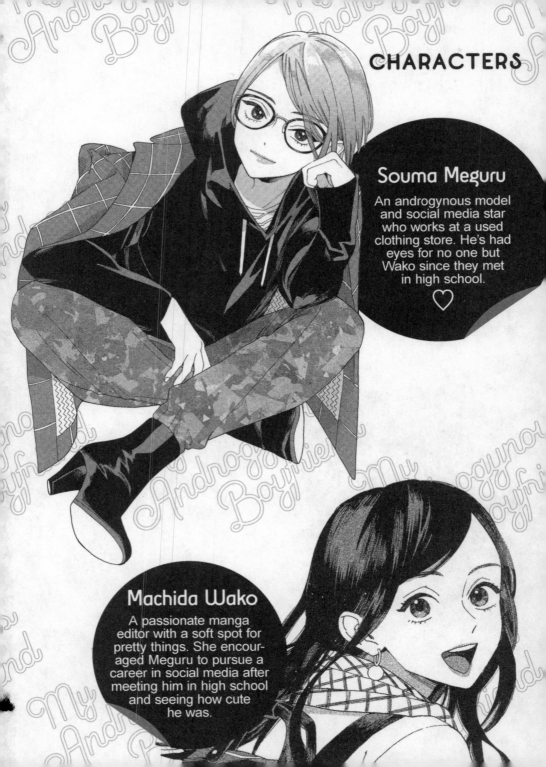

CHARACTERS

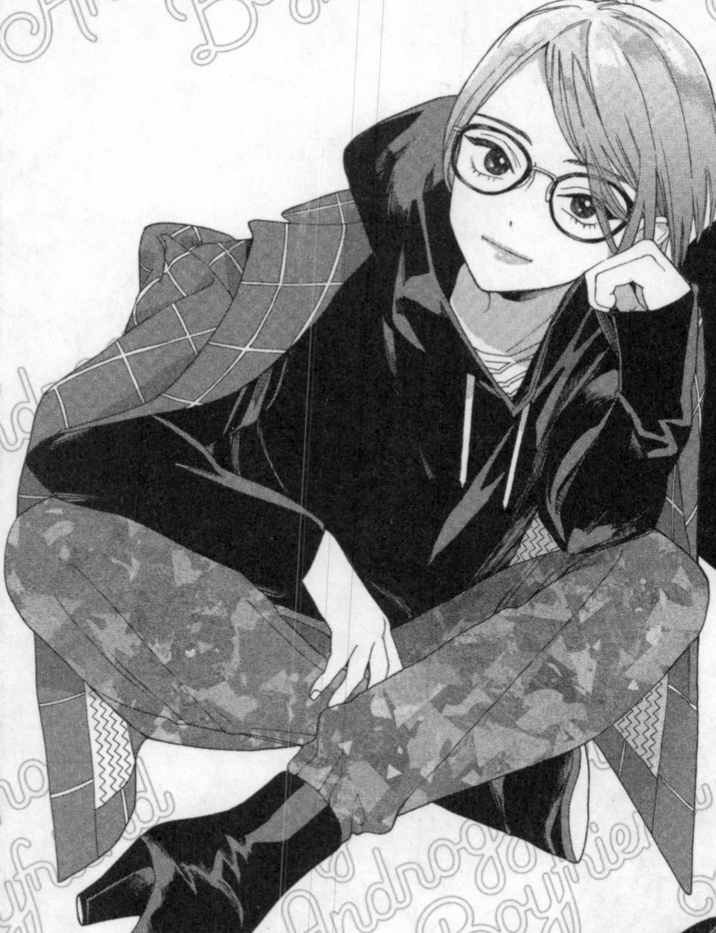

Souma Meguru

An androgynous model and social media star who works at a used clothing store. He's had eyes for no one but Wako since they met in high school.

♡

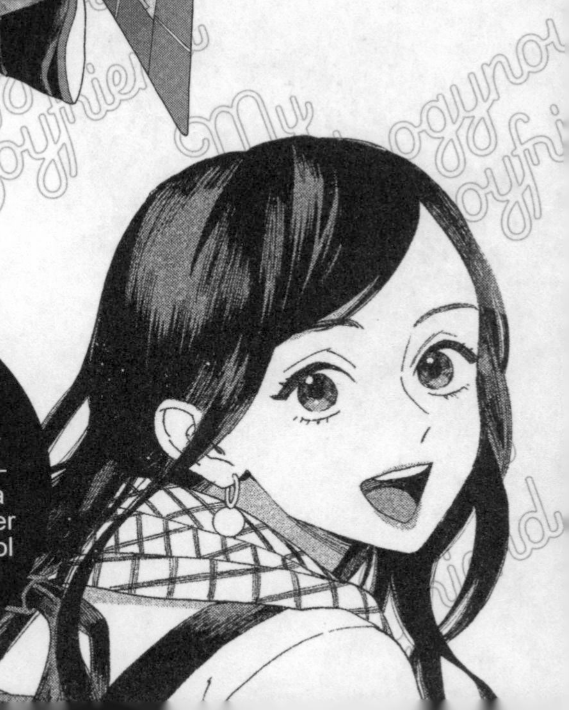

Machida Wako

A passionate manga editor with a soft spot for pretty things. She encouraged Meguru to pursue a career in social media after meeting him in high school and seeing how cute he was.

Kira

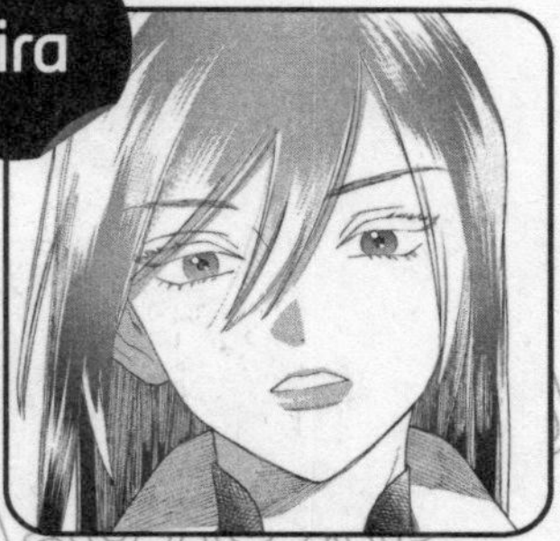

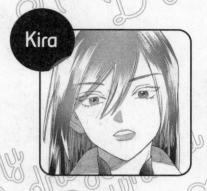

A model at the same agency as Meguru, this unique, androgynous man only pays attention to beautiful things.

Nanami

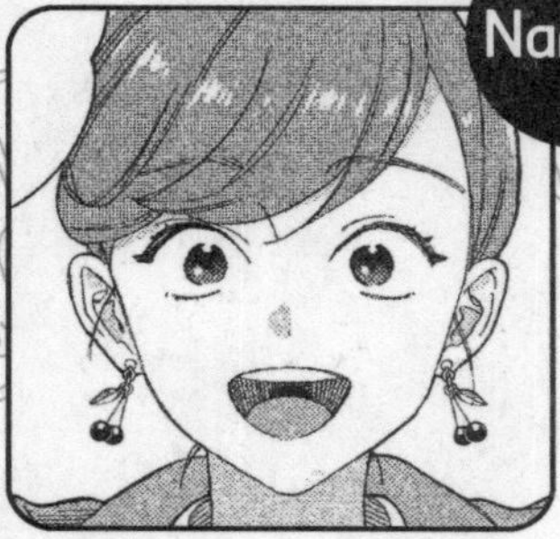

A junior editor who works with Wako. She thinks Meguru is Wako's girlfriend.

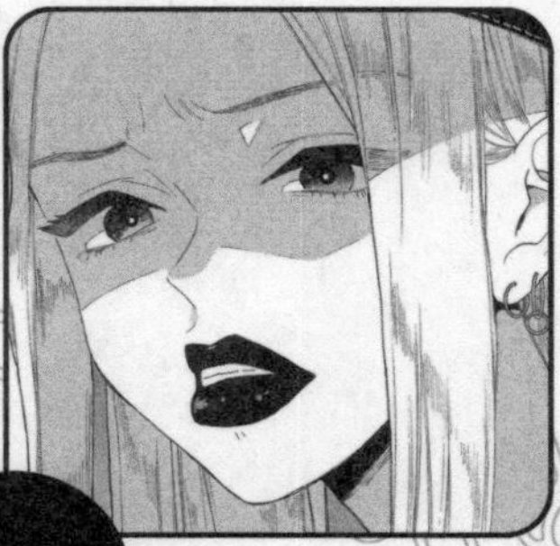

Boss

Manager of Yonto 1/5, the used clothing store where Meguru works.

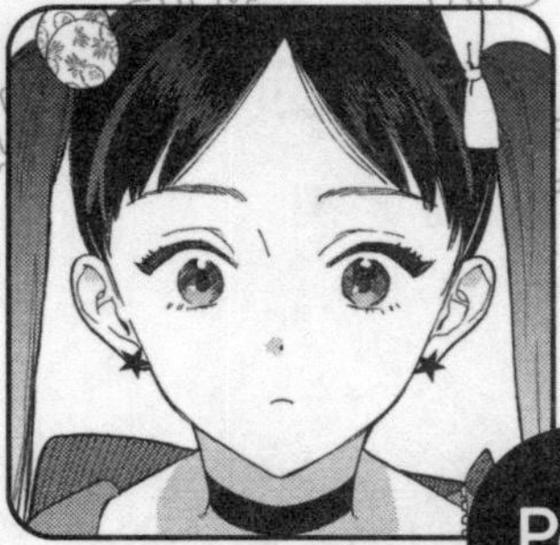

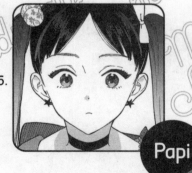

Papi

Clerk at Yonto 1/5.

STORY

From his makeup to his fingernails, Meguru is one hundred percent adorable—and androgynous! However, his girlfriend Wako is an ordinary office worker. She's his biggest fan, and he's always trying to better himself for her. This is the story of their sweet, love-filled life!

CONTENTS

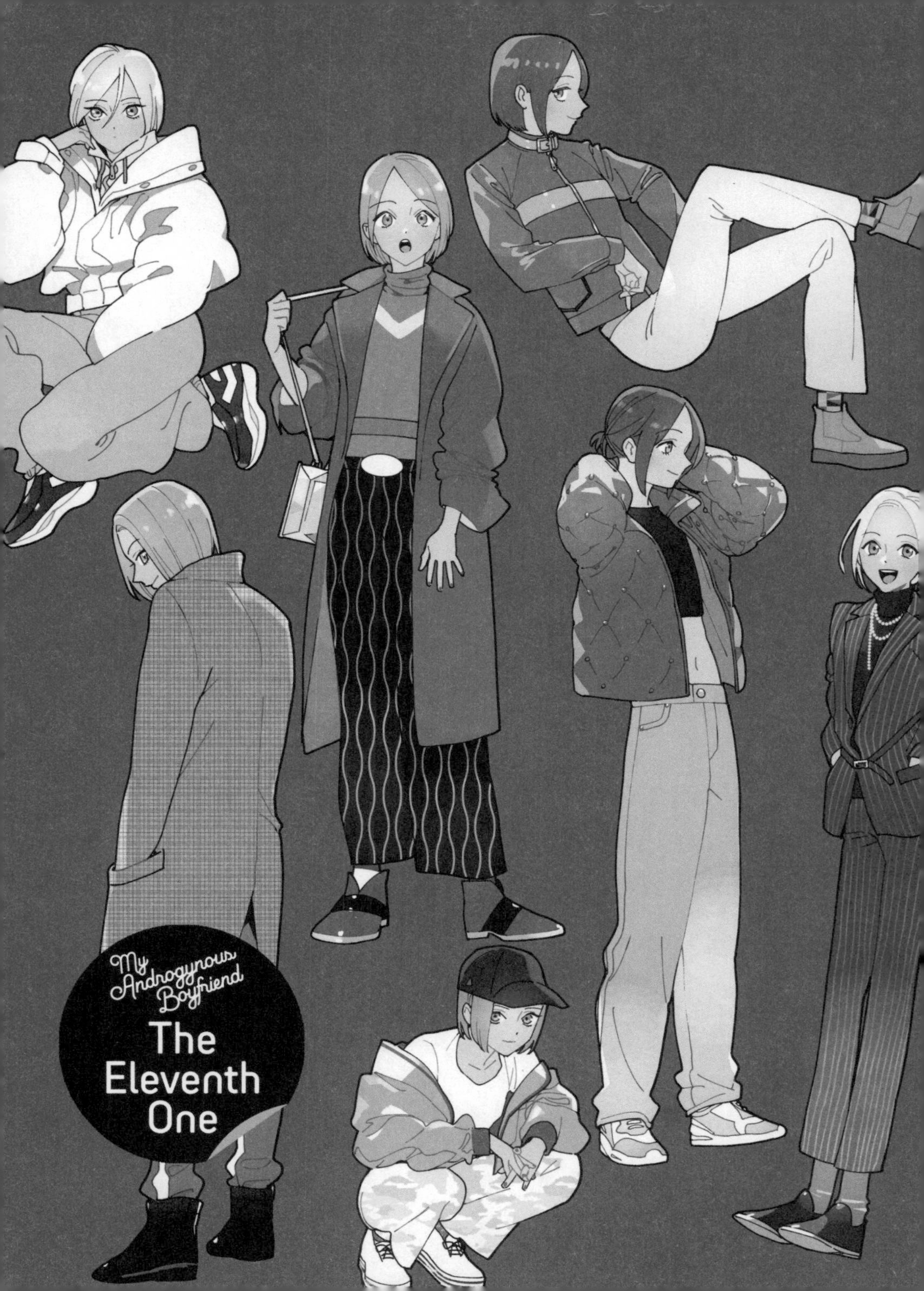
My Androgynous Boyfriend
The Eleventh One

My Androgynous Boyfriend

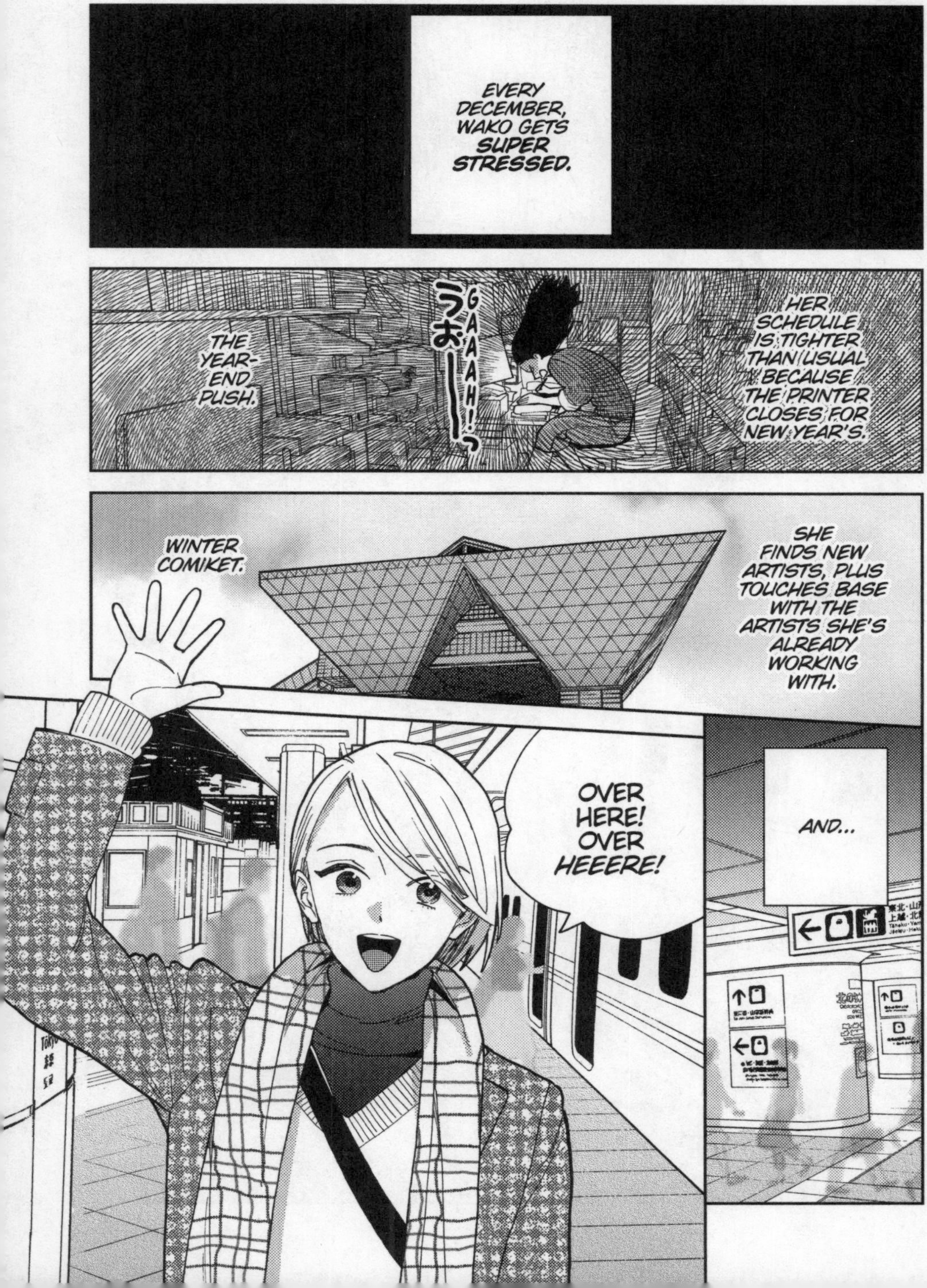
EVERY DECEMBER, WAKO GETS SUPER STRESSED.
HER SCHEDULE IS TIGHTER THAN USUAL BECAUSE THE PRINTER CLOSES FOR NEW YEAR'S.
うおーーっ
GAAAH!!
THE YEAR-END PUSH.
SHE FINDS NEW ARTISTS, PLUS TOUCHES BASE WITH THE ARTISTS SHE'S ALREADY WORKING WITH.
WINTER COMIKET.
AND...
OVER HERE! OVER HEEERE!

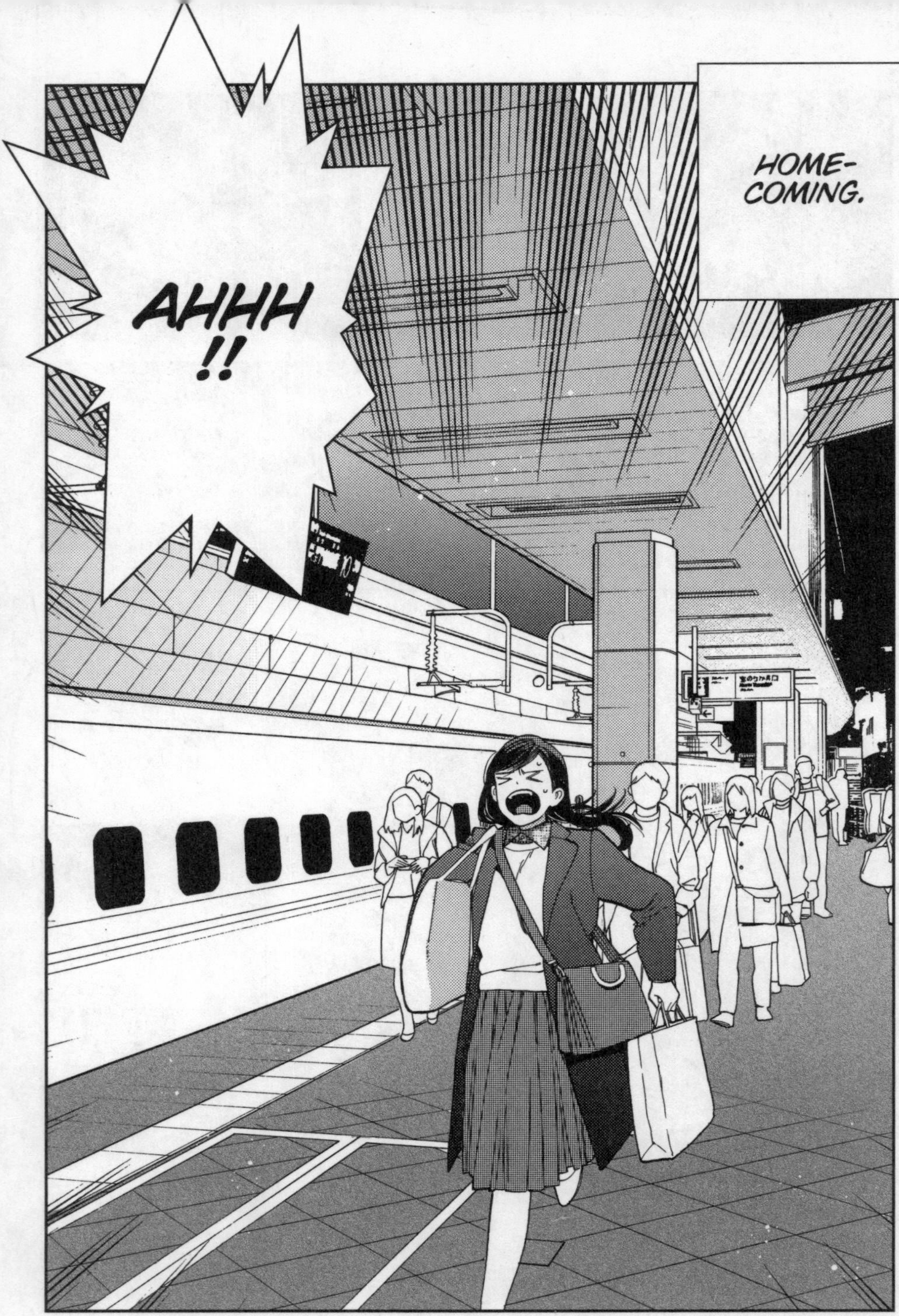
HOME-
COMING.
AHHH
!!

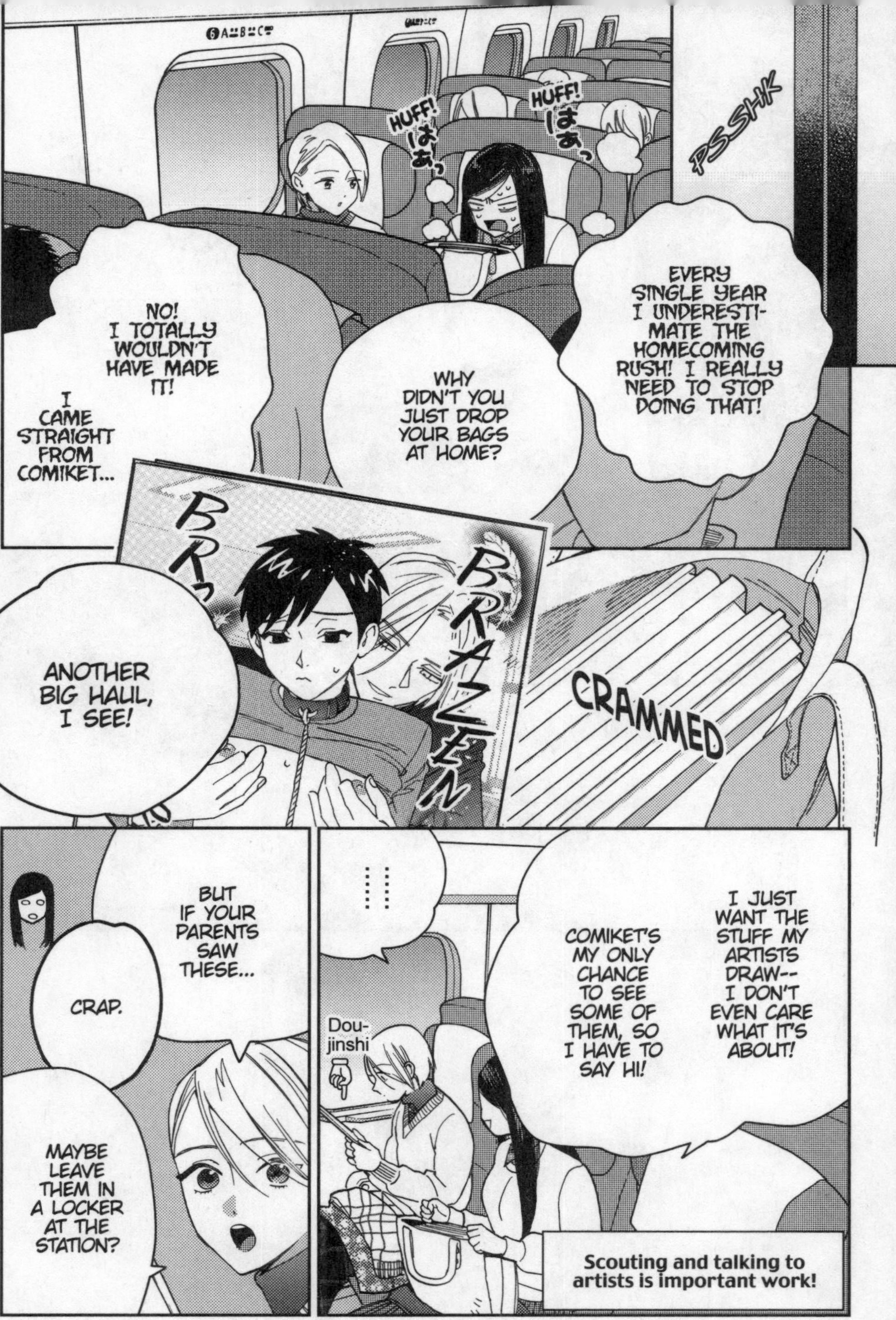
PSSHK
HUFF! はぁっ
HUFF! はぁっ
EVERY SINGLE YEAR I UNDERESTI-MATE THE HOMECOMING RUSH! I REALLY NEED TO STOP DOING THAT!
WHY DIDN'T YOU JUST DROP YOUR BAGS AT HOME?
NO! I TOTALLY WOULDN'T HAVE MADE IT!
I CAME STRAIGHT FROM COMIKET...
CRAMMED
BRAZEN
ANOTHER BIG HAUL, I SEE!
......
I JUST WANT THE STUFF MY ARTISTS DRAW-- I DON'T EVEN CARE WHAT IT'S ABOUT!
COMIKET'S MY ONLY CHANCE TO SEE SOME OF THEM, SO I HAVE TO SAY HI!
Doujinshi
Scouting and talking to artists is important work!
BUT IF YOUR PARENTS SAW THESE...
CRAP.
MAYBE LEAVE THEM IN A LOCKER AT THE STATION?

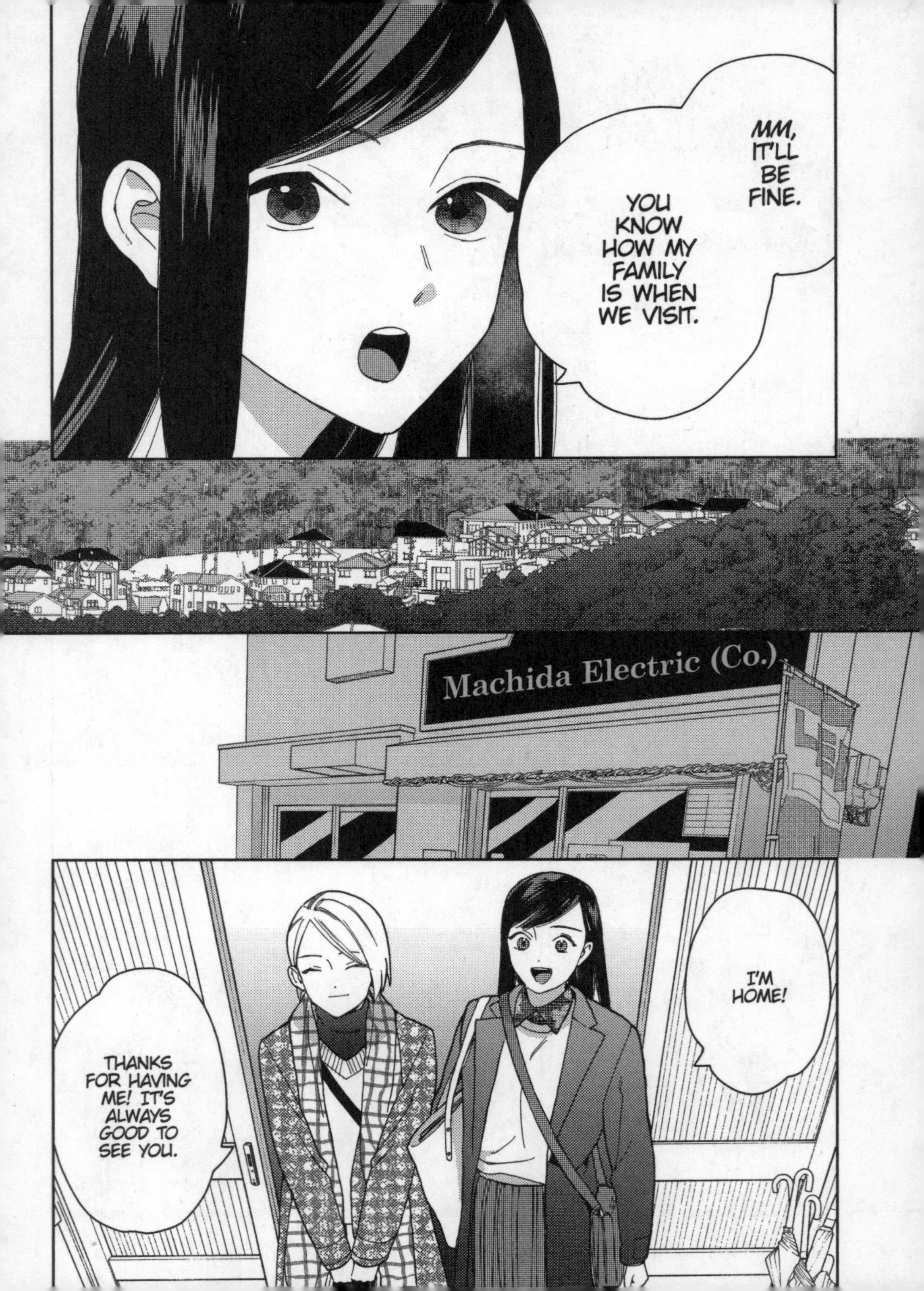
MM, IT'LL BE FINE.
YOU KNOW HOW MY FAMILY IS WHEN WE VISIT.
Machida Electric (Co.)
I'M HOME!
THANKS FOR HAVING ME! IT'S ALWAYS GOOD TO SEE YOU.

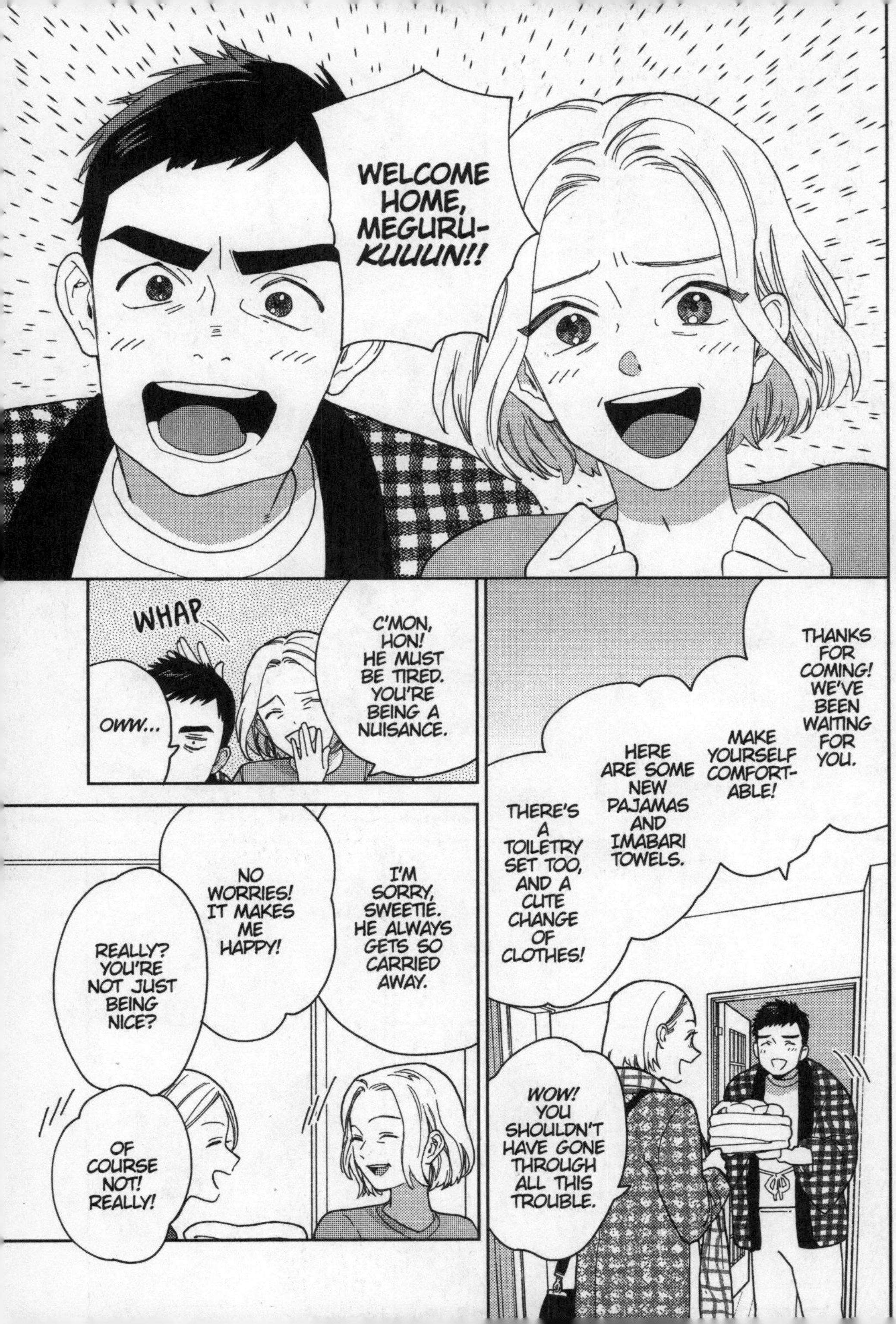
WELCOME HOME, MEGURU-KUUUN!!
THANKS FOR COMING! WE'VE BEEN WAITING FOR YOU.
MAKE YOURSELF COMFORT-ABLE!
HERE ARE SOME NEW PAJAMAS AND IMABARI TOWELS.
THERE'S A TOILETRY SET TOO, AND A CUTE CHANGE OF CLOTHES!
WOW! YOU SHOULDN'T HAVE GONE THROUGH ALL THIS TROUBLE.
WHAP
C'MON, HON! HE MUST BE TIRED. YOU'RE BEING A NUISANCE.
OWW...
I'M SORRY, SWEETIE. HE ALWAYS GETS SO CARRIED AWAY.
NO WORRIES! IT MAKES ME HAPPY!
REALLY? YOU'RE NOT JUST BEING NICE?
OF COURSE NOT! REALLY!

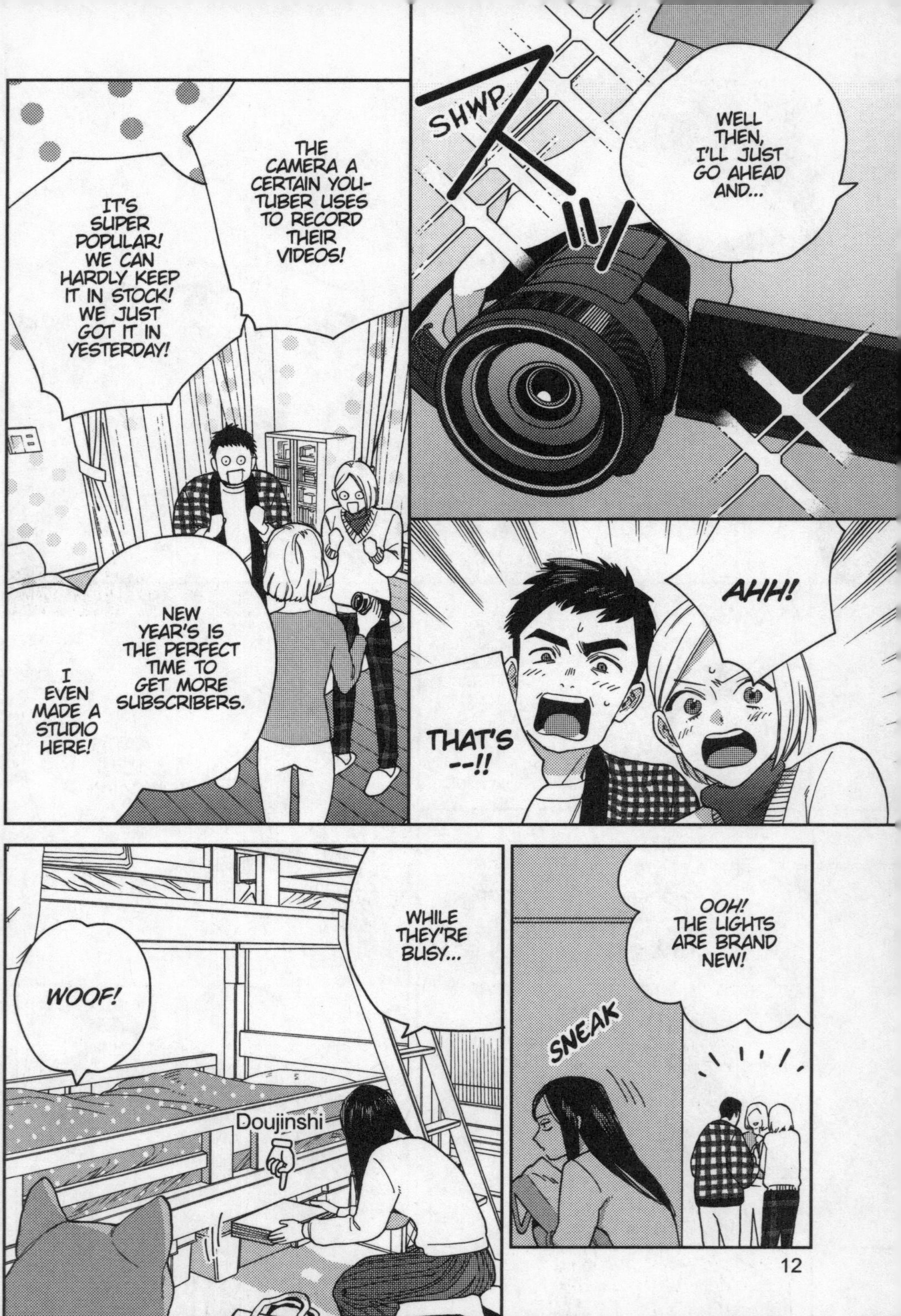
SHWP
WELL THEN, I'LL JUST GO AHEAD AND...
AHH!
THAT'S --!!
THE CAMERA A CERTAIN YOU-TUBER USES TO RECORD THEIR VIDEOS!
IT'S SUPER POPULAR! WE CAN HARDLY KEEP IT IN STOCK! WE JUST GOT IT IN YESTERDAY!
NEW YEAR'S IS THE PERFECT TIME TO GET MORE SUBSCRIBERS.
I EVEN MADE A STUDIO HERE!
OOH! THE LIGHTS ARE BRAND NEW!
SNEAK
WHILE THEY'RE BUSY...
WOOF!
Doujinshi

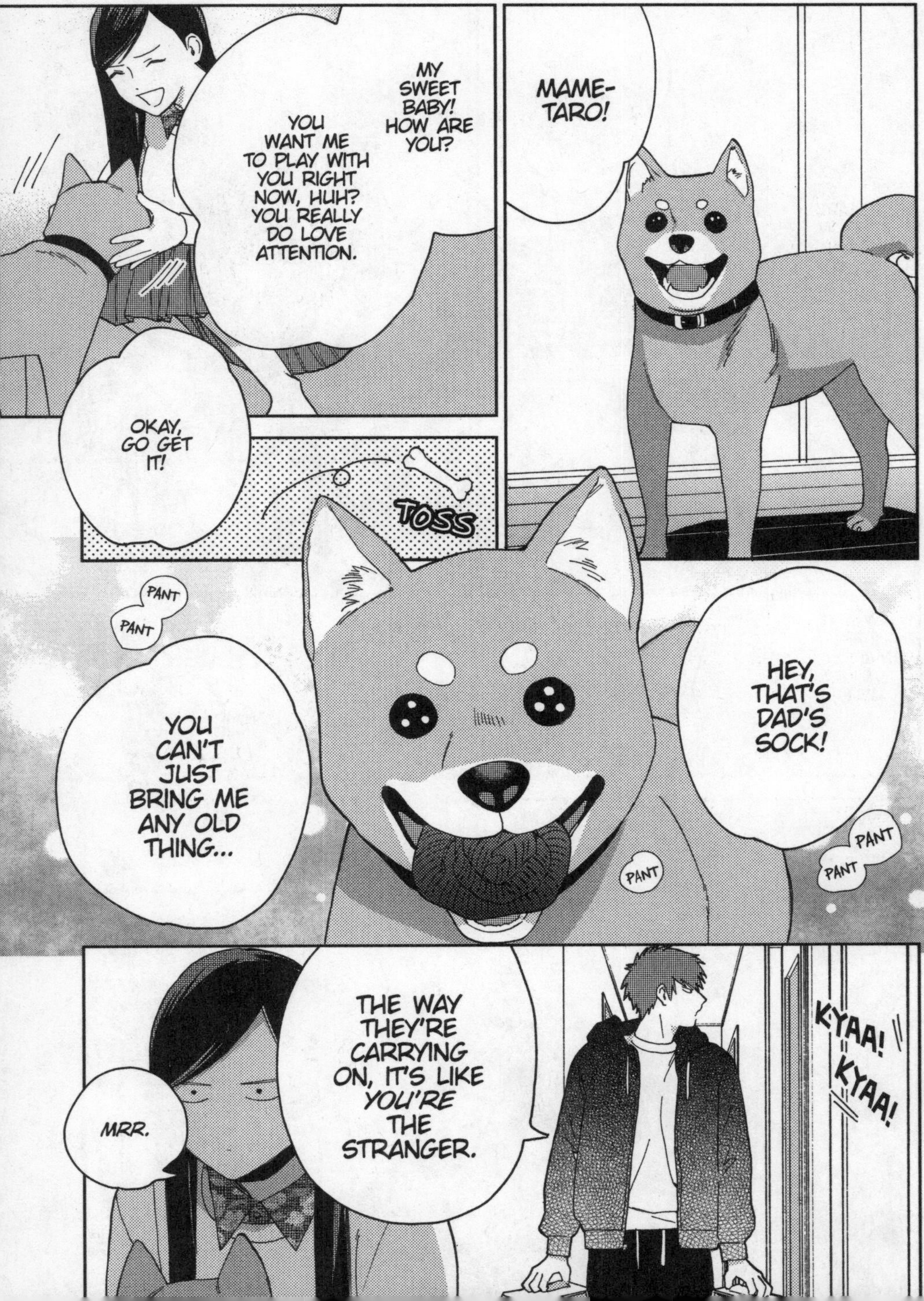
MAME-TARO!
MY SWEET BABY! HOW ARE YOU?
YOU WANT ME TO PLAY WITH YOU RIGHT NOW, HUH? YOU REALLY DO LOVE ATTENTION.
OKAY, GO GET IT!
TOSS
HEY, THAT'S DAD'S SOCK!
PANT PANT
PANT
PANT PANT
YOU CAN'T JUST BRING ME ANY OLD THING...
KYAA! KYAA!
THE WAY THEY'RE CARRYING ON, IT'S LIKE *YOU'RE* THE STRANGER.
MRR.

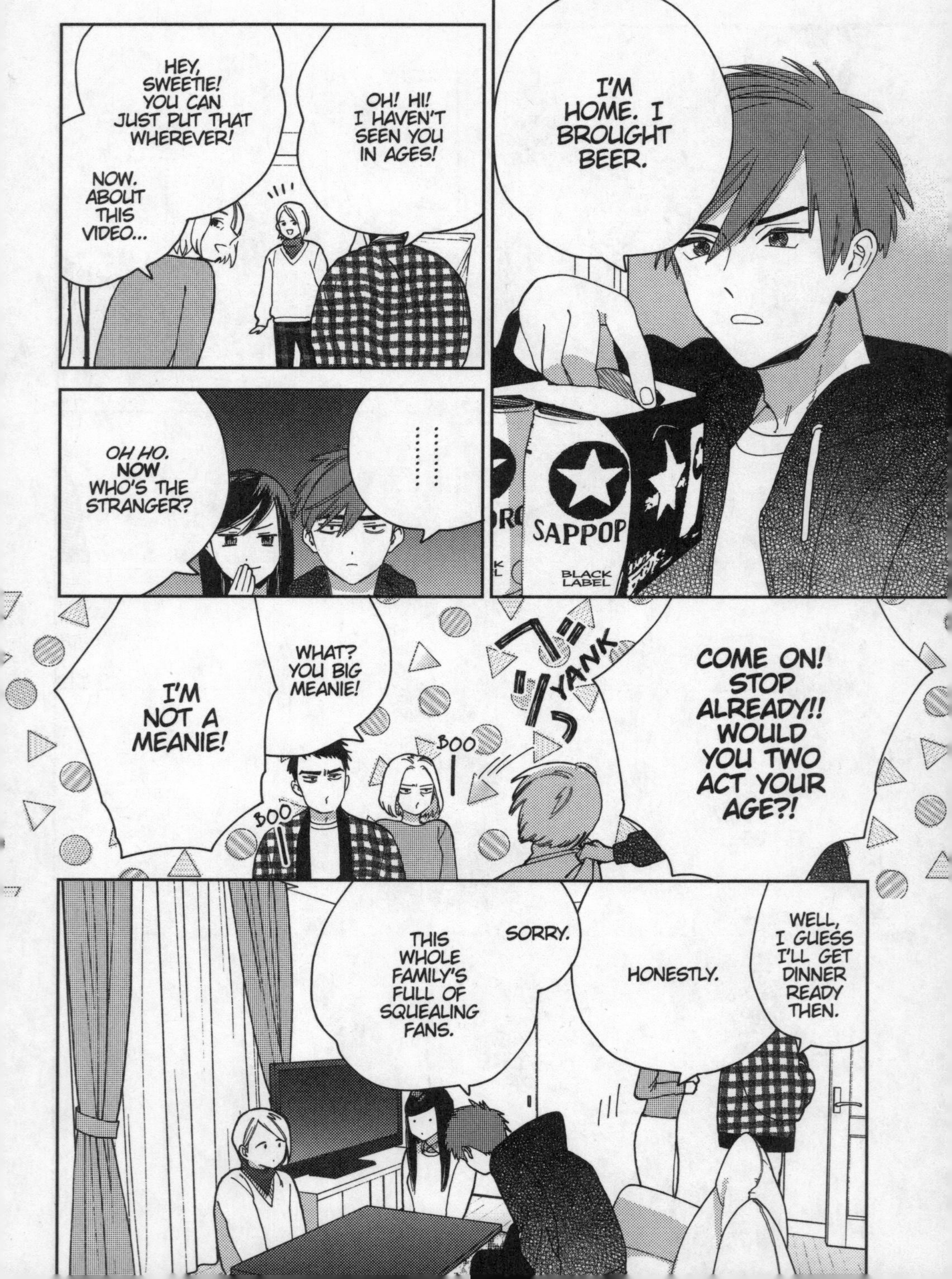
I'M HOME. I BROUGHT BEER.
OH! HI! I HAVEN'T SEEN YOU IN AGES!
HEY, SWEETIE! YOU CAN JUST PUT THAT WHEREVER!
NOW. ABOUT THIS VIDEO...
......
OH HO. NOW WHO'S THE STRANGER?
COME ON! STOP ALREADY!! WOULD YOU TWO ACT YOUR AGE?!
YANK
WHAT? YOU BIG MEANIE!
I'M NOT A MEANIE!
BOO
BOO
WELL, I GUESS I'LL GET DINNER READY THEN.
HONESTLY.
SORRY.
THIS WHOLE FAMILY'S FULL OF SQUEALING FANS.

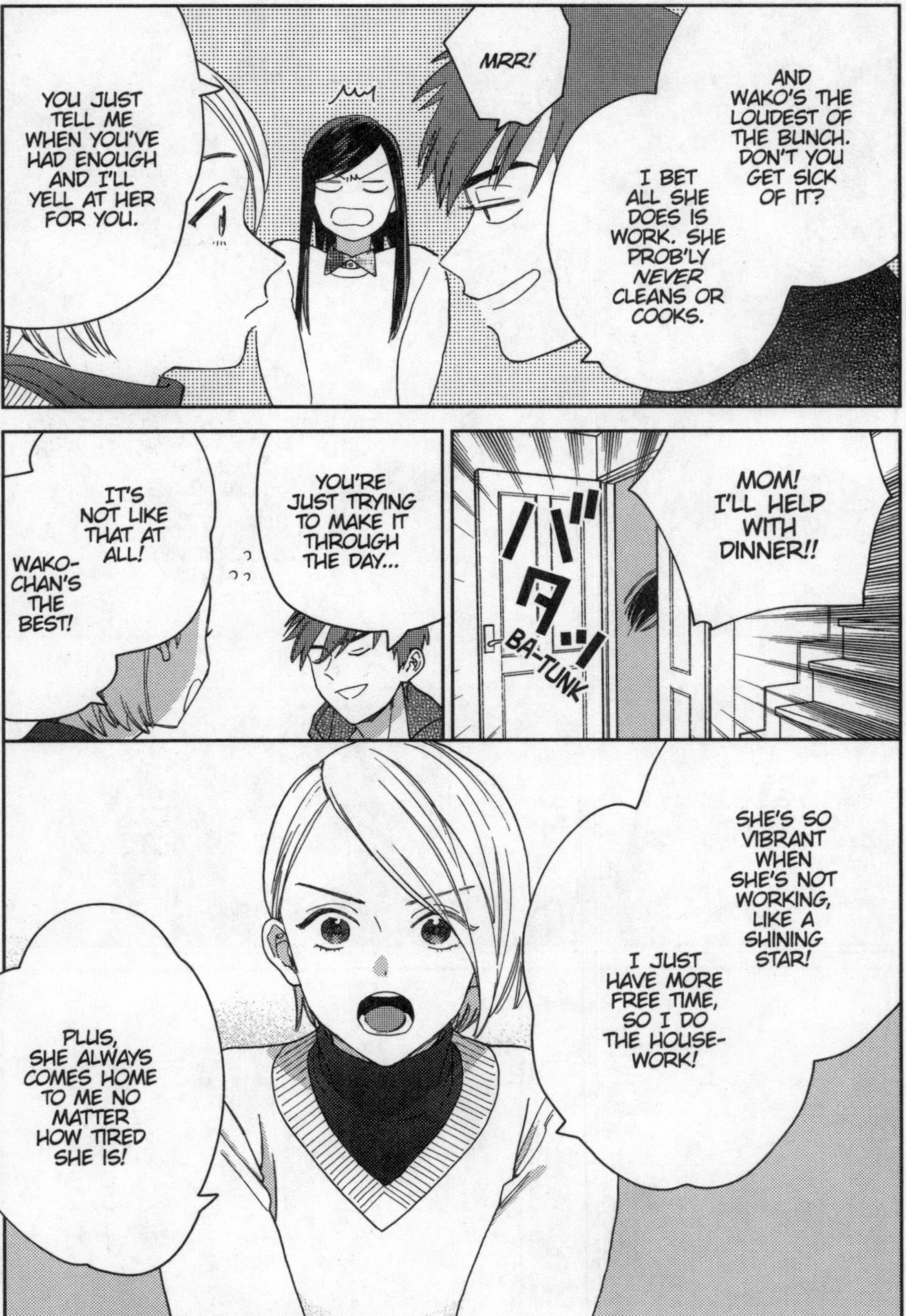
AND WAKO'S THE LOUDEST OF THE BUNCH. DON'T YOU GET SICK OF IT?
I BET ALL SHE DOES IS WORK. SHE PROB'LY *NEVER* CLEANS OR COOKS.
MRR!
YOU JUST TELL ME WHEN YOU'VE HAD ENOUGH AND I'LL YELL AT HER FOR YOU.
MOM! I'LL HELP WITH DINNER!!
バタッ!
BA-TUNK
YOU'RE JUST TRYING TO MAKE IT THROUGH THE DAY...
IT'S NOT LIKE THAT AT ALL!
WAKO-CHAN'S THE BEST!
SHE'S SO VIBRANT WHEN SHE'S NOT WORKING, LIKE A SHINING STAR!
I JUST HAVE MORE FREE TIME, SO I DO THE HOUSE-WORK!
PLUS, SHE ALWAYS COMES HOME TO ME NO MATTER HOW TIRED SHE IS!

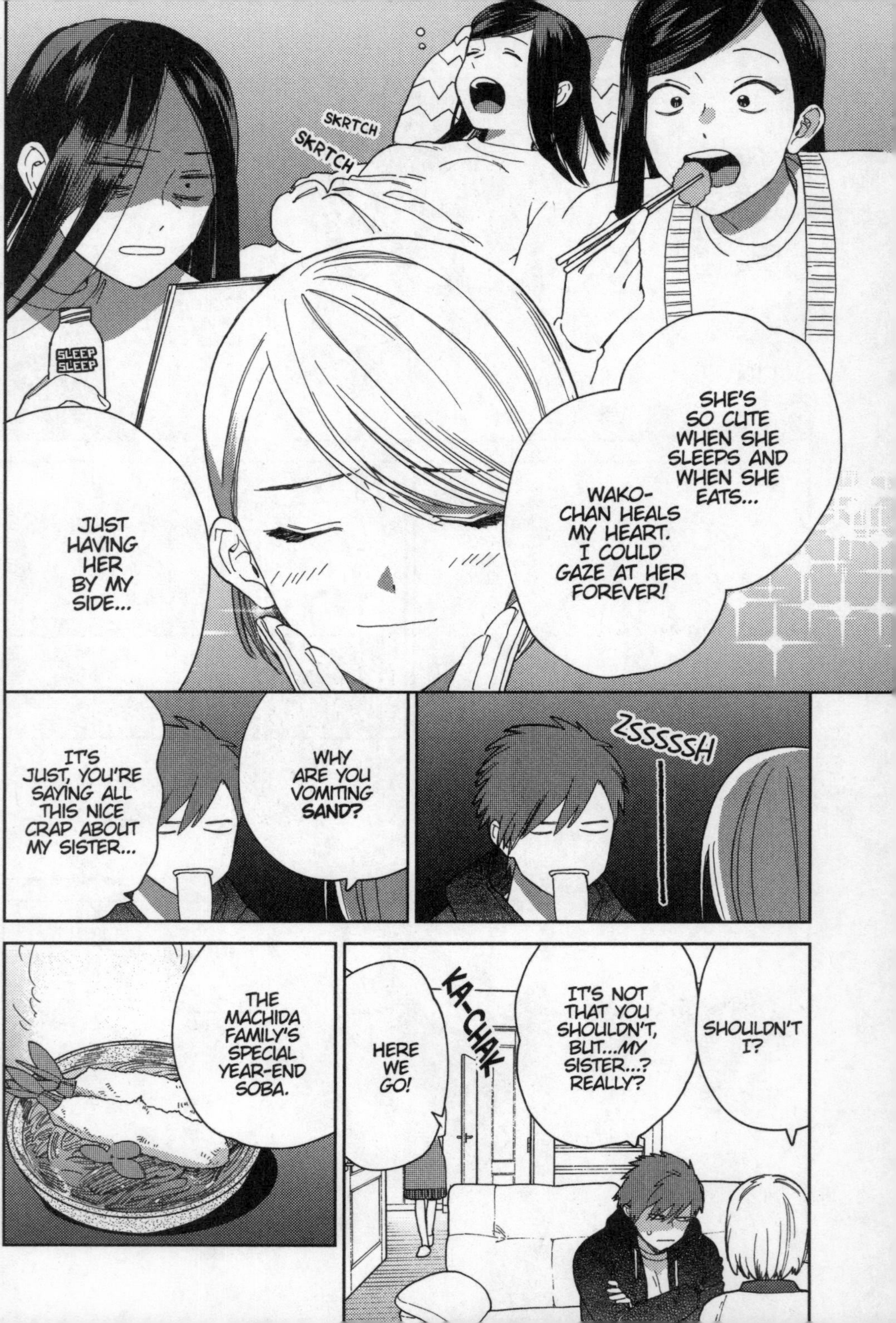
SKRTCH
SKRTCH
SLEEP SLEEP
SHE'S SO CUTE WHEN SHE SLEEPS AND WHEN SHE EATS...
WAKO-CHAN HEALS MY HEART. I COULD GAZE AT HER FOREVER!
JUST HAVING HER BY MY SIDE...
ZSSSSSH
WHY ARE YOU VOMITING SAND?
IT'S JUST, YOU'RE SAYING ALL THIS NICE CRAP ABOUT MY SISTER...
SHOULDN'T I?
IT'S NOT THAT YOU SHOULDN'T, BUT...MY SISTER...? REALLY?
KA-CHAK
HERE WE GO!
THE MACHIDA FAMILY'S SPECIAL YEAR-END SOBA.

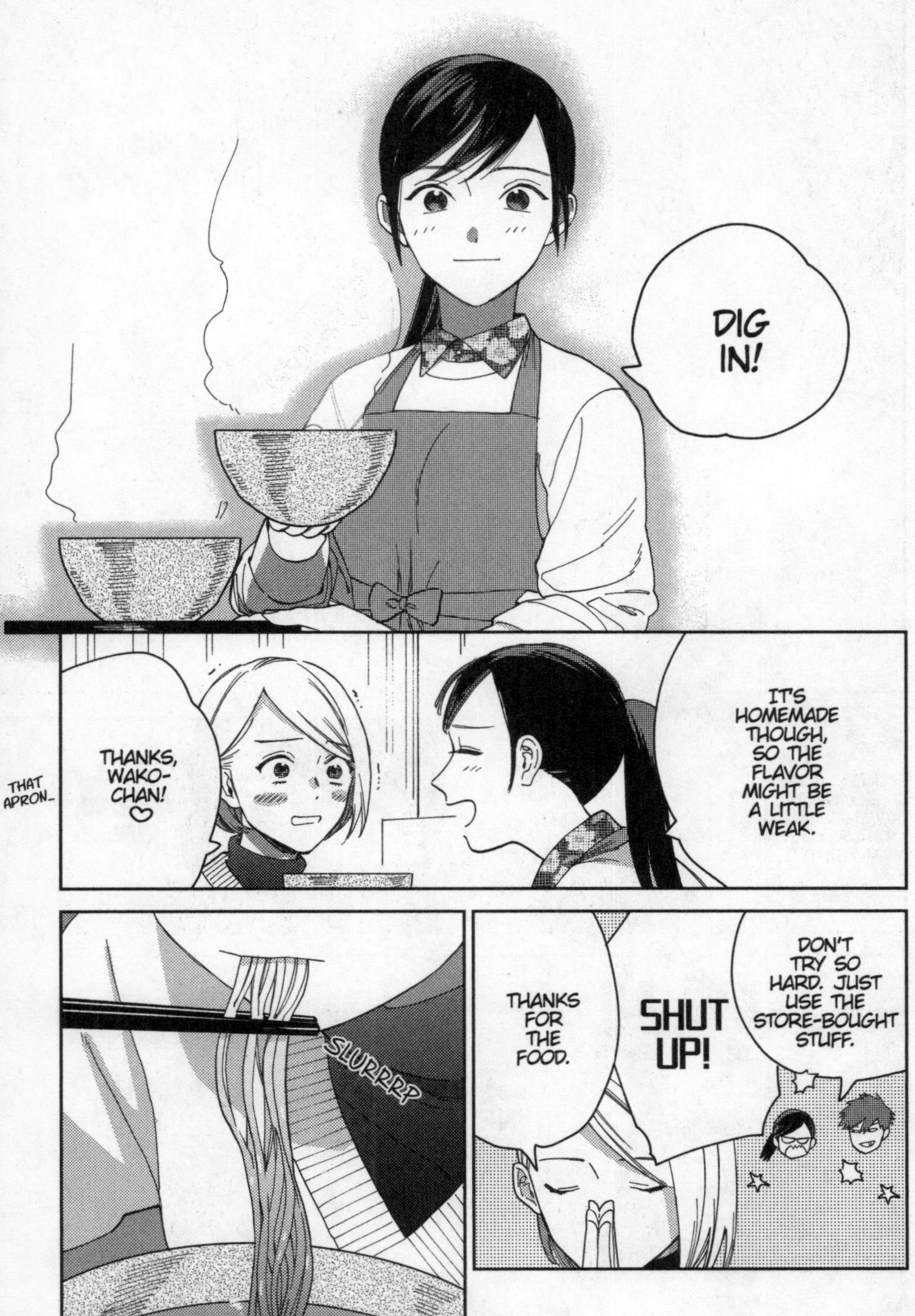
DIG IN!
IT'S HOMEMADE THOUGH, SO THE FLAVOR MIGHT BE A LITTLE WEAK.
THANKS, WAKO-CHAN! ♡
THAT APRON...
DON'T TRY SO HARD. JUST USE THE STORE-BOUGHT STUFF.
SHUT UP!
THANKS FOR THE FOOD.
SLURRRP

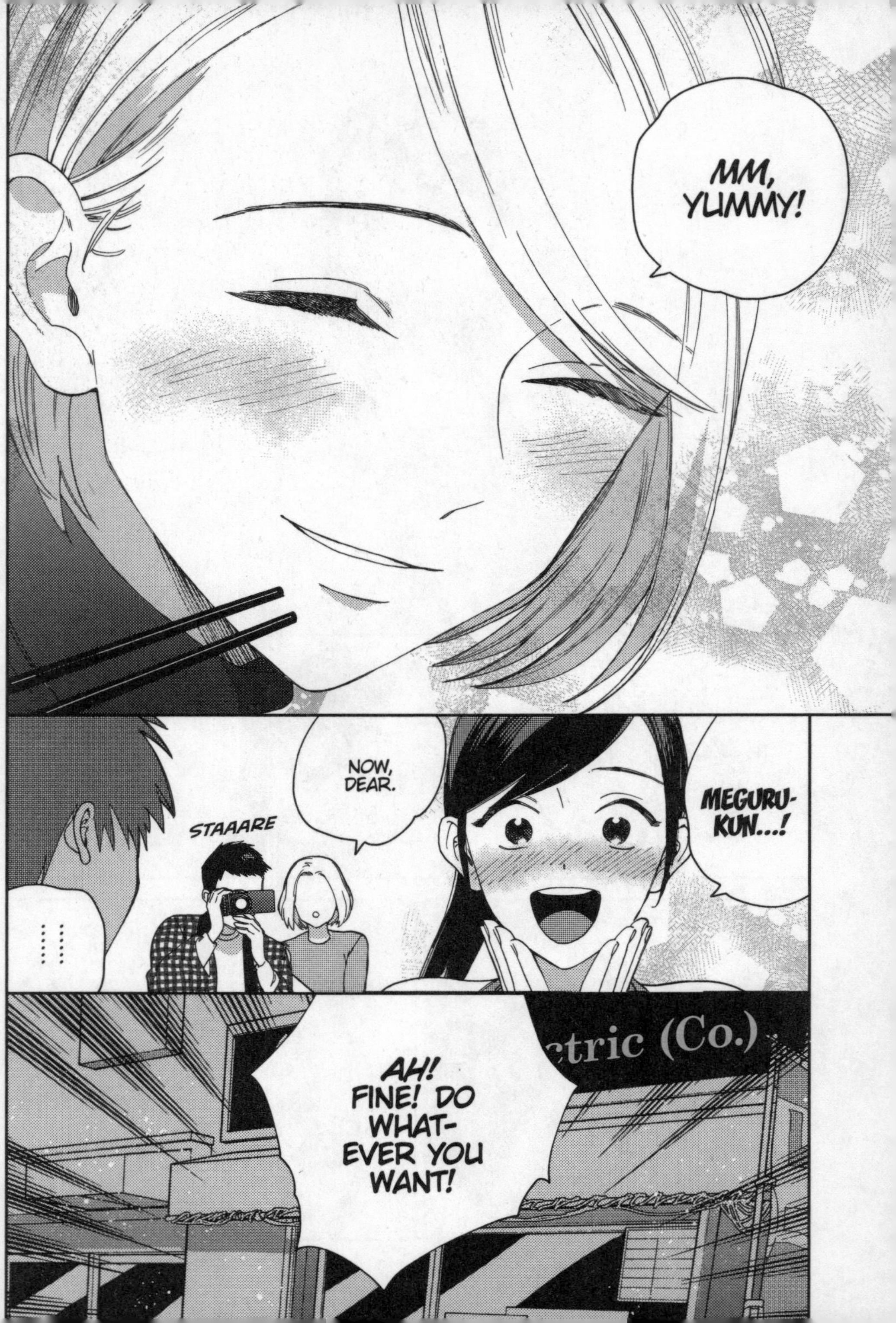
MM, YUMMY!
MEGURU-KUN...!
NOW, DEAR.
STAAARE
......
electric (Co.)
AH! FINE! DO WHAT-EVER YOU WANT!

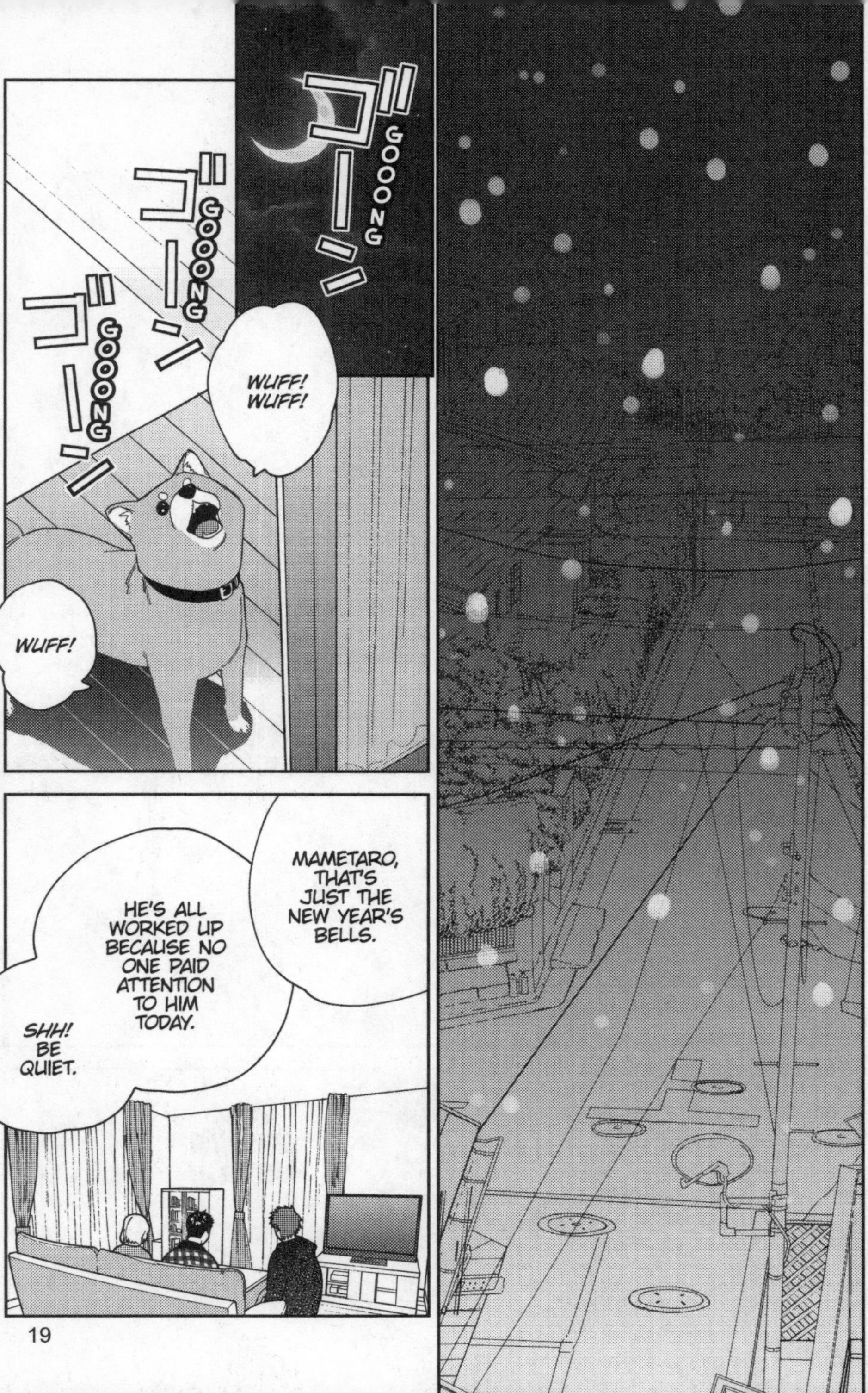
GOOOONG
GOOOONG
GOOOONG
WUFF! WUFF!
WUFF!
MAMETARO, THAT'S JUST THE NEW YEAR'S BELLS.
HE'S ALL WORKED UP BECAUSE NO ONE PAID ATTENTION TO HIM TODAY.
SHH! BE QUIET.

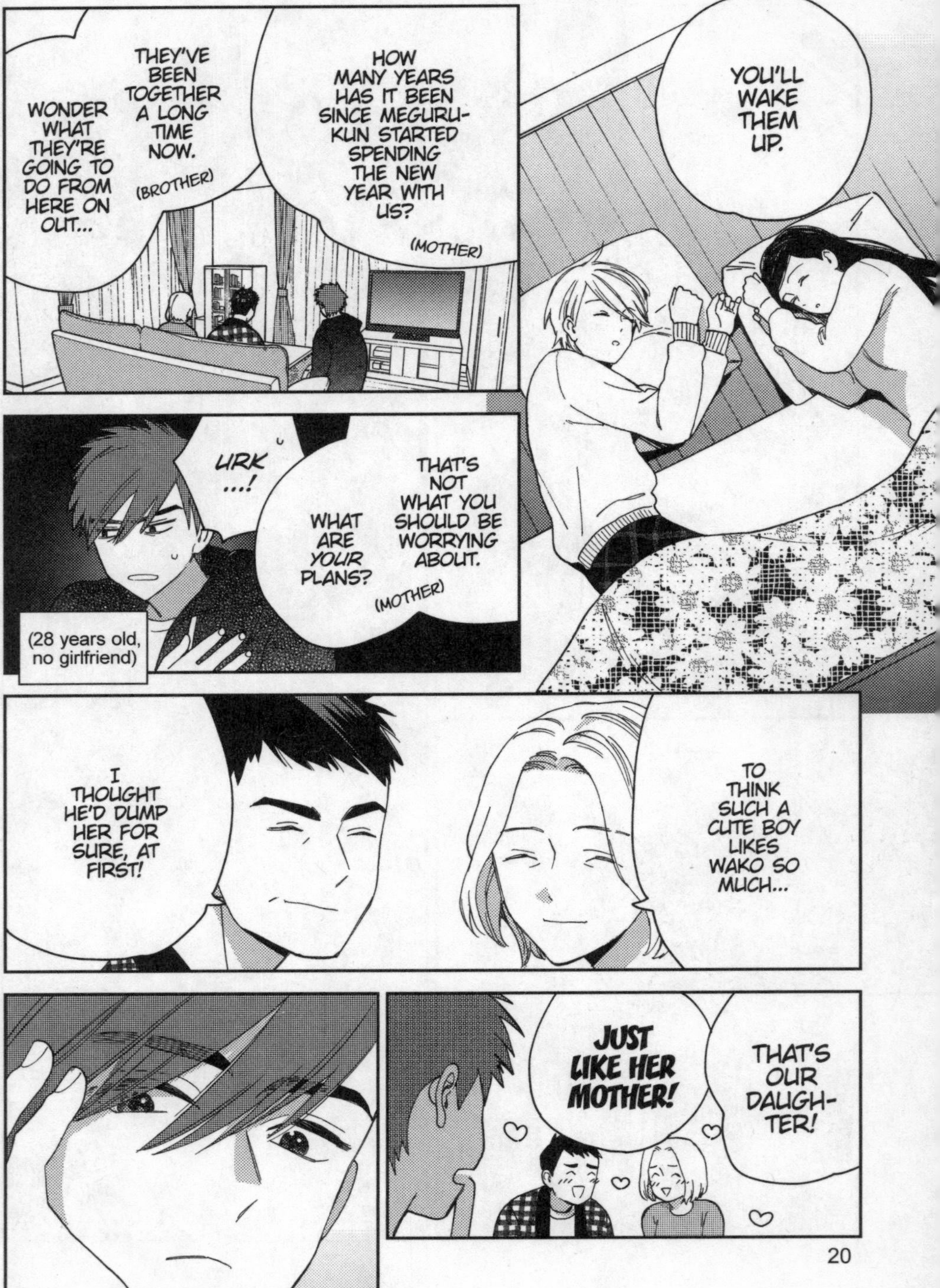
YOU'LL WAKE THEM UP.
HOW MANY YEARS HAS IT BEEN SINCE MEGURU-KUN STARTED SPENDING THE NEW YEAR WITH US?
(MOTHER)
THEY'VE BEEN TOGETHER A LONG TIME NOW.
(BROTHER)
WONDER WHAT THEY'RE GOING TO DO FROM HERE ON OUT...
THAT'S NOT WHAT YOU SHOULD BE WORRYING ABOUT.
WHAT ARE *YOUR* PLANS?
(MOTHER)
URK ...!
(28 years old, no girlfriend)
TO THINK SUCH A CUTE BOY LIKES WAKO SO MUCH...
I THOUGHT HE'D DUMP HER FOR SURE, AT FIRST!
THAT'S OUR DAUGH-TER!
JUST LIKE HER MOTHER!

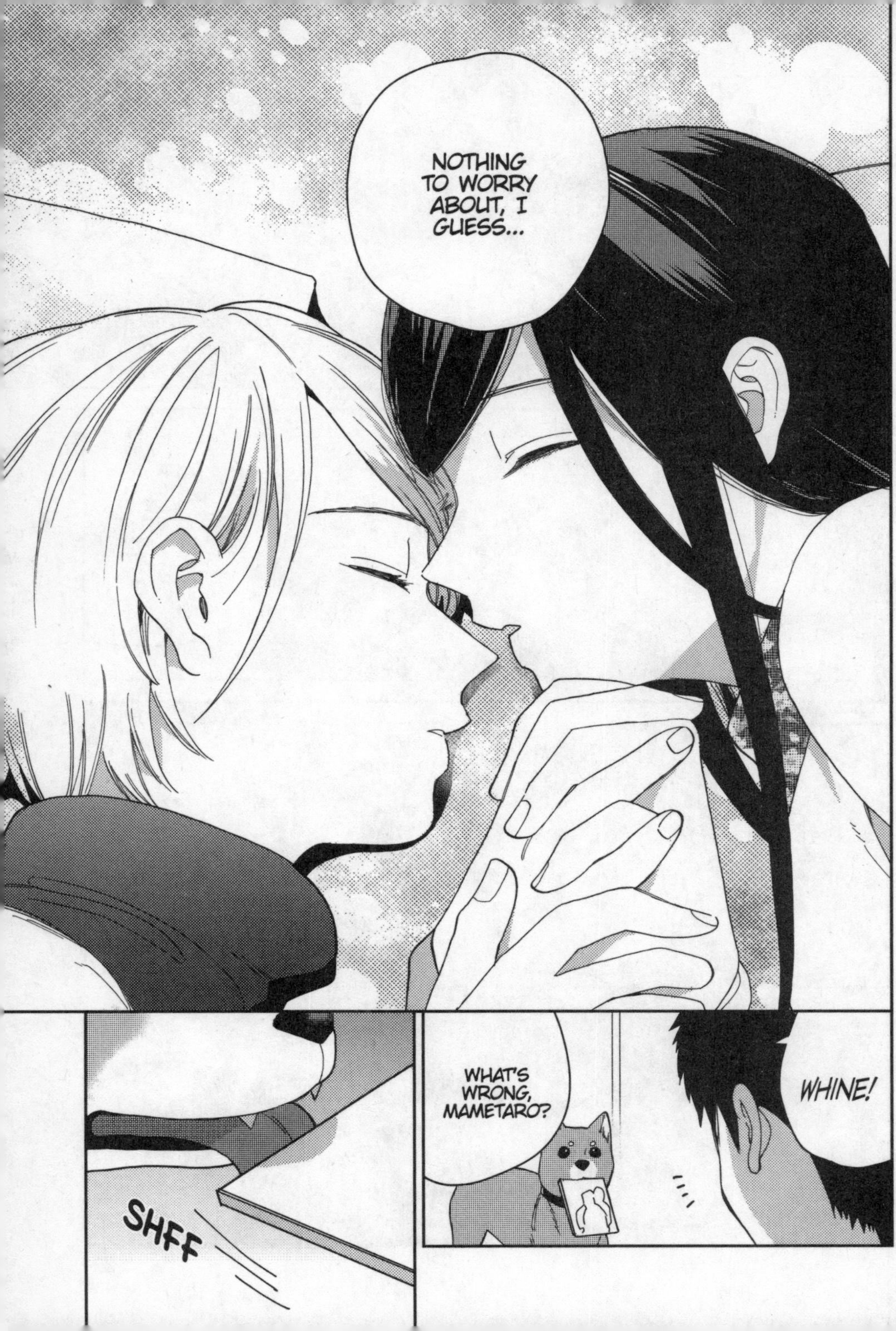
NOTHING TO WORRY ABOUT, I GUESS...
WHINE!
WHAT'S WRONG, MAMETARO?
SHFF

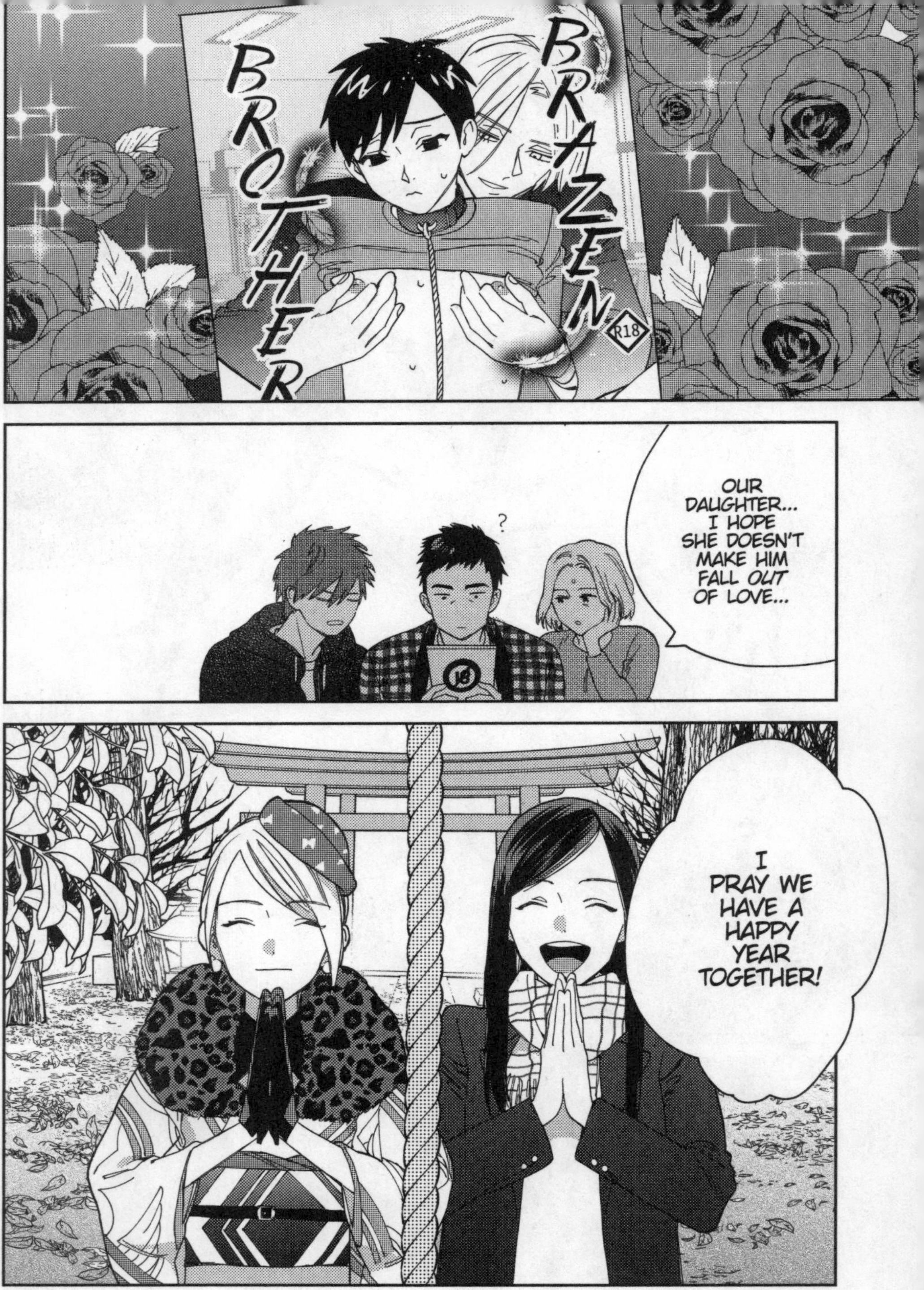
BRAZEN
BROTHER
R18
?
OUR DAUGHTER... I HOPE SHE DOESN'T MAKE HIM FALL *OUT* OF LOVE...
I PRAY WE HAVE A HAPPY YEAR TOGETHER!

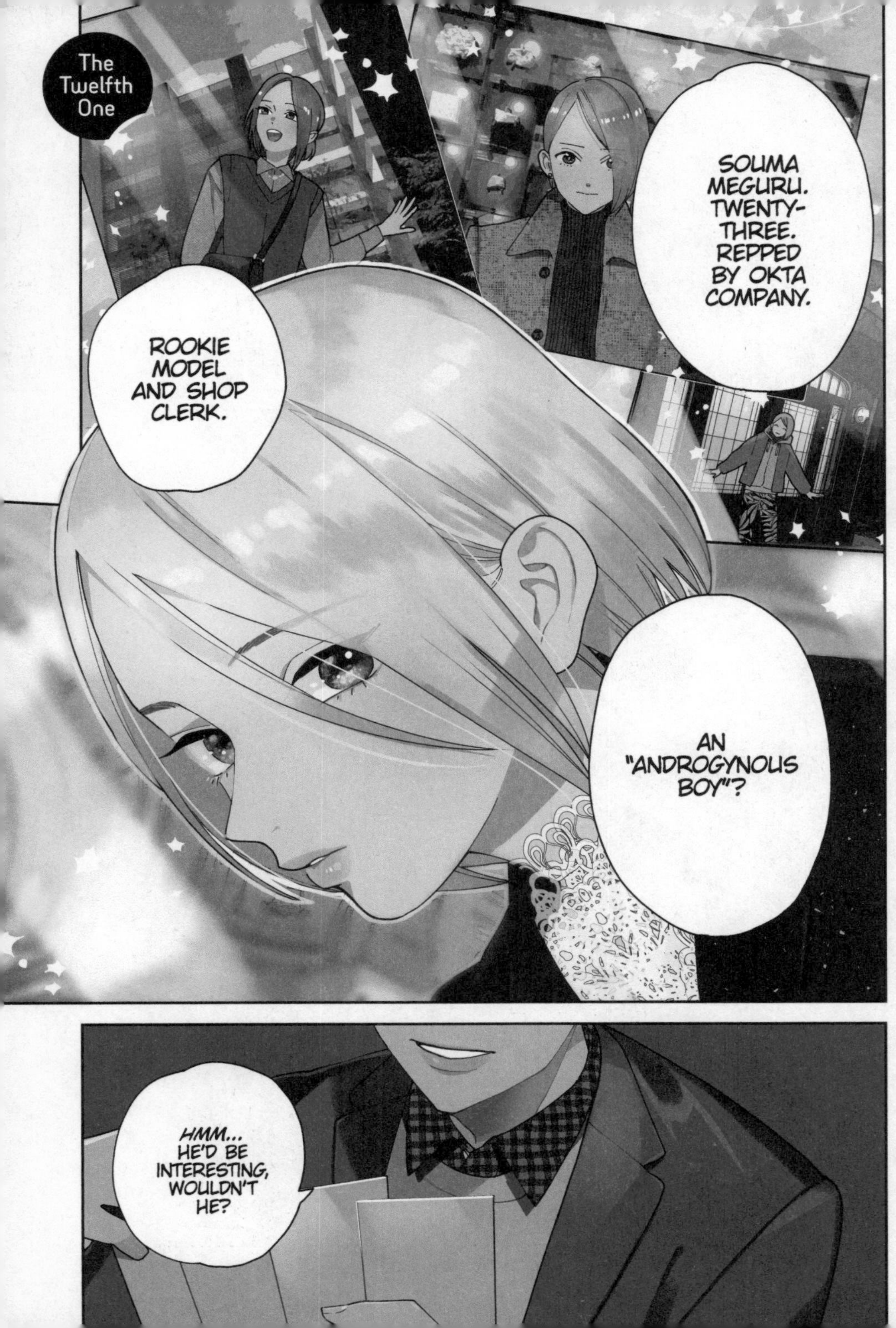
The Twelfth One
SOUMA MEGURU. TWENTY-THREE. REPPED BY OKTA COMPANY.
ROOKIE MODEL AND SHOP CLERK.
AN "ANDROGYNOUS BOY"?
HMM... HE'D BE INTERESTING, WOULDN'T HE?

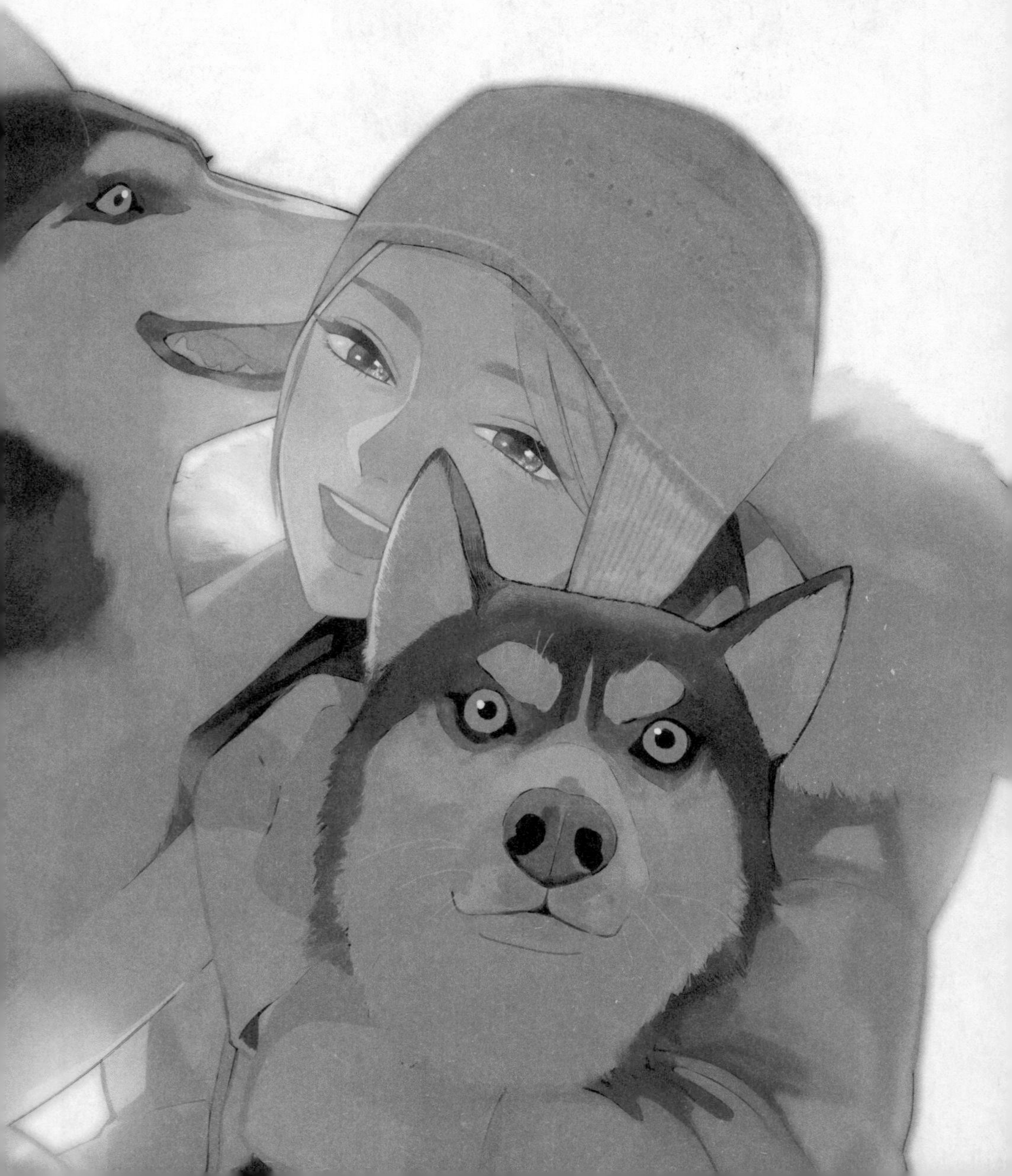

My Androgynous Boyfriend

The Twelfth One

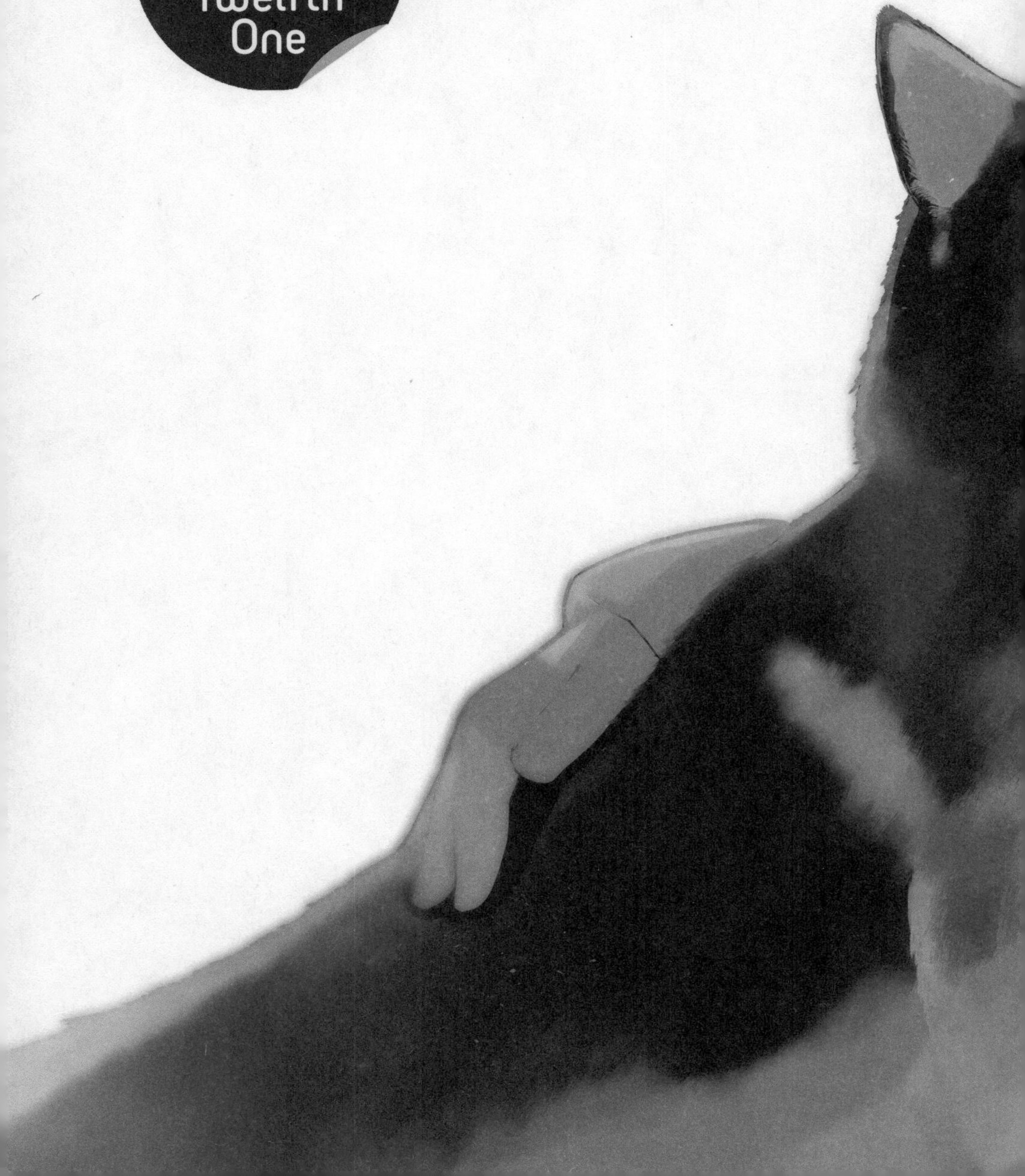

My Androgynous Boyfriend

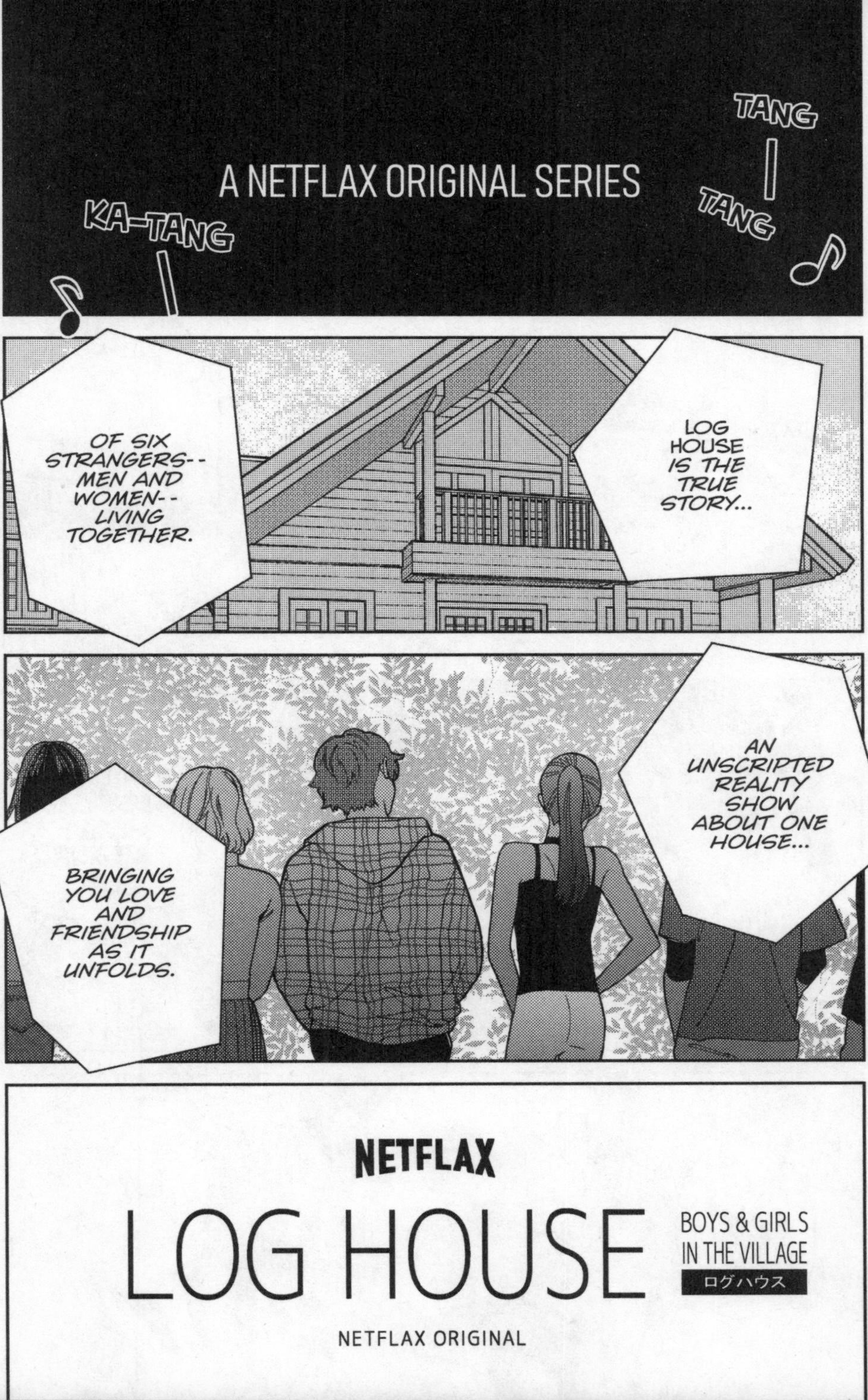
A NETFLAX ORIGINAL SERIES
TANG TANG
KA-TANG
LOG HOUSE IS THE TRUE STORY...
OF SIX STRANGERS--MEN AND WOMEN--LIVING TOGETHER.
AN UNSCRIPTED REALITY SHOW ABOUT ONE HOUSE...
BRINGING YOU LOVE AND FRIENDSHIP AS IT UNFOLDS.
NETFLAX
LOG HOUSE
BOYS & GIRLS IN THE VILLAGE
ログハウス
NETFLAX ORIGINAL

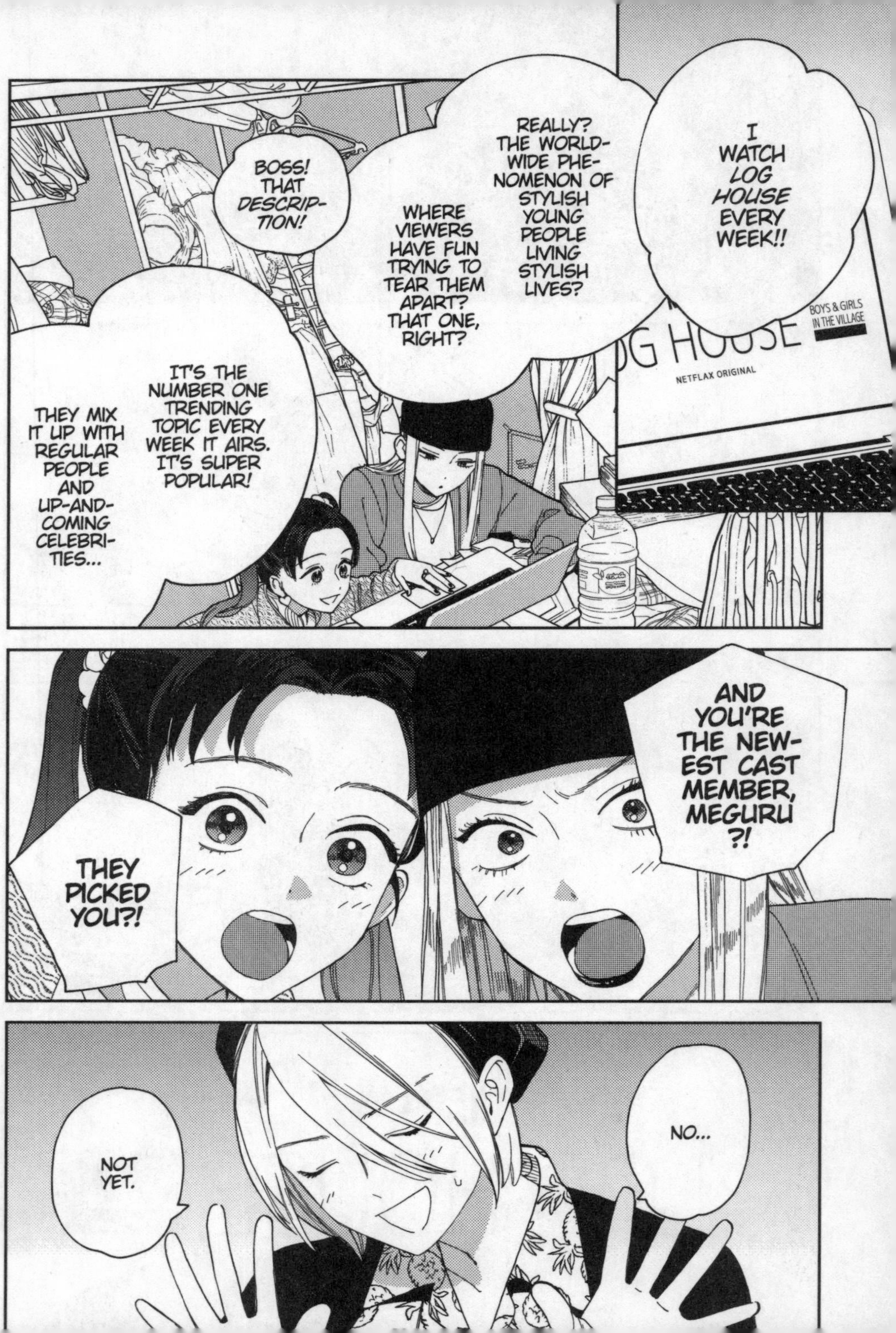
I WATCH LOG HOUSE EVERY WEEK!!
REALLY? THE WORLD-WIDE PHENOMENON OF STYLISH YOUNG PEOPLE LIVING STYLISH LIVES?
WHERE VIEWERS HAVE FUN TRYING TO TEAR THEM APART? THAT ONE, RIGHT?
BOSS! THAT DESCRIPTION!
BOYS & GIRLS IN THE VILLAGE
OG HOUSE
NETFLAX ORIGINAL
IT'S THE NUMBER ONE TRENDING TOPIC EVERY WEEK IT AIRS. IT'S SUPER POPULAR!
THEY MIX IT UP WITH REGULAR PEOPLE AND UP-AND-COMING CELEBRITIES...
AND YOU'RE THE NEWEST CAST MEMBER, MEGURU?!
THEY PICKED YOU?!
NO...
NOT YET.

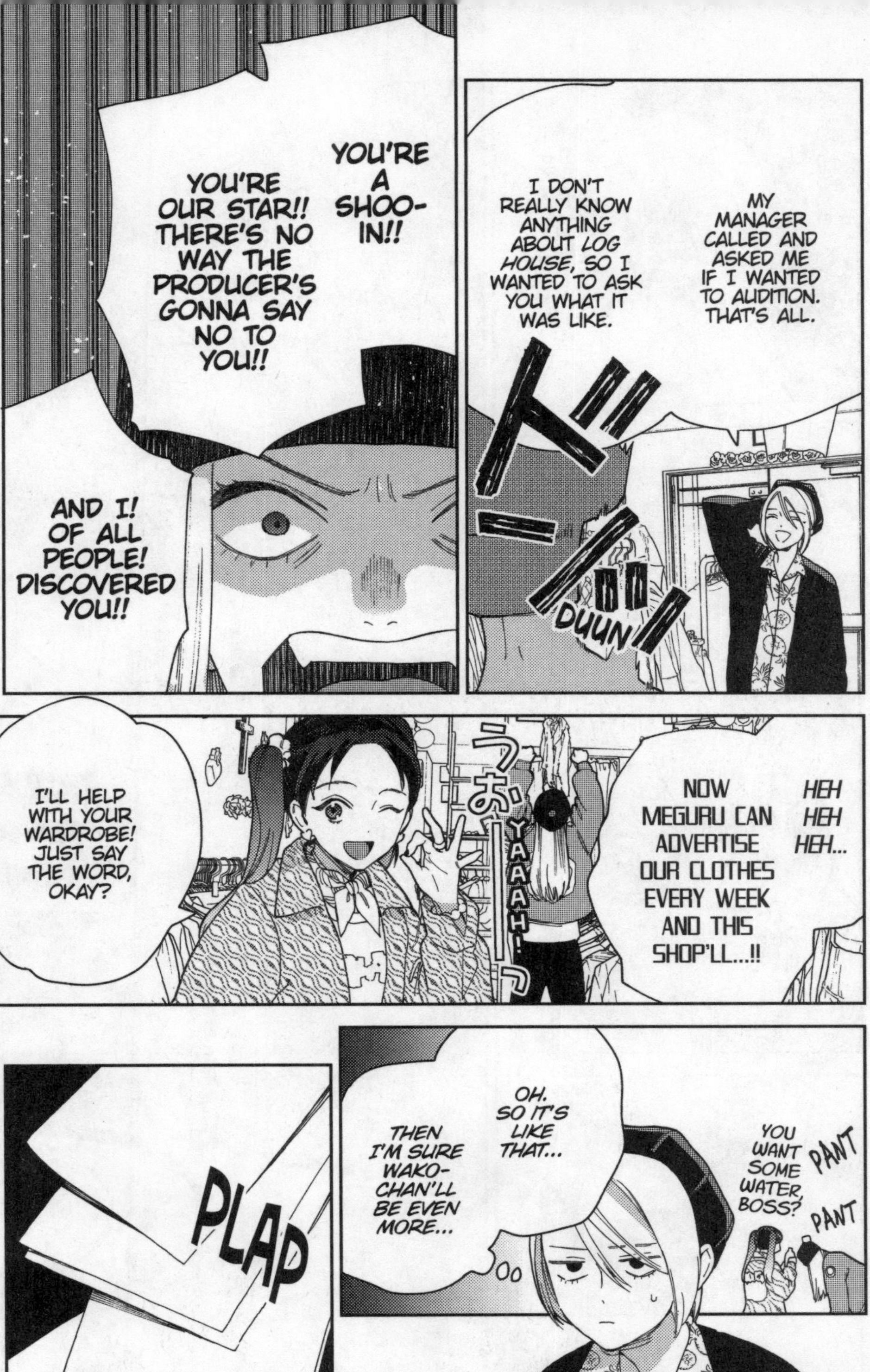
MY MANAGER CALLED AND ASKED ME IF I WANTED TO AUDITION. THAT'S ALL.
I DON'T REALLY KNOW ANYTHING ABOUT *LOG HOUSE*, SO I WANTED TO ASK YOU WHAT IT WAS LIKE.
DUUN
YOU'RE A SHOO-IN!!
YOU'RE OUR STAR!! THERE'S NO WAY THE PRODUCER'S GONNA SAY NO TO YOU!!
AND I! OF ALL PEOPLE! DISCOVERED YOU!!
HEH HEH HEH...
NOW MEGURU CAN ADVERTISE OUR CLOTHES EVERY WEEK AND THIS SHOP'LL...!!
YAAAAH!!
I'LL HELP WITH YOUR WARDROBE! JUST SAY THE WORD, OKAY?
PANT PANT
YOU WANT SOME WATER, BOSS?
OH. SO IT'S LIKE THAT...
THEN I'M SURE WAKO-CHAN'LL BE EVEN MORE...
PLAP

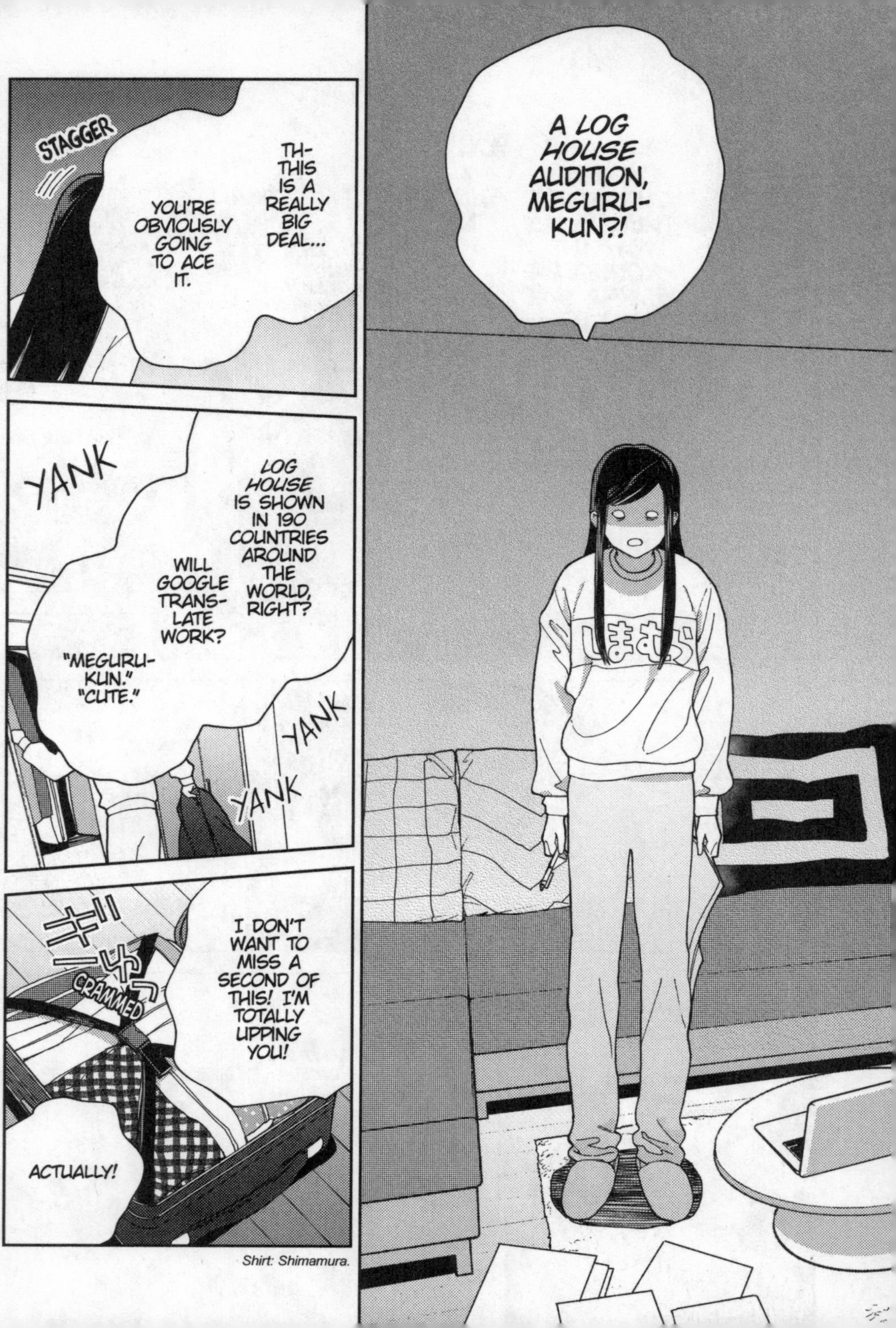
A LOG HOUSE AUDITION, MEGURU-KUN?!
しまむら
TH-THIS IS A REALLY BIG DEAL...
YOU'RE OBVIOUSLY GOING TO ACE IT.
STAGGER
LOG HOUSE IS SHOWN IN 190 COUNTRIES AROUND THE WORLD, RIGHT?
WILL GOOGLE TRANSLATE WORK?
YANK
YANK
"MEGURU-KUN." "CUTE."
YANK
I DON'T WANT TO MISS A SECOND OF THIS! I'M TOTALLY UPPING YOU!
CRAMMED
ACTUALLY!

Shirt: Shimamura.

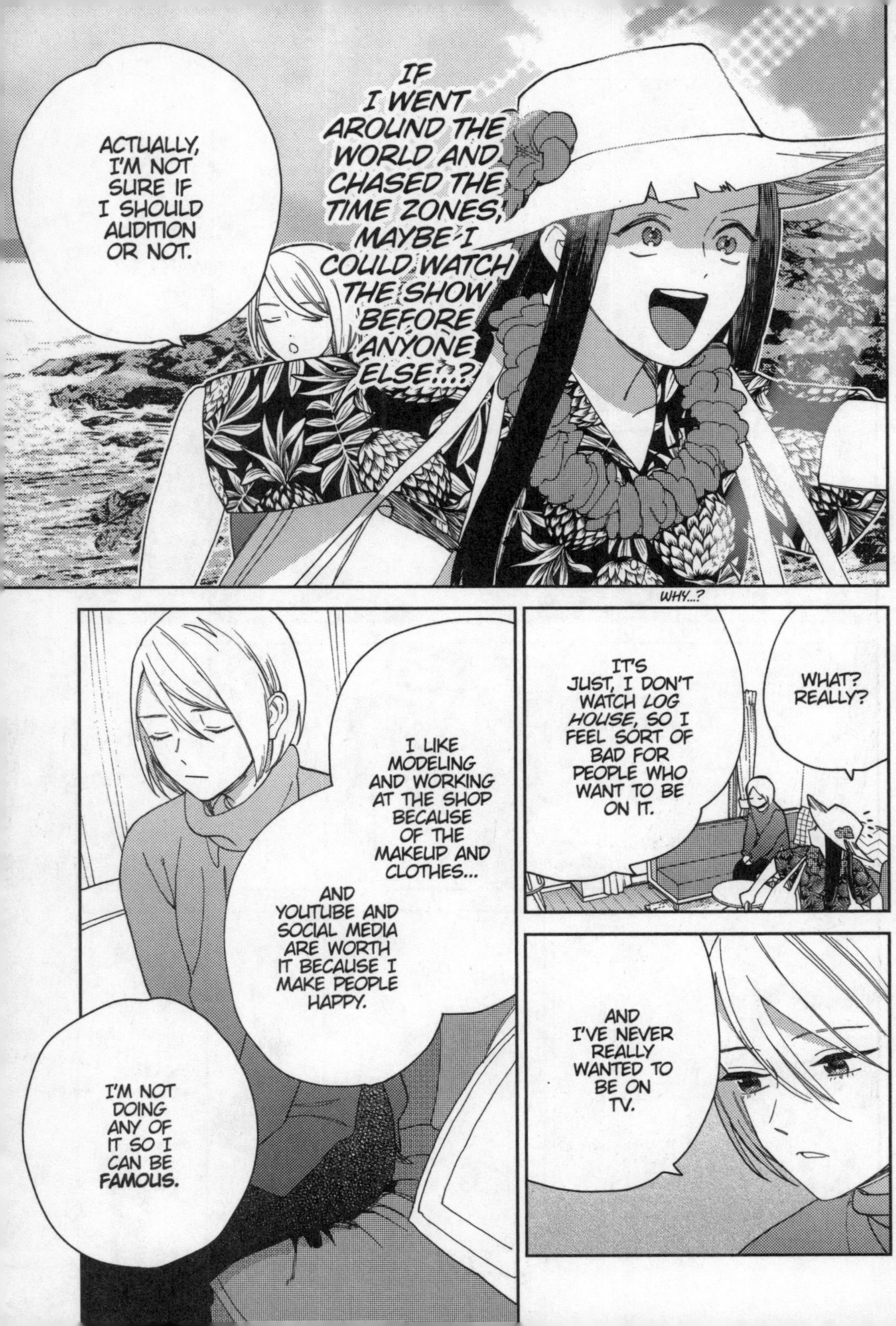
IF I WENT AROUND THE WORLD AND CHASED THE TIME ZONES, MAYBE I COULD WATCH THE SHOW BEFORE ANYONE ELSE...?
ACTUALLY, I'M NOT SURE IF I SHOULD AUDITION OR NOT.
WHY...?
WHAT? REALLY?
IT'S JUST, I DON'T WATCH *LOG HOUSE*, SO I FEEL SORT OF BAD FOR PEOPLE WHO WANT TO BE ON IT.
AND I'VE NEVER REALLY WANTED TO BE ON TV.
I LIKE MODELING AND WORKING AT THE SHOP BECAUSE OF THE MAKEUP AND CLOTHES...
AND YOUTUBE AND SOCIAL MEDIA ARE WORTH IT BECAUSE I MAKE PEOPLE HAPPY.
I'M NOT DOING ANY OF IT SO I CAN BE FAMOUS.

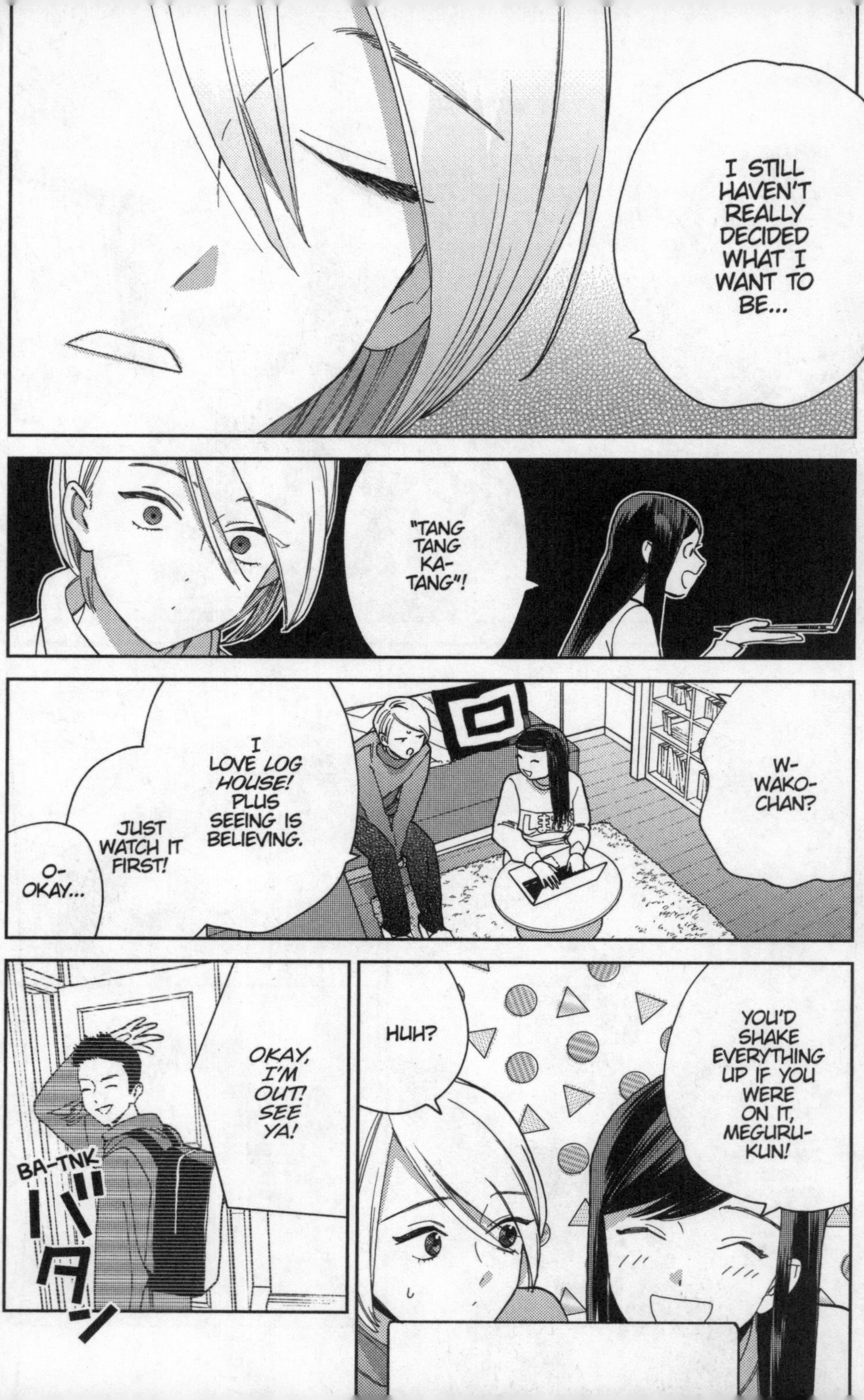
I STILL HAVEN'T REALLY DECIDED WHAT I WANT TO BE...
"TANG TANG KA-TANG"!
W-WAKO-CHAN?
I LOVE LOG HOUSE! PLUS SEEING IS BELIEVING.
JUST WATCH IT FIRST!
O-OKAY...
YOU'D SHAKE EVERYTHING UP IF YOU WERE ON IT, MEGURU-KUN!
HUH?
OKAY, I'M OUT! SEE YA!
BA-TNK

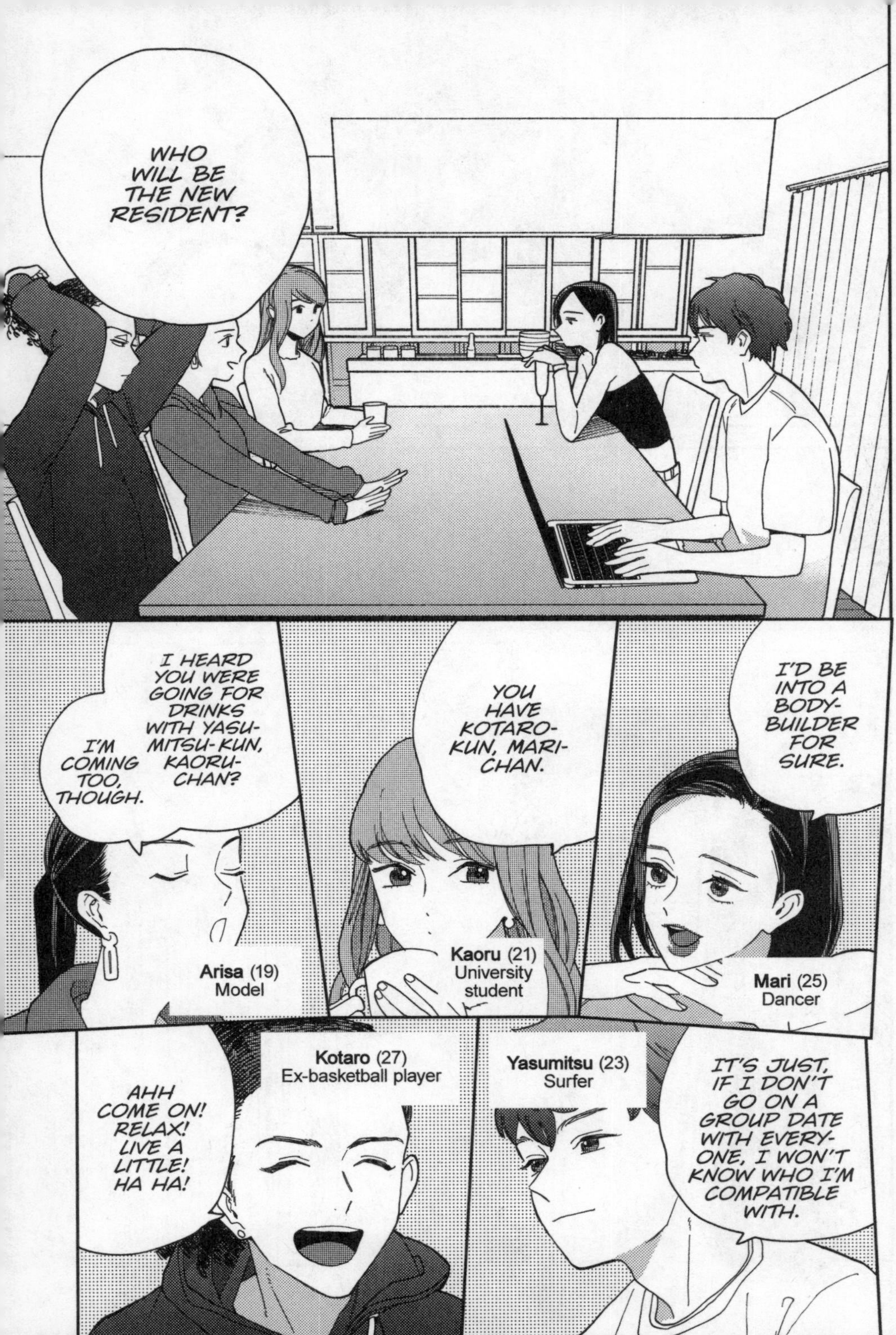
WHO WILL BE THE NEW RESIDENT?
I'D BE INTO A BODY-BUILDER FOR SURE.
Mari (25) Dancer
YOU HAVE KOTARO-KUN, MARI-CHAN.
Kaoru (21) University student
I HEARD YOU WERE GOING FOR DRINKS WITH YASU-MITSU-KUN, KAORU-CHAN?
I'M COMING TOO, THOUGH.
Arisa (19) Model
Yasumitsu (23) Surfer
IT'S JUST, IF I DON'T GO ON A GROUP DATE WITH EVERY-ONE, I WON'T KNOW WHO I'M COMPATIBLE WITH.
Kotaro (27) Ex-basketball player
AHH COME ON! RELAX! LIVE A LITTLE! HA HA!

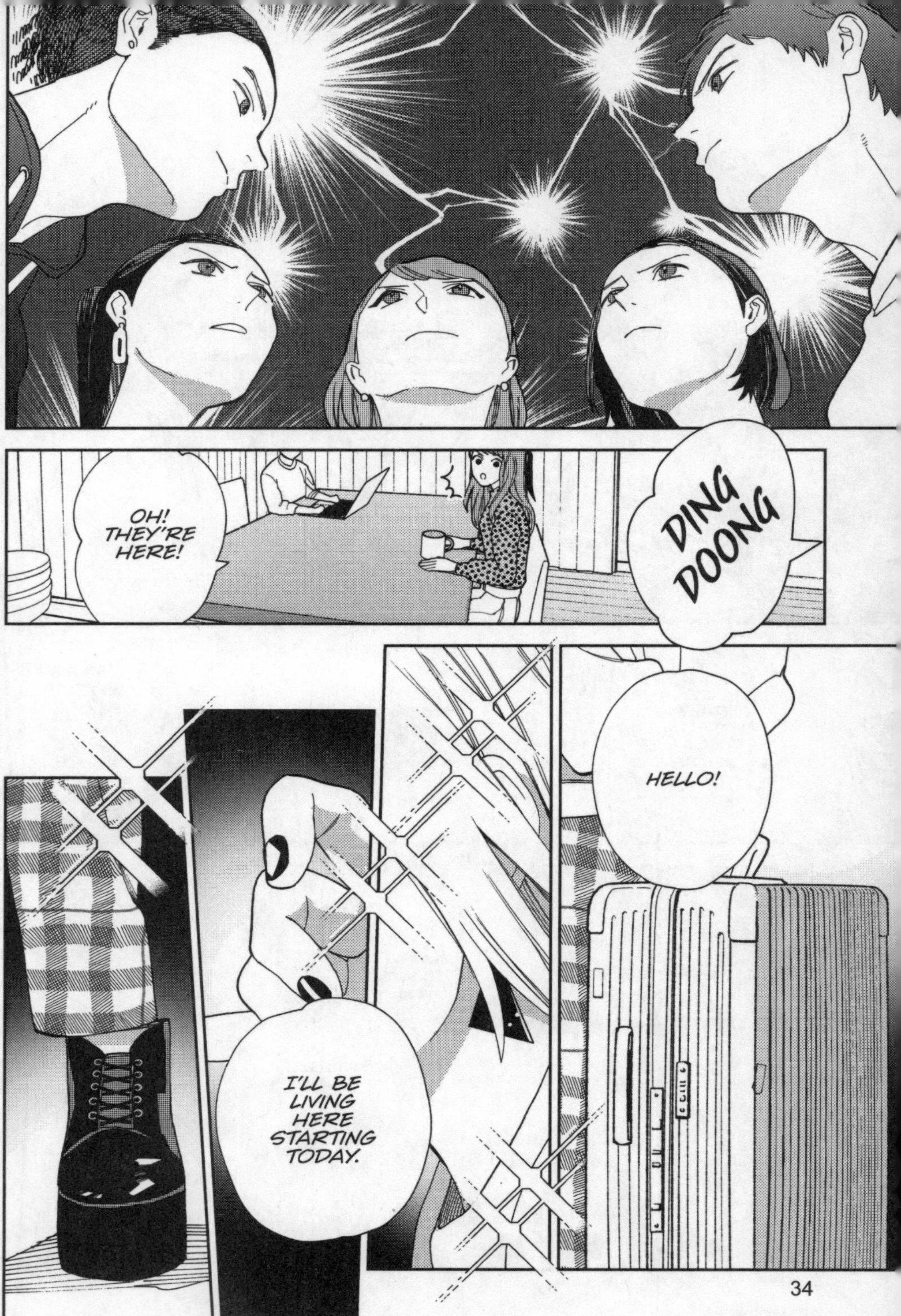
DING DOONG
OH! THEY'RE HERE!
HELLO!
I'LL BE LIVING HERE STARTING TODAY.

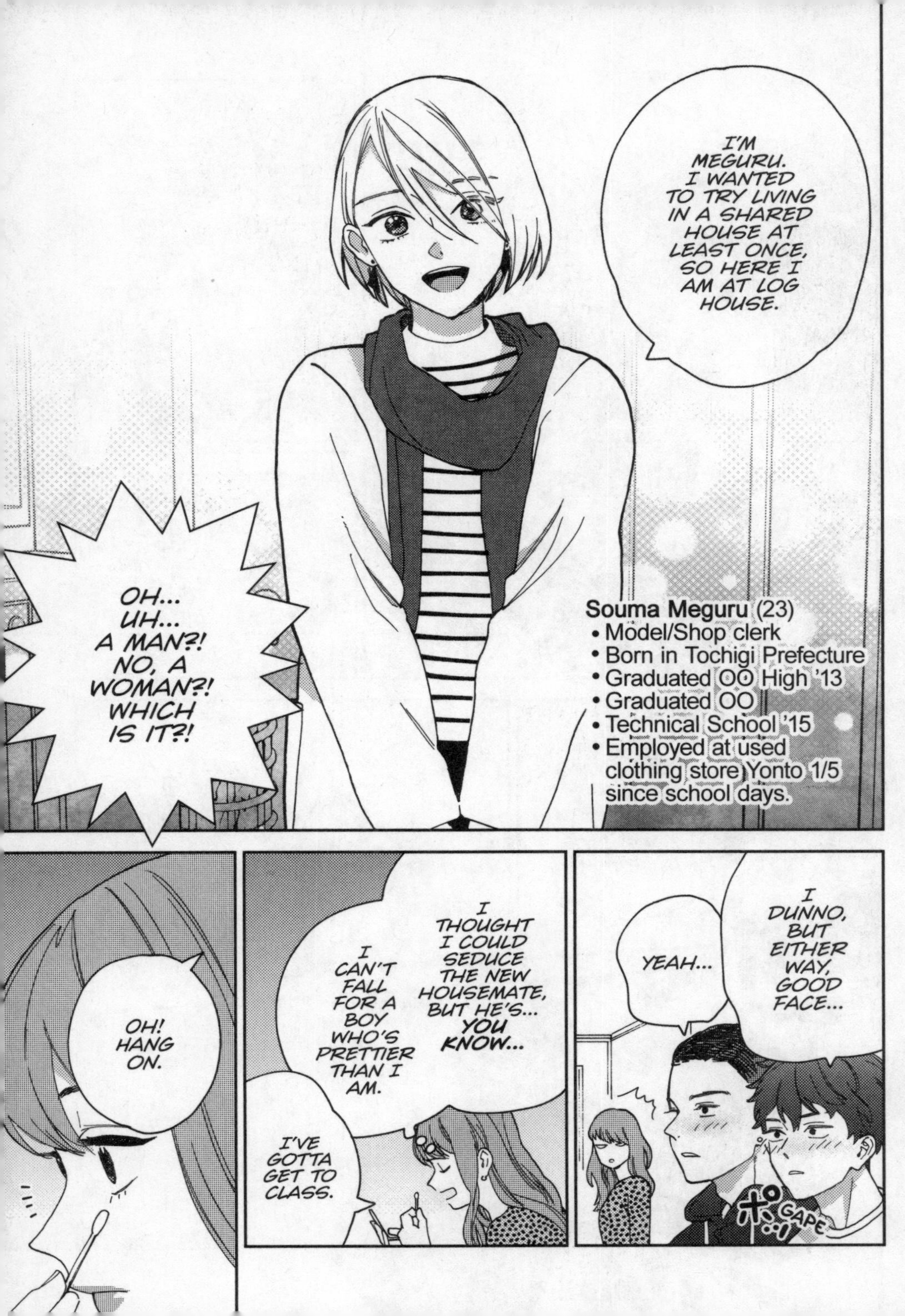
I'M MEGURU. I WANTED TO TRY LIVING IN A SHARED HOUSE AT LEAST ONCE, SO HERE I AM AT LOG HOUSE.
Souma Meguru (23)
• Model/Shop clerk
• Born in Tochigi Prefecture
• Graduated OO High '13
• Graduated OO
• Technical School '15
• Employed at used clothing store Yonto 1/5 since school days.
OH... UH... A MAN?! NO, A WOMAN?! WHICH IS IT?!
I DUNNO, BUT EITHER WAY, GOOD FACE...
YEAH...
GAPE
I THOUGHT I COULD SEDUCE THE NEW HOUSEMATE, BUT HE'S... YOU KNOW...
I CAN'T FALL FOR A BOY WHO'S PRETTIER THAN I AM.
I'VE GOTTA GET TO CLASS.
OH! HANG ON.

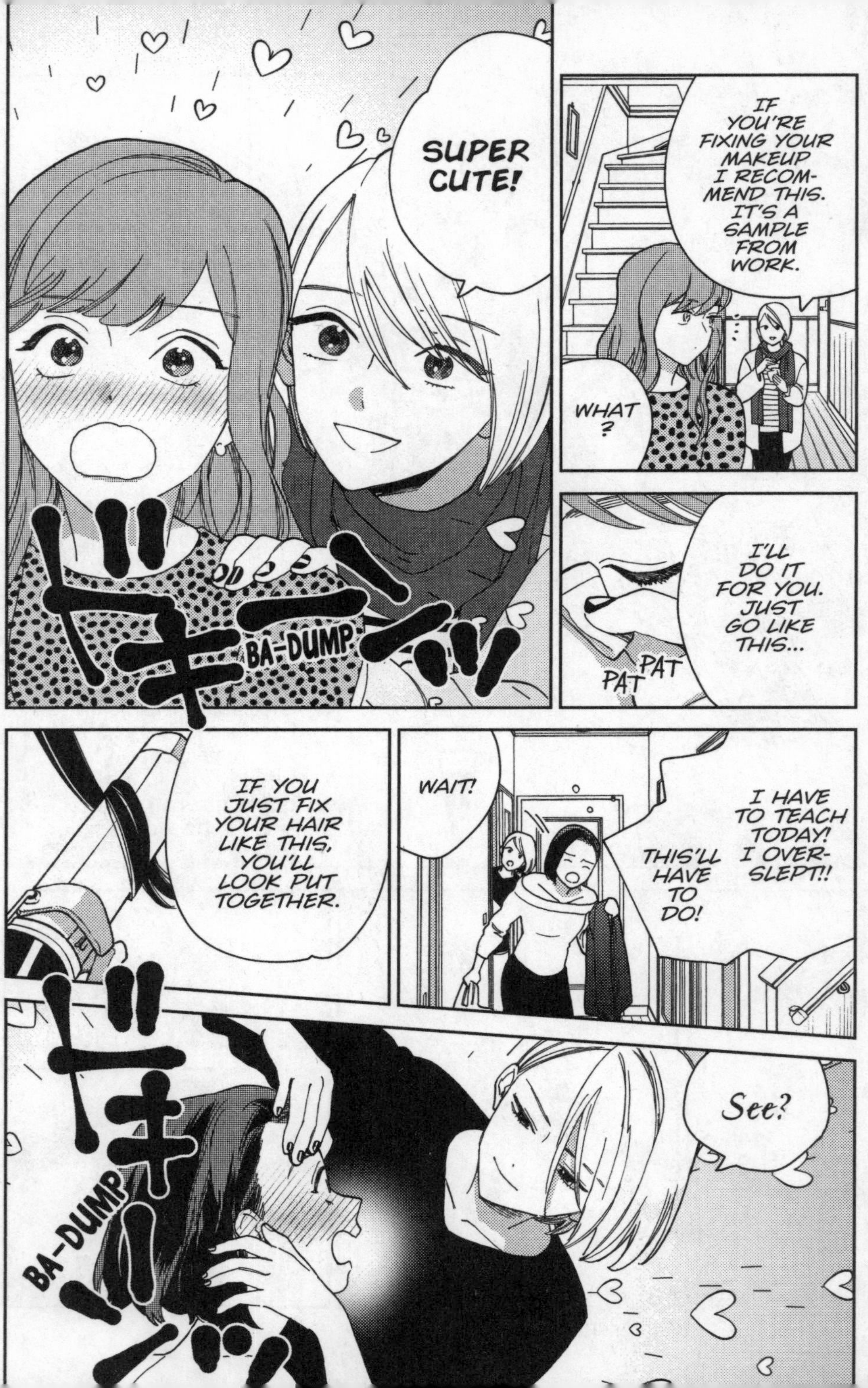
IF YOU'RE FIXING YOUR MAKEUP I RECOMMEND THIS. IT'S A SAMPLE FROM WORK.
WHAT?
I'LL DO IT FOR YOU. JUST GO LIKE THIS...
PAT PAT
SUPER CUTE!
BA-DUMP
I HAVE TO TEACH TODAY! I OVERSLEPT!!
THIS'LL HAVE TO DO!
WAIT!
IF YOU JUST FIX YOUR HAIR LIKE THIS, YOU'LL LOOK PUT TOGETHER.
See?
BA-DUMP

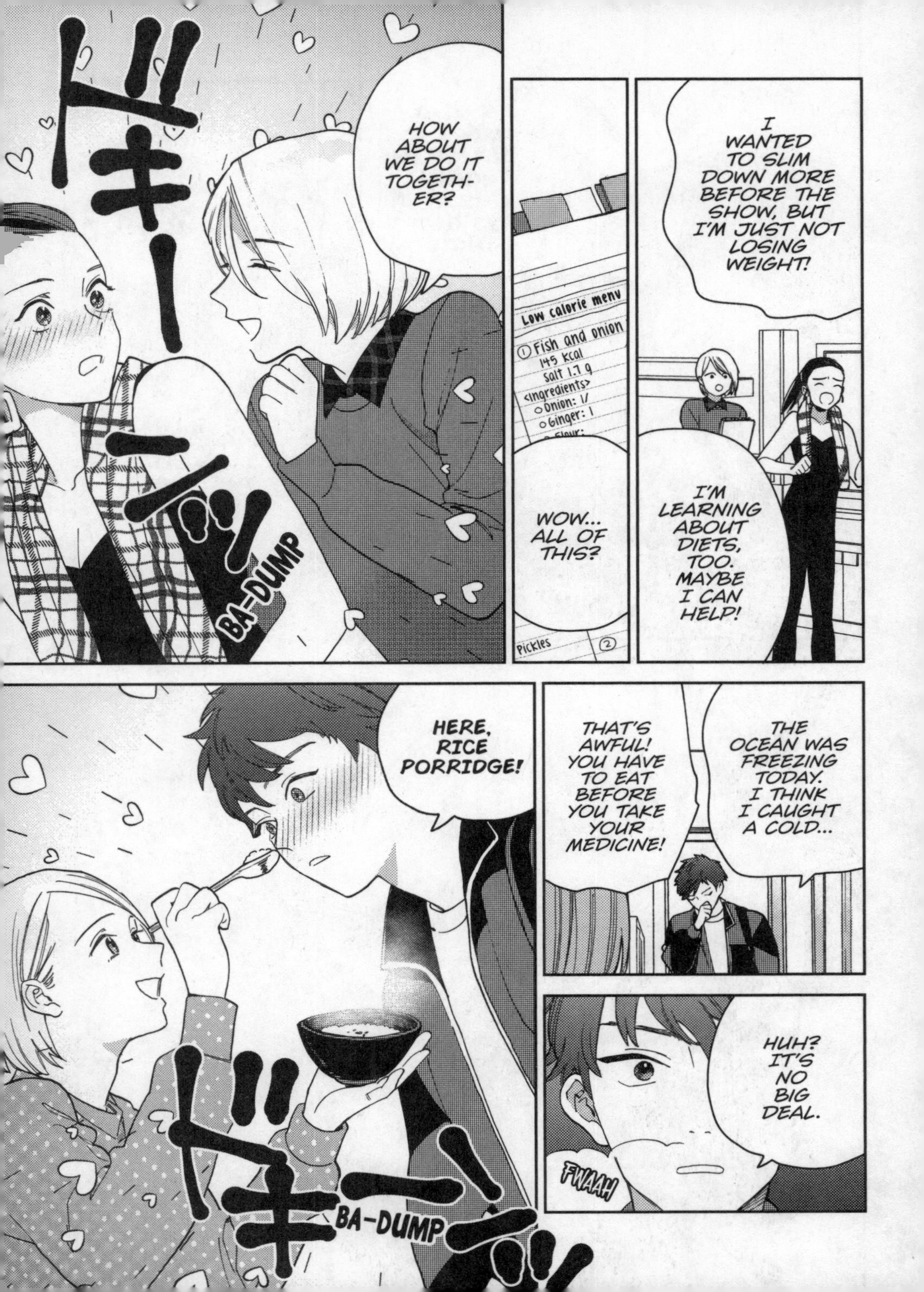
I WANTED TO SLIM DOWN MORE BEFORE THE SHOW, BUT I'M JUST NOT LOSING WEIGHT!
I'M LEARNING ABOUT DIETS, TOO. MAYBE I CAN HELP!
Low calorie menu
① Fish and onion
145 kcal
Salt 1.7 g
<Ingredients>
○Onion: 1/
○Ginger: 1
Pickles
②
WOW... ALL OF THIS?
HOW ABOUT WE DO IT TOGETHER?
ドキーッ
BA-DUMP
THE OCEAN WAS FREEZING TODAY. I THINK I CAUGHT A COLD...
THAT'S AWFUL! YOU HAVE TO EAT BEFORE YOU TAKE YOUR MEDICINE!
HUH? IT'S NO BIG DEAL.
FWAAH
HERE, RICE PORRIDGE!
ドキーッ
BA-DUMP

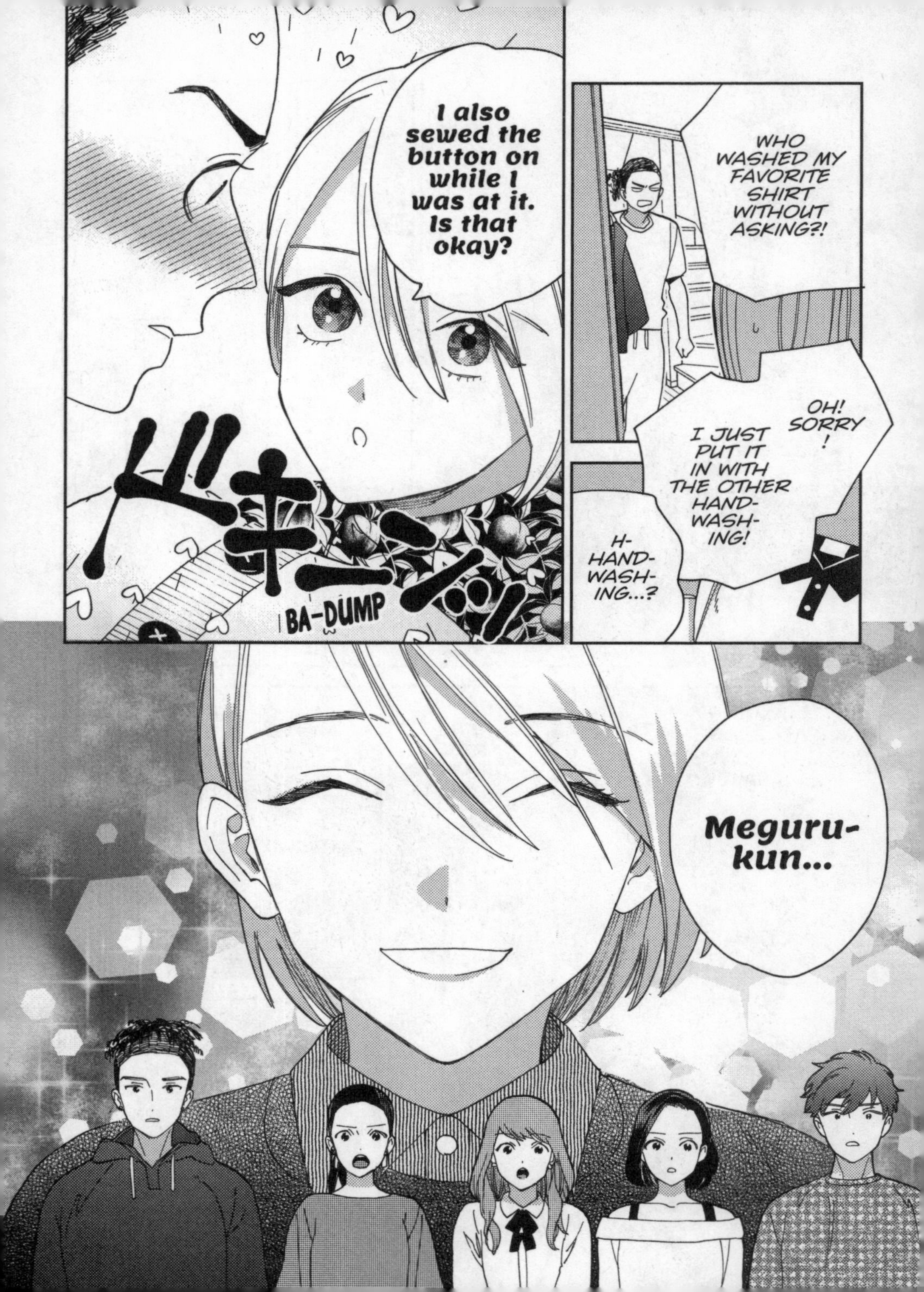
WHO WASHED MY FAVORITE SHIRT WITHOUT ASKING?!
OH! SORRY!
I JUST PUT IT IN WITH THE OTHER HAND-WASHING!
H-HAND-WASH-ING...?
I also sewed the button on while I was at it. Is that okay?
BA-DUMP
Meguru-kun...

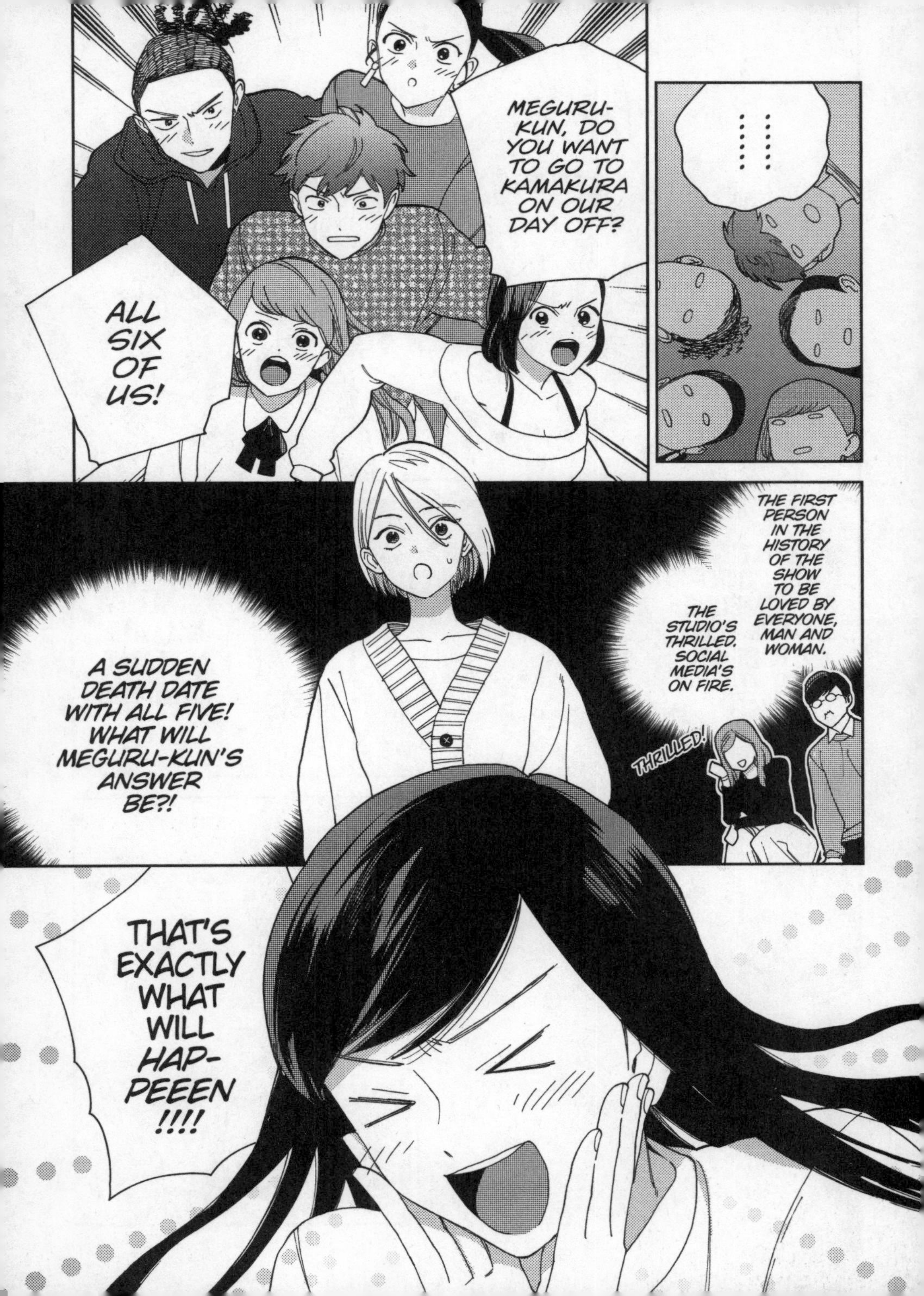
......
MEGURU-KUN, DO YOU WANT TO GO TO KAMAKURA ON OUR DAY OFF?
ALL SIX OF US!
THE FIRST PERSON IN THE HISTORY OF THE SHOW TO BE LOVED BY EVERYONE, MAN AND WOMAN.
THE STUDIO'S THRILLED. SOCIAL MEDIA'S ON FIRE.
THRILLED!
A SUDDEN DEATH DATE WITH ALL FIVE! WHAT WILL MEGURU-KUN'S ANSWER BE?!
THAT'S EXACTLY WHAT WILL HAP-PEEEN!!!!

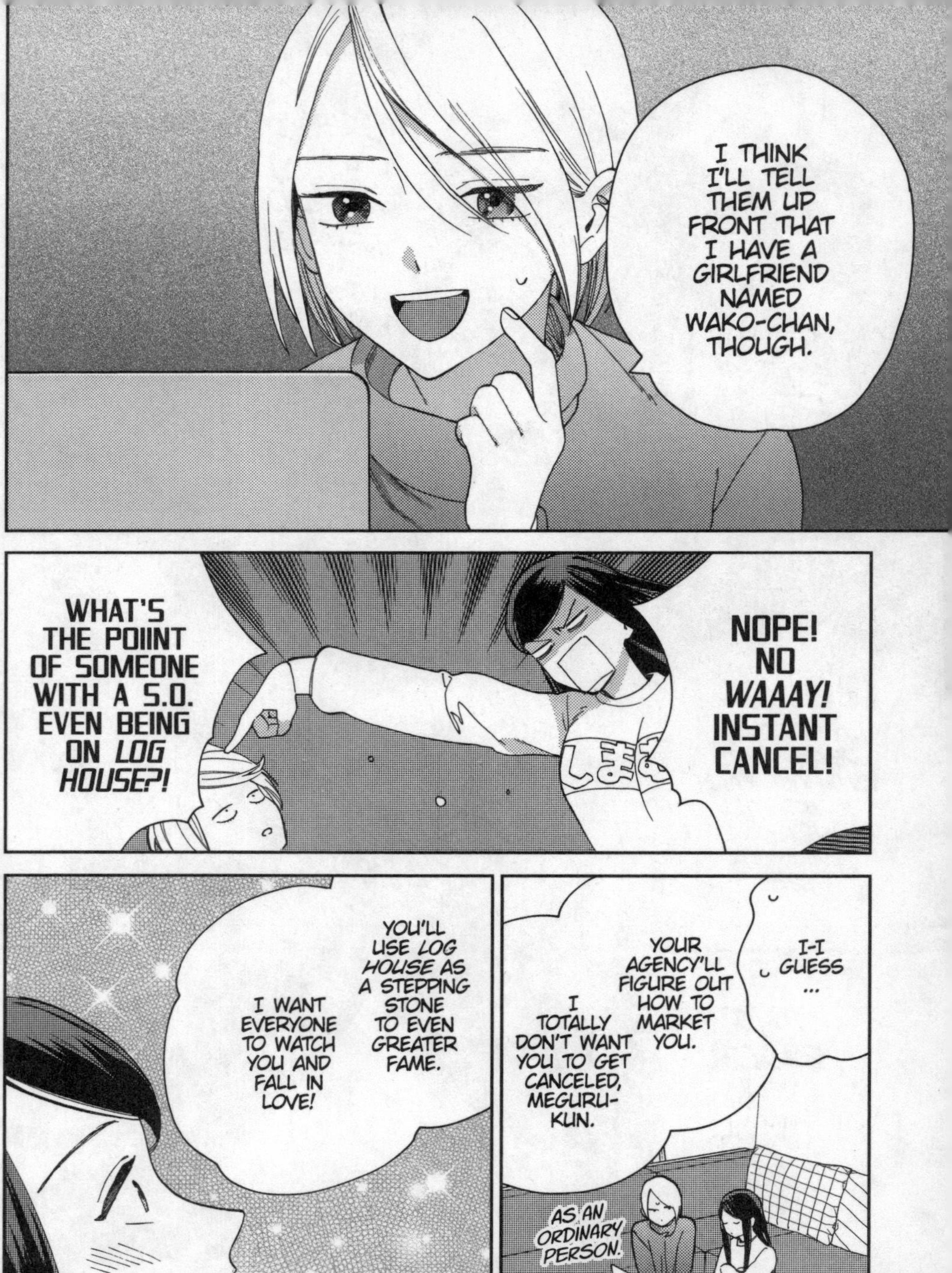
I THINK I'LL TELL THEM UP FRONT THAT I HAVE A GIRLFRIEND NAMED WAKO-CHAN, THOUGH.
NOPE! NO *WAAAY!* INSTANT CANCEL!
WHAT'S THE POIINT OF SOMEONE WITH A S.O. EVEN BEING ON *LOG HOUSE*?!
I-I GUESS ...
YOUR AGENCY'LL FIGURE OUT HOW TO MARKET YOU.
I TOTALLY DON'T WANT YOU TO GET CANCELED, MEGURU-KUN.
AS AN ORDINARY PERSON.
YOU'LL USE *LOG HOUSE* AS A STEPPING STONE TO EVEN GREATER FAME.
I WANT EVERYONE TO WATCH YOU AND FALL IN LOVE!

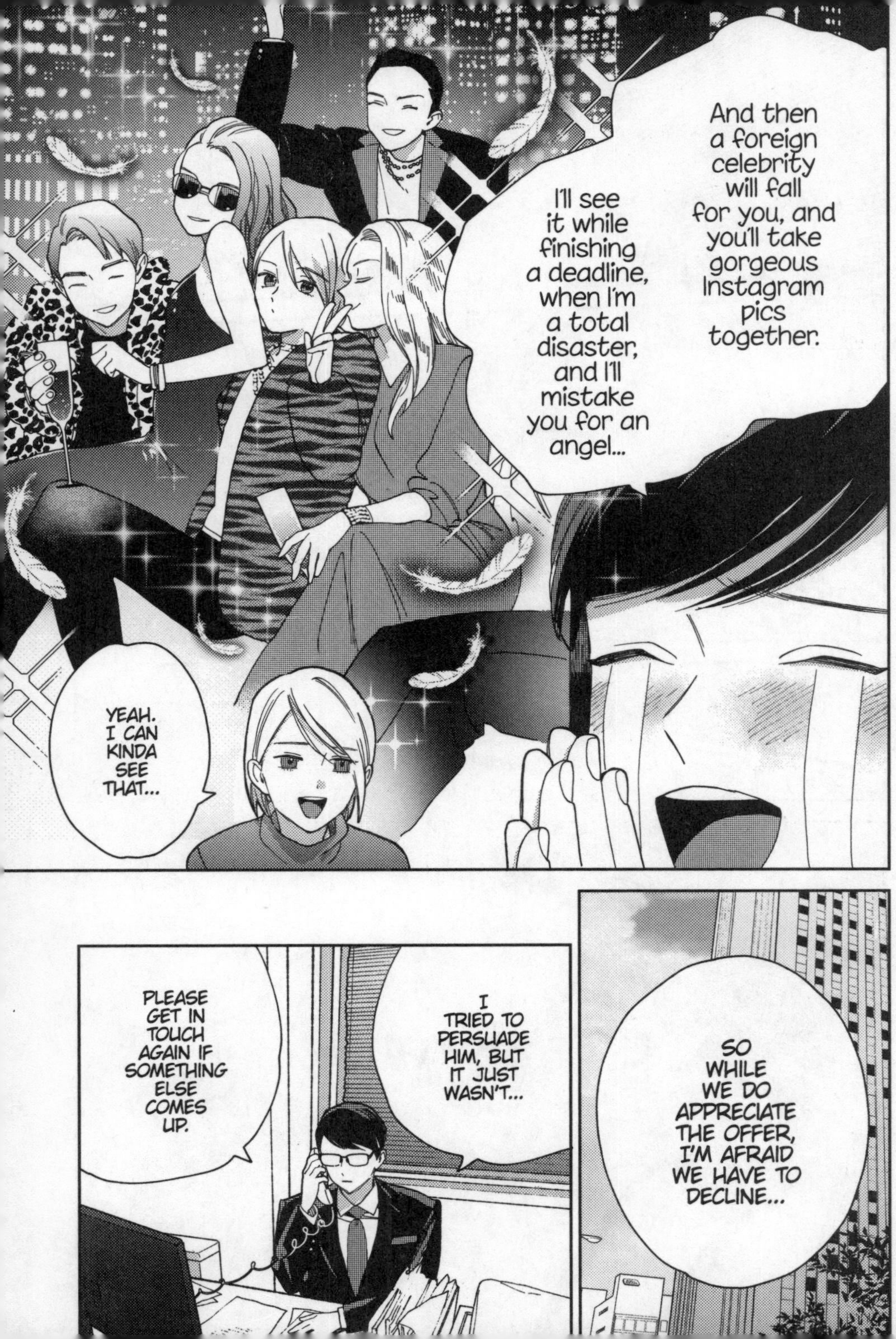
I'll see it while finishing a deadline, when I'm a total disaster, and I'll mistake you for an angel...
And then a foreign celebrity will fall for you, and you'll take gorgeous Instagram pics together.
YEAH. I CAN KINDA SEE THAT...
SO WHILE WE DO APPRECIATE THE OFFER, I'M AFRAID WE HAVE TO DECLINE...
I TRIED TO PERSUADE HIM, BUT IT JUST WASN'T...
PLEASE GET IN TOUCH AGAIN IF SOMETHING ELSE COMES UP.

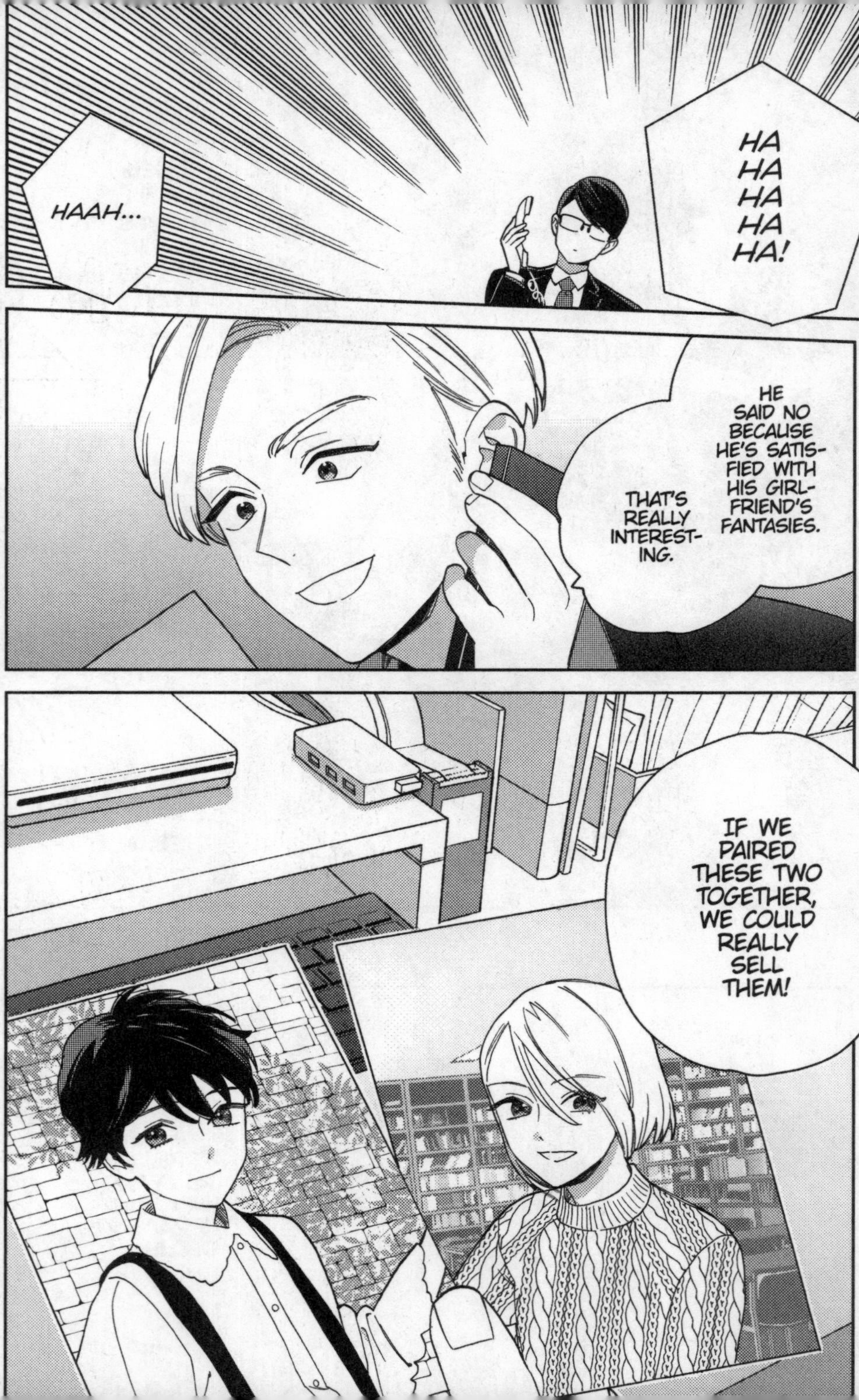
HA HA HA HA HA!
HAAH...
HE SAID NO BECAUSE HE'S SATISFIED WITH HIS GIRLFRIEND'S FANTASIES.
THAT'S REALLY INTERESTING.
IF WE PAIRED THESE TWO TOGETHER, WE COULD REALLY SELL THEM!

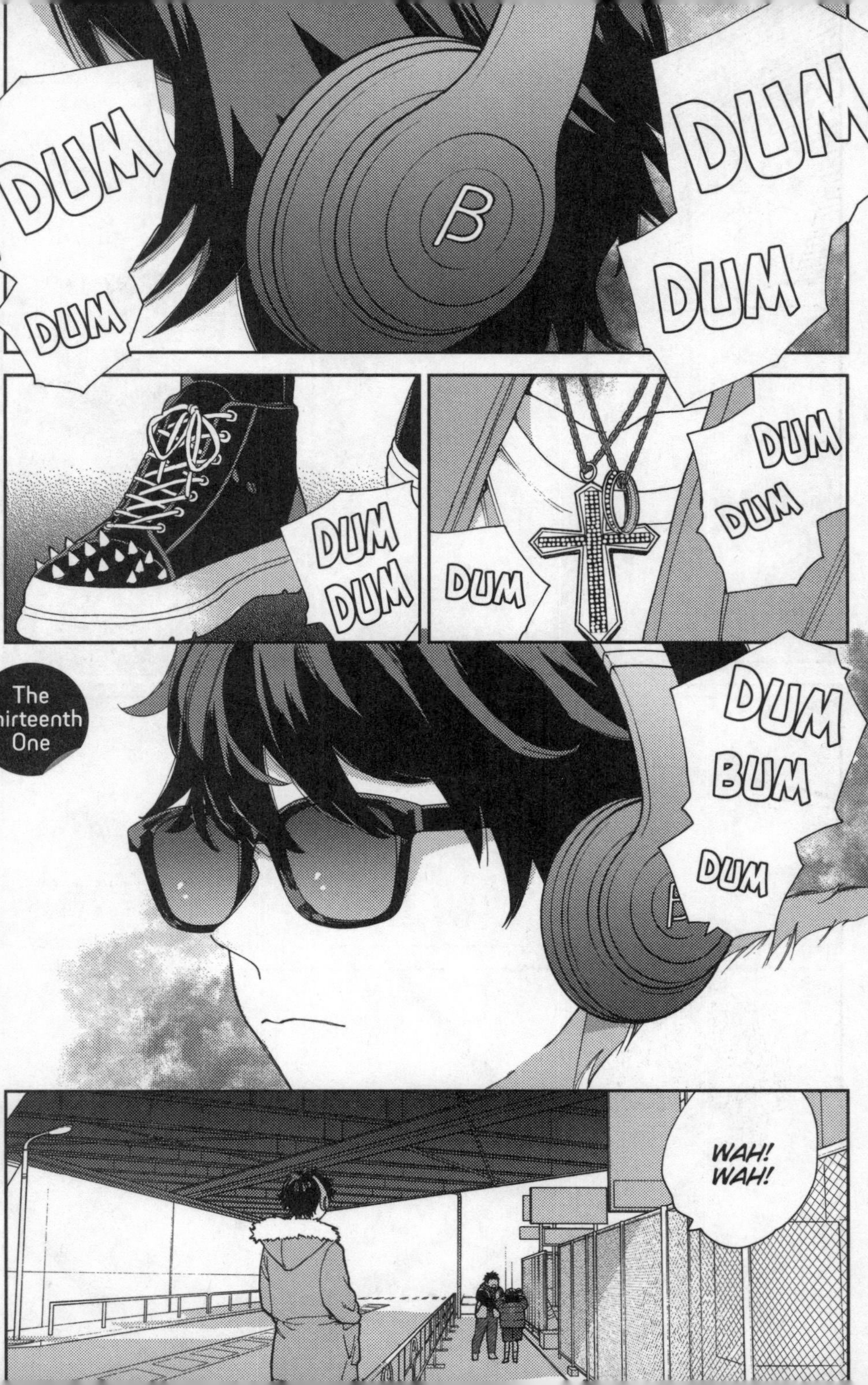
DUM
DUM
DUM
DUM
DUM
DUM
DUM
DUM
DUM
The Thirteenth One
DUM
BUM
DUM
WAH!
WAH!

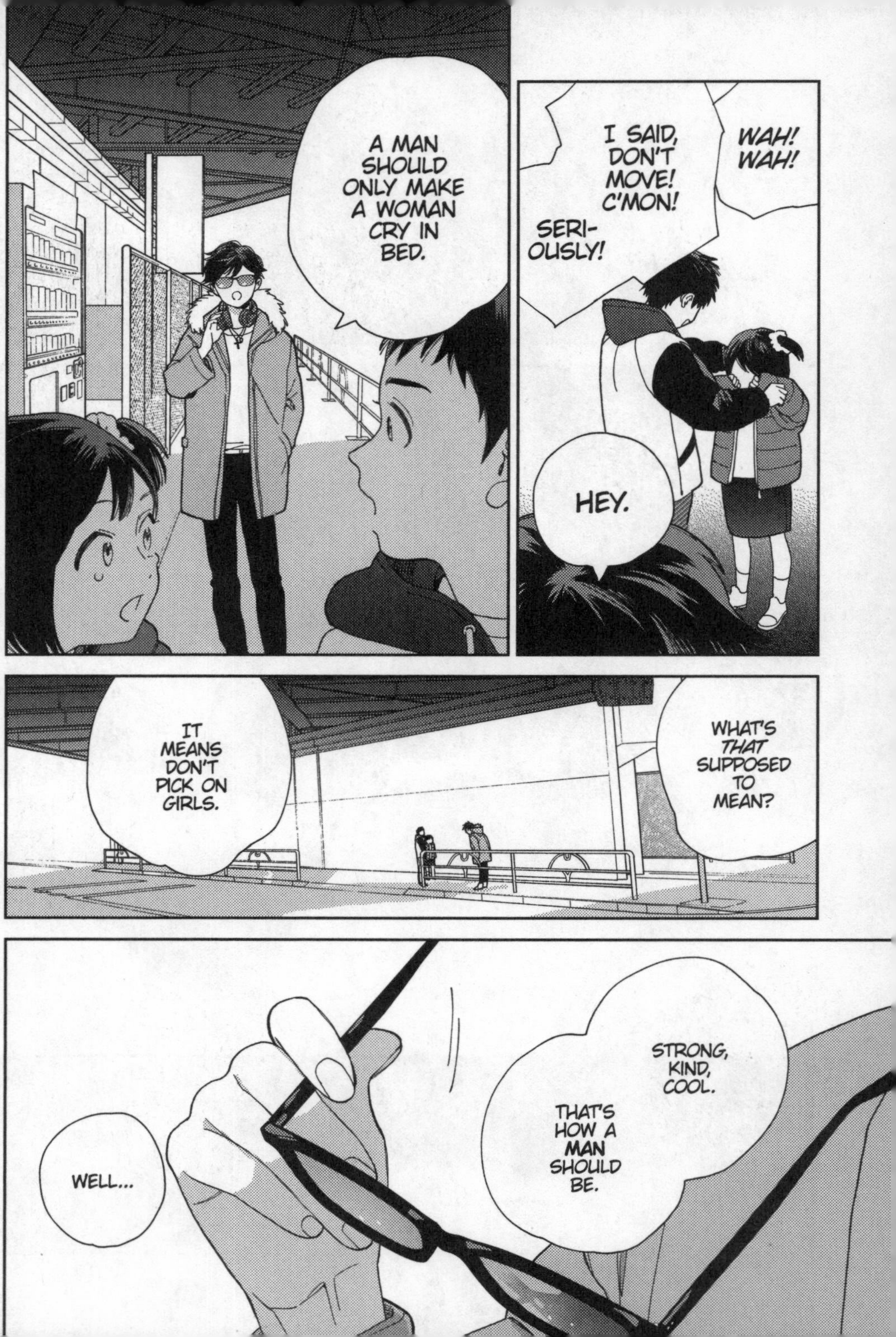
WAH! WAH!
I SAID, DON'T MOVE! C'MON!
SERI-OUSLY!
HEY.
A MAN SHOULD ONLY MAKE A WOMAN CRY IN BED.
WHAT'S *THAT* SUPPOSED TO MEAN?
IT MEANS DON'T PICK ON GIRLS.
STRONG, KIND, COOL.
THAT'S HOW A MAN SHOULD BE.
WELL...

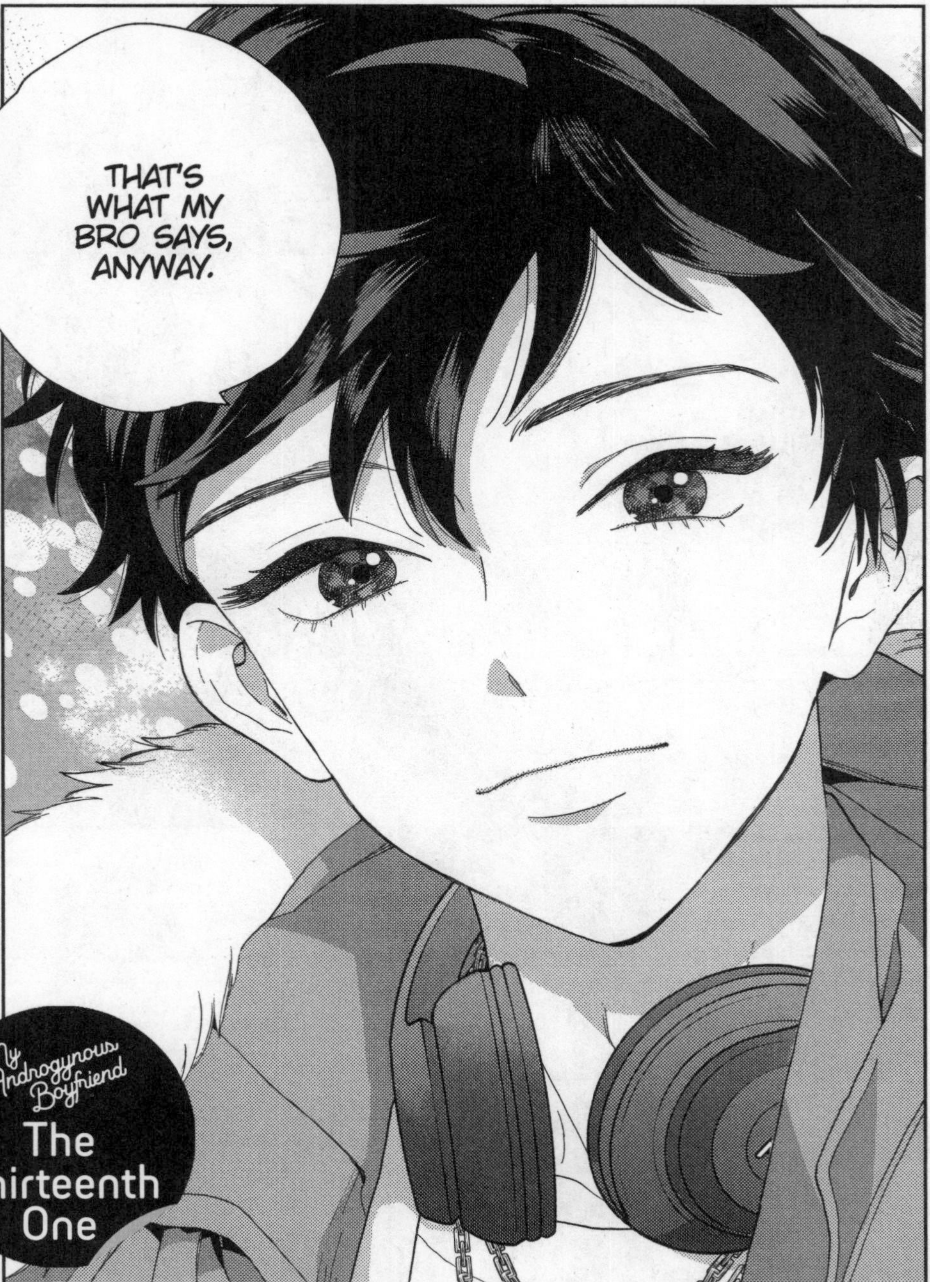
THAT'S WHAT MY BRO SAYS, ANYWAY.
My Androgynous Boyfriend
The Thirteenth One

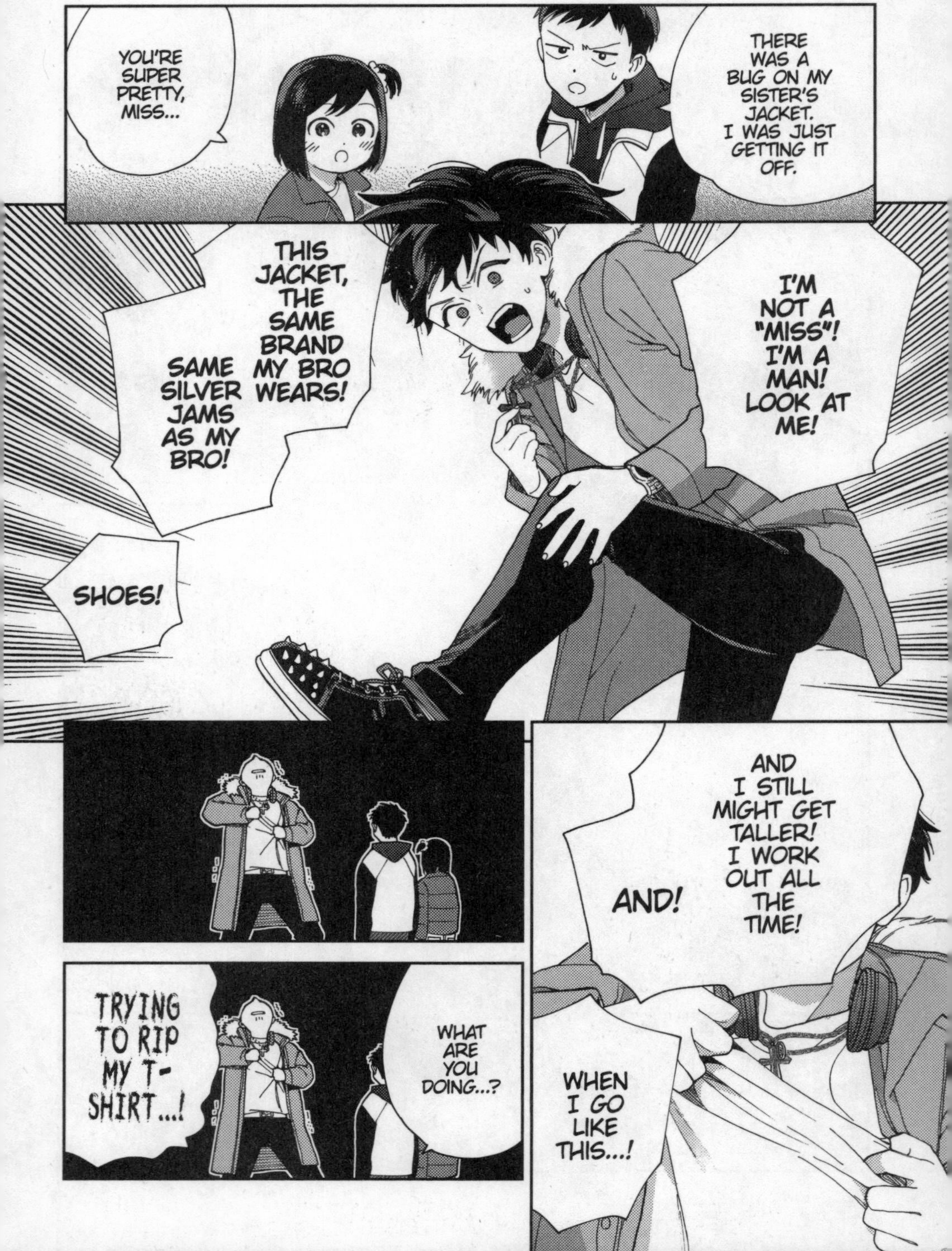
THERE WAS A BUG ON MY SISTER'S JACKET. I WAS JUST GETTING IT OFF.
YOU'RE SUPER PRETTY, MISS...
I'M NOT A "MISS"! I'M A MAN! LOOK AT ME!
THIS JACKET, THE SAME BRAND MY BRO WEARS!
SAME SILVER JAMS AS MY BRO!
SHOES!
AND I STILL MIGHT GET TALLER! I WORK OUT ALL THE TIME!
AND!
WHEN I GO LIKE THIS...!
WHAT ARE YOU DOING...?
TRYING TO RIP MY T-SHIRT...!

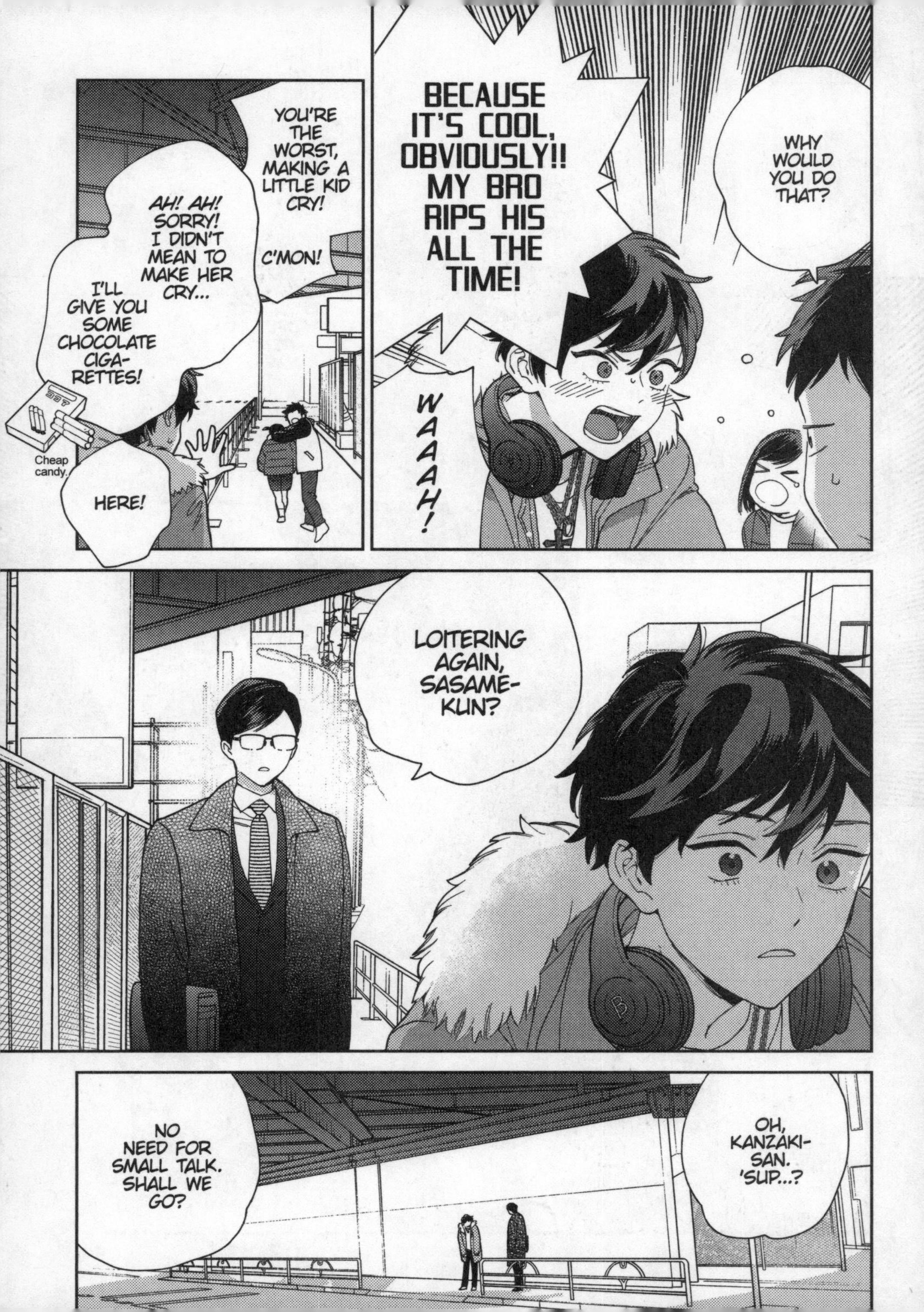
WHY WOULD YOU DO THAT?
BECAUSE IT'S COOL, OBVIOUSLY!! MY BRO RIPS HIS ALL THE TIME!
WAAAAH!
YOU'RE THE WORST, MAKING A LITTLE KID CRY!
C'MON!
AH! AH! SORRY! I DIDN'T MEAN TO MAKE HER CRY...
I'LL GIVE YOU SOME CHOCOLATE CIGARETTES!
HERE!
Cheap candy.
LOITERING AGAIN, SASAME-KUN?
OH, KANZAKI-SAN. 'SUP...?
NO NEED FOR SMALL TALK. SHALL WE GO?

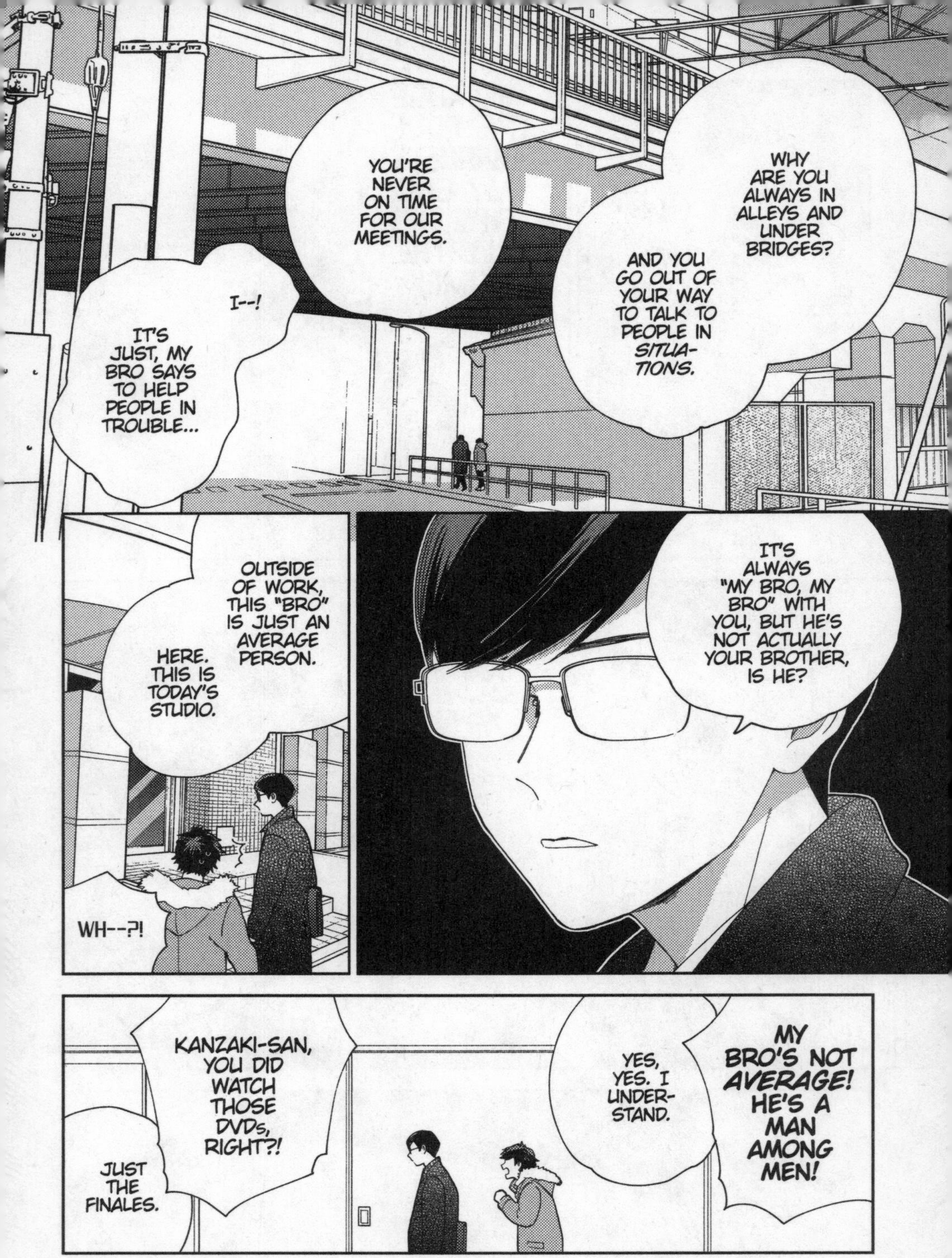
WHY ARE YOU ALWAYS IN ALLEYS AND UNDER BRIDGES?
AND YOU GO OUT OF YOUR WAY TO TALK TO PEOPLE IN SITUATIONS.
YOU'RE NEVER ON TIME FOR OUR MEETINGS.
I--!
IT'S JUST, MY BRO SAYS TO HELP PEOPLE IN TROUBLE...
IT'S ALWAYS "MY BRO, MY BRO" WITH YOU, BUT HE'S NOT ACTUALLY YOUR BROTHER, IS HE?
OUTSIDE OF WORK, THIS "BRO" IS JUST AN AVERAGE PERSON.
HERE. THIS IS TODAY'S STUDIO.
WH--?!
MY BRO'S NOT AVERAGE! HE'S A MAN AMONG MEN!
YES, YES. I UNDERSTAND.
KANZAKI-SAN, YOU DID WATCH THOSE DVDs, RIGHT?!
JUST THE FINALES.

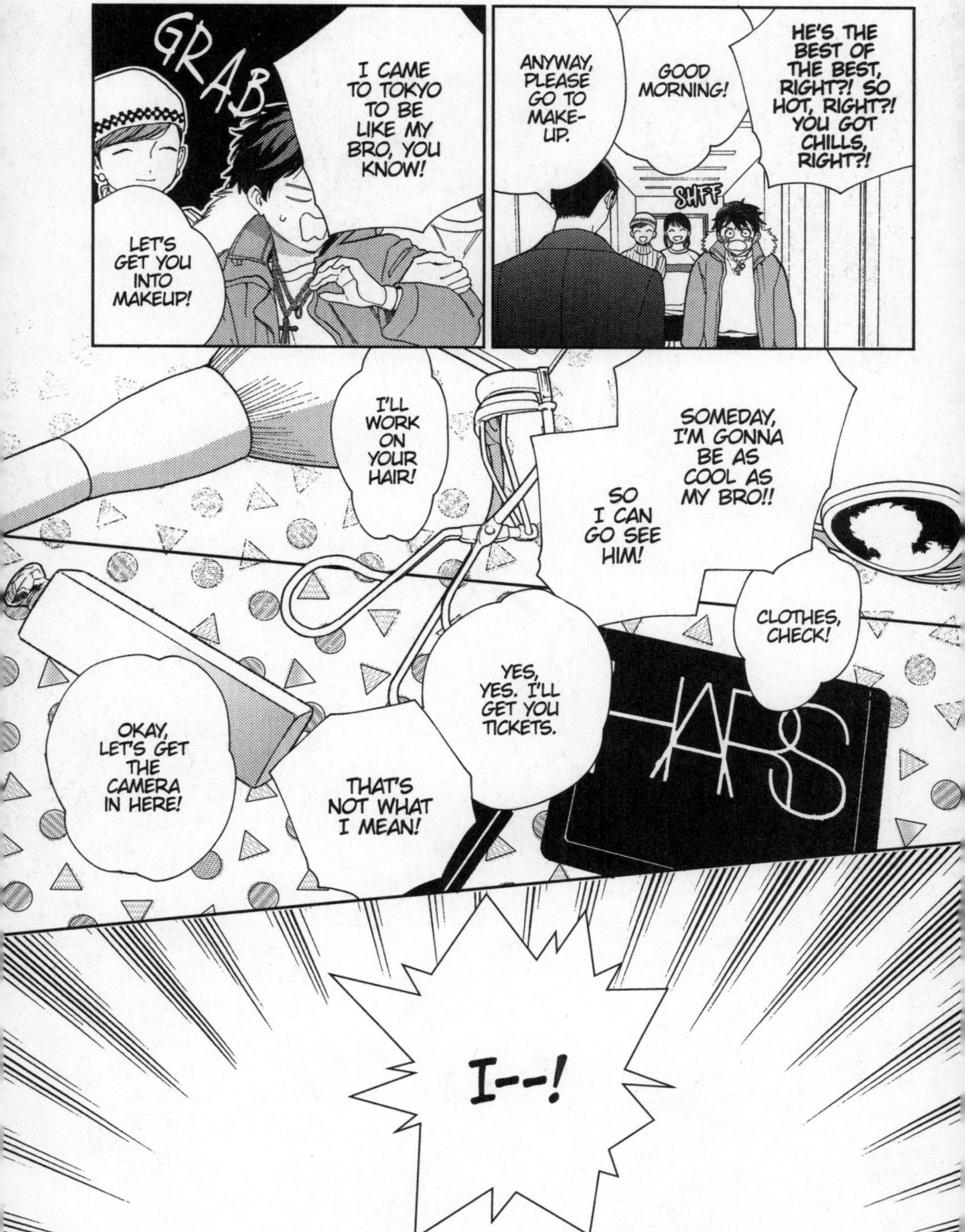
HE'S THE BEST OF THE BEST, RIGHT?! SO HOT, RIGHT?! YOU GOT CHILLS, RIGHT?!
GOOD MORNING!
ANYWAY, PLEASE GO TO MAKE-UP.
SHFF
I CAME TO TOKYO TO BE LIKE MY BRO, YOU KNOW!
GRAB
LET'S GET YOU INTO MAKEUP!
SOMEDAY, I'M GONNA BE AS COOL AS MY BRO!!
SO I CAN GO SEE HIM!
I'LL WORK ON YOUR HAIR!
CLOTHES, CHECK!
YES, YES. I'LL GET YOU TICKETS.
THAT'S NOT WHAT I MEAN!
OKAY, LET'S GET THE CAMERA IN HERE!
I--!

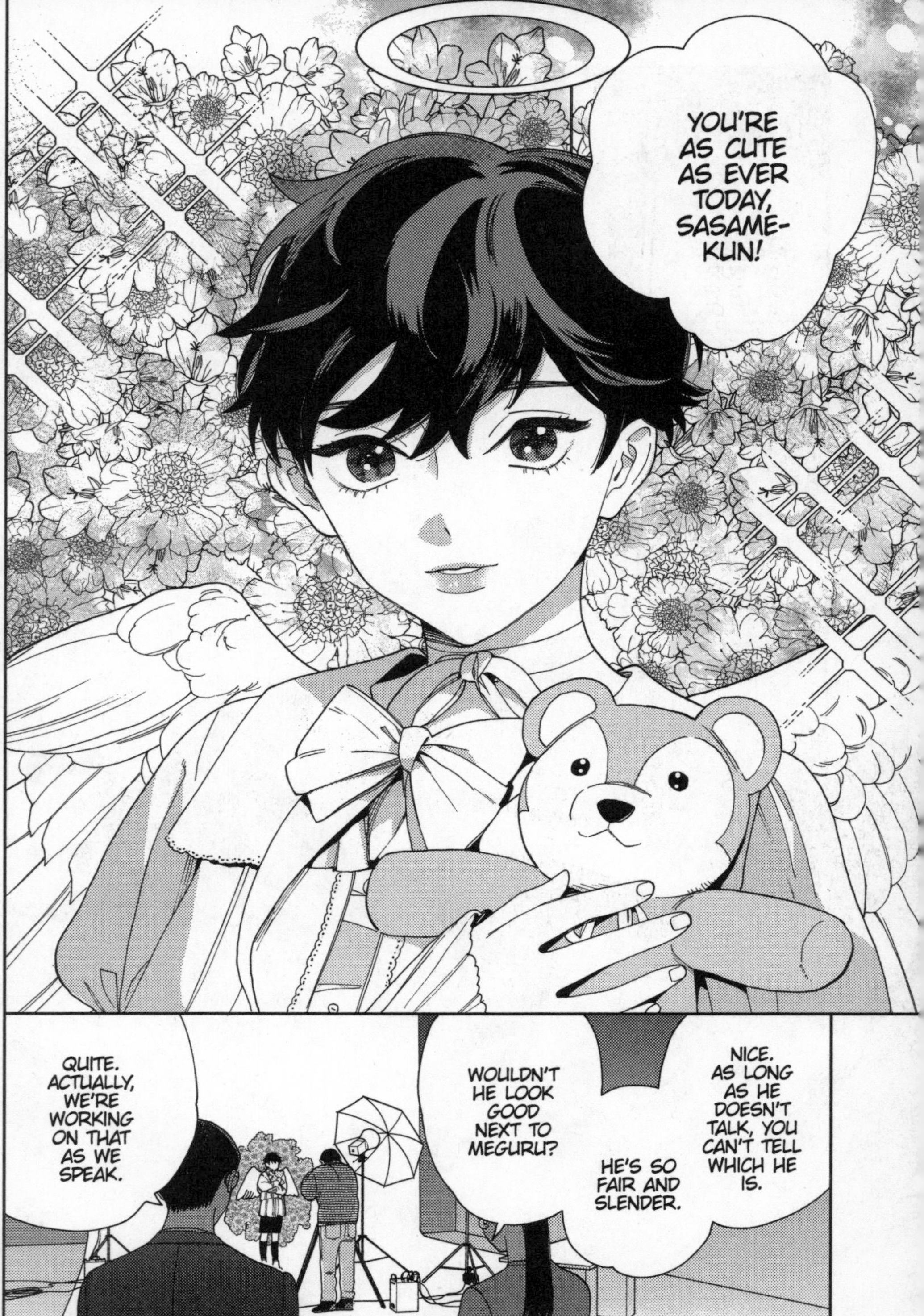
YOU'RE AS CUTE AS EVER TODAY, SASAME-KUN!
NICE. AS LONG AS HE DOESN'T TALK, YOU CAN'T TELL WHICH HE IS.
HE'S SO FAIR AND SLENDER.
WOULDN'T HE LOOK GOOD NEXT TO MEGURU?
QUITE. ACTUALLY, WE'RE WORKING ON THAT AS WE SPEAK.

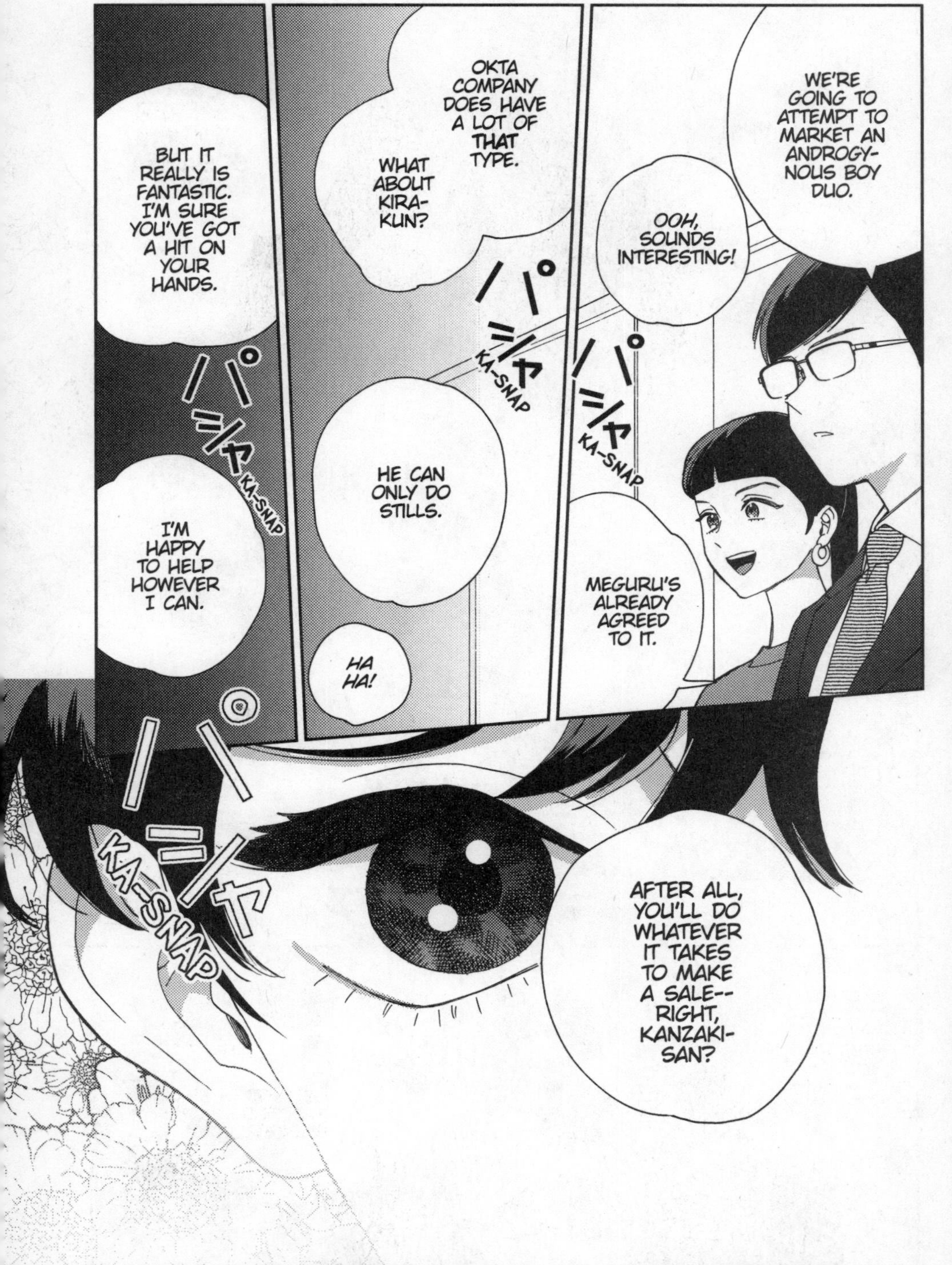

WE'RE GOING TO ATTEMPT TO MARKET AN ANDROGYNOUS BOY DUO.
OOH, SOUNDS INTERESTING!
パシャ
KA-SNAP
MEGURU'S ALREADY AGREED TO IT.
OKTA COMPANY DOES HAVE A LOT OF THAT TYPE.
WHAT ABOUT KIRA-KUN?
パシャ
KA-SNAP
HE CAN ONLY DO STILLS.
HA HA!
BUT IT REALLY IS FANTASTIC. I'M SURE YOU'VE GOT A HIT ON YOUR HANDS.
パシャ
KA-SNAP
I'M HAPPY TO HELP HOWEVER I CAN.
パシャ
KA-SNAP
AFTER ALL, YOU'LL DO WHATEVER IT TAKES TO MAKE A SALE--RIGHT, KANZAKI-SAN?

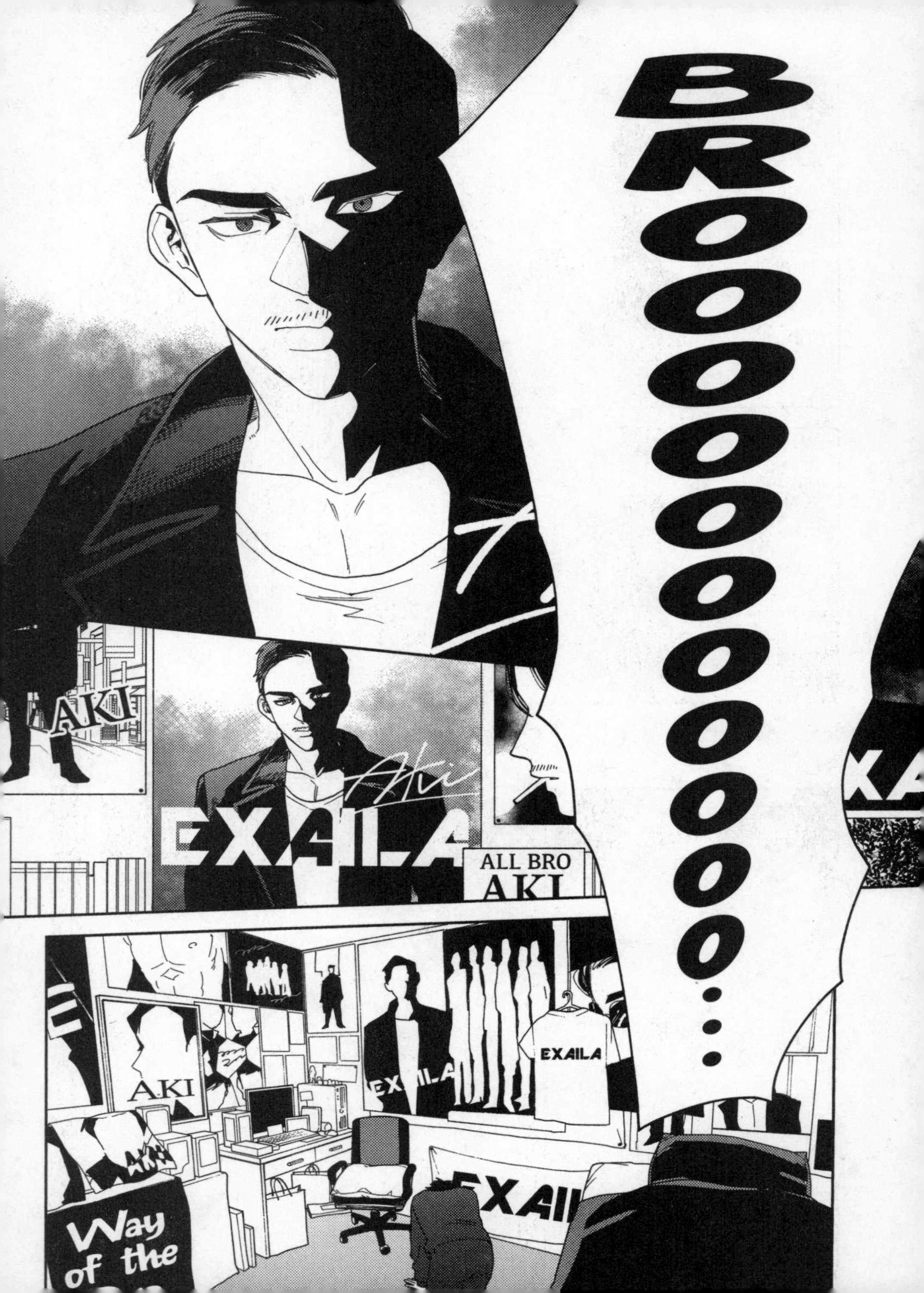
BROOOOOOOOOOO...
AKI
EXAILA
ALL BRO
AKI
EXAILA
AKI
EXAILA
Way
of the

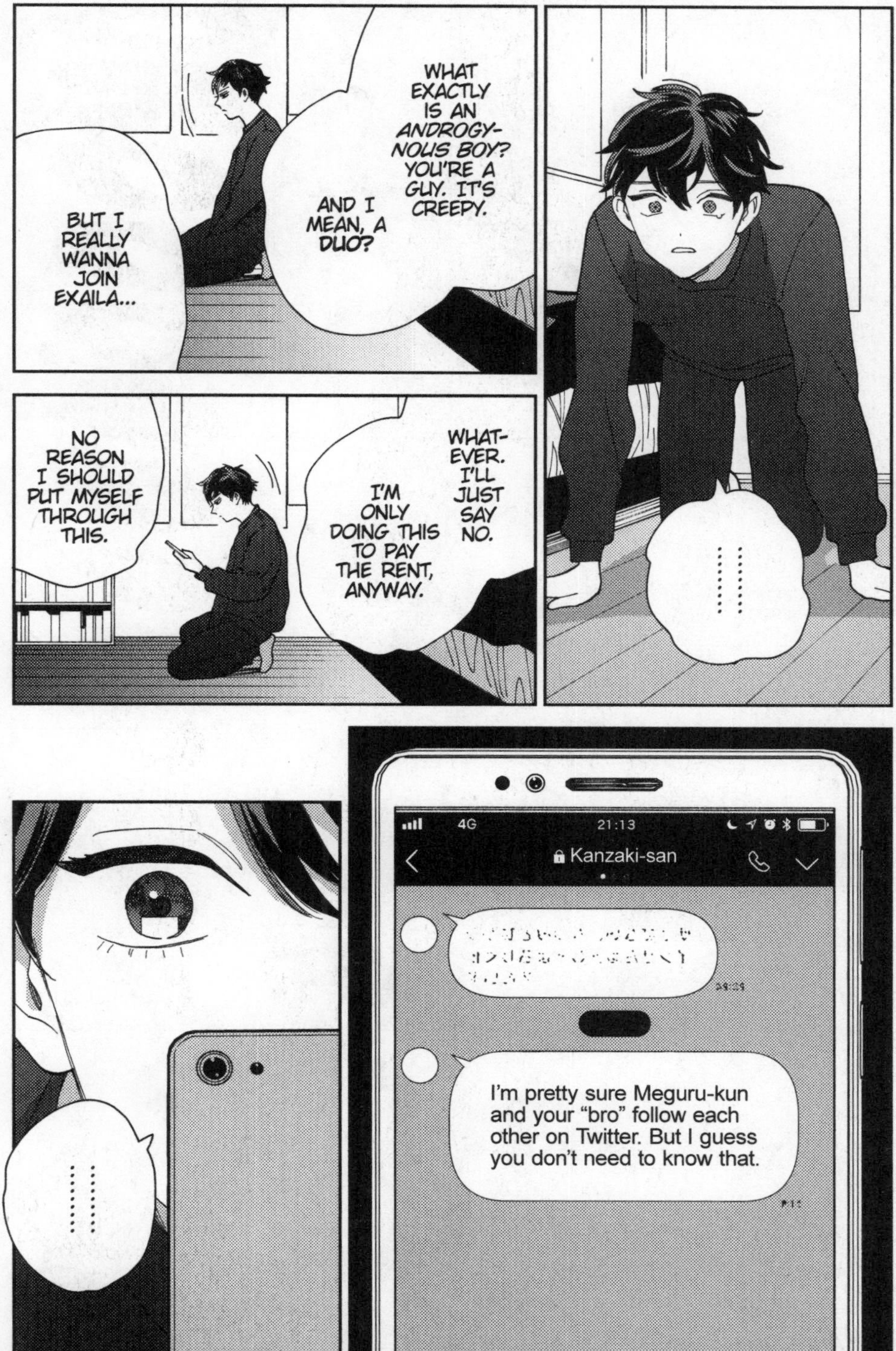
……
WHAT EXACTLY IS AN ANDROGYNOUS BOY? YOU'RE A GUY. IT'S CREEPY.
AND I MEAN, A DUO?
BUT I REALLY WANNA JOIN EXAILA...
WHATEVER. I'LL JUST SAY NO.
I'M ONLY DOING THIS TO PAY THE RENT, ANYWAY.
NO REASON I SHOULD PUT MYSELF THROUGH THIS.
4G 21:13
Kanzaki-san
I'm pretty sure Meguru-kun and your "bro" follow each other on Twitter. But I guess you don't need to know that.
……

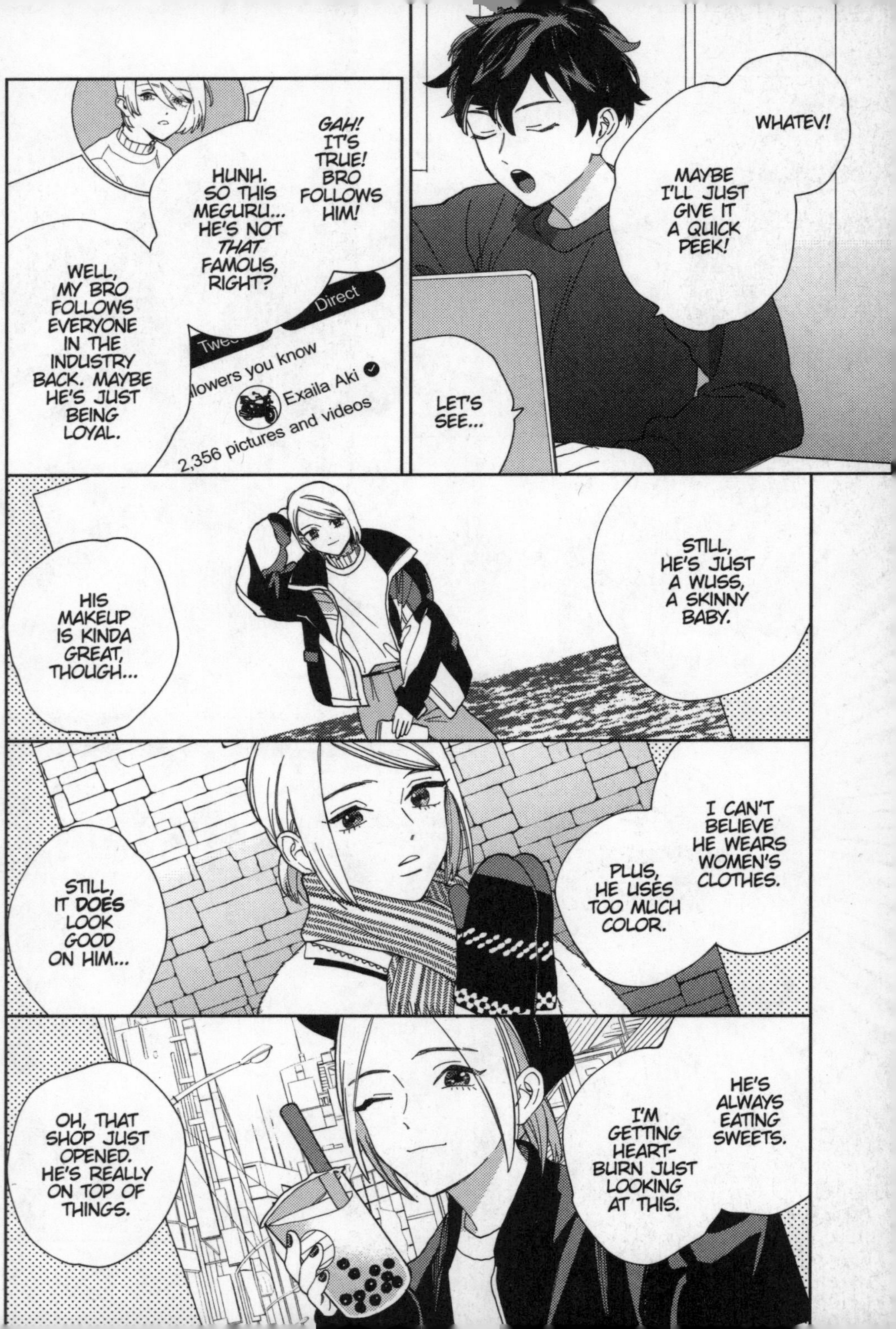
WHATEV!
MAYBE I'LL JUST GIVE IT A QUICK PEEK!
LET'S SEE...
GAH! IT'S TRUE! BRO FOLLOWS HIM!
HUNH. SO THIS MEGURU... HE'S NOT *THAT* FAMOUS, RIGHT?
Direct
Exaila Aki
2,356 pictures and videos
WELL, MY BRO FOLLOWS EVERYONE IN THE INDUSTRY BACK. MAYBE HE'S JUST BEING LOYAL.
STILL, HE'S JUST A WUSS, A SKINNY BABY.
HIS MAKEUP IS KINDA GREAT, THOUGH...
I CAN'T BELIEVE HE WEARS WOMEN'S CLOTHES.
PLUS, HE USES TOO MUCH COLOR.
STILL, IT **DOES** LOOK GOOD ON HIM...
HE'S ALWAYS EATING SWEETS.
I'M GETTING HEART-BURN JUST LOOKING AT THIS.
OH, THAT SHOP JUST OPENED. HE'S REALLY ON TOP OF THINGS.

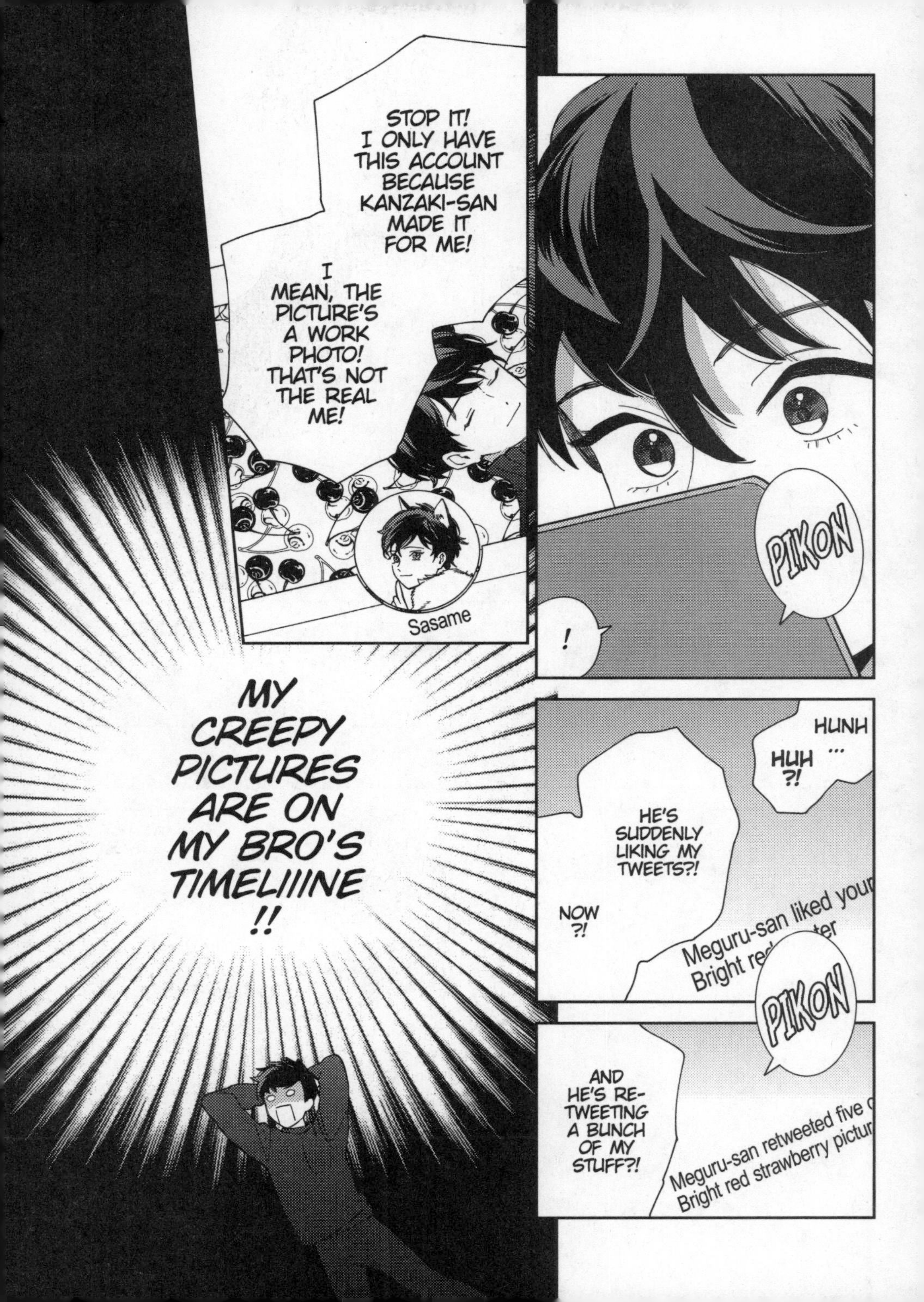
PIKON
!
STOP IT! I ONLY HAVE THIS ACCOUNT BECAUSE KANZAKI-SAN MADE IT FOR ME!
I MEAN, THE PICTURE'S A WORK PHOTO! THAT'S NOT THE REAL ME!
Sasame
HUNH ...
HUH ?!
HE'S SUDDENLY LIKING MY TWEETS?!
NOW ?!
Meguru-san liked your
Bright red
PIKON
AND HE'S RE-TWEETING A BUNCH OF MY STUFF?!
Meguru-san retweeted five
Bright red strawberry
MY CREEPY PICTURES ARE ON MY BRO'S TIMELIIINE !!

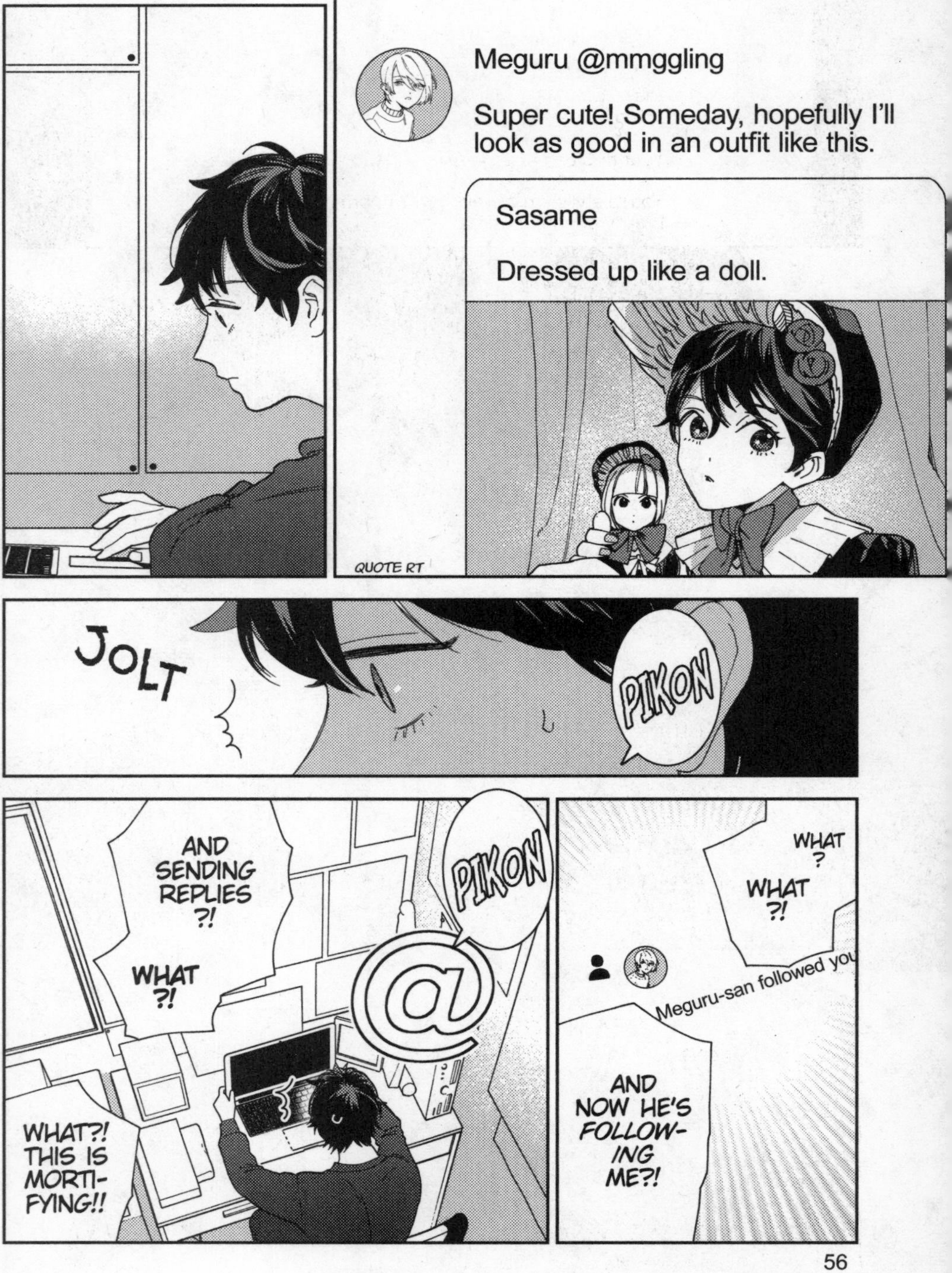
Meguru @mmggling
Super cute! Someday, hopefully I'll look as good in an outfit like this.
Sasame
Dressed up like a doll.
QUOTE RT
PIKON
JOLT
WHAT?
WHAT?!
Meguru-san followed you
AND NOW HE'S FOLLOWING ME?!
PIKON
@
AND SENDING REPLIES?!
WHAT?!
WHAT?! THIS IS MORTIFYING!!

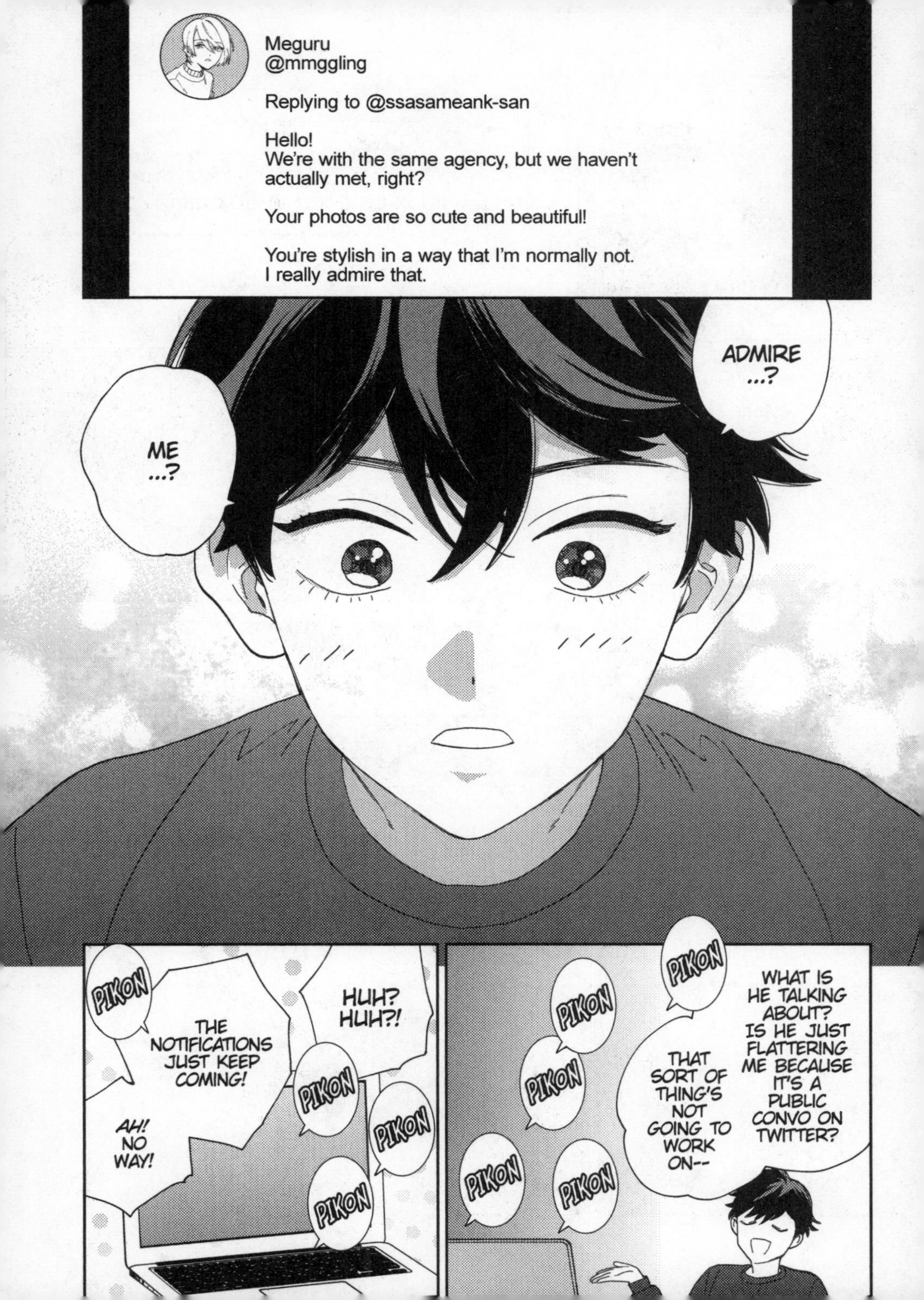
Meguru
@mmggling
Replying to @ssasameank-san
Hello!
We're with the same agency, but we haven't actually met, right?
Your photos are so cute and beautiful!
You're stylish in a way that I'm normally not.
I really admire that.
ADMIRE ...?
ME ...?
PIKON
WHAT IS HE TALKING ABOUT? IS HE JUST FLATTERING ME BECAUSE IT'S A PUBLIC CONVO ON TWITTER?
PIKON
THAT SORT OF THING'S NOT GOING TO WORK ON--
PIKON
PIKON
PIKON
HUH? HUH?!
PIKON
THE NOTIFICATIONS JUST KEEP COMING!
PIKON
PIKON
AH! NO WAY!
PIKON

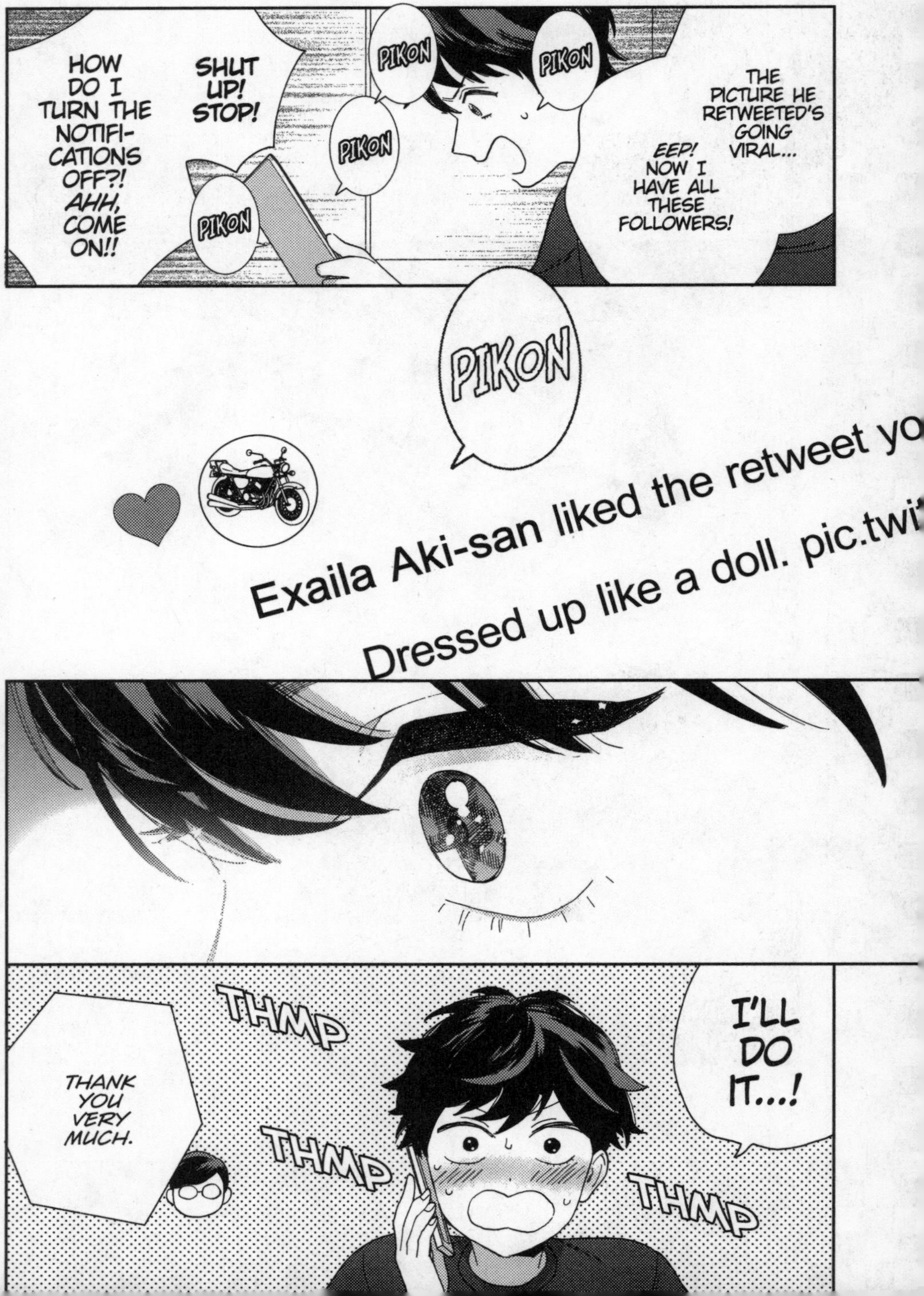
THE PICTURE HE RETWEETED'S GOING VIRAL...
EEP! NOW I HAVE ALL THESE FOLLOWERS!
PIKON
PIKON
PIKON
PIKON
SHUT UP! STOP!
HOW DO I TURN THE NOTIFICATIONS OFF?! AHH, COME ON!!
PIKON
Exaila Aki-san liked the retweet yo
Dressed up like a doll. pic.twi
I'LL DO IT...!
THMP
THMP
THMP
THANK YOU VERY MUCH.

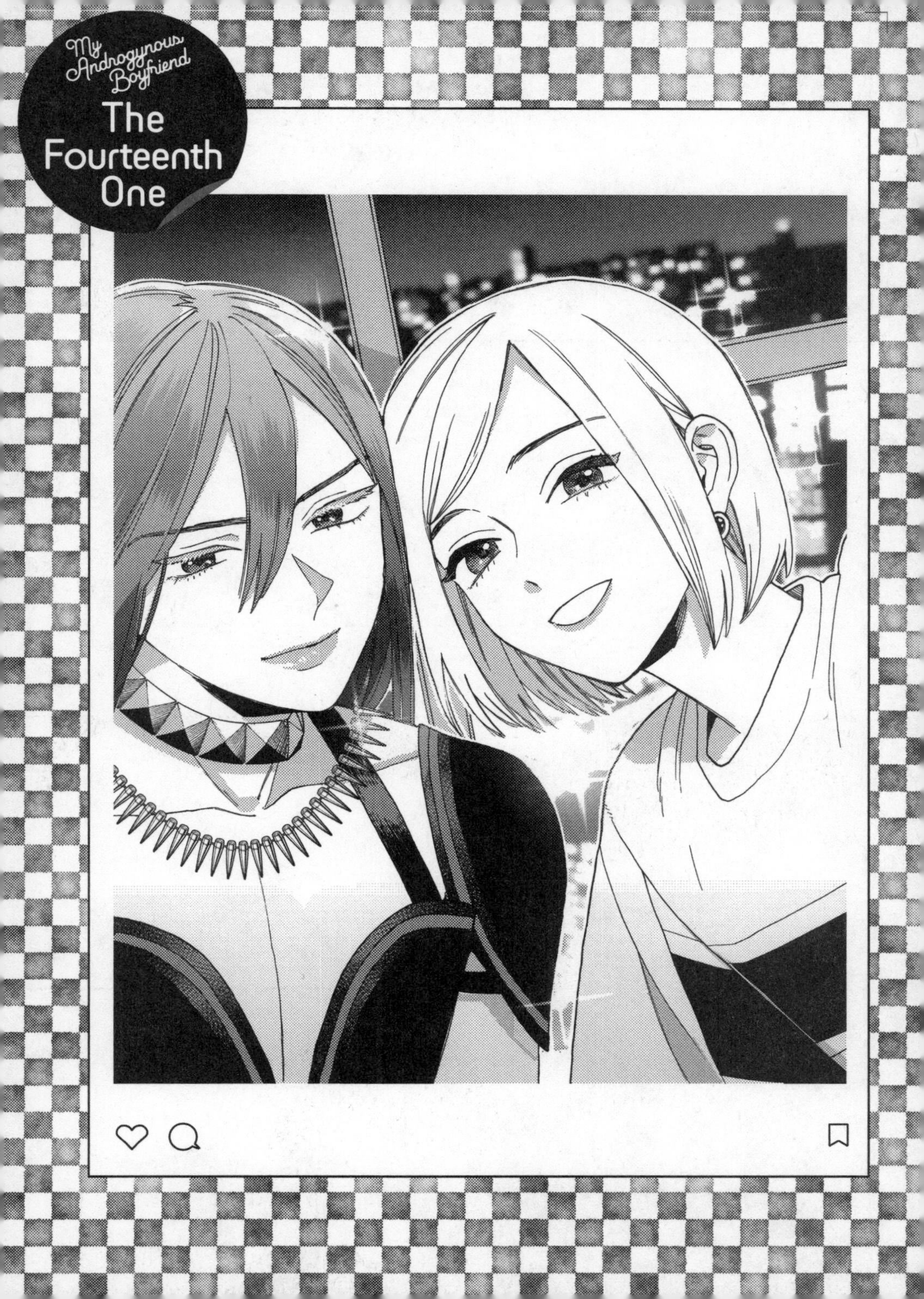
My Androgynous Boyfriend
The Fourteenth One

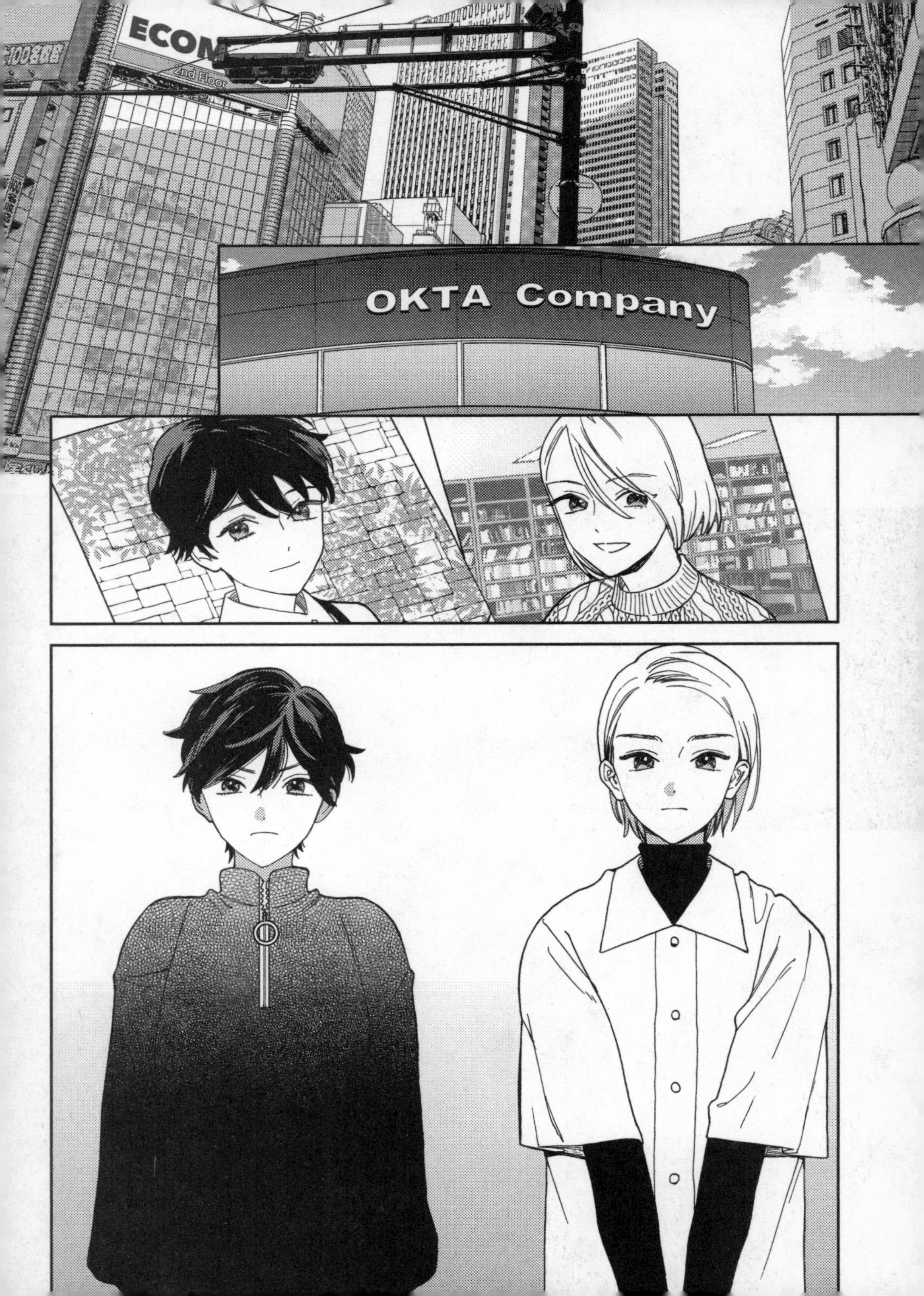
ECOM
2nd Floor
OKTA Company

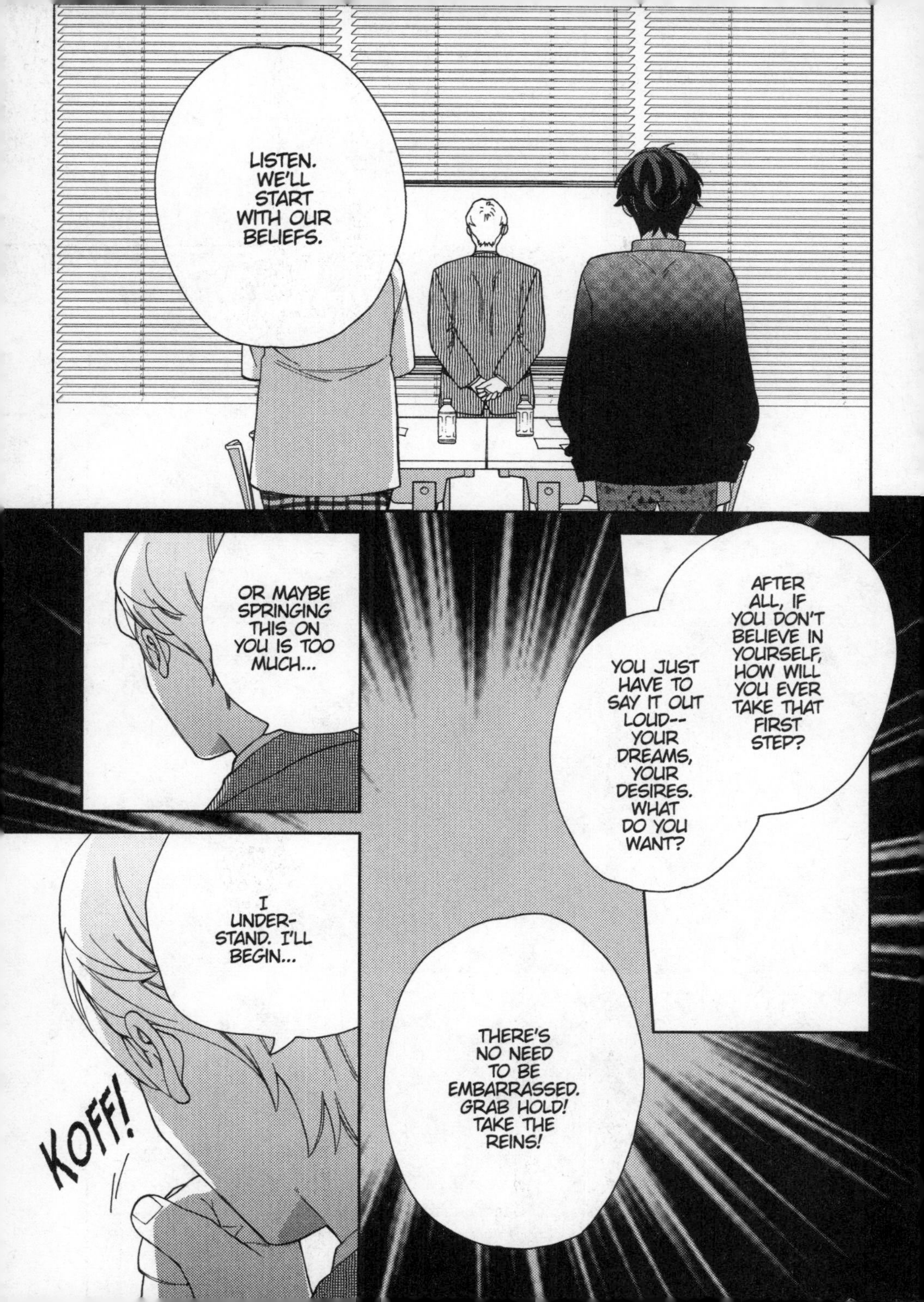
LISTEN. WE'LL START WITH OUR BELIEFS.
AFTER ALL, IF YOU DON'T BELIEVE IN YOURSELF, HOW WILL YOU EVER TAKE THAT FIRST STEP?
YOU JUST HAVE TO SAY IT OUT LOUD-- YOUR DREAMS, YOUR DESIRES. WHAT DO YOU WANT?
THERE'S NO NEED TO BE EMBARRASSED. GRAB HOLD! TAKE THE REINS!
OR MAYBE SPRINGING THIS ON YOU IS TOO MUCH...
I UNDER-STAND. I'LL BEGIN...
KOFF!

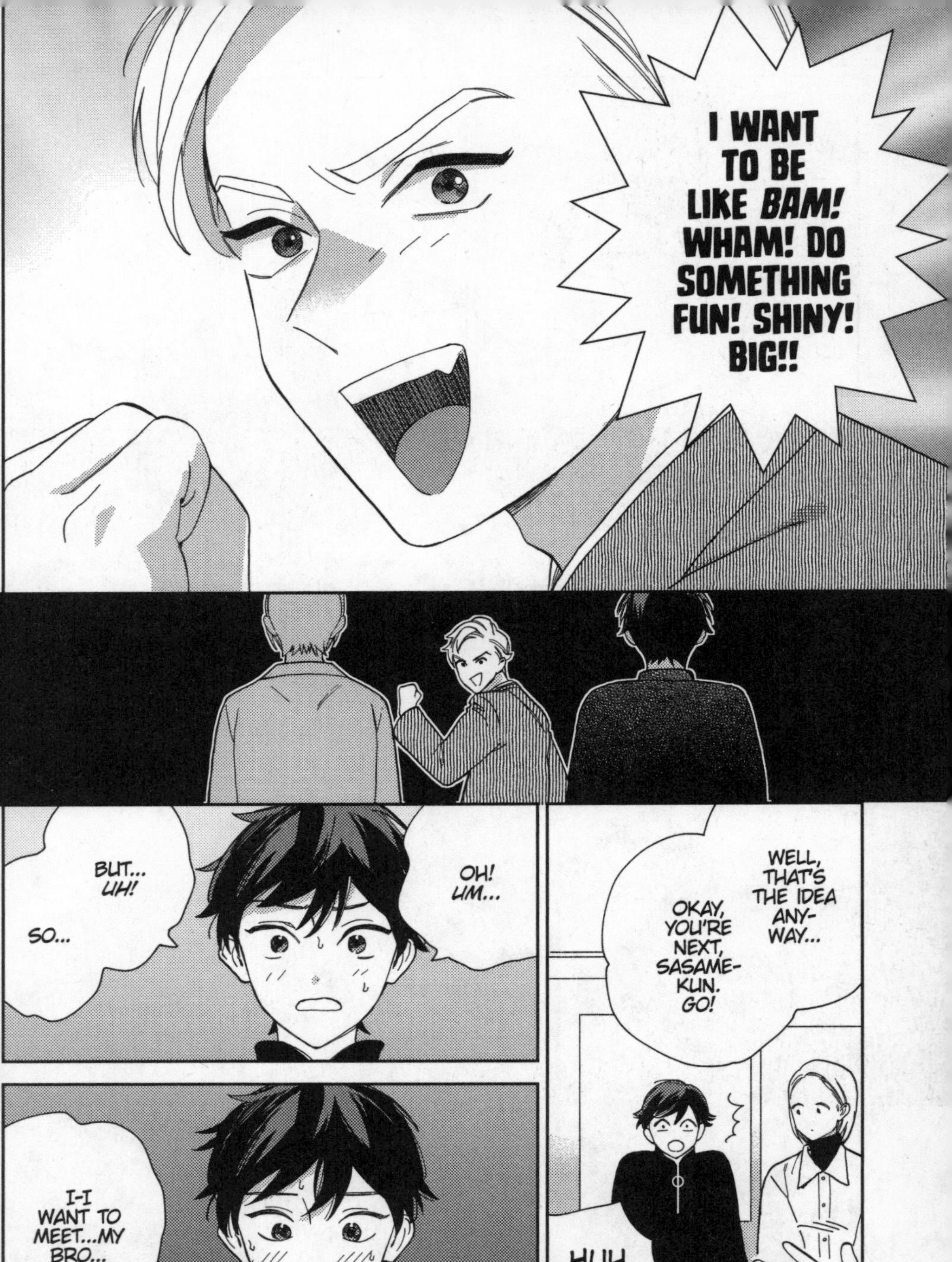
I WANT TO BE LIKE *BAM!* WHAM! DO SOMETHING FUN! SHINY! BIG!!
WELL, THAT'S THE IDEA ANYWAY...
OKAY, YOU'RE NEXT, SASAME-KUN. GO!
HUH ?!
OH! UM...
BUT... UH!
SO...
I-I WANT TO MEET...MY BRO...

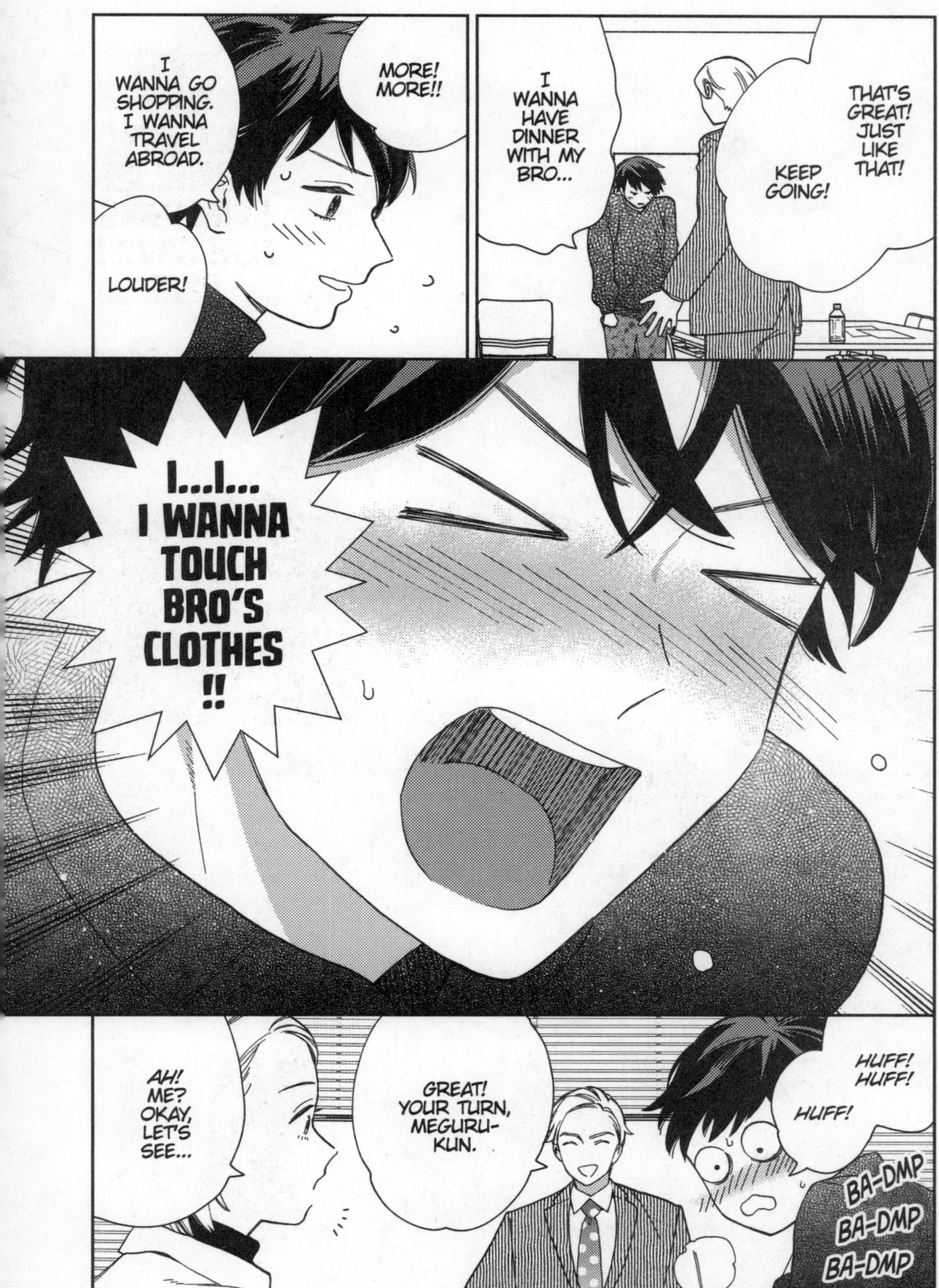
THAT'S GREAT! JUST LIKE THAT!
KEEP GOING!
I WANNA HAVE DINNER WITH MY BRO...
MORE! MORE!!
I WANNA GO SHOPPING. I WANNA TRAVEL ABROAD.
LOUDER!
I...I... I WANNA TOUCH BRO'S CLOTHES !!
HUFF! HUFF!
HUFF!
BA-DMP BA-DMP BA-DMP
GREAT! YOUR TURN, MEGURU-KUN.
AH! ME? OKAY, LET'S SEE...

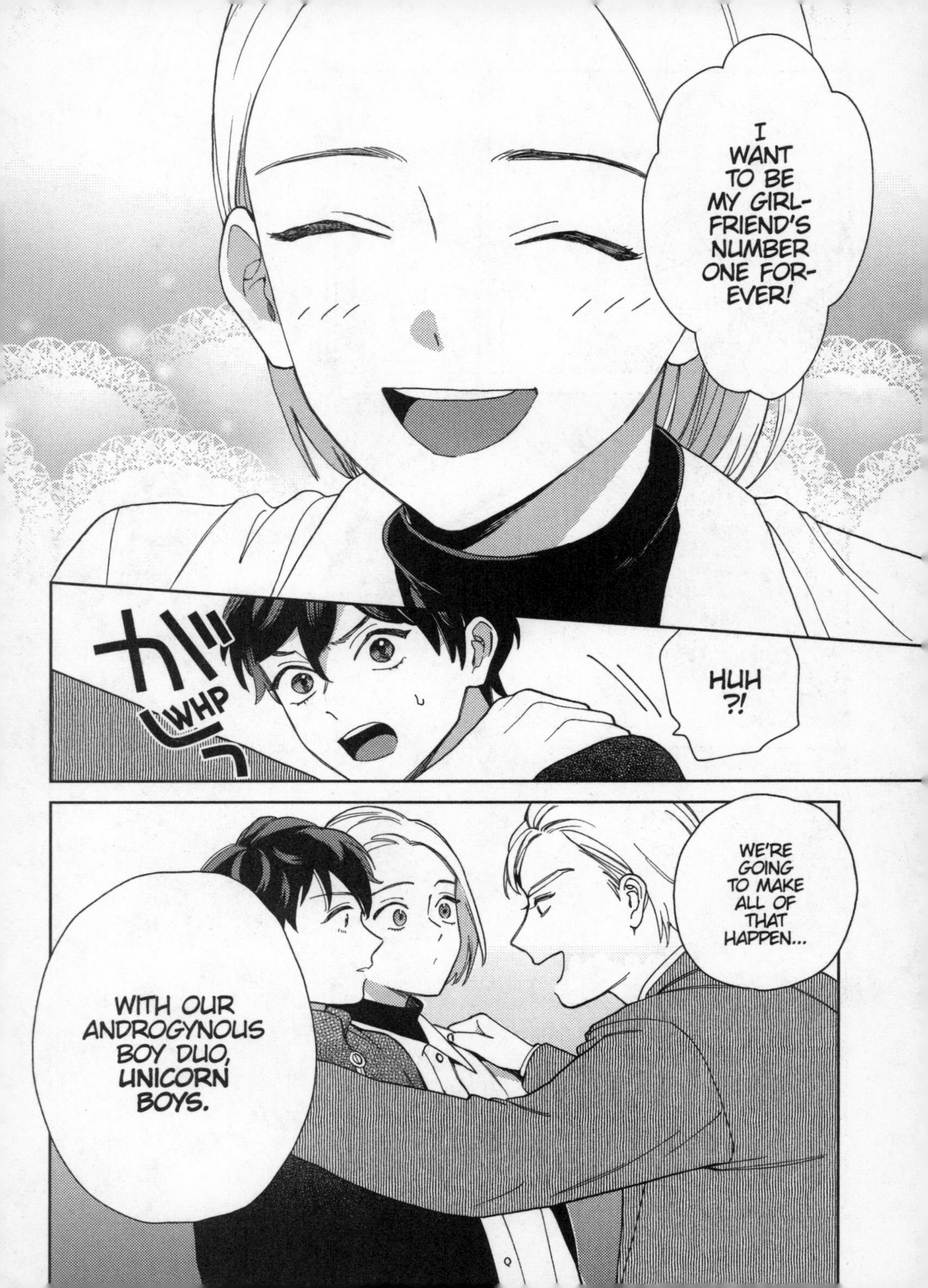
I WANT TO BE MY GIRL-FRIEND'S NUMBER ONE FOR-EVER!
HUH?!
カバ
WHP
WE'RE GOING TO MAKE ALL OF THAT HAPPEN...
WITH OUR ANDROGYNOUS BOY DUO, UNICORN BOYS.

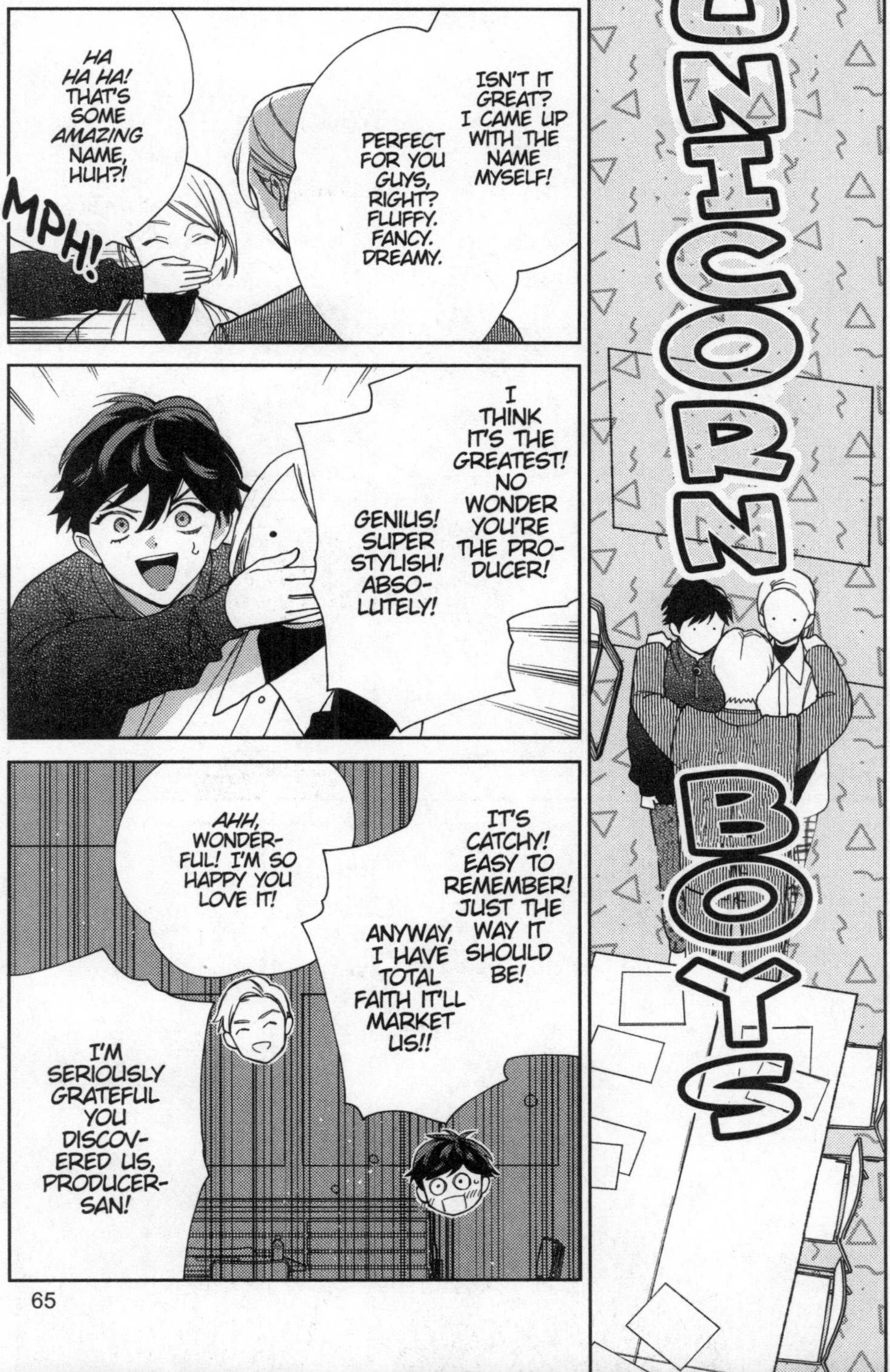
UNICORN BOYS
ISN'T IT GREAT? I CAME UP WITH THE NAME MYSELF!
PERFECT FOR YOU GUYS, RIGHT? FLUFFY. FANCY. DREAMY.
HA HA HA! THAT'S SOME AMAZING NAME, HUH?!
MPH!
I THINK IT'S THE GREATEST! NO WONDER YOU'RE THE PRODUCER!
GENIUS! SUPER STYLISH! ABSOLUTELY!
IT'S CATCHY! EASY TO REMEMBER! JUST THE WAY IT SHOULD BE!
ANYWAY, I HAVE TOTAL FAITH IT'LL MARKET US!!
AHH, WONDERFUL! I'M SO HAPPY YOU LOVE IT!
I'M SERIOUSLY GRATEFUL YOU DISCOVERED US, PRODUCER-SAN!

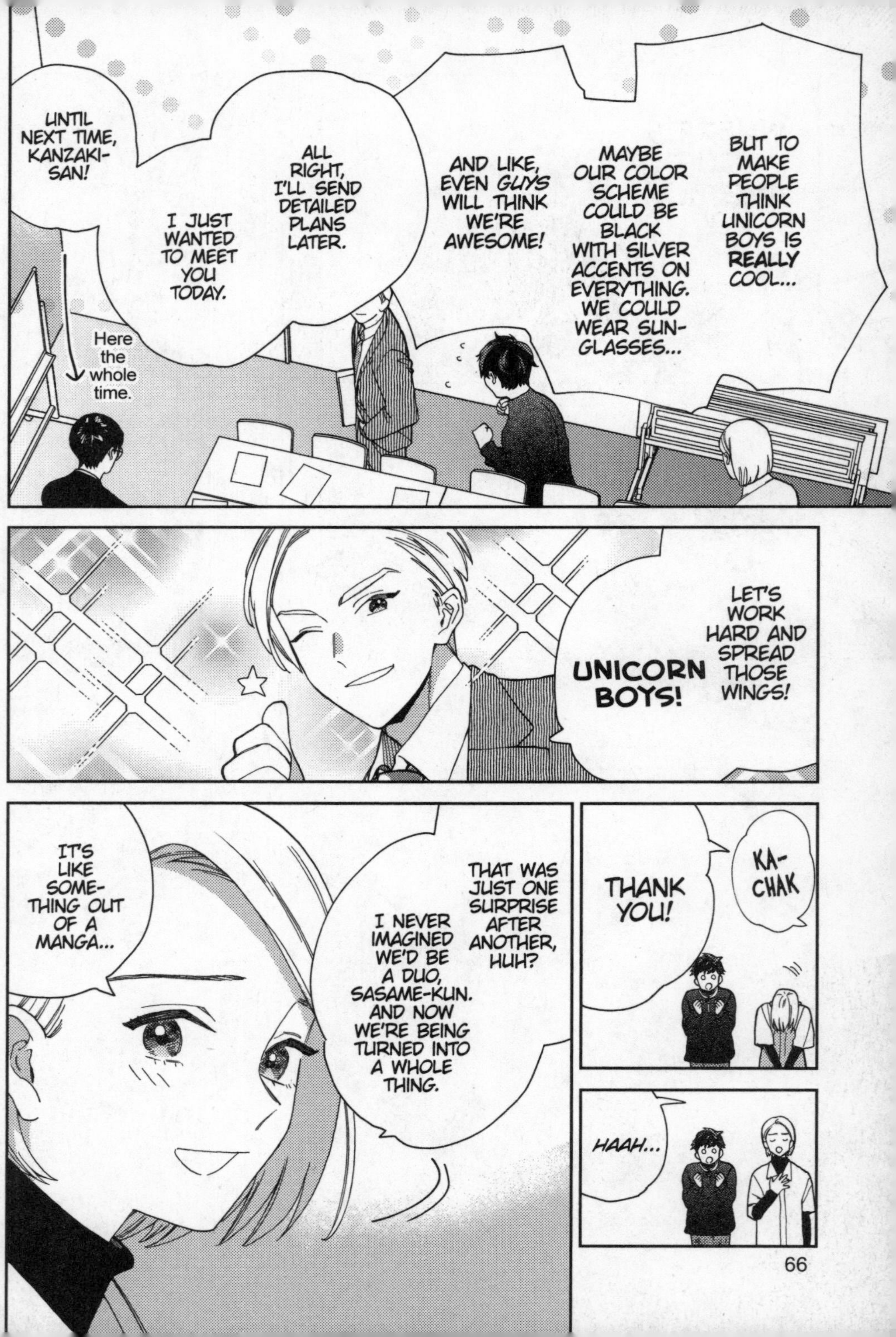
BUT TO MAKE PEOPLE THINK UNICORN BOYS IS REALLY COOL...
MAYBE OUR COLOR SCHEME COULD BE BLACK WITH SILVER ACCENTS ON EVERYTHING. WE COULD WEAR SUN-GLASSES...
AND LIKE, EVEN GUYS WILL THINK WE'RE AWESOME!
ALL RIGHT, I'LL SEND DETAILED PLANS LATER.
I JUST WANTED TO MEET YOU TODAY.
UNTIL NEXT TIME, KANZAKI-SAN!
Here the whole time.
LET'S WORK HARD AND SPREAD THOSE WINGS!
UNICORN BOYS!
KA-CHAK
THANK YOU!
HAAH...
THAT WAS JUST ONE SURPRISE AFTER ANOTHER, HUH?
I NEVER IMAGINED WE'D BE A DUO, SASAME-KUN. AND NOW WE'RE BEING TURNED INTO A WHOLE THING.
IT'S LIKE SOME-THING OUT OF A MANGA...

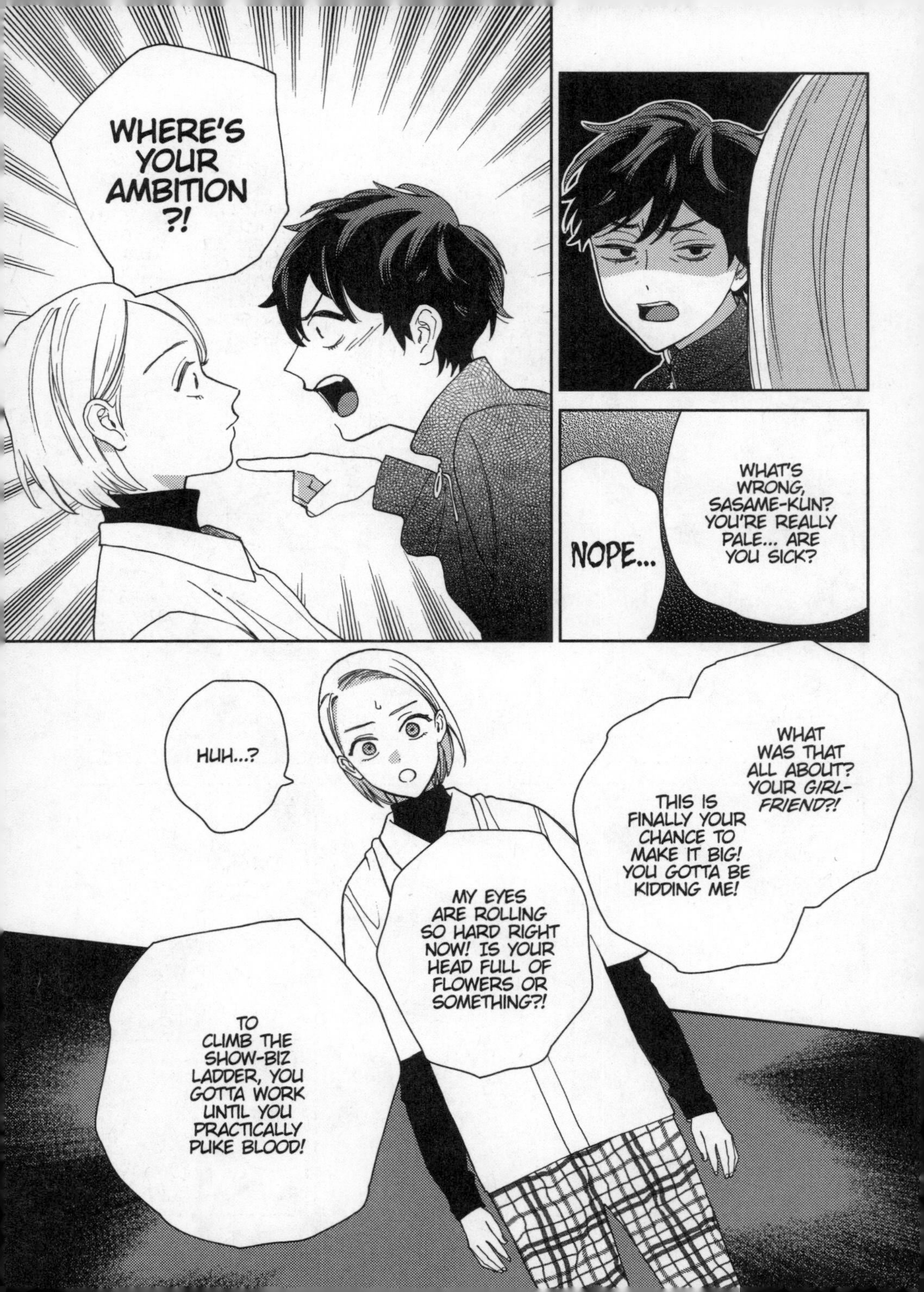
WHAT'S WRONG, SASAME-KUN? YOU'RE REALLY PALE... ARE YOU SICK?
NOPE...
WHERE'S YOUR AMBITION ?!
WHAT WAS THAT ALL ABOUT? YOUR GIRL-FRIEND?!
THIS IS FINALLY YOUR CHANCE TO MAKE IT BIG! YOU GOTTA BE KIDDING ME!
HUH...?
MY EYES ARE ROLLING SO HARD RIGHT NOW! IS YOUR HEAD FULL OF FLOWERS OR SOMETHING?!
TO CLIMB THE SHOW-BIZ LADDER, YOU GOTTA WORK UNTIL YOU PRACTICALLY PUKE BLOOD!

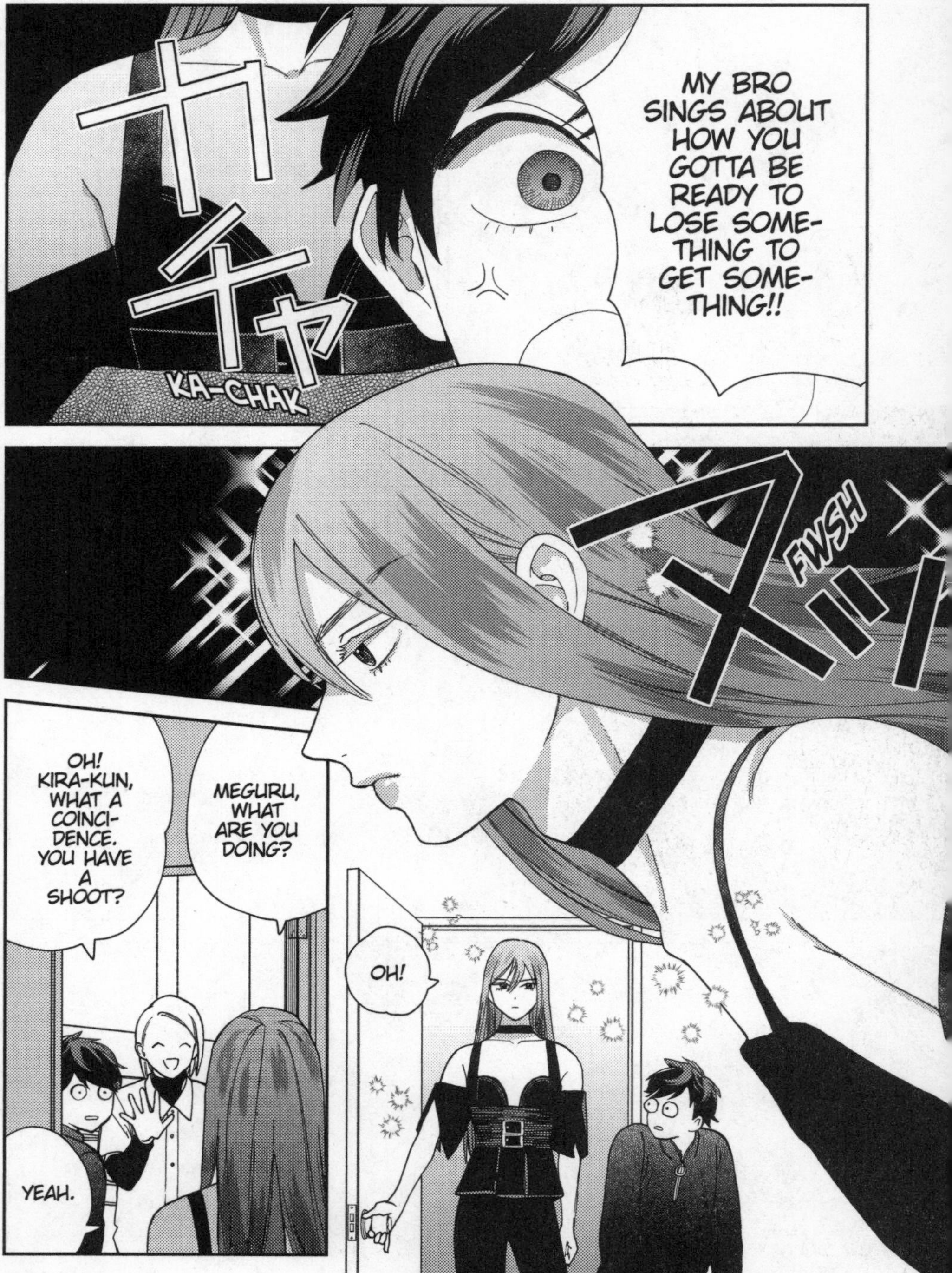
MY BRO SINGS ABOUT HOW YOU GOTTA BE READY TO LOSE SOME-THING TO GET SOME-THING!!
KA-CHAK
FWSH
OH!
MEGURU, WHAT ARE YOU DOING?
OH! KIRA-KUN, WHAT A COINCI-DENCE. YOU HAVE A SHOOT?
YEAH.

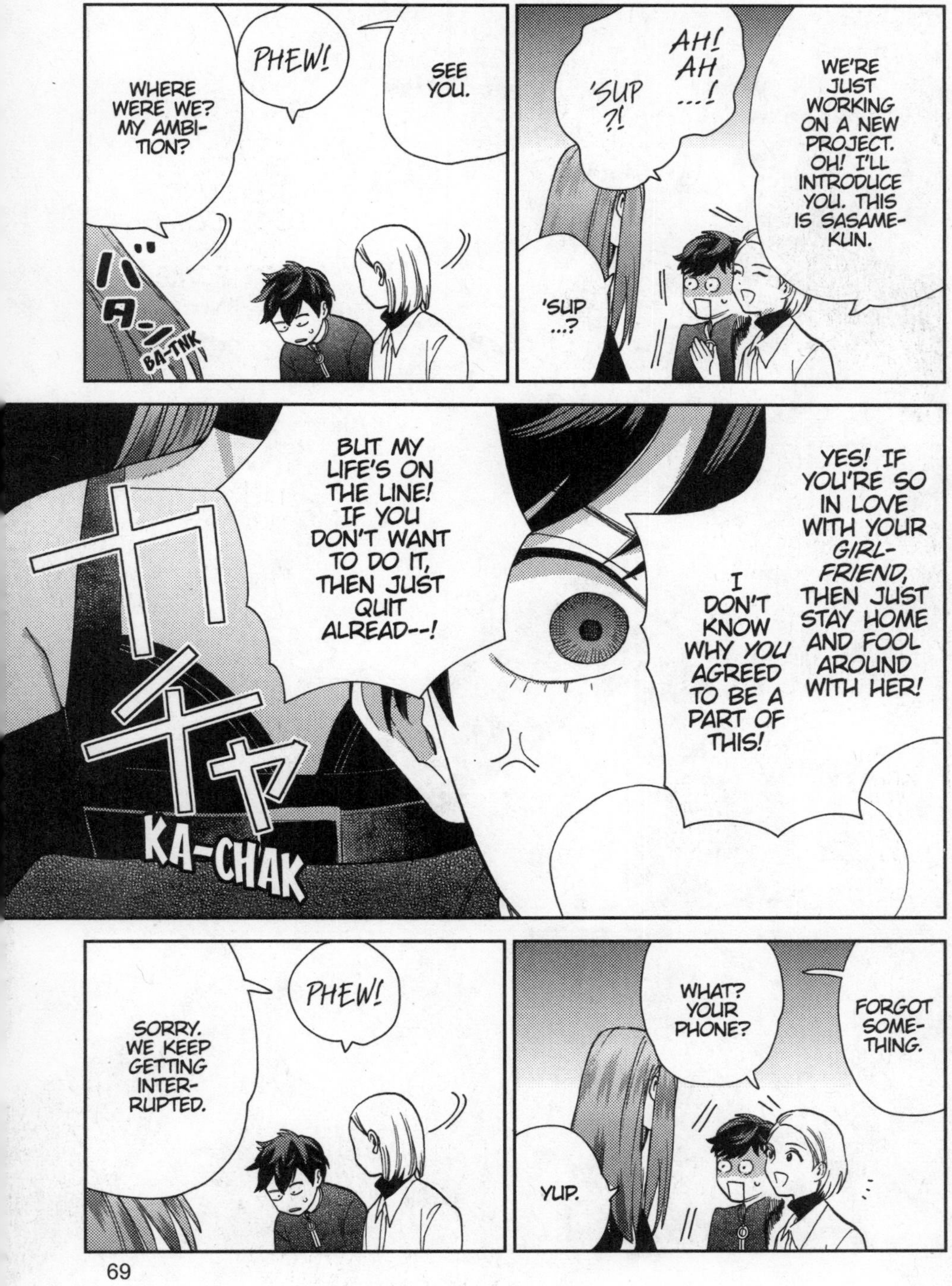

WE'RE JUST WORKING ON A NEW PROJECT. OH! I'LL INTRODUCE YOU. THIS IS SASAME-KUN.
AH! AH ...!
'SUP ?!
'SUP ...?
SEE YOU.
PHEW!
WHERE WERE WE? MY AMBITION?
バターン
BA-TNK
YES! IF YOU'RE SO IN LOVE WITH YOUR GIRLFRIEND, THEN JUST STAY HOME AND FOOL AROUND WITH HER!
I DON'T KNOW WHY YOU AGREED TO BE A PART OF THIS!
BUT MY LIFE'S ON THE LINE! IF YOU DON'T WANT TO DO IT, THEN JUST QUIT ALREAD--!
ガチャ
KA-CHAK
FORGOT SOMETHING.
WHAT? YOUR PHONE?
YUP.
PHEW!
SORRY. WE KEEP GETTING INTERRUPTED.

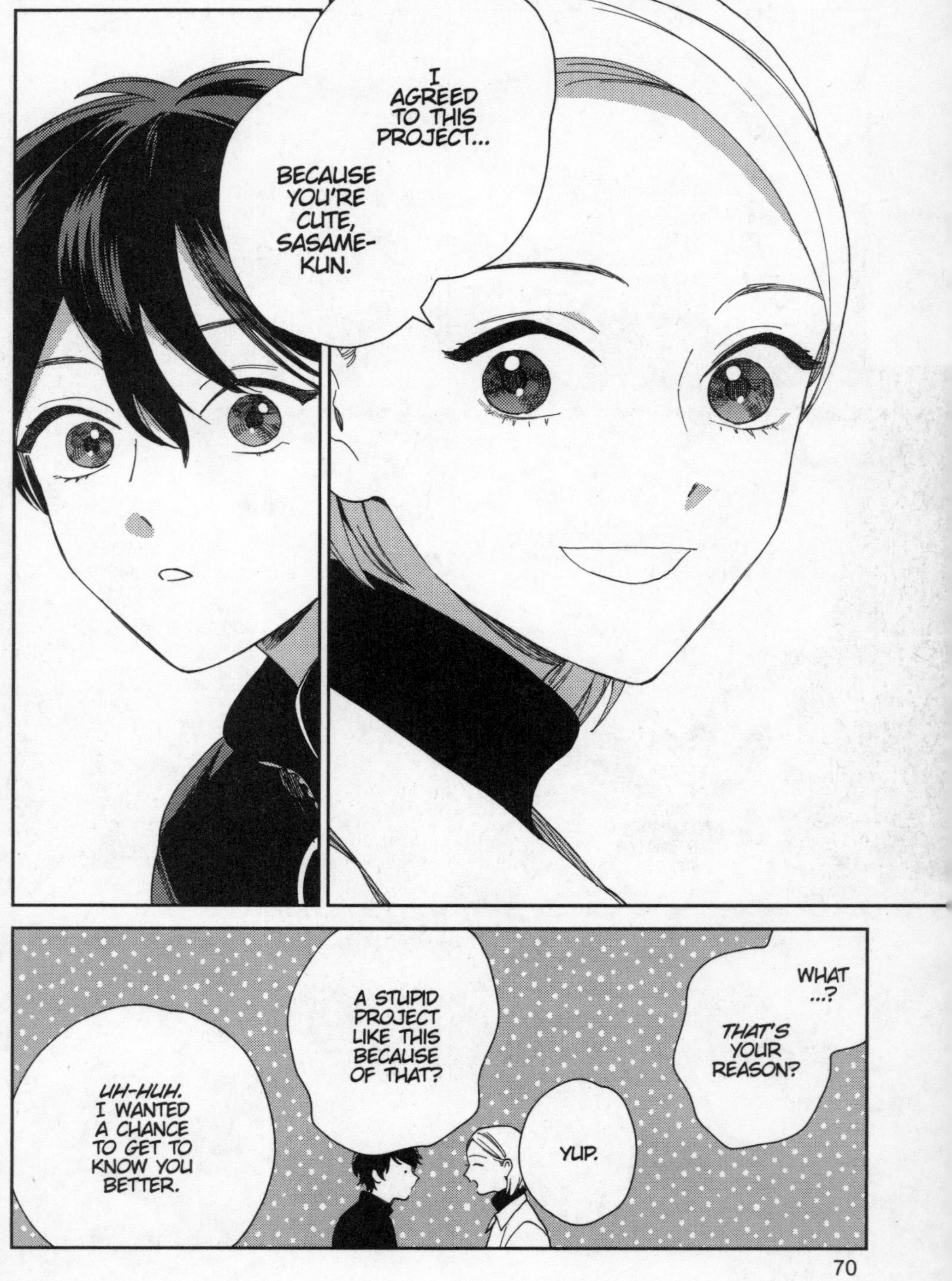
I AGREED TO THIS PROJECT...
BECAUSE YOU'RE CUTE, SASAME-KUN.
WHAT ...? *THAT'S* YOUR REASON?
YUP.
A STUPID PROJECT LIKE THIS BECAUSE OF THAT?
UH-HUH. I WANTED A CHANCE TO GET TO KNOW YOU BETTER.

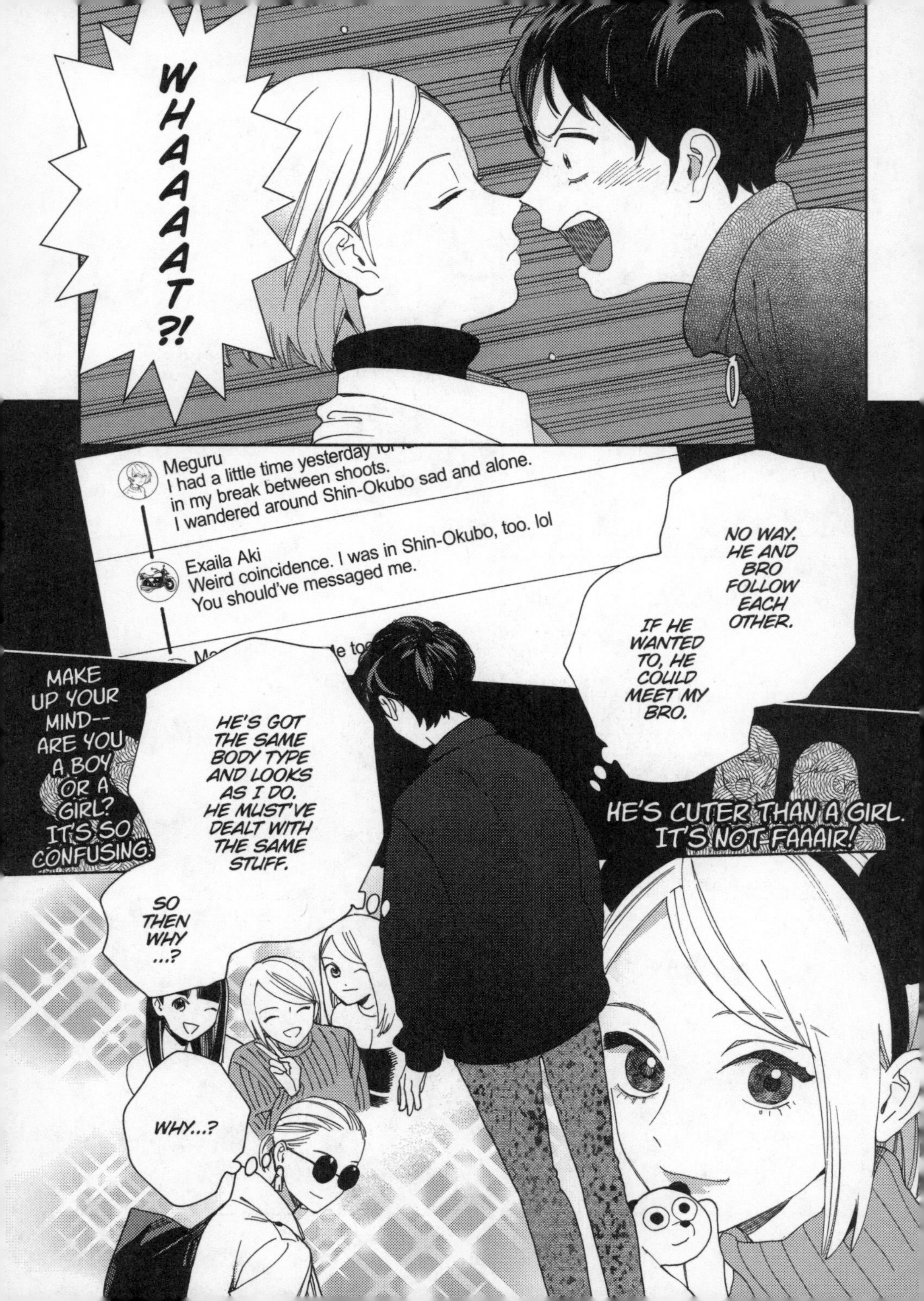
WHAAAAAT?!
Meguru
I had a little time yesterday
in my break between shoots.
I wandered around Shin-Okubo sad and alone.
Exaila Aki
Weird coincidence. I was in Shin-Okubo, too. lol
You should've messaged me.
NO WAY. HE AND BRO FOLLOW EACH OTHER.
IF HE WANTED TO, HE COULD MEET MY BRO.
HE'S CUTER THAN A GIRL. IT'S NOT FAAAIR!
HE'S GOT THE SAME BODY TYPE AND LOOKS AS I DO. HE MUST'VE DEALT WITH THE SAME STUFF.
MAKE UP YOUR MIND-- ARE YOU A BOY OR A GIRL? IT'S SO CONFUSING.
SO THEN WHY ...?
WHY...?

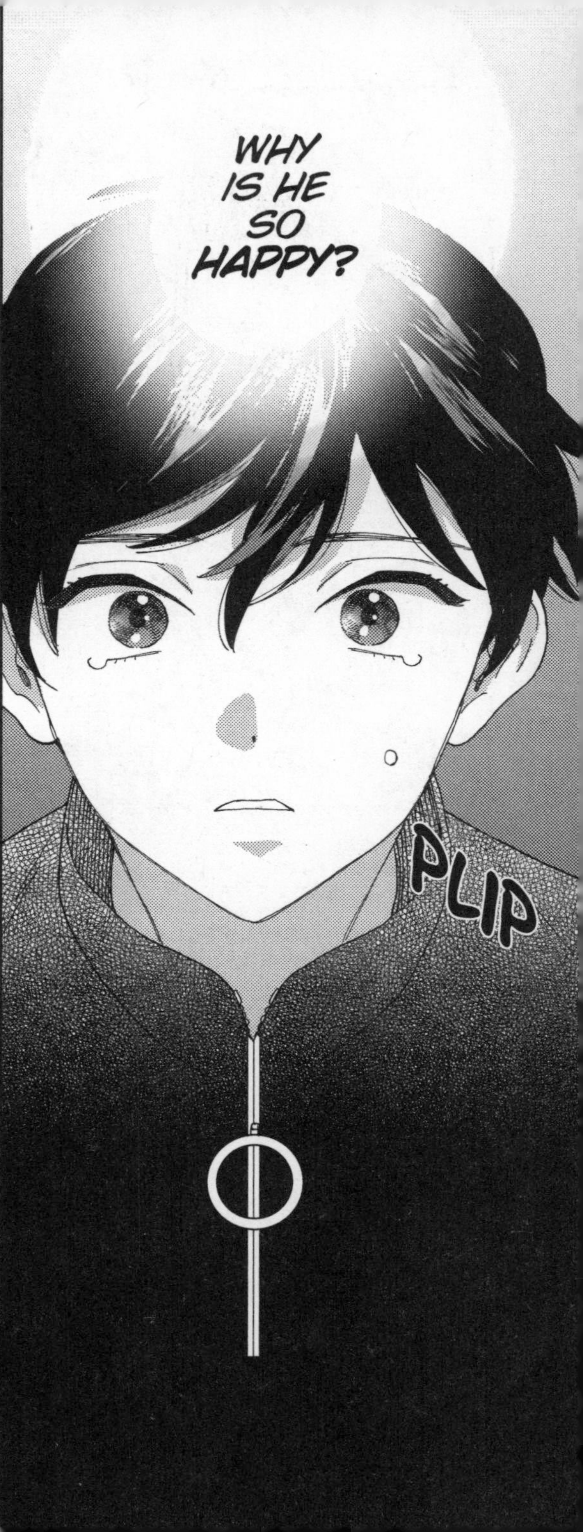
WHY IS HE SO HAPPY?
PLIP

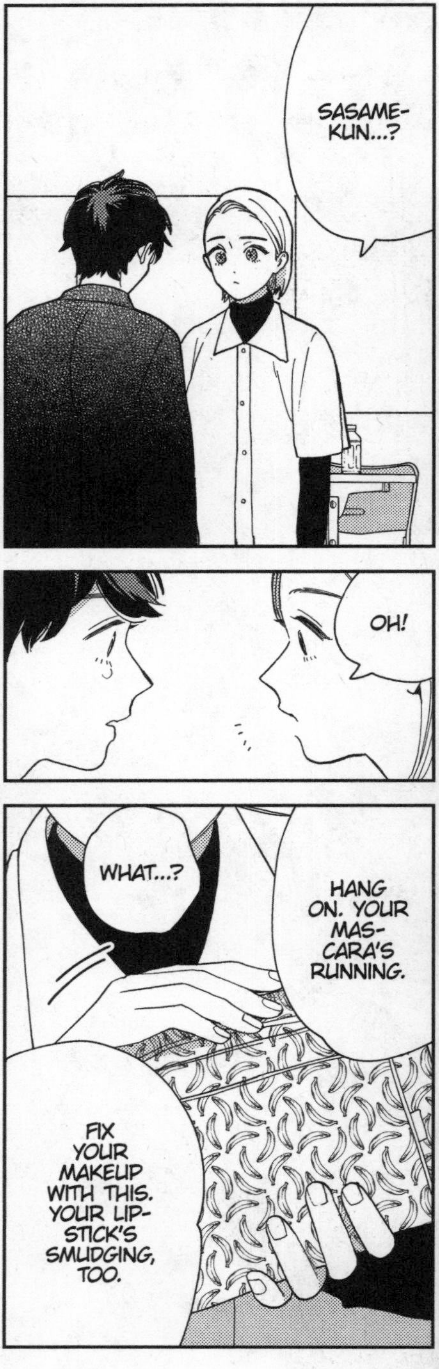
SASAME-KUN...?
OH!
HANG ON. YOUR MAS-CARA'S RUNNING.
WHAT...?
FIX YOUR MAKEUP WITH THIS. YOUR LIP-STICK'S SMUDGING, TOO.

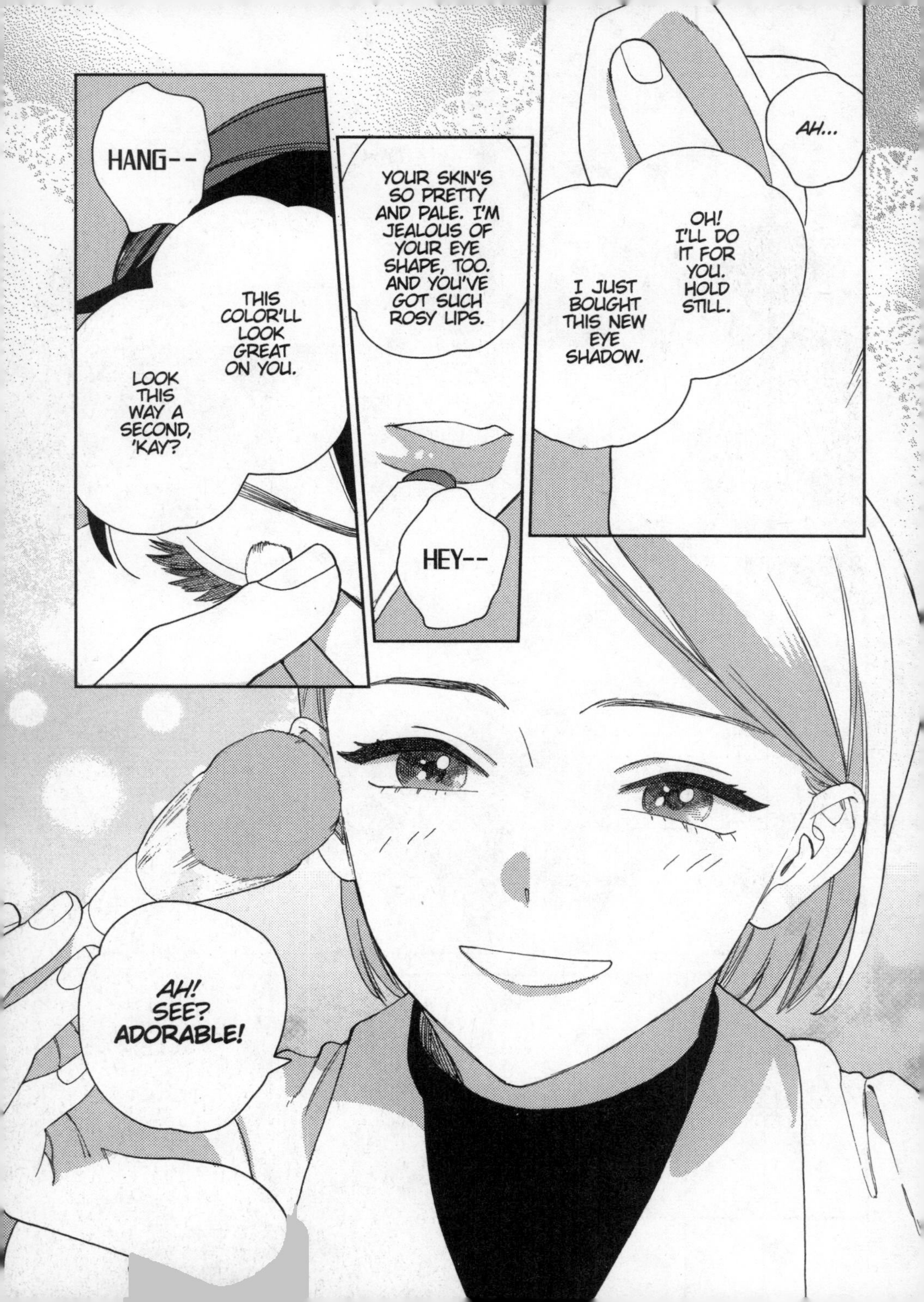
AH...
OH! I'LL DO IT FOR YOU. HOLD STILL.
I JUST BOUGHT THIS NEW EYE SHADOW.
YOUR SKIN'S SO PRETTY AND PALE. I'M JEALOUS OF YOUR EYE SHAPE, TOO. AND YOU'VE GOT SUCH ROSY LIPS.
HEY--
HANG--
THIS COLOR'LL LOOK GREAT ON YOU.
LOOK THIS WAY A SECOND, 'KAY?
AH! SEE? ADORABLE!

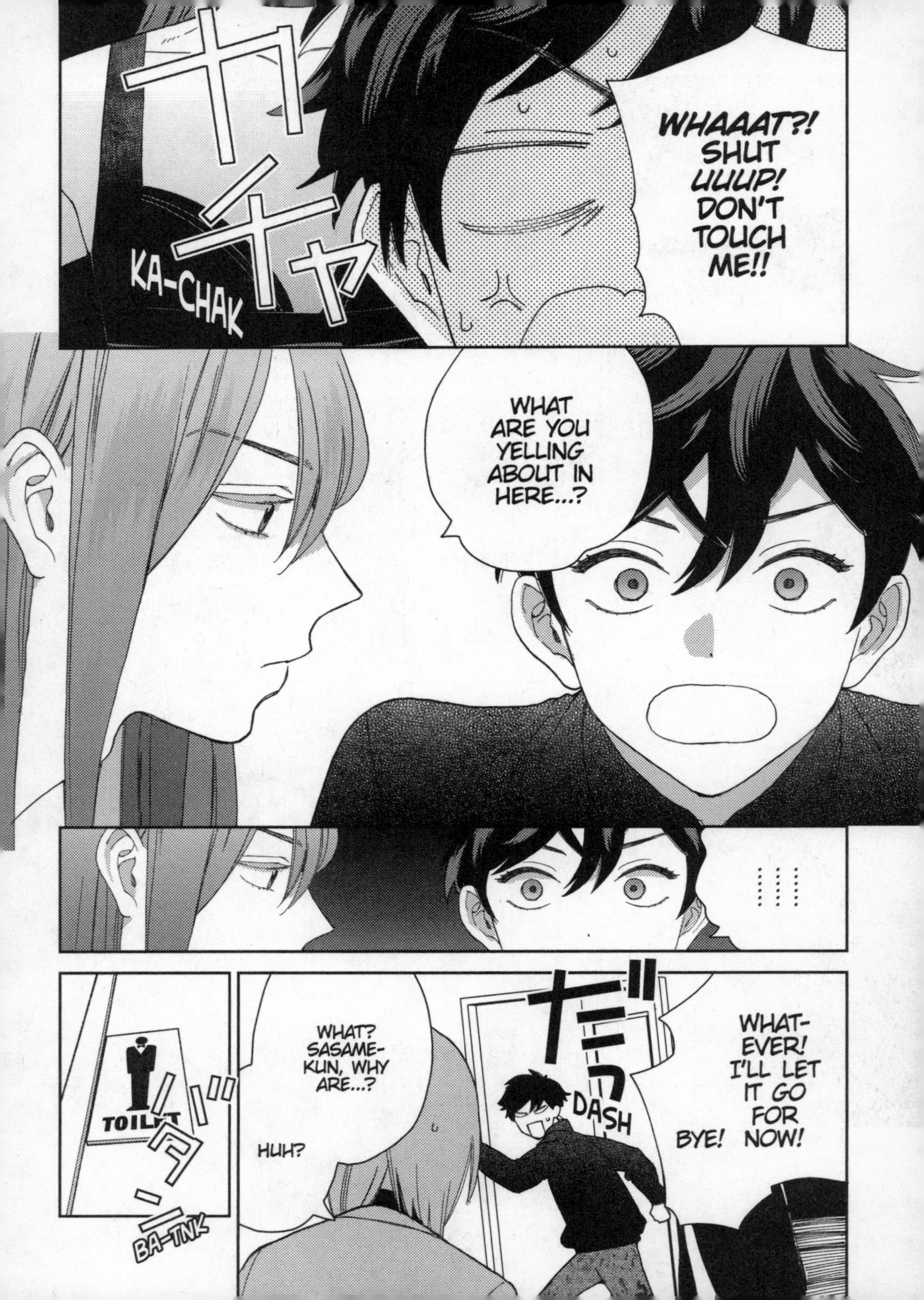
WHAAAT?! SHUT UUUP! DON'T TOUCH ME!!
KA-CHAK
WHAT ARE YOU YELLING ABOUT IN HERE...?
WHAT-EVER! I'LL LET IT GO FOR NOW!
BYE!
DASH
WHAT? SASAME-KUN, WHY ARE...?
HUH?
BA-TNK

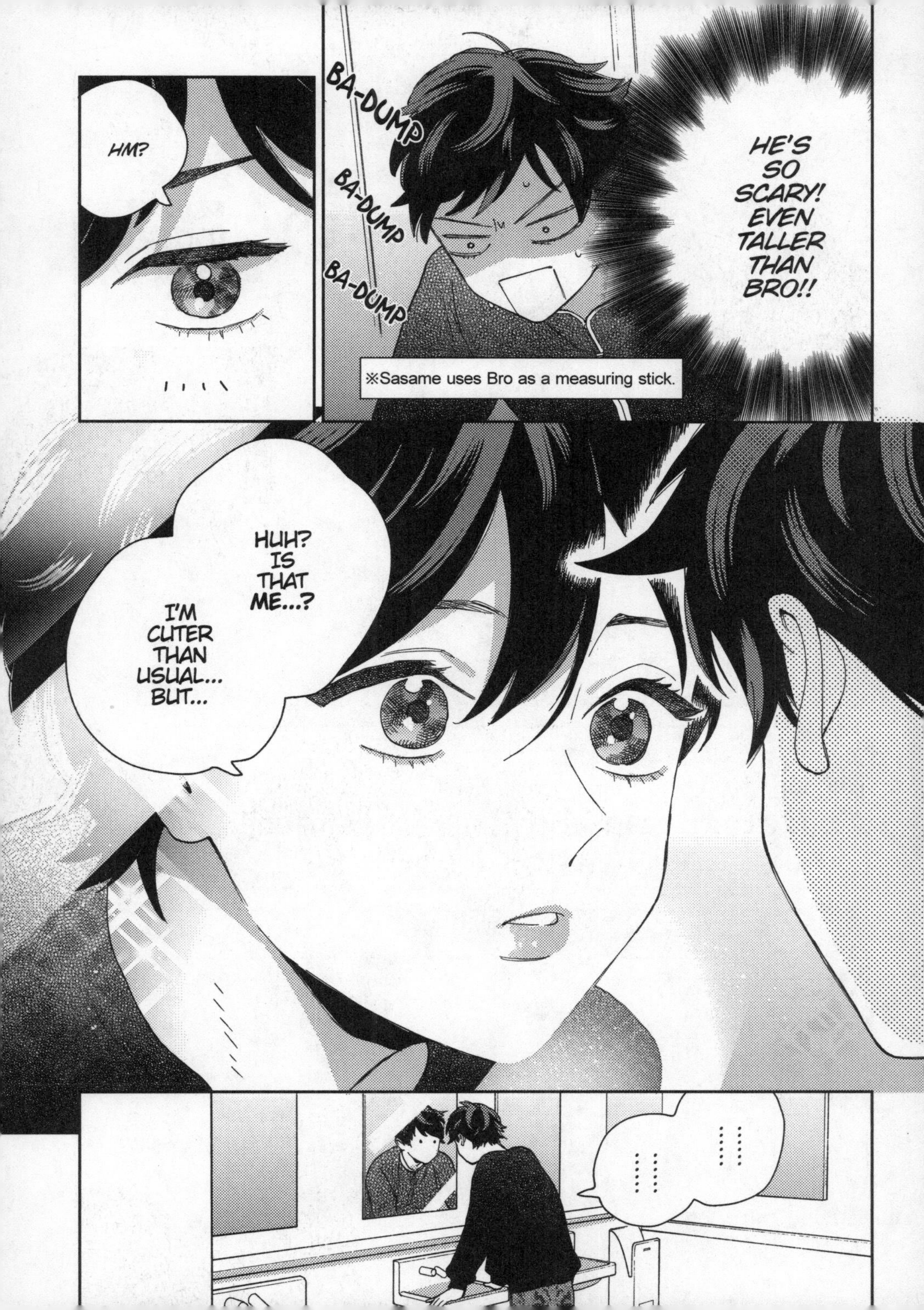
BA-DUMP
BA-DUMP
BA-DUMP
HE'S SO SCARY! EVEN TALLER THAN BRO!!
※Sasame uses Bro as a measuring stick.
HM?
HUH? IS THAT ME...?
I'M CUTER THAN USUAL... BUT...
......
......

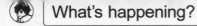 What's happening?

 Sasame @ssasameank • 55s
Meguru did my makeup for me.

PIRON

 Meguru-san and Exaila Aki-san liked your tweet.

MEGURU-KUN'S DOING MAKEUP FOR THIS CUTE BOY?!

EX

AHHHH!

My Androgynous Boyfriend

The Fifteenth One

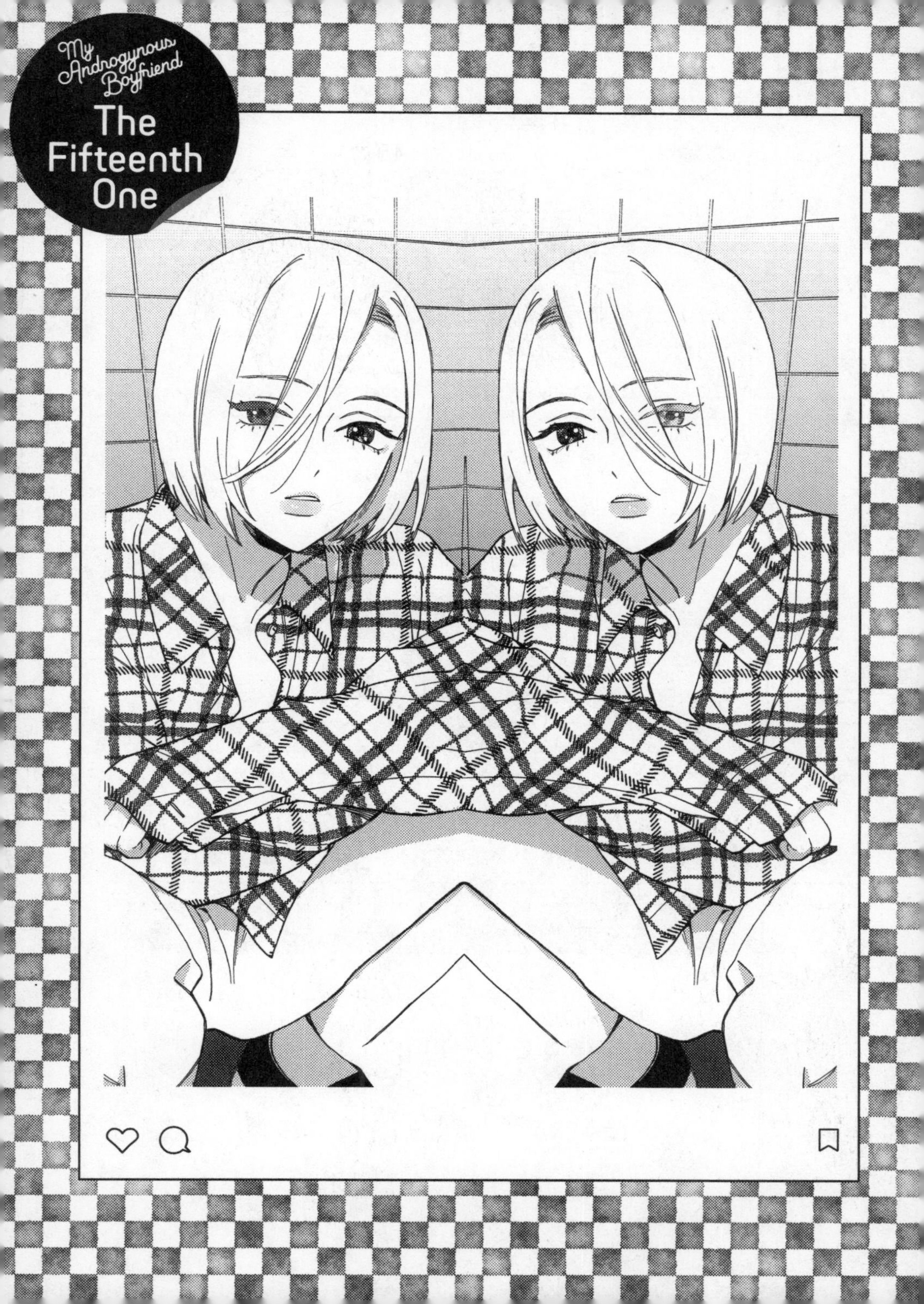

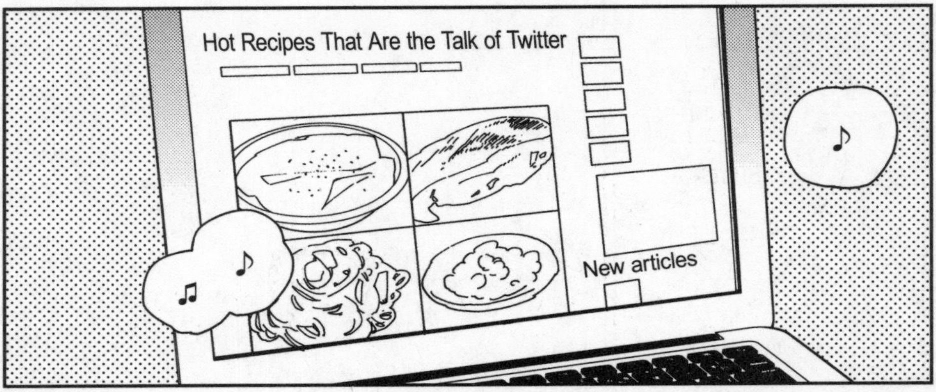
Hot Recipes That Are the Talk of Twitter
New articles

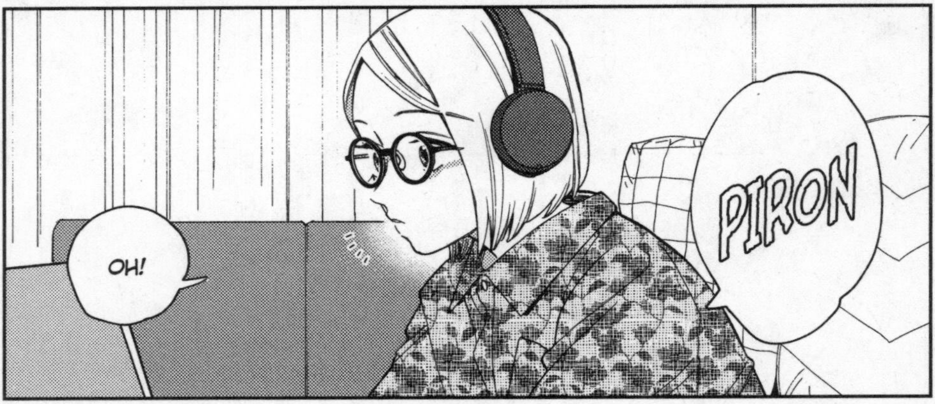
PIRON
OH!

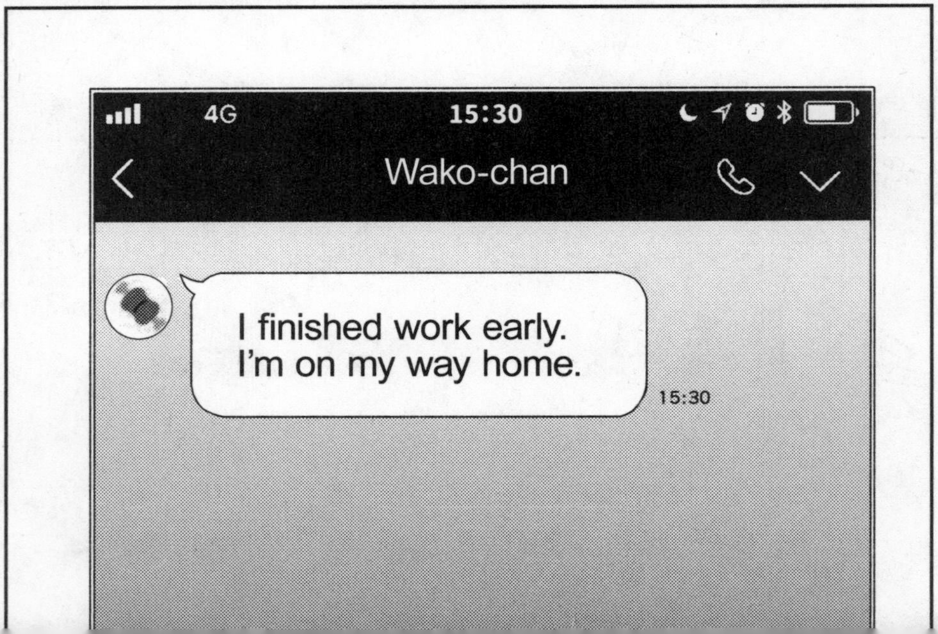
4G
15:30
Wako-chan
I finished work early.
I'm on my way home.
15:30

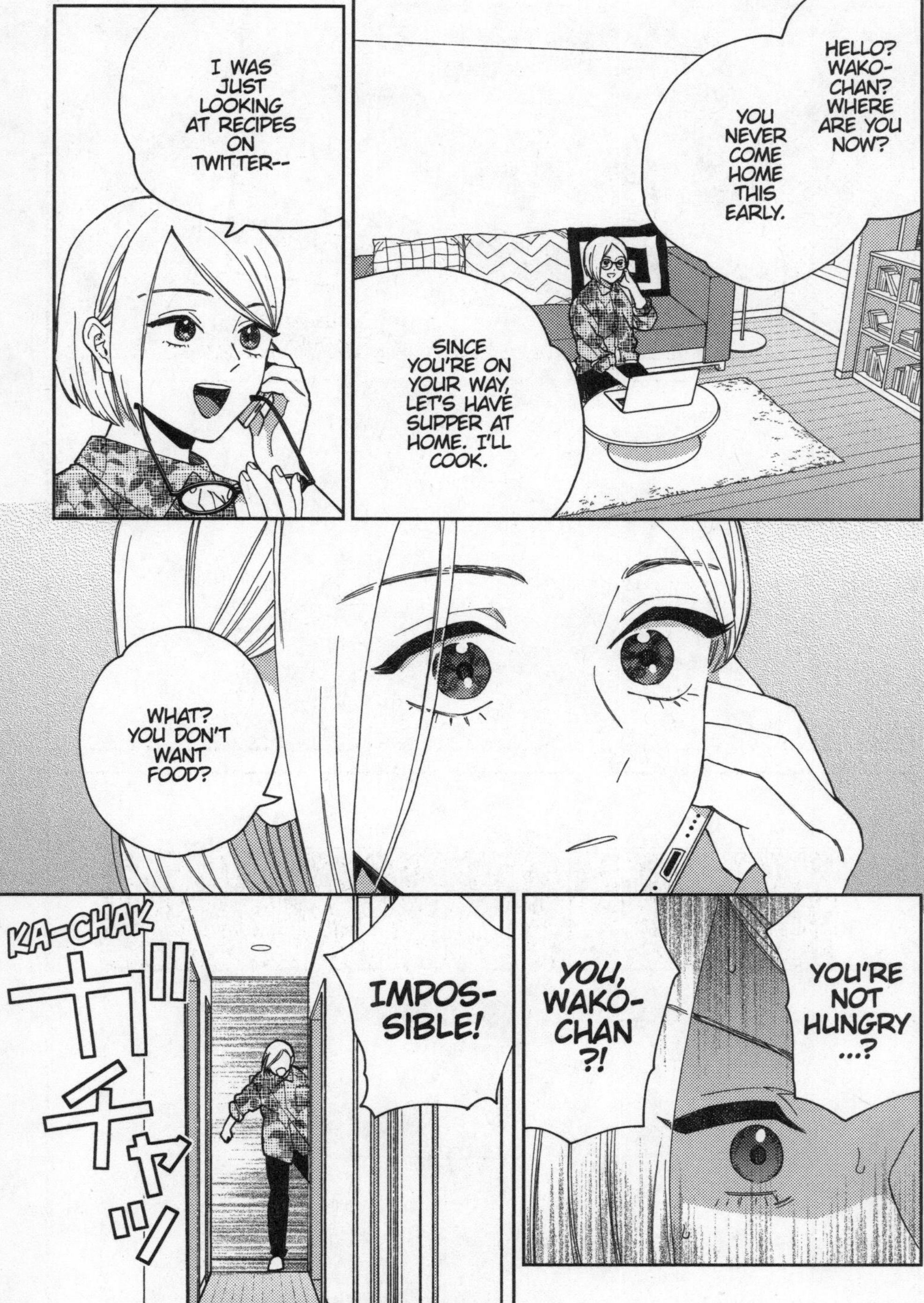
HELLO? WAKO-CHAN? WHERE ARE YOU NOW?
YOU NEVER COME HOME THIS EARLY.
SINCE YOU'RE ON YOUR WAY, LET'S HAVE SUPPER AT HOME. I'LL COOK.
I WAS JUST LOOKING AT RECIPES ON TWITTER--
WHAT? YOU DON'T WANT FOOD?
YOU'RE NOT HUNGRY ...?
YOU, WAKO-CHAN ?!
IMPOS-SIBLE!
KA-CHAK

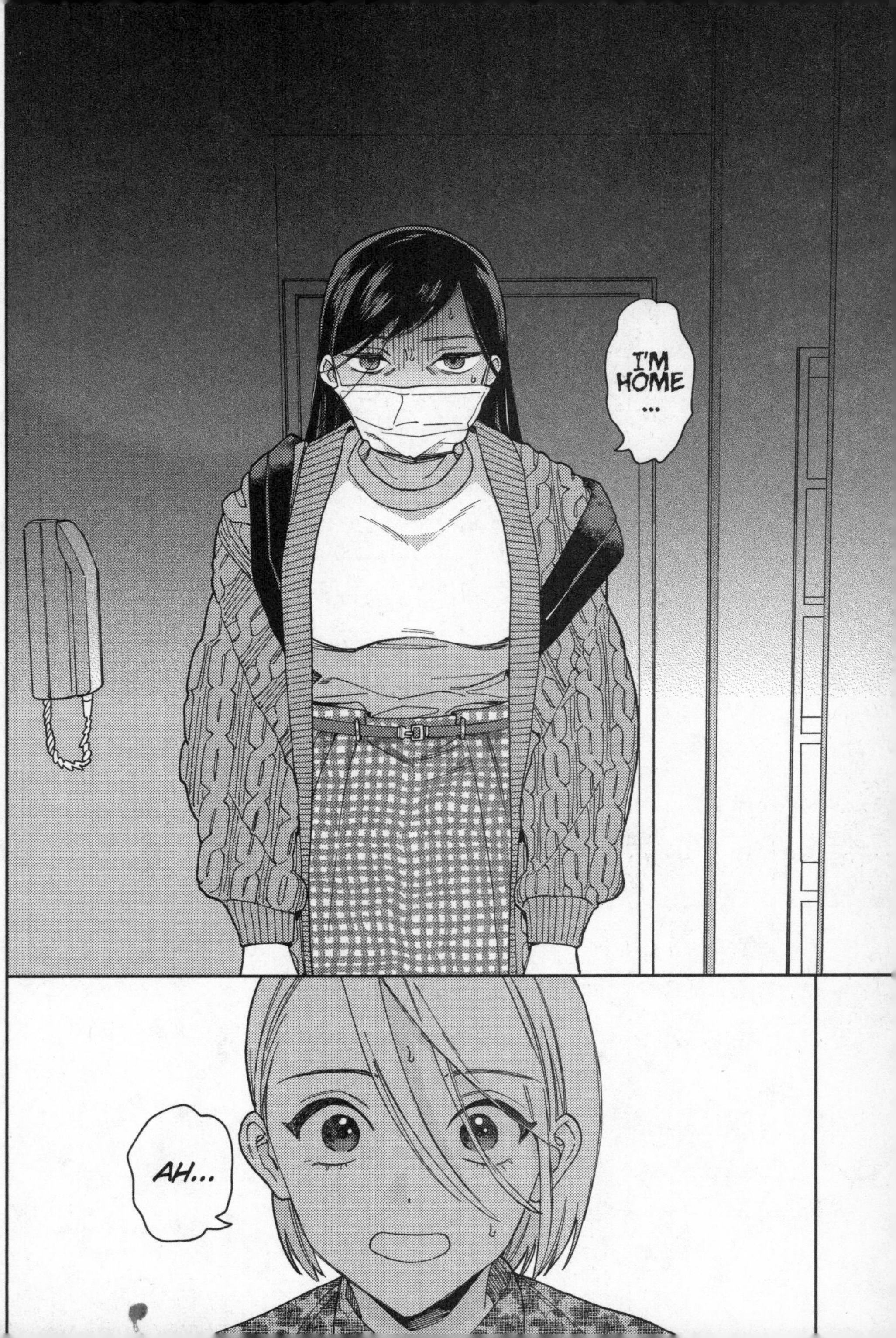
I'M HOME ...
AH...

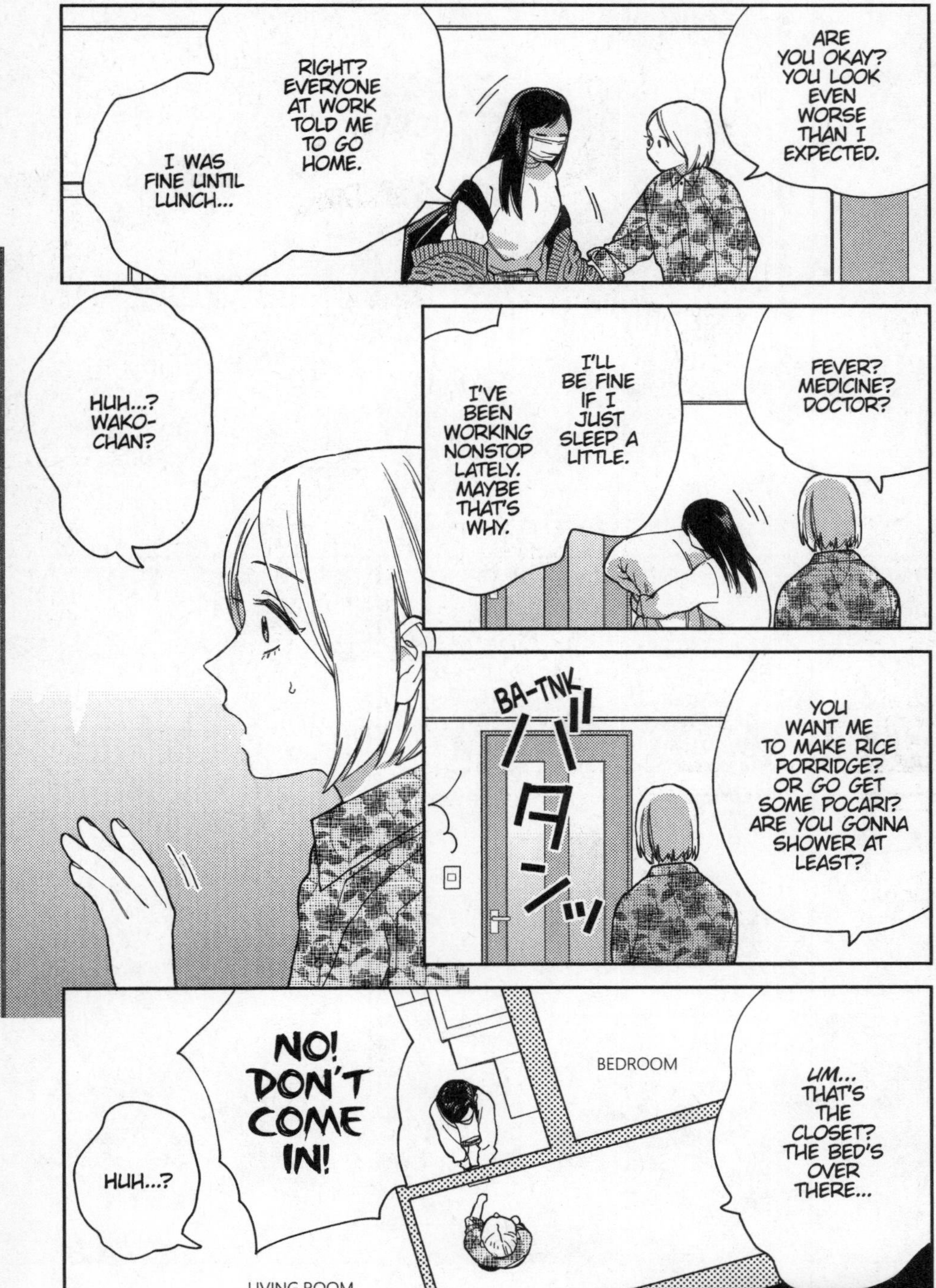
ARE YOU OKAY? YOU LOOK EVEN WORSE THAN I EXPECTED.
RIGHT? EVERYONE AT WORK TOLD ME TO GO HOME.
I WAS FINE UNTIL LUNCH...
FEVER? MEDICINE? DOCTOR?
I'LL BE FINE IF I JUST SLEEP A LITTLE.
I'VE BEEN WORKING NONSTOP LATELY. MAYBE THAT'S WHY.
YOU WANT ME TO MAKE RICE PORRIDGE? OR GO GET SOME POCARI? ARE YOU GONNA SHOWER AT LEAST?
BA-TNK
バタンッ
HUH...? WAKO-CHAN?
UM... THAT'S THE CLOSET? THE BED'S OVER THERE...
BEDROOM
NO! DON'T COME IN!
HUH...?
LIVING ROOM

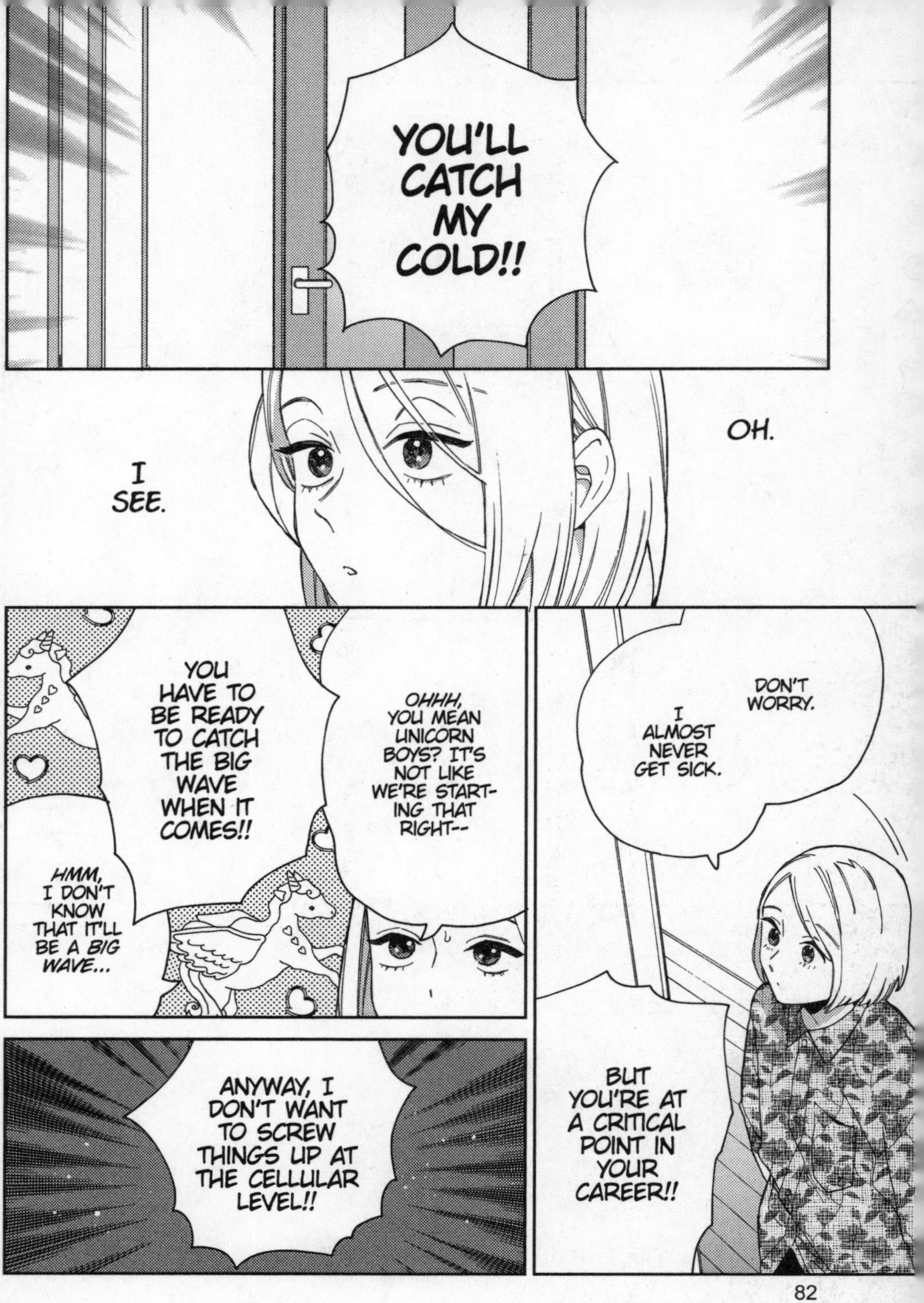
YOU'LL CATCH MY COLD!!
OH.
I SEE.
DON'T WORRY.
I ALMOST NEVER GET SICK.
BUT YOU'RE AT A CRITICAL POINT IN YOUR CAREER!!
OHHH, YOU MEAN UNICORN BOYS? IT'S NOT LIKE WE'RE STARTING THAT RIGHT--
YOU HAVE TO BE READY TO CATCH THE BIG WAVE WHEN IT COMES!!
HMM, I DON'T KNOW THAT IT'LL BE A BIG *WAVE...*
ANYWAY, I DON'T WANT TO SCREW THINGS UP AT THE CELLULAR LEVEL!!

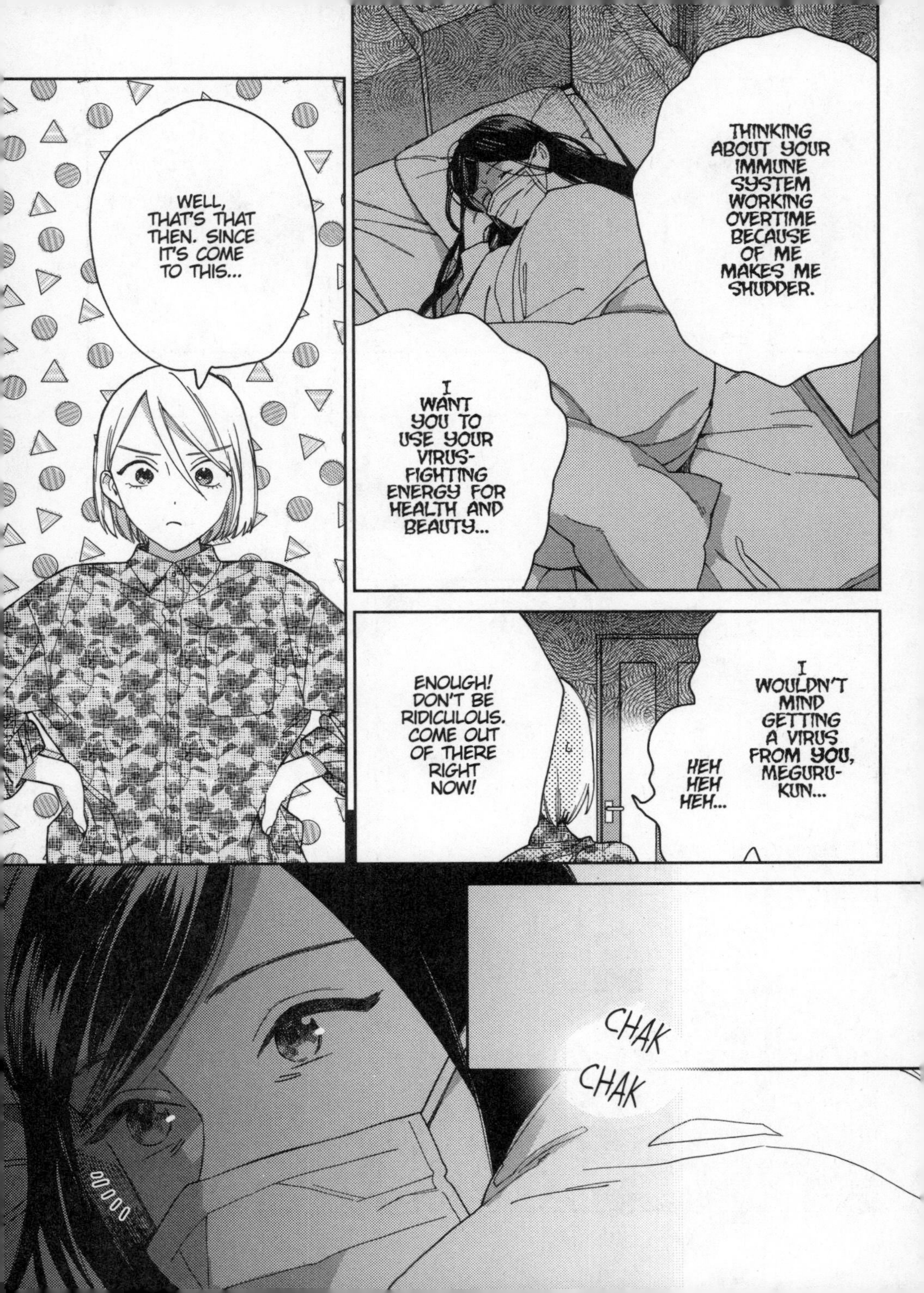
THINKING ABOUT YOUR IMMUNE SYSTEM WORKING OVERTIME BECAUSE OF ME MAKES ME SHUDDER.
I WANT YOU TO USE YOUR VIRUS-FIGHTING ENERGY FOR HEALTH AND BEAUTY...
I WOULDN'T MIND GETTING A VIRUS FROM YOU, MEGURU-KUN...
HEH HEH HEH...
ENOUGH! DON'T BE RIDICULOUS. COME OUT OF THERE RIGHT NOW!
WELL, THAT'S THAT THEN. SINCE IT'S COME TO THIS...
CHAK
CHAK

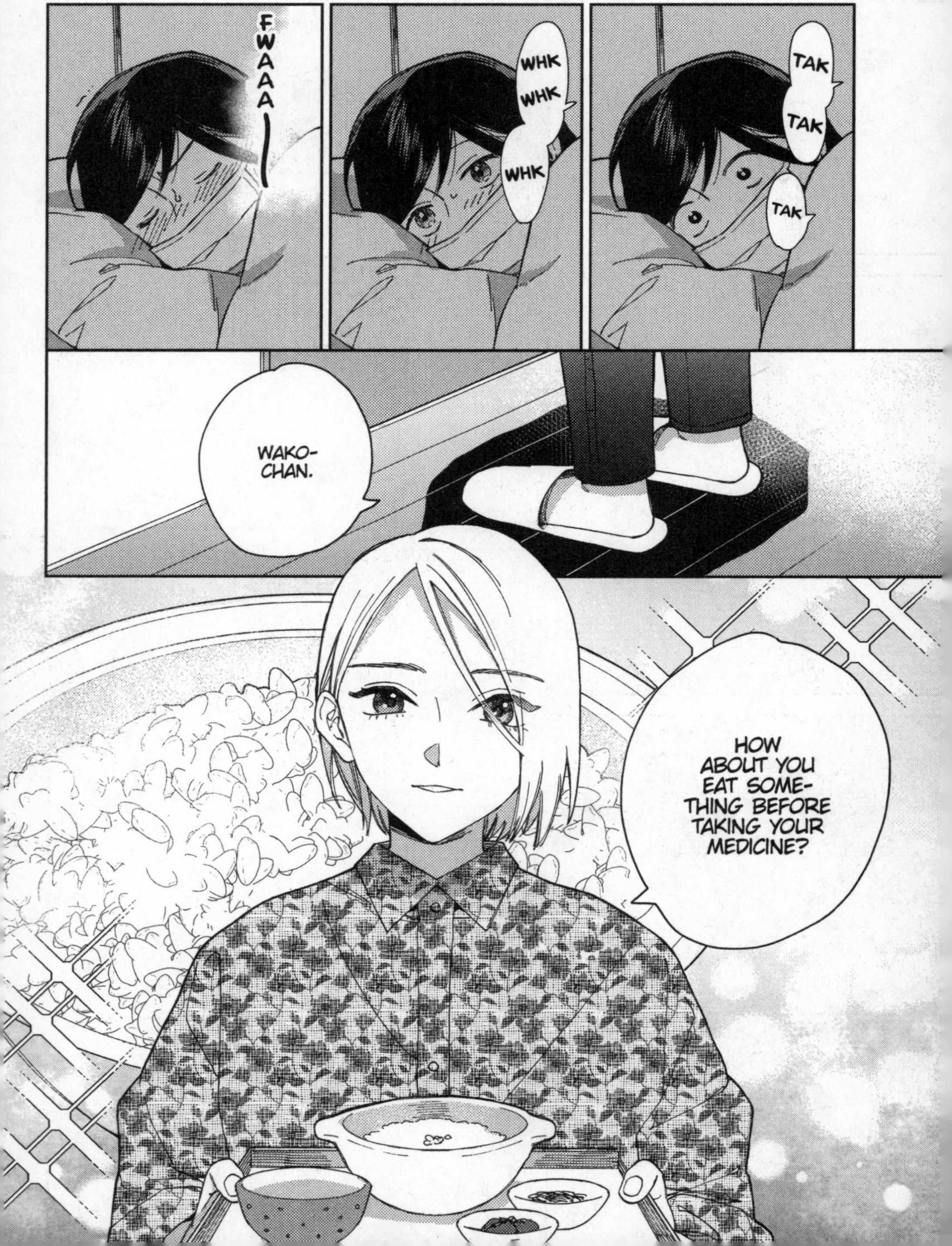
TAK
TAK
TAK
WHK
WHK
WHK
FWAAAA—
WAKO-CHAN.
HOW ABOUT YOU EAT SOME-THING BEFORE TAKING YOUR MEDICINE?

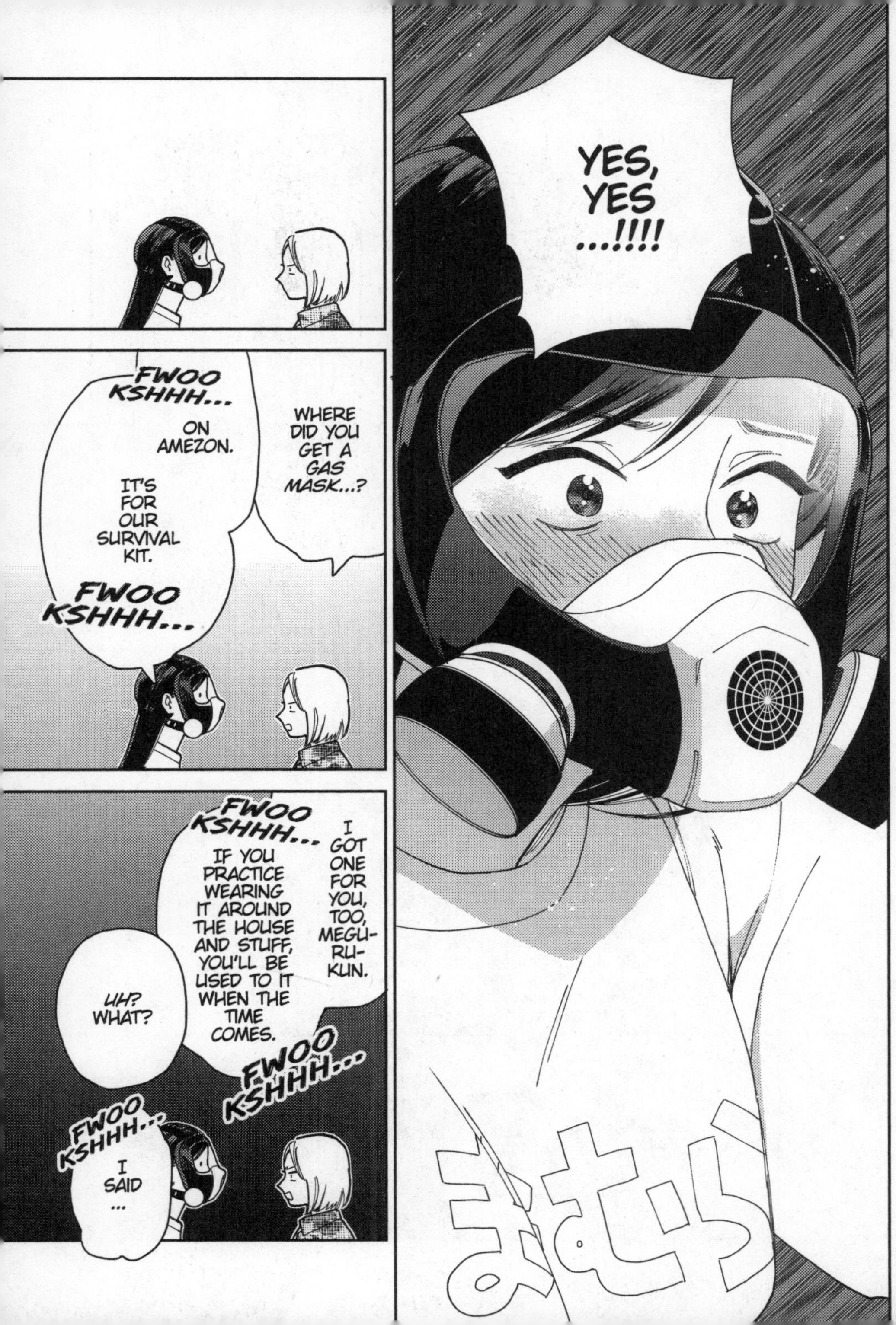
YES, YES ...!!!!
WHERE DID YOU GET A GAS MASK...?
FWOO KSHHH...
ON AMEZON.
IT'S FOR OUR SURVIVAL KIT.
FWOO KSHHH...
I GOT ONE FOR YOU, TOO, MEGURU-KUN.
FWOO KSHHH...
IF YOU PRACTICE WEARING IT AROUND THE HOUSE AND STUFF, YOU'LL BE USED TO IT WHEN THE TIME COMES.
FWOO KSHHH...
UH? WHAT?
FWOO KSHHH...
I SAID ...

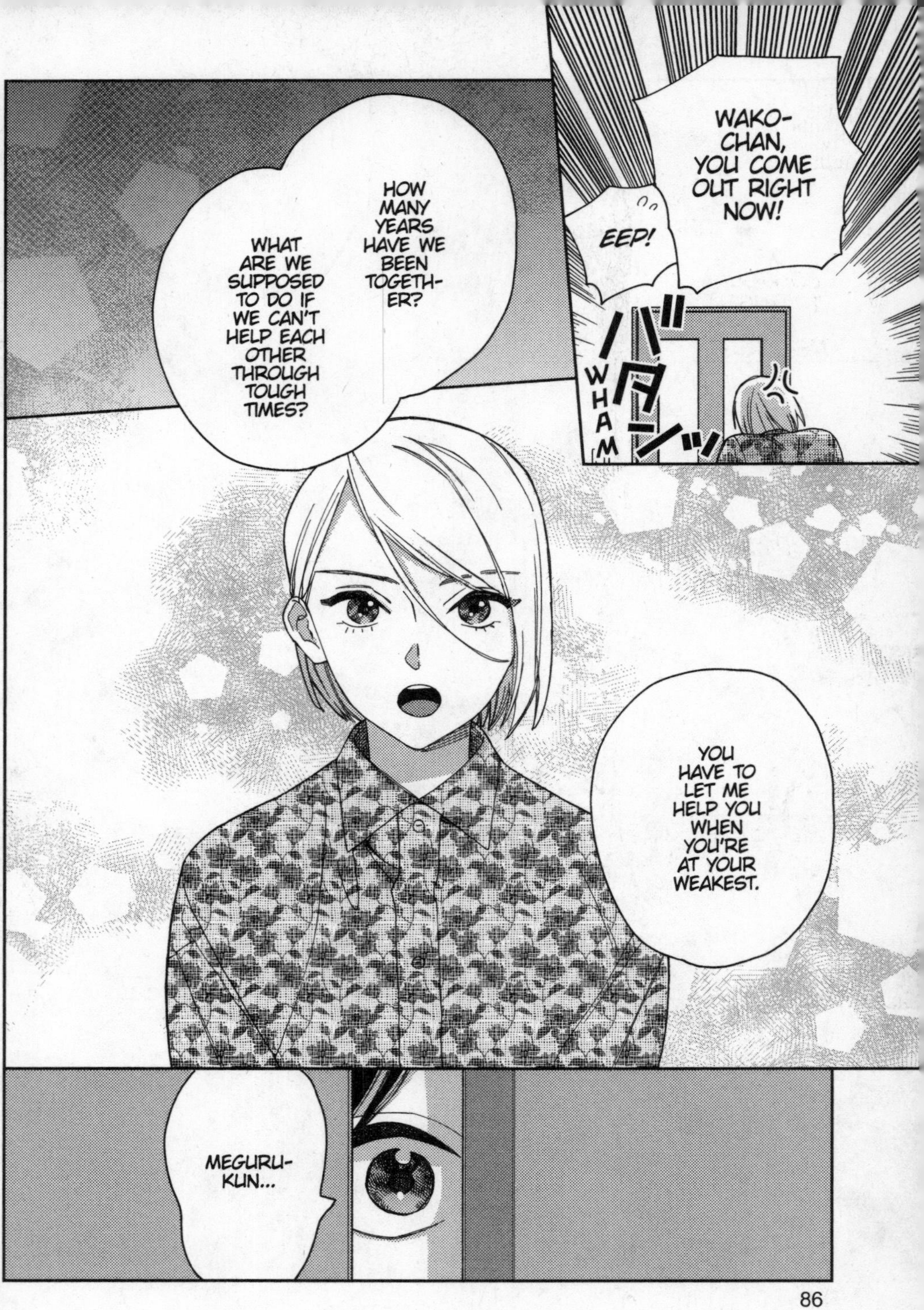
WAKO-CHAN, YOU COME OUT RIGHT NOW!
EEP!
WHAM
HOW MANY YEARS HAVE WE BEEN TOGETH-ER?
WHAT ARE WE SUPPOSED TO DO IF WE CAN'T HELP EACH OTHER THROUGH TOUGH TIMES?
YOU HAVE TO LET ME HELP YOU WHEN YOU'RE AT YOUR WEAKEST.
MEGURU-KUN...

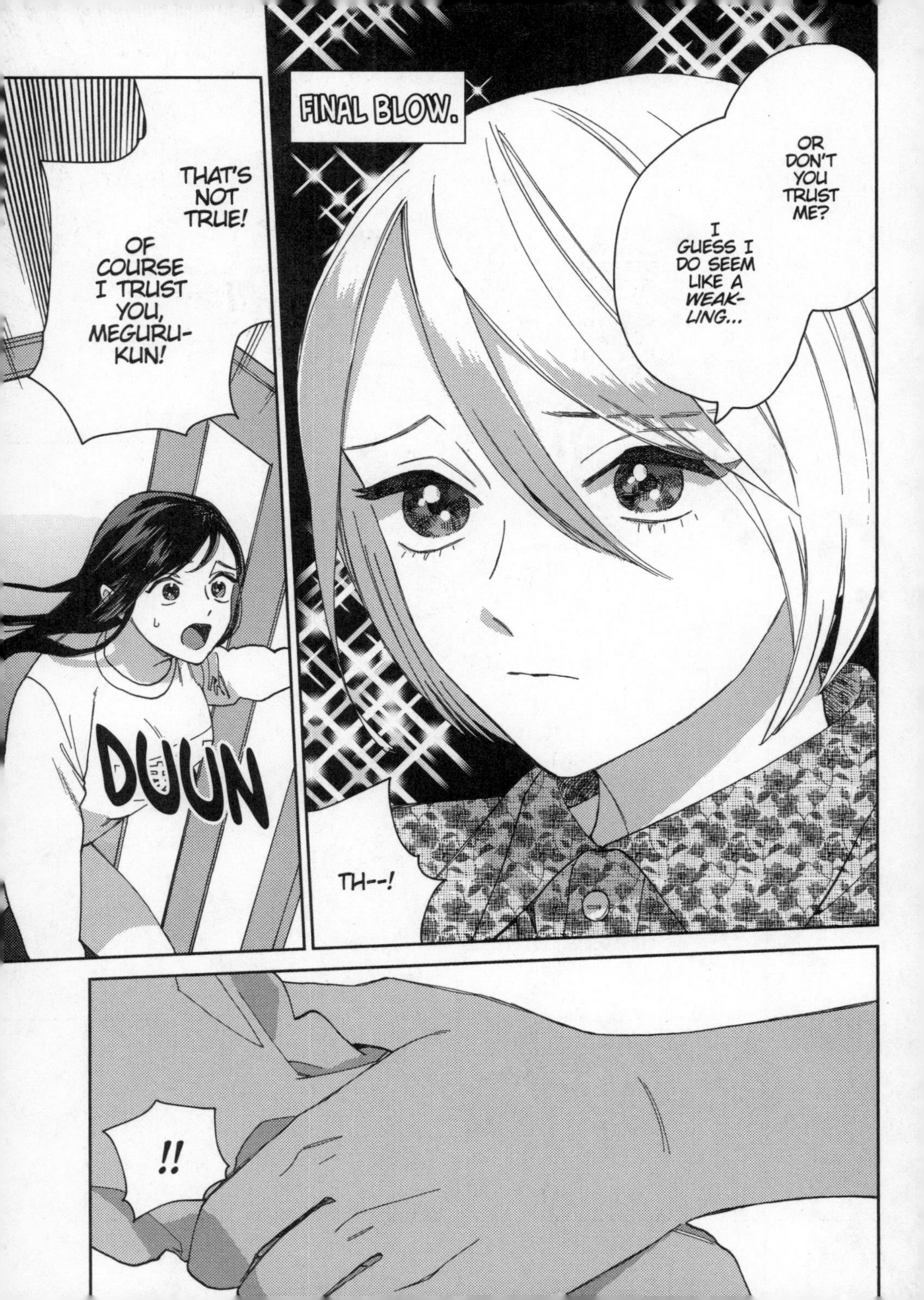
OR DON'T YOU TRUST ME?
I GUESS I DO SEEM LIKE A WEAK-LING...
FINAL BLOW.
TH--!
THAT'S NOT TRUE!
OF COURSE I TRUST YOU, MEGURU-KUN!
DUUN
!!

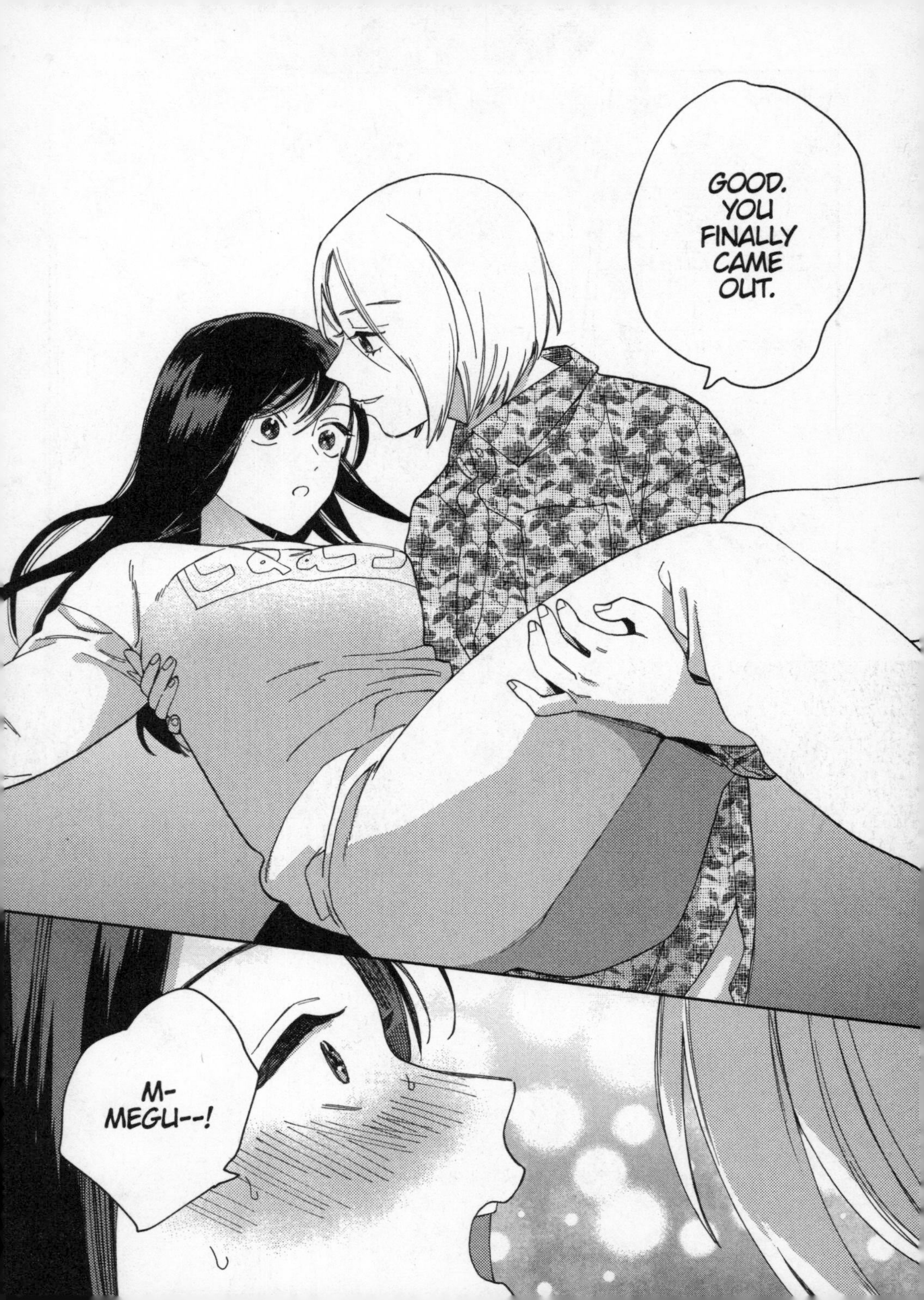
GOOD. YOU FINALLY CAME OUT.
M-MEGU--!

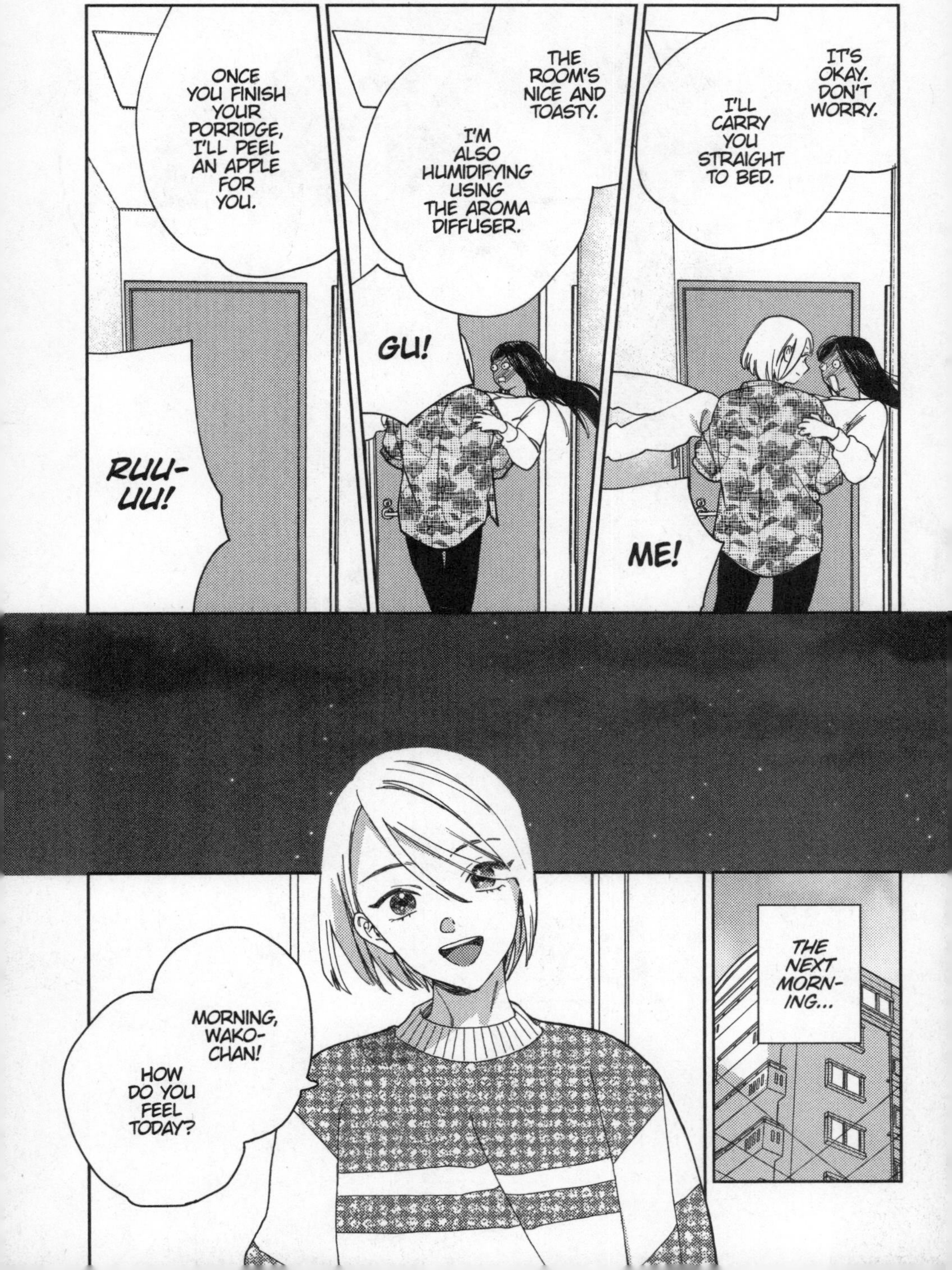
IT'S OKAY. DON'T WORRY.
I'LL CARRY YOU STRAIGHT TO BED.
ME!
THE ROOM'S NICE AND TOASTY.
I'M ALSO HUMIDIFYING USING THE AROMA DIFFUSER.
GU!
ONCE YOU FINISH YOUR PORRIDGE, I'LL PEEL AN APPLE FOR YOU.
RUU-UU!
THE NEXT MORN-ING...
MORNING, WAKO-CHAN!
HOW DO YOU FEEL TODAY?

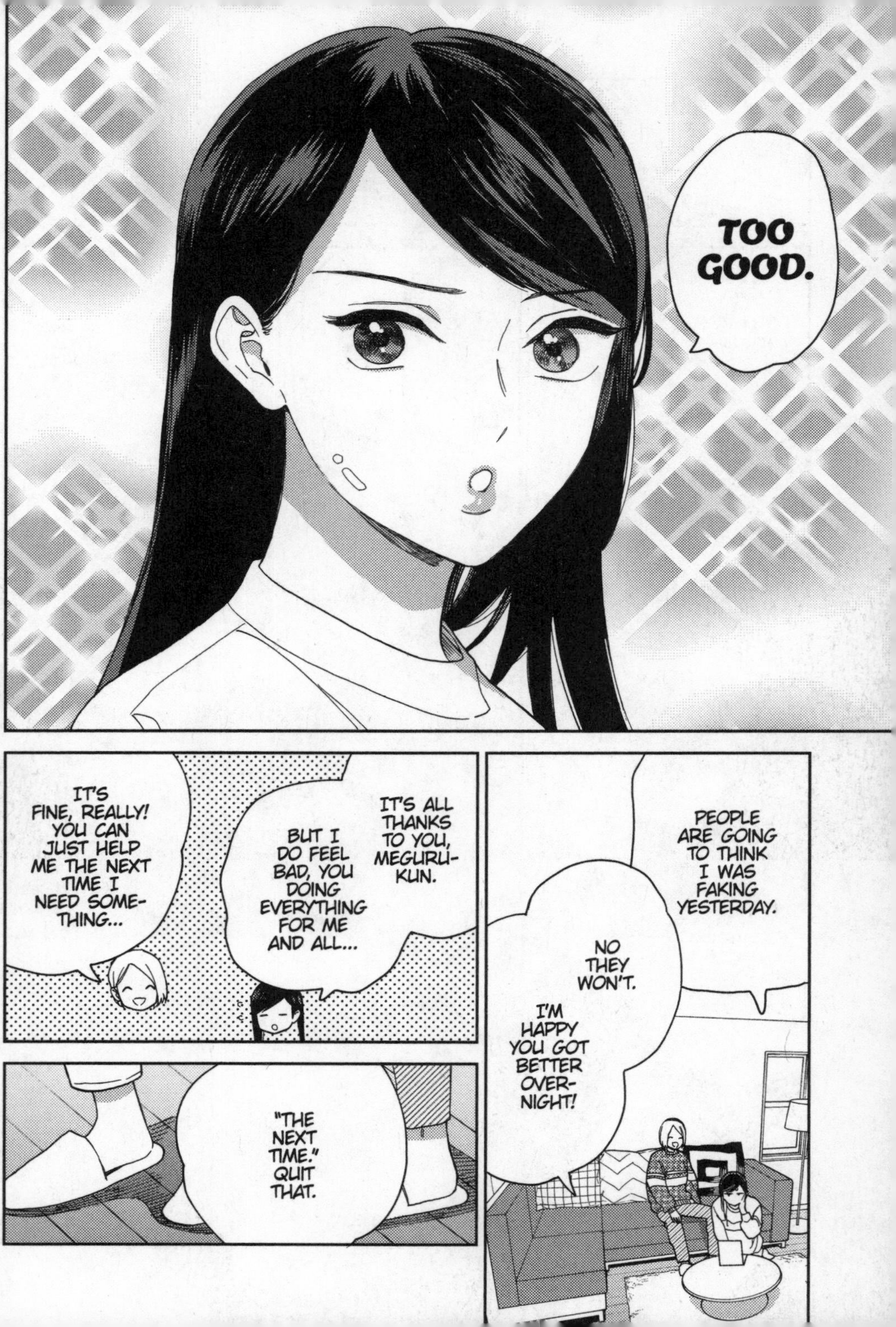
TOO GOOD.
PEOPLE ARE GOING TO THINK I WAS FAKING YESTERDAY.
NO THEY WON'T.
I'M HAPPY YOU GOT BETTER OVER-NIGHT!
IT'S ALL THANKS TO YOU, MEGURU-KUN.
BUT I DO FEEL BAD, YOU DOING EVERYTHING FOR ME AND ALL...
IT'S FINE, REALLY! YOU CAN JUST HELP ME THE NEXT TIME I NEED SOME-THING...
"THE NEXT TIME." QUIT THAT.

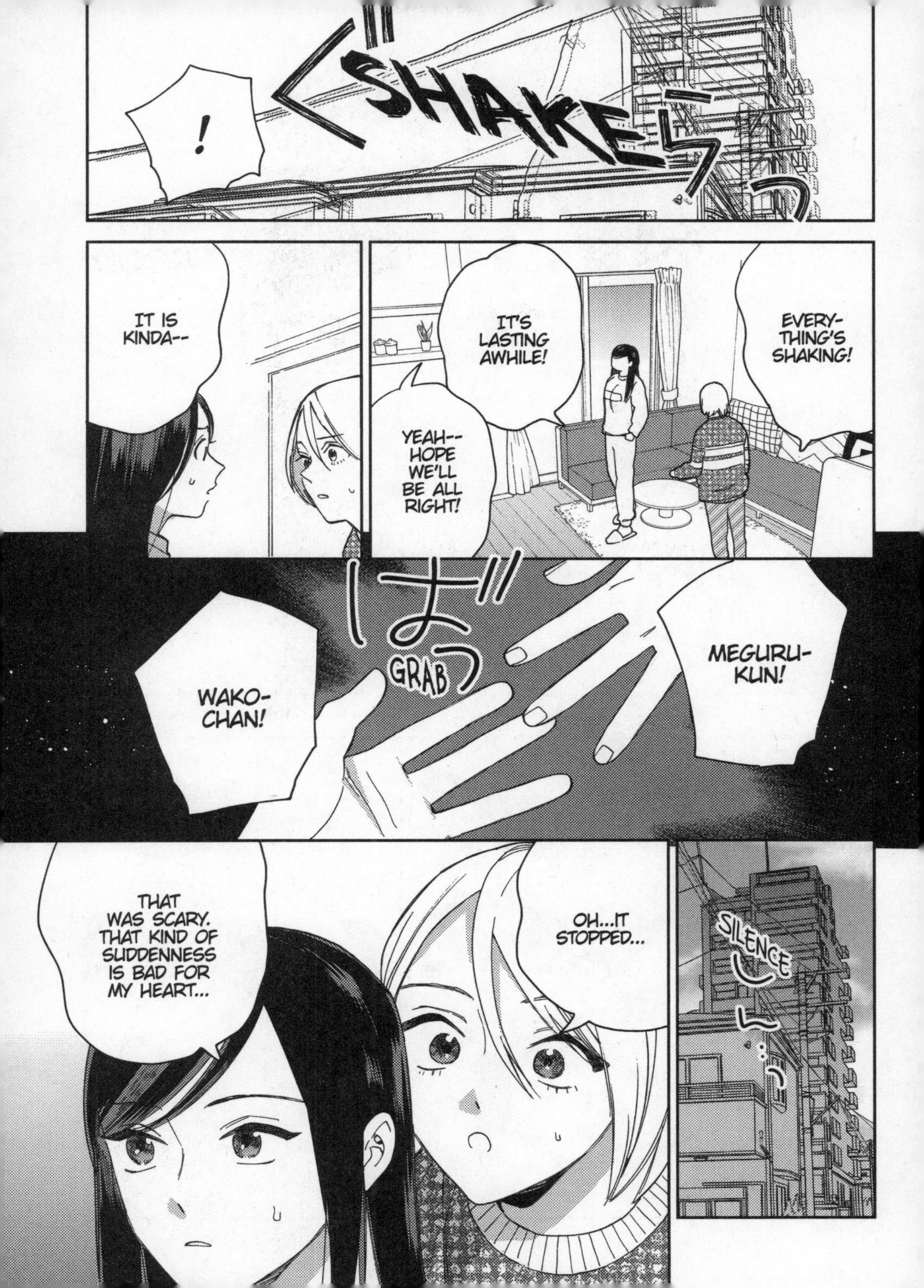
SHAKE
!
EVERY-THING'S SHAKING!
IT'S LASTING AWHILE!
YEAH-- HOPE WE'LL BE ALL RIGHT!
IT IS KINDA--
MEGURU-KUN!
GRAB
WAKO-CHAN!
SILENCE
OH...IT STOPPED...
THAT WAS SCARY. THAT KIND OF SUDDENNESS IS BAD FOR MY HEART...

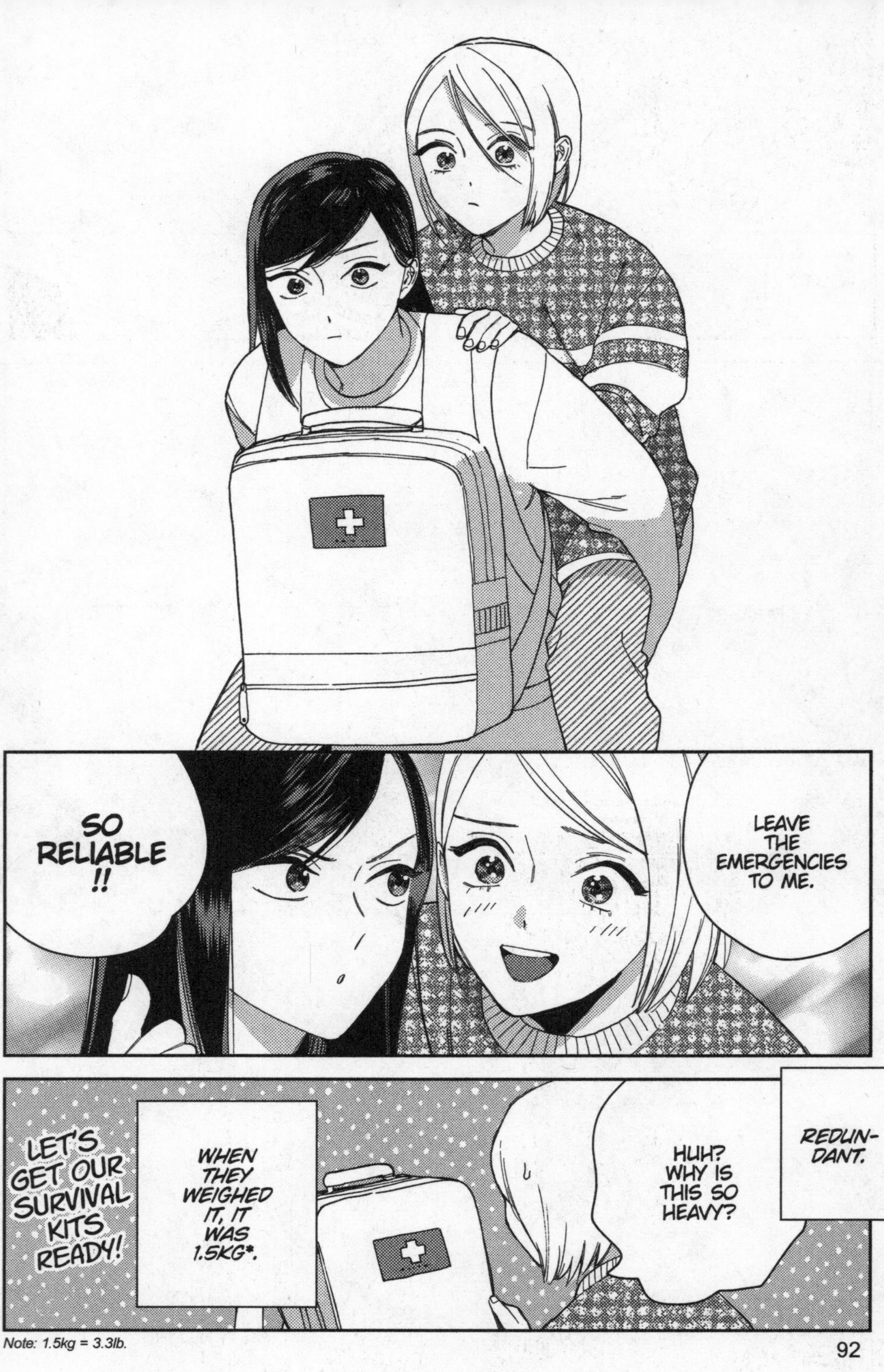
LEAVE THE EMERGENCIES TO ME.
SO RELIABLE !!
REDUN-DANT.
HUH? WHY IS THIS SO HEAVY?
WHEN THEY WEIGHED IT, IT WAS 1.5KG*.
LET'S GET OUR SURVIVAL KITS READY!

Note: 1.5kg = 3.3lb.

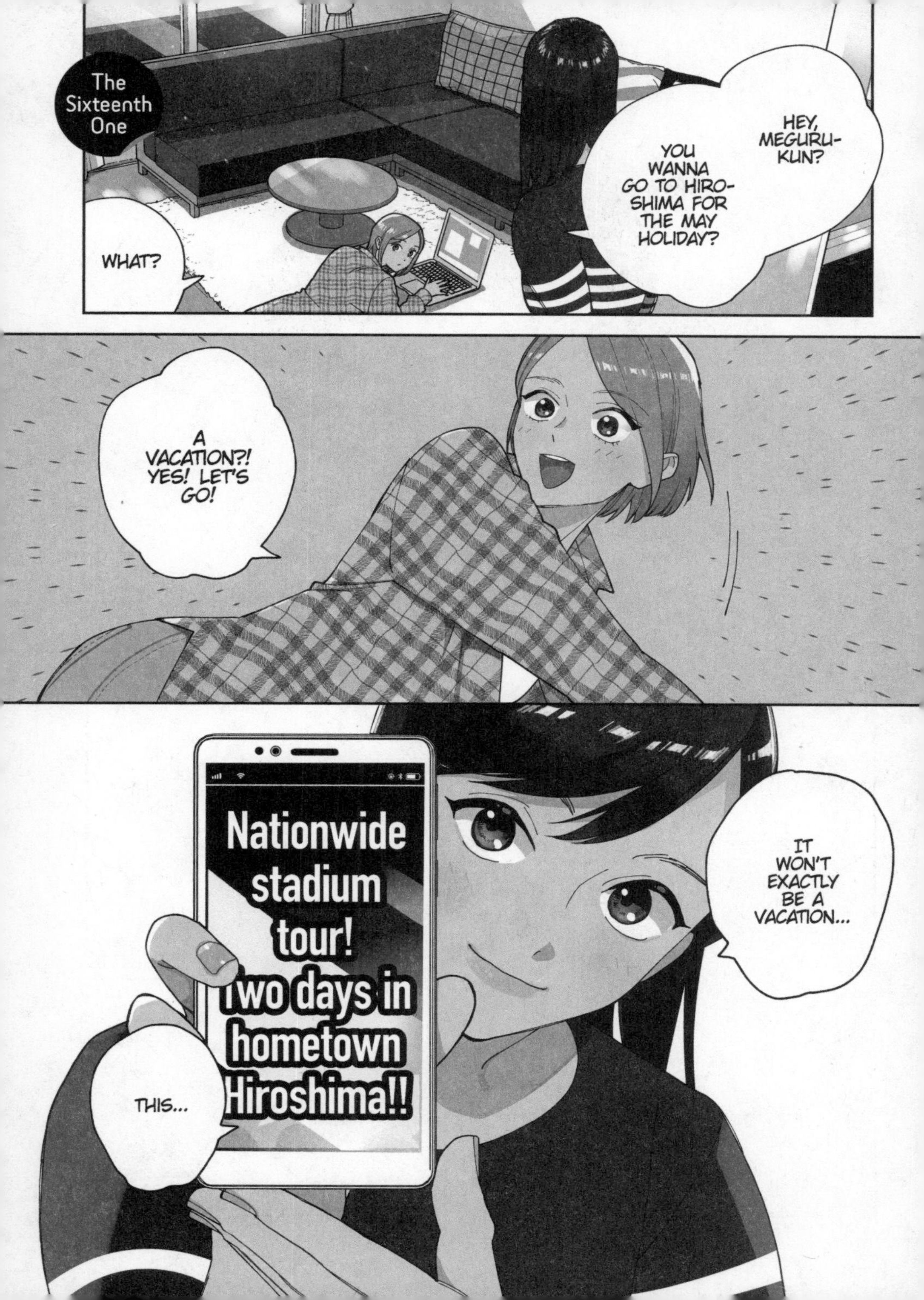
The Sixteenth One
HEY, MEGURU-KUN? YOU WANNA GO TO HIROSHIMA FOR THE MAY HOLIDAY?
WHAT?
A VACATION?! YES! LET'S GO!
IT WON'T EXACTLY BE A VACATION...
Nationwide stadium tour! Two days in hometown Hiroshima!!
THIS...

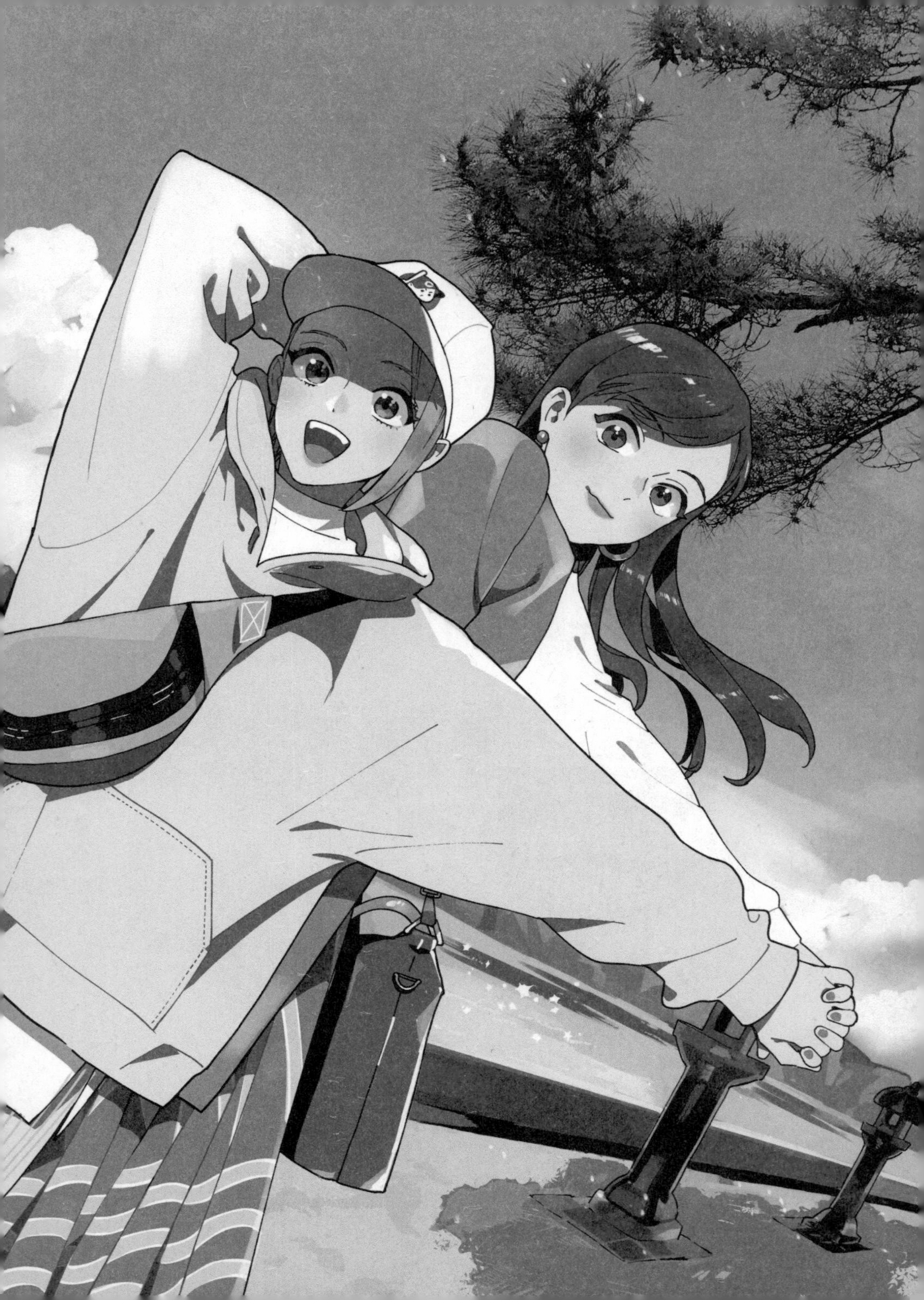

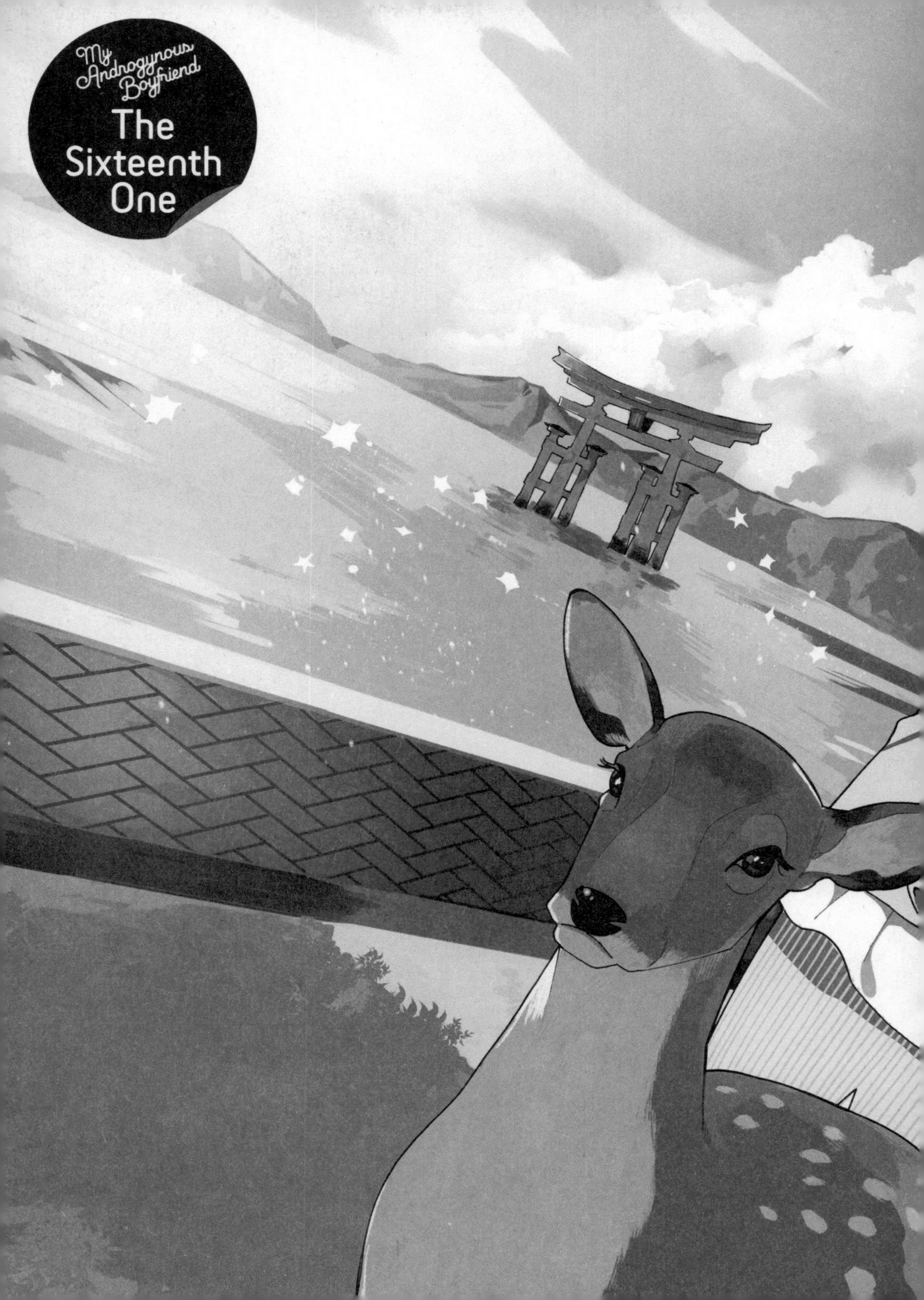
My Androgynous Boyfriend
The Sixteenth One

My Androgynous Boyfriend

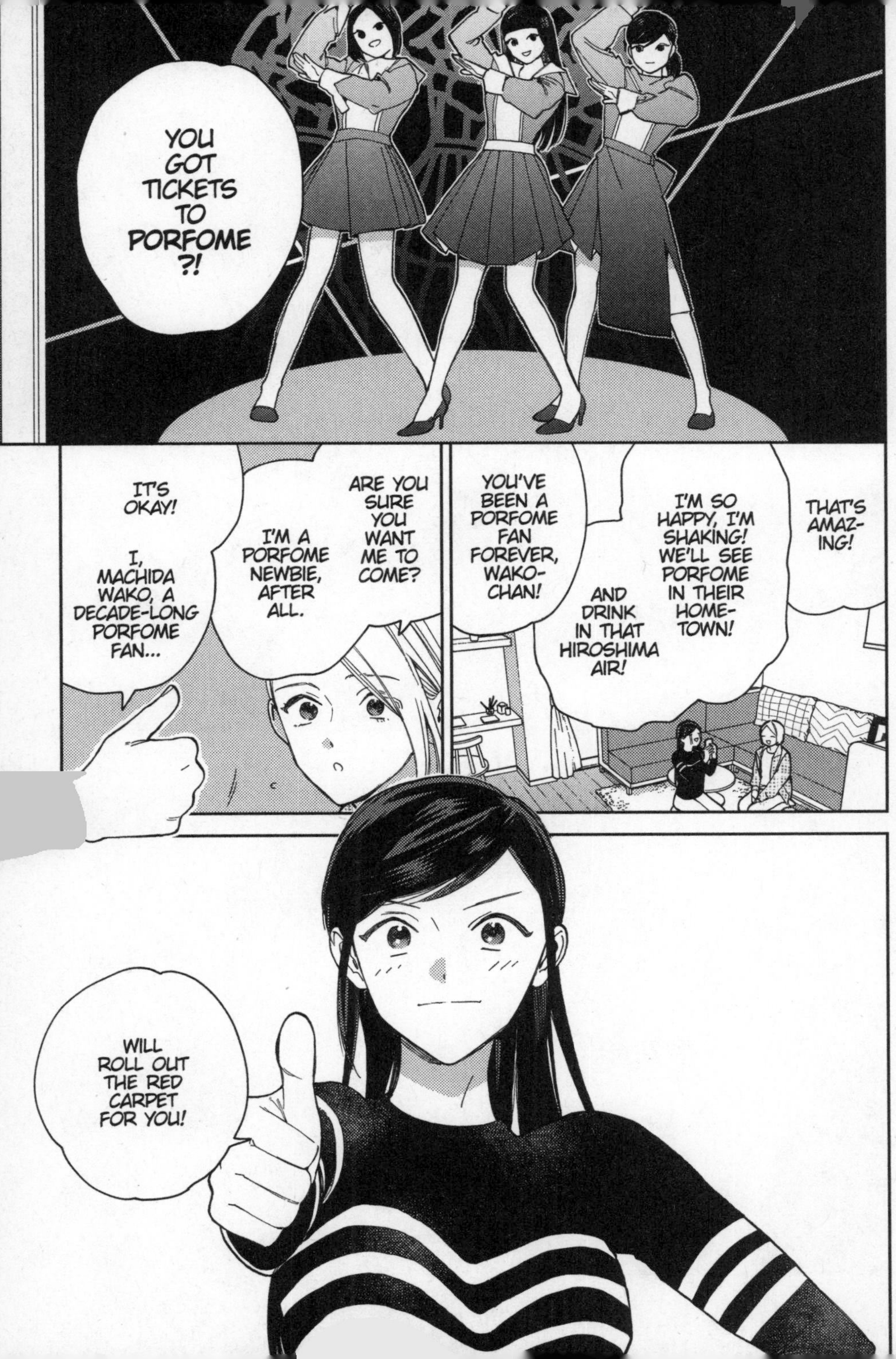
YOU GOT TICKETS TO PORFOME ?!
THAT'S AMAZ-ING!
I'M SO HAPPY, I'M SHAKING! WE'LL SEE PORFOME IN THEIR HOME-TOWN!
AND DRINK IN THAT HIROSHIMA AIR!
YOU'VE BEEN A PORFOME FAN FOREVER, WAKO-CHAN!
ARE YOU SURE YOU WANT ME TO COME?
I'M A PORFOME NEWBIE, AFTER ALL.
IT'S OKAY!
I, MACHIDA WAKO, A DECADE-LONG PORFOME FAN...
WILL ROLL OUT THE RED CARPET FOR YOU!

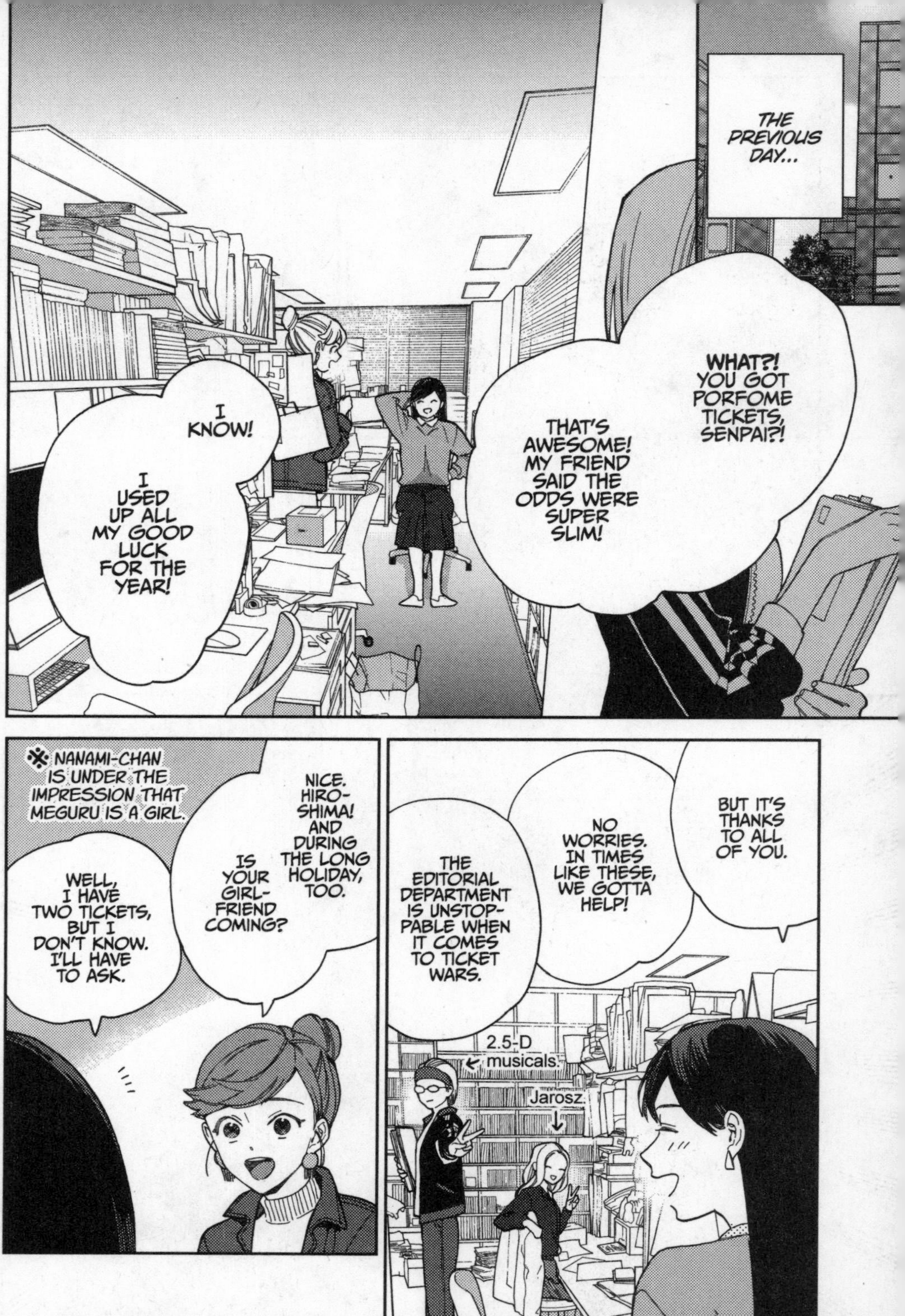
THE PREVIOUS DAY...
WHAT?! YOU GOT PORFOME TICKETS, SENPAI?!
THAT'S AWESOME! MY FRIEND SAID THE ODDS WERE SUPER SLIM!
I KNOW!
I USED UP ALL MY GOOD LUCK FOR THE YEAR!
BUT IT'S THANKS TO ALL OF YOU.
NO WORRIES. IN TIMES LIKE THESE, WE GOTTA HELP!
THE EDITORIAL DEPARTMENT IS UNSTOPPABLE WHEN IT COMES TO TICKET WARS.
2.5-D musicals.
Jarosz.
NICE. HIROSHIMA! AND DURING THE LONG HOLIDAY, TOO.
IS YOUR GIRLFRIEND COMING?
※ NANAMI-CHAN IS UNDER THE IMPRESSION THAT MEGURU IS A GIRL.
WELL, I HAVE TWO TICKETS, BUT I DON'T KNOW. I'LL HAVE TO ASK.

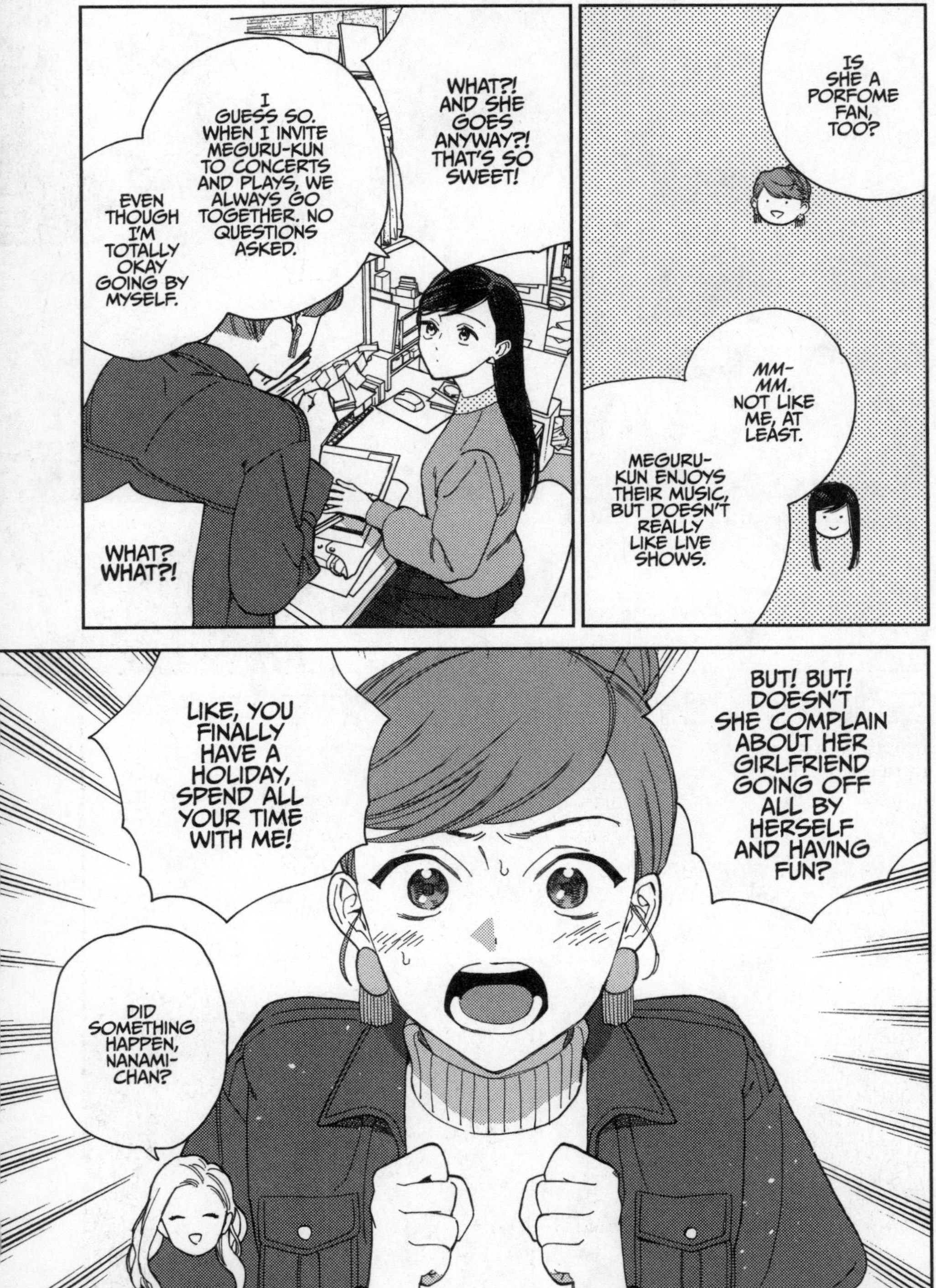
IS SHE A PORFOME FAN, TOO?
MM-MM. NOT LIKE ME, AT LEAST.
MEGURU-KUN ENJOYS THEIR MUSIC, BUT DOESN'T REALLY LIKE LIVE SHOWS.
WHAT?! AND SHE GOES ANYWAY?! THAT'S SO SWEET!
I GUESS SO. WHEN I INVITE MEGURU-KUN TO CONCERTS AND PLAYS, WE ALWAYS GO TOGETHER. NO QUESTIONS ASKED.
EVEN THOUGH I'M TOTALLY OKAY GOING BY MYSELF.
WHAT? WHAT?!
BUT! BUT! DOESN'T SHE COMPLAIN ABOUT HER GIRLFRIEND GOING OFF ALL BY HERSELF AND HAVING FUN?
LIKE, YOU FINALLY HAVE A HOLIDAY, SPEND ALL YOUR TIME WITH ME!
DID SOMETHING HAPPEN, NANAMI-CHAN?

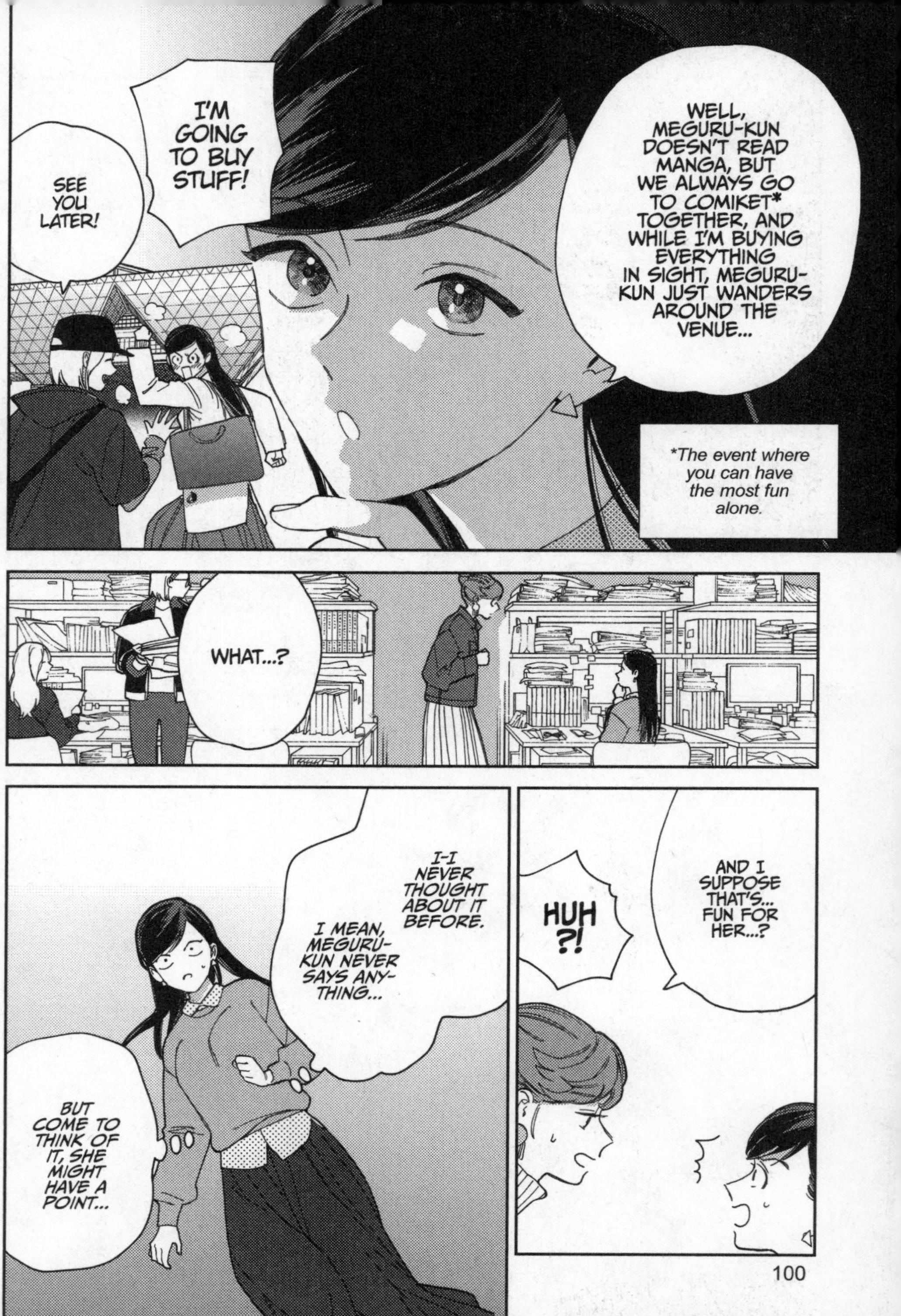
WELL, MEGURU-KUN DOESN'T READ MANGA, BUT WE ALWAYS GO TO COMIKET* TOGETHER, AND WHILE I'M BUYING EVERYTHING IN SIGHT, MEGURU-KUN JUST WANDERS AROUND THE VENUE...
*The event where you can have the most fun alone.
I'M GOING TO BUY STUFF!
SEE YOU LATER!
WHAT...?
AND I SUPPOSE THAT'S... FUN FOR HER...?
HUH?!
I-I NEVER THOUGHT ABOUT IT BEFORE.
I MEAN, MEGURU-KUN NEVER SAYS ANYTHING...
BUT COME TO THINK OF IT, SHE MIGHT HAVE A POINT...

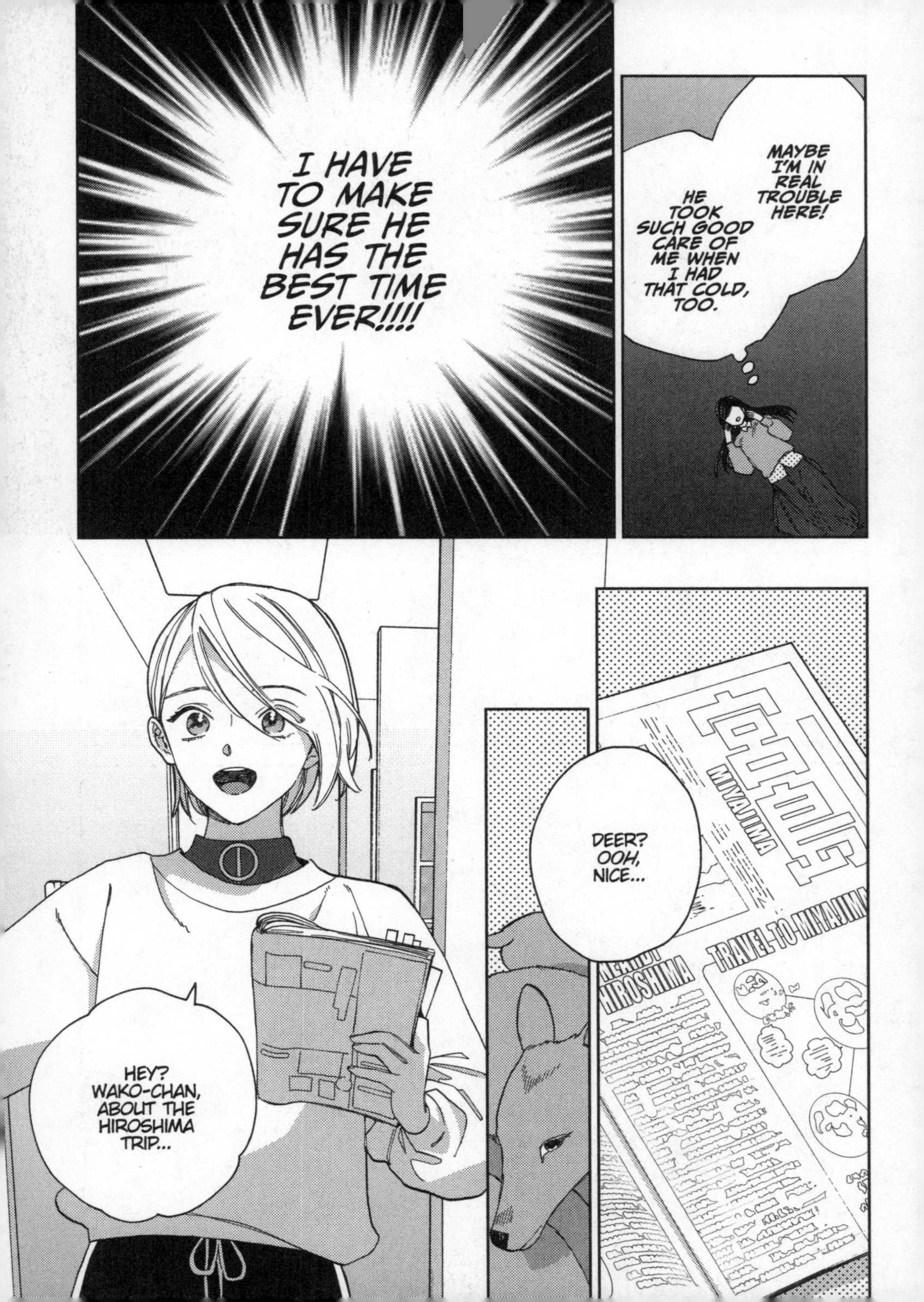
MAYBE I'M IN REAL TROUBLE HERE!
HE TOOK SUCH GOOD CARE OF ME WHEN I HAD THAT COLD, TOO.
I HAVE TO MAKE SURE HE HAS THE BEST TIME EVER!!!!
MIYAJIMA
HIROSHIMA
DEER? OOH, NICE...
HEY? WAKO-CHAN, ABOUT THE HIROSHIMA TRIP...

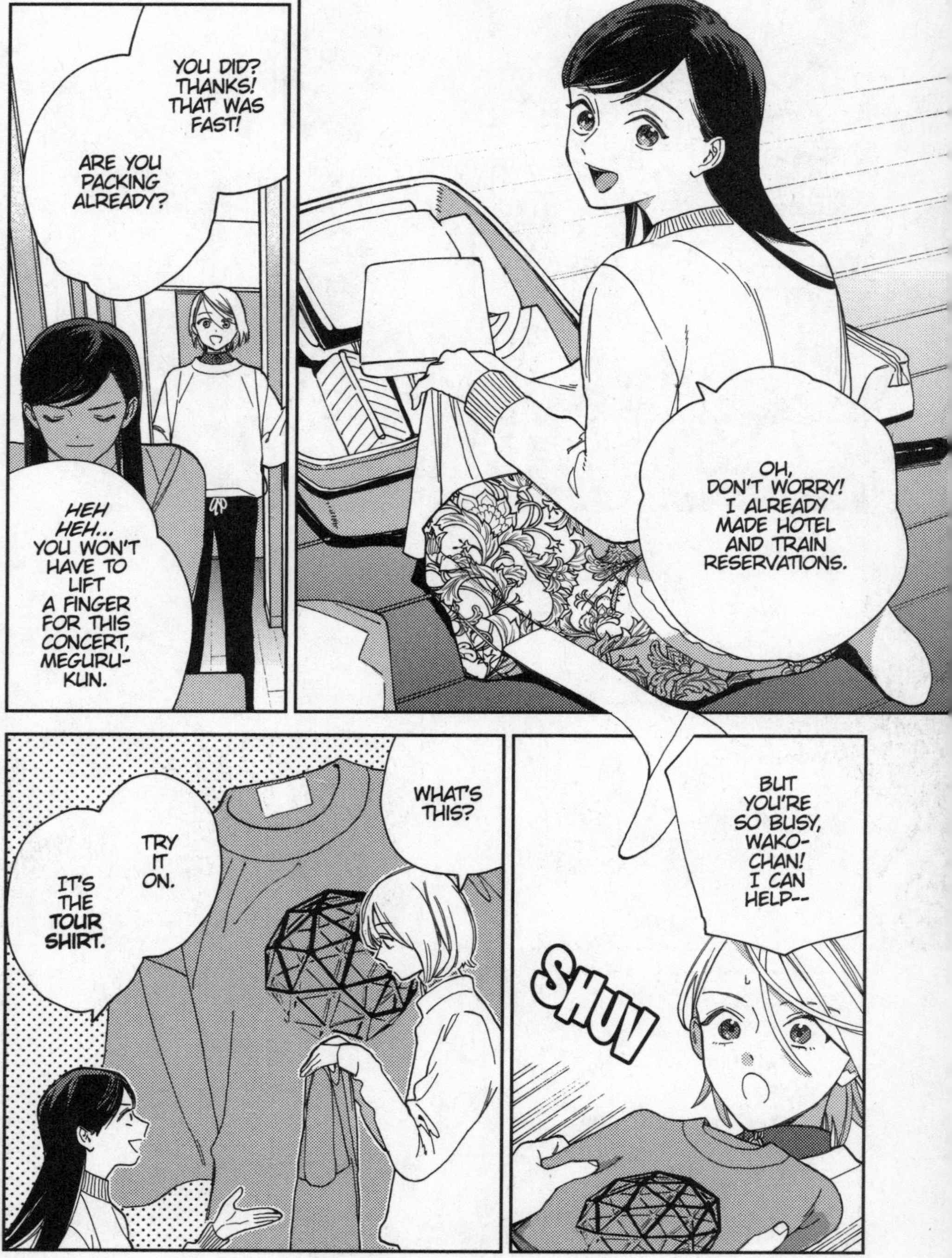
OH, DON'T WORRY! I ALREADY MADE HOTEL AND TRAIN RESERVATIONS.
YOU DID? THANKS! THAT WAS FAST!
ARE YOU PACKING ALREADY?
HEH HEH... YOU WON'T HAVE TO LIFT A FINGER FOR THIS CONCERT, MEGURU-KUN.
BUT YOU'RE SO BUSY, WAKO-CHAN! I CAN HELP--
SHUV
WHAT'S THIS?
TRY IT ON.
IT'S THE TOUR SHIRT.

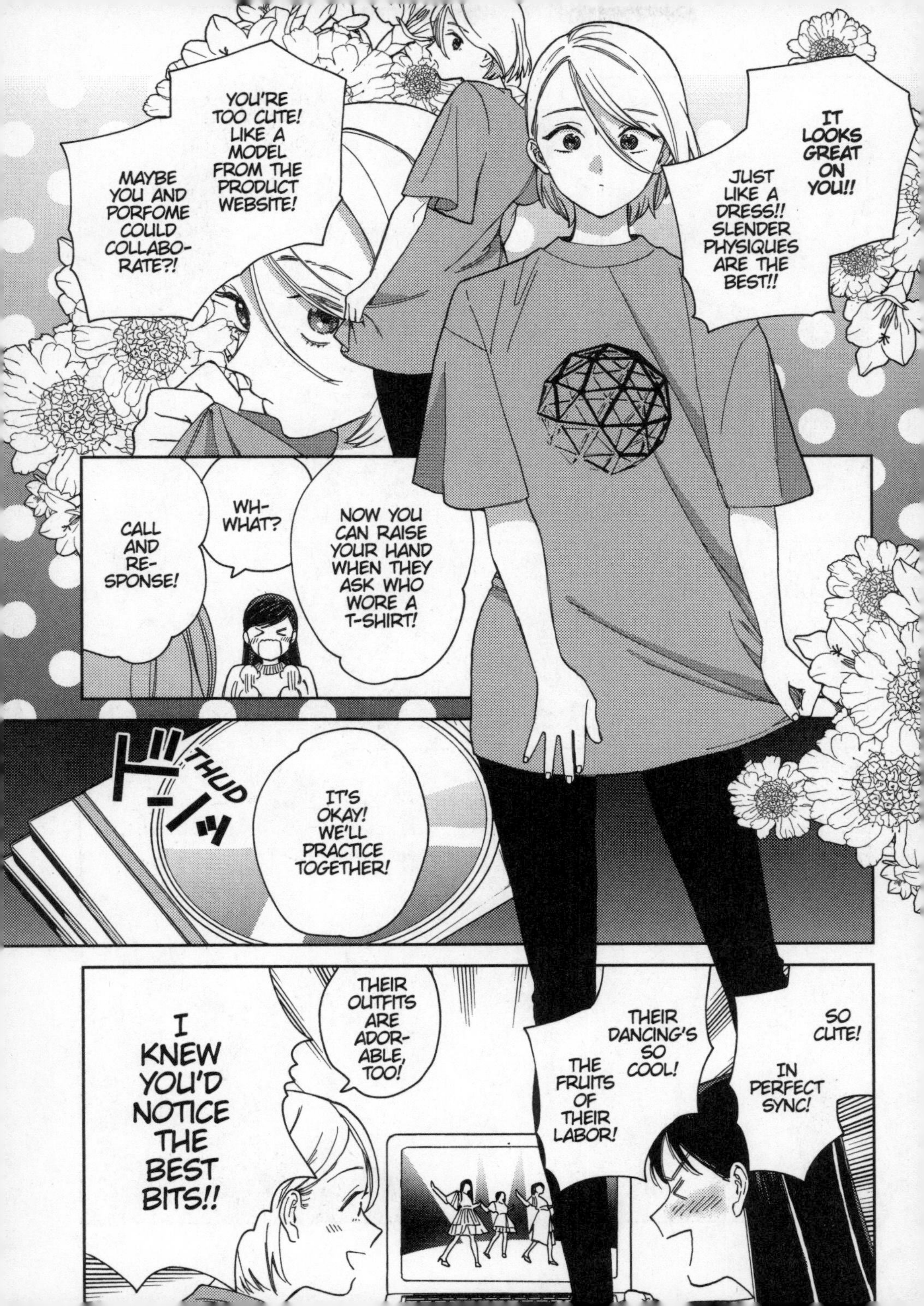
IT LOOKS GREAT ON YOU!!
JUST LIKE A DRESS!! SLENDER PHYSIQUES ARE THE BEST!!
YOU'RE TOO CUTE! LIKE A MODEL FROM THE PRODUCT WEBSITE!
MAYBE YOU AND PORFOME COULD COLLABO-RATE?!
NOW YOU CAN RAISE YOUR HAND WHEN THEY ASK WHO WORE A T-SHIRT!
WH-WHAT?
CALL AND RE-SPONSE!
THUD
IT'S OKAY! WE'LL PRACTICE TOGETHER!
SO CUTE!
IN PERFECT SYNC!
THEIR DANCING'S SO COOL!
THE FRUITS OF THEIR LABOR!
THEIR OUTFITS ARE ADOR-ABLE, TOO!
I KNEW YOU'D NOTICE THE BEST BITS!!

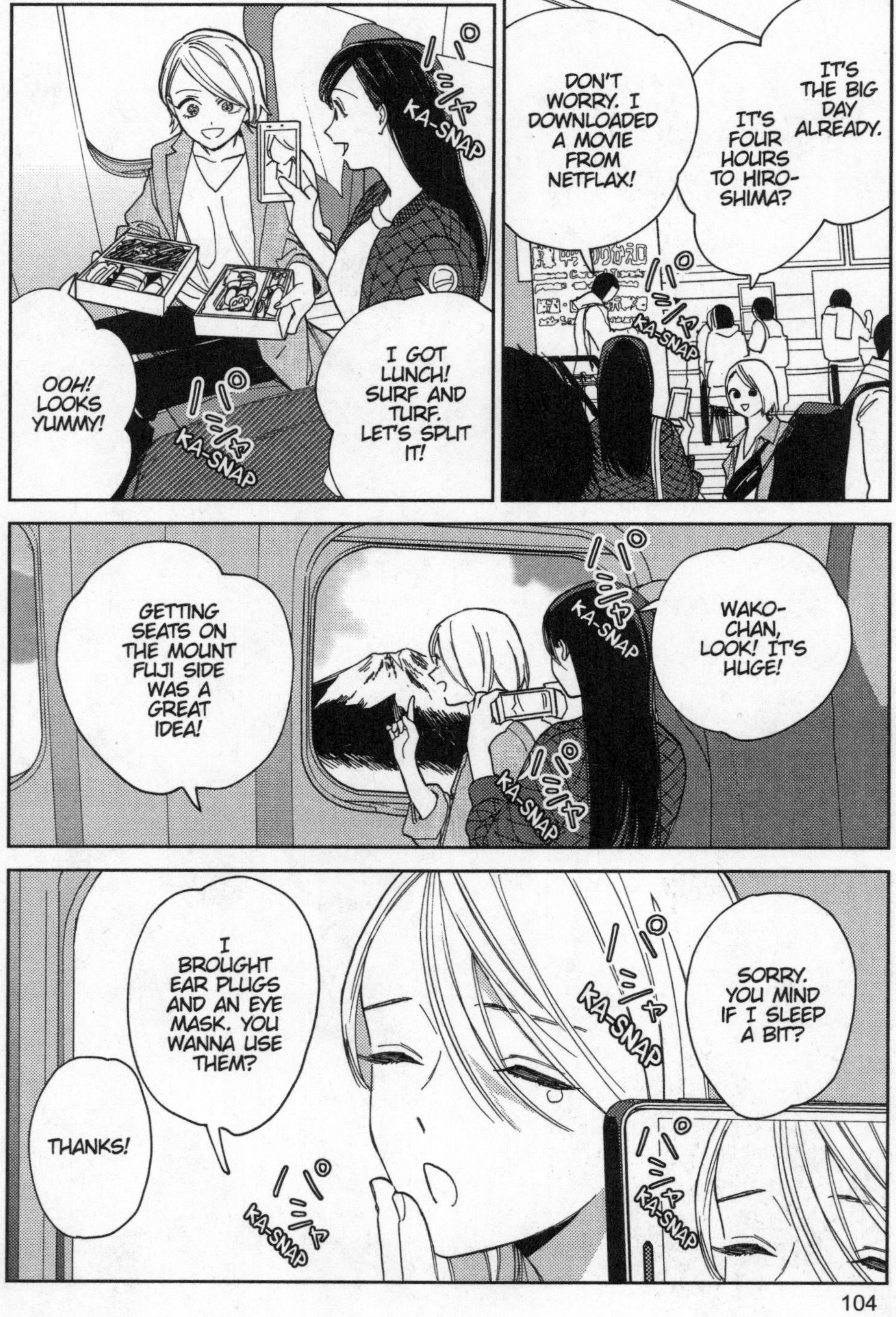
IT'S THE BIG DAY ALREADY.
IT'S FOUR HOURS TO HIRO-SHIMA?
DON'T WORRY. I DOWNLOADED A MOVIE FROM NETFLAX!
KA-SNAP
KA-SNAP
I GOT LUNCH! SURF AND TURF. LET'S SPLIT IT!
OOH! LOOKS YUMMY!
KA-SNAP
WAKO-CHAN, LOOK! IT'S HUGE!
KA-SNAP
GETTING SEATS ON THE MOUNT FUJI SIDE WAS A GREAT IDEA!
KA-SNAP
SORRY. YOU MIND IF I SLEEP A BIT?
KA-SNAP
I BROUGHT EAR PLUGS AND AN EYE MASK. YOU WANNA USE THEM?
KA-SNAP
THANKS!
KA-SNAP

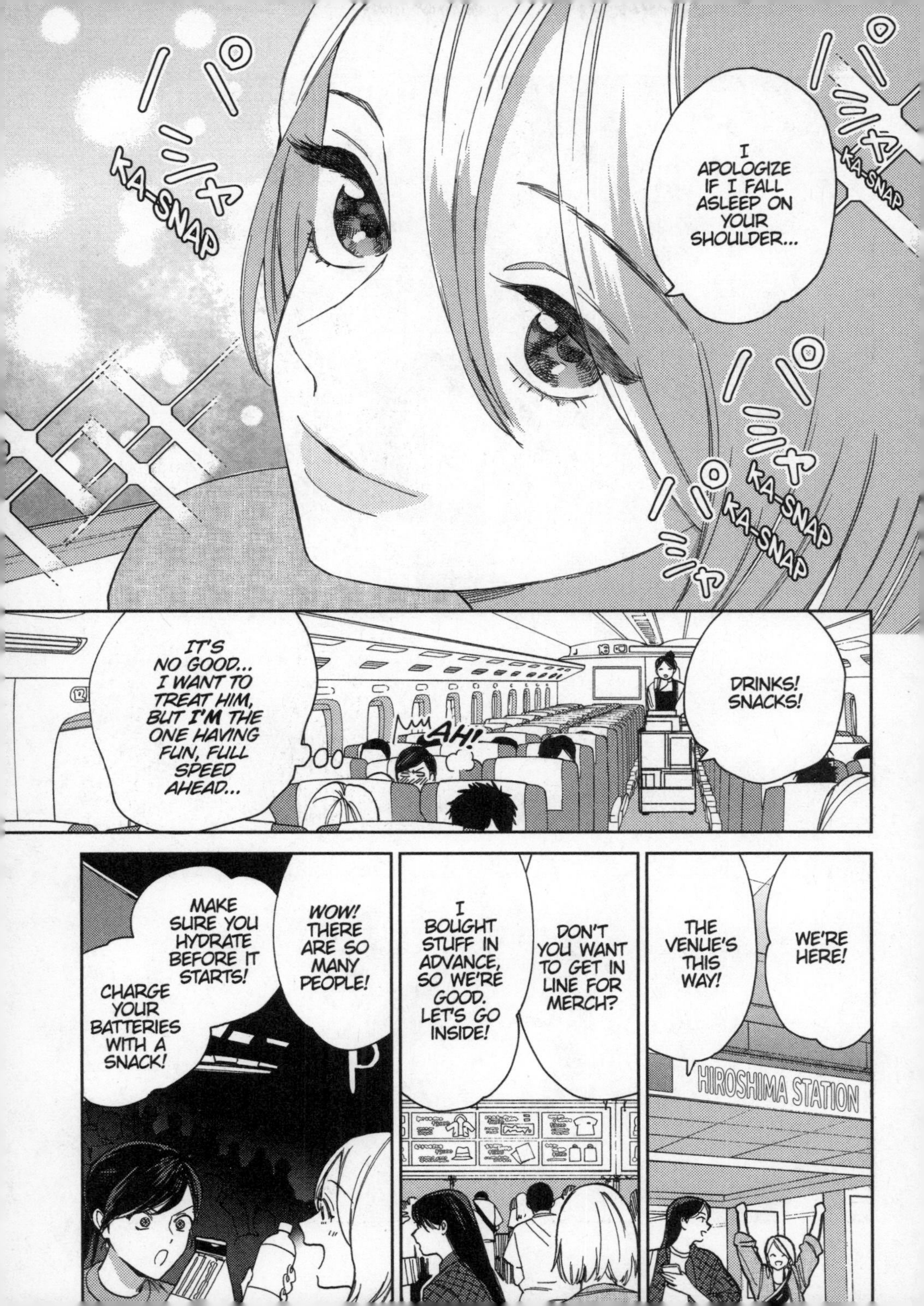
KA-SNAP
I APOLOGIZE IF I FALL ASLEEP ON YOUR SHOULDER...
KA-SNAP
KA-SNAP
KA-SNAP
DRINKS! SNACKS!
AH!
IT'S NO GOOD... I WANT TO TREAT HIM, BUT I'M THE ONE HAVING FUN, FULL SPEED AHEAD...
WE'RE HERE!
THE VENUE'S THIS WAY!
HIROSHIMA STATION
DON'T YOU WANT TO GET IN LINE FOR MERCH?
I BOUGHT STUFF IN ADVANCE, SO WE'RE GOOD. LET'S GO INSIDE!
WOW! THERE ARE SO MANY PEOPLE!
MAKE SURE YOU HYDRATE BEFORE IT STARTS!
CHARGE YOUR BATTERIES WITH A SNACK!

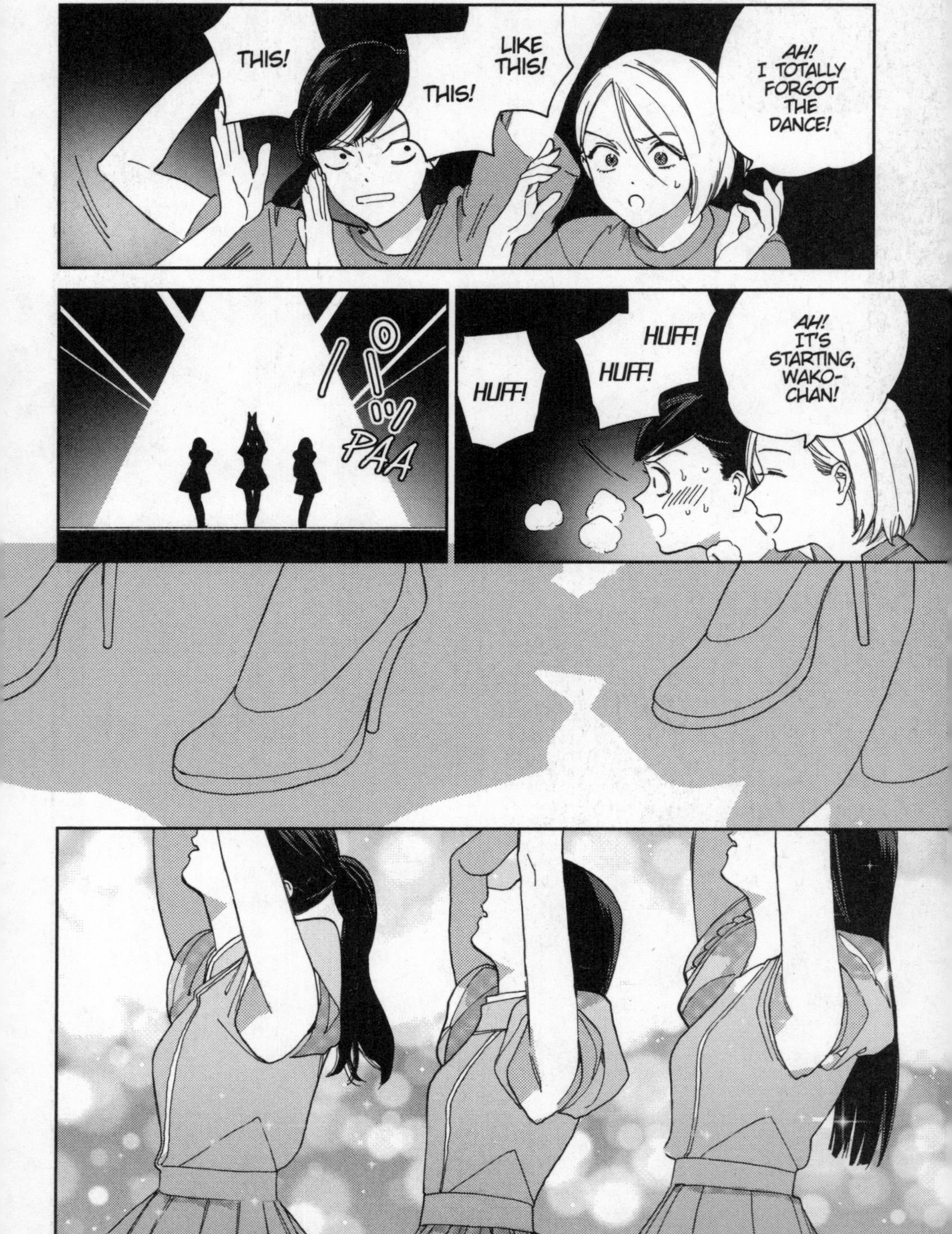
AH! I TOTALLY FORGOT THE DANCE!
LIKE THIS!
THIS!
THIS!
AH! IT'S STARTING, WAKO-CHAN!
HUFF!
HUFF!
HUFF!
PAA

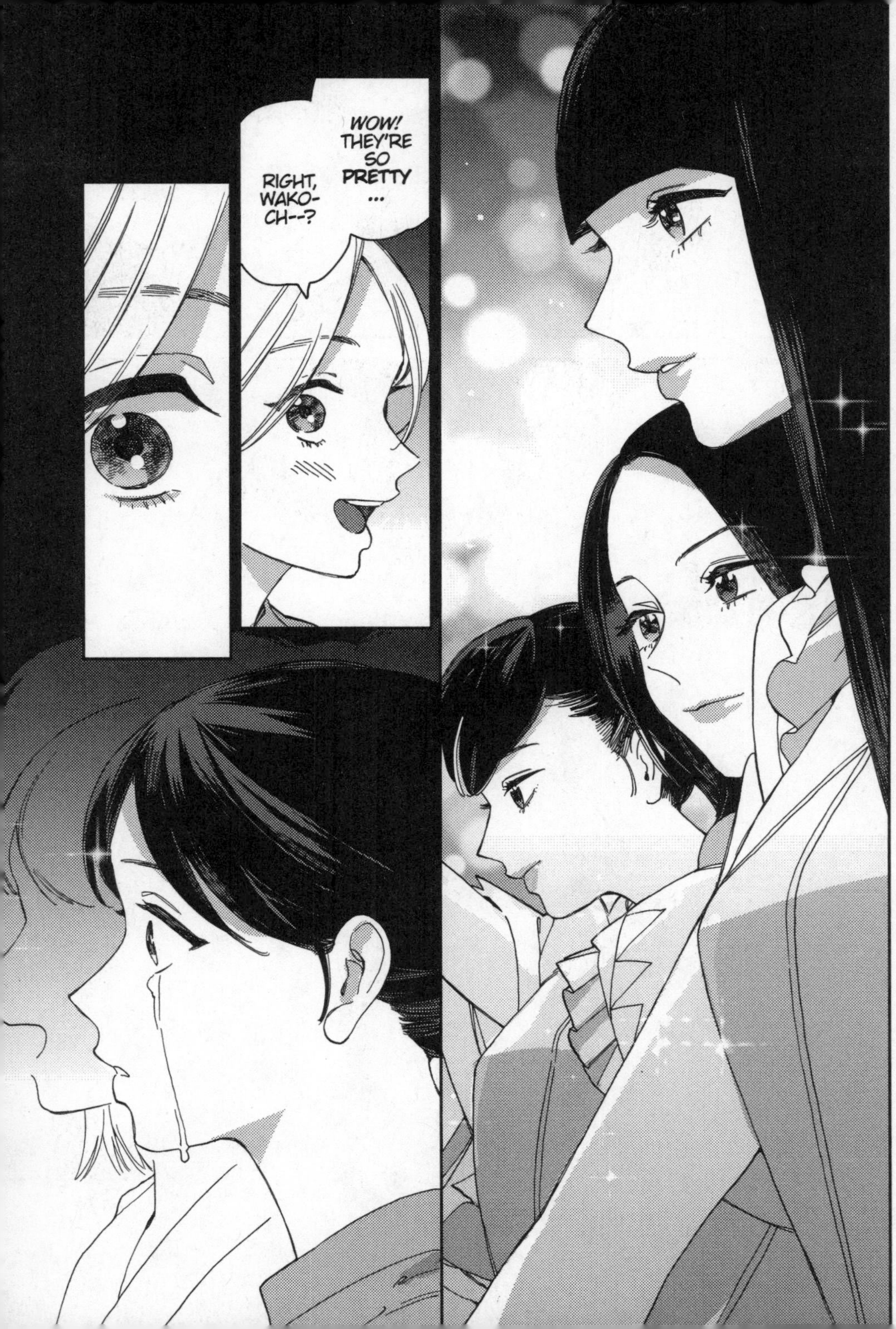
WOW! THEY'RE SO PRETTY ... RIGHT, WAKO-CH--?

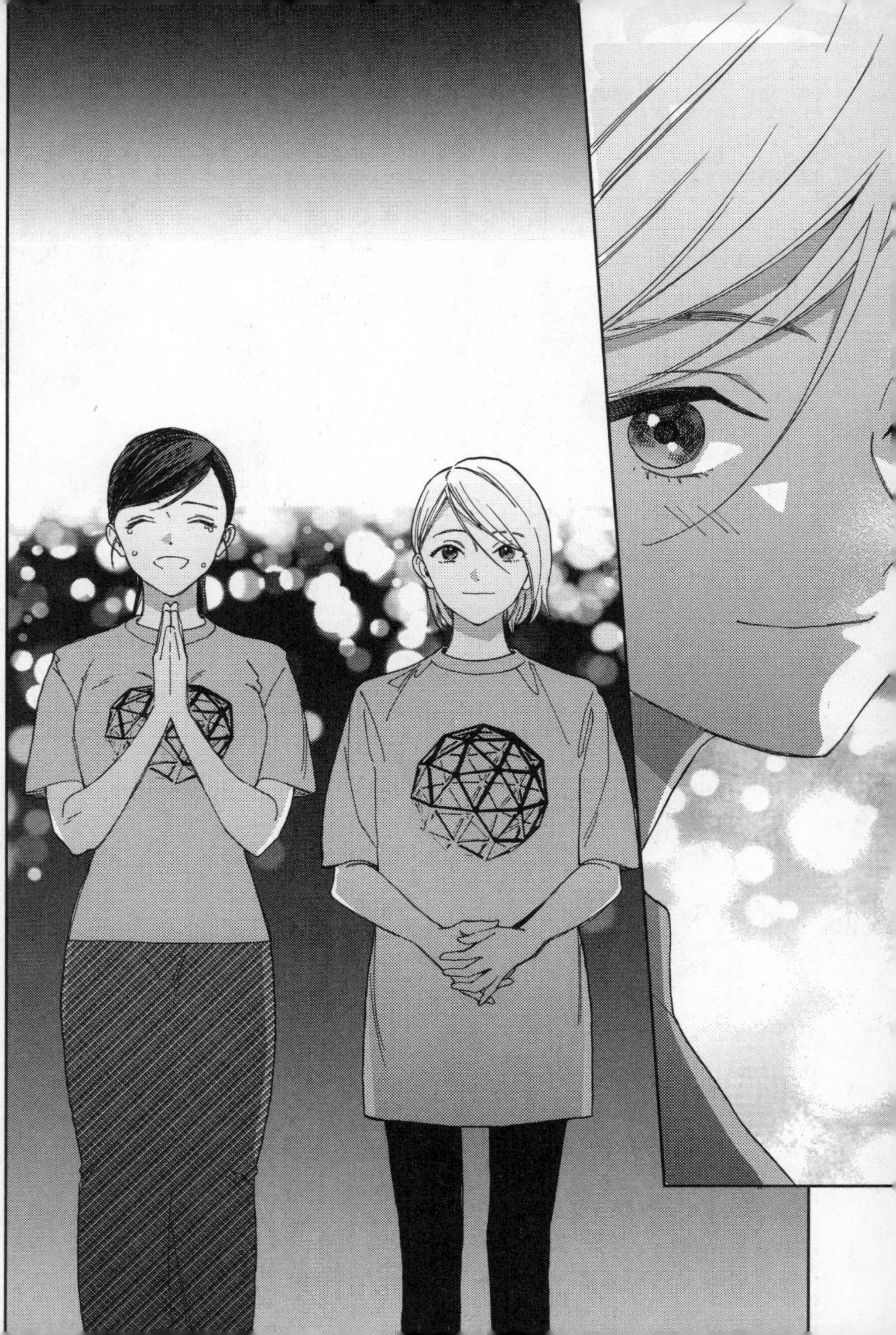

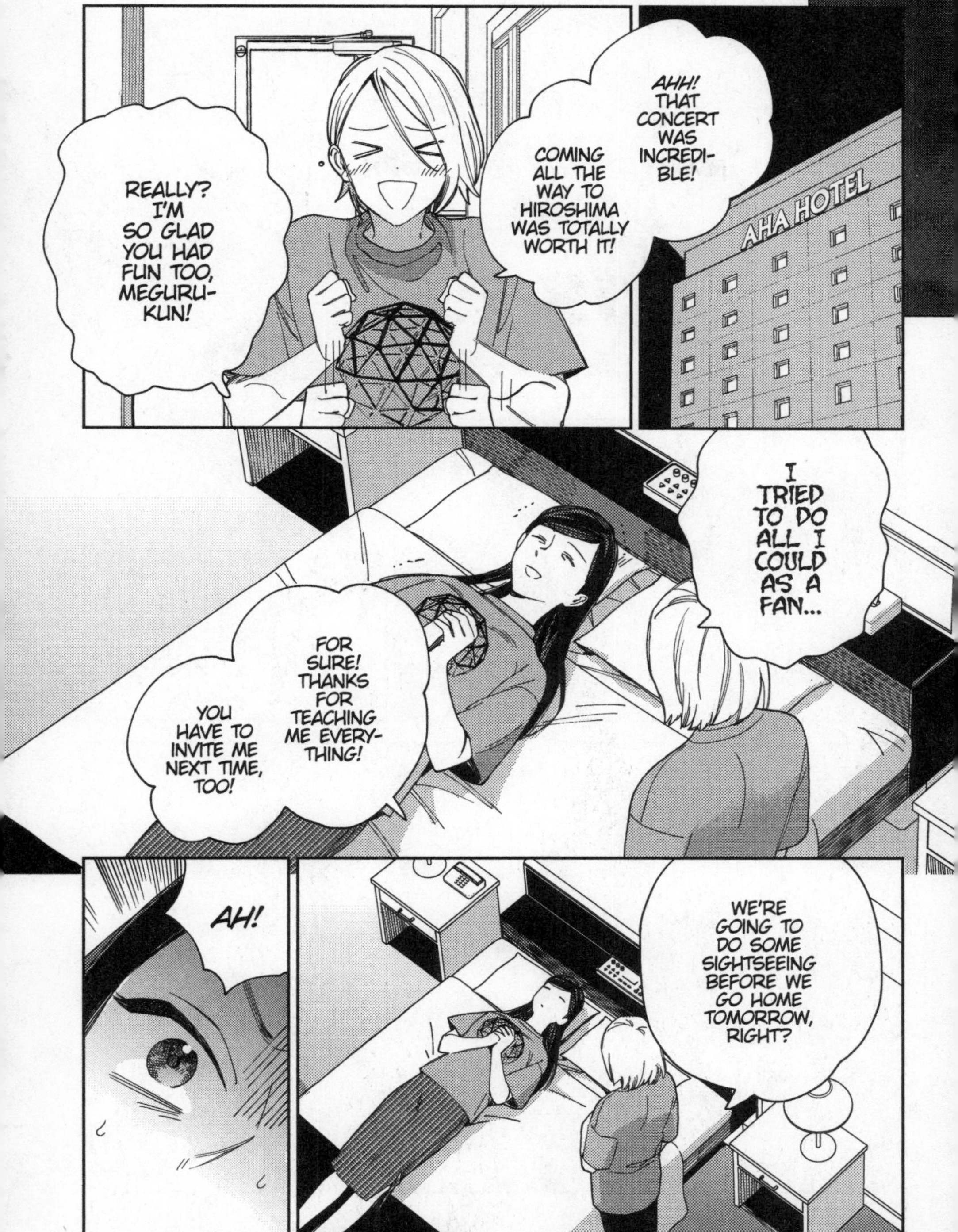
AHA HOTEL
AHH! THAT CONCERT WAS INCREDI-BLE!
COMING ALL THE WAY TO HIROSHIMA WAS TOTALLY WORTH IT!
REALLY? I'M SO GLAD YOU HAD FUN TOO, MEGURU-KUN!
I TRIED TO DO ALL I COULD AS A FAN...
FOR SURE! THANKS FOR TEACHING ME EVERY-THING!
YOU HAVE TO INVITE ME NEXT TIME, TOO!
WE'RE GOING TO DO SOME SIGHTSEEING BEFORE WE GO HOME TOMORROW, RIGHT?
AH!

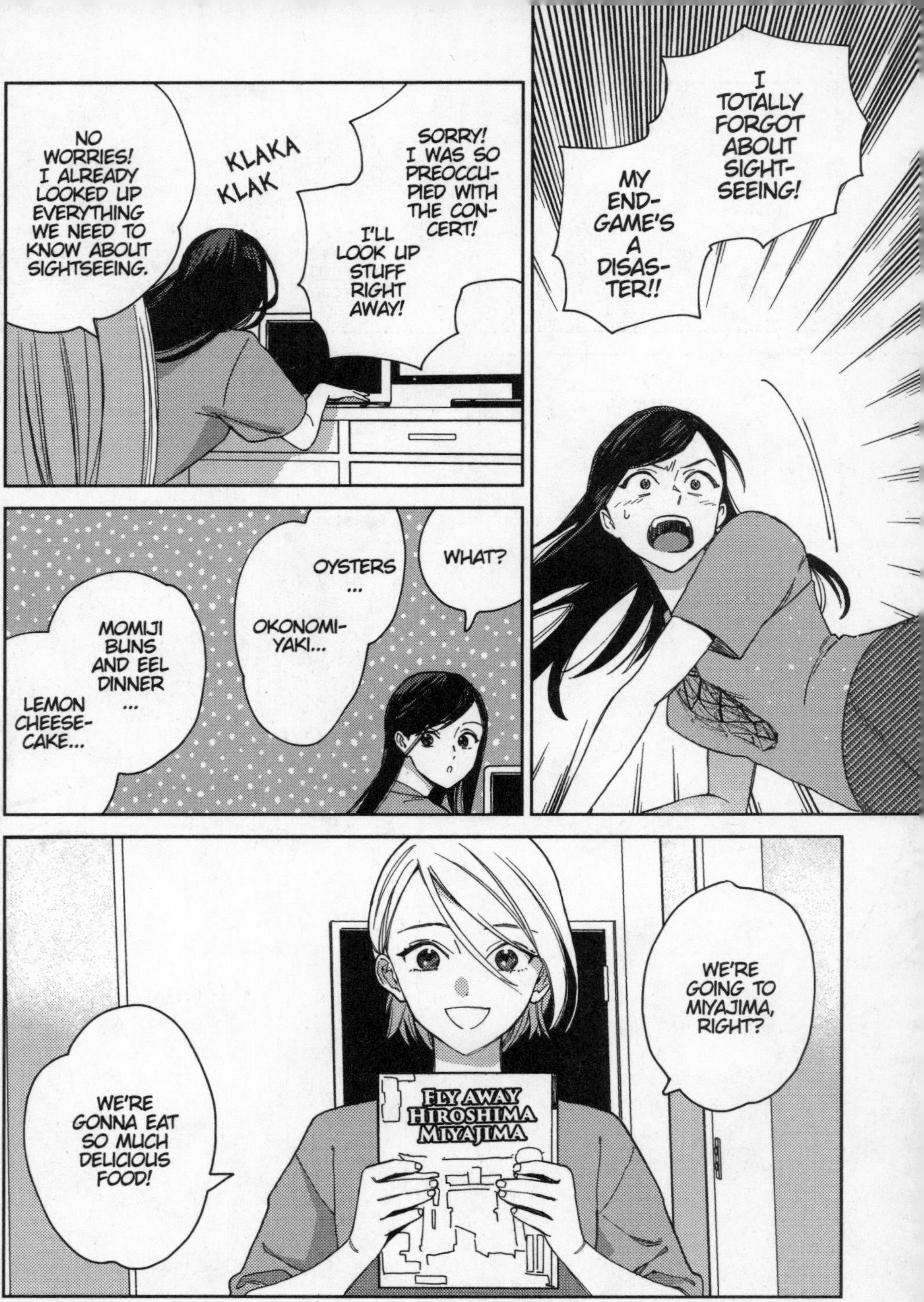
I TOTALLY FORGOT ABOUT SIGHT-SEEING!
MY END-GAME'S A DISASTER!!
SORRY! I WAS SO PREOCCU-PIED WITH THE CON-CERT!
I'LL LOOK UP STUFF RIGHT AWAY!
KLAKA KLAK
NO WORRIES! I ALREADY LOOKED UP EVERYTHING WE NEED TO KNOW ABOUT SIGHTSEEING.
WHAT?
OYSTERS ...
OKONOMI-YAKI...
MOMIJI BUNS AND EEL DINNER ...
LEMON CHEESE-CAKE...
WE'RE GOING TO MIYAJIMA, RIGHT?
FLY AWAY HIROSHIMA MIYAJIMA
WE'RE GONNA EAT SO MUCH DELICIOUS FOOD!

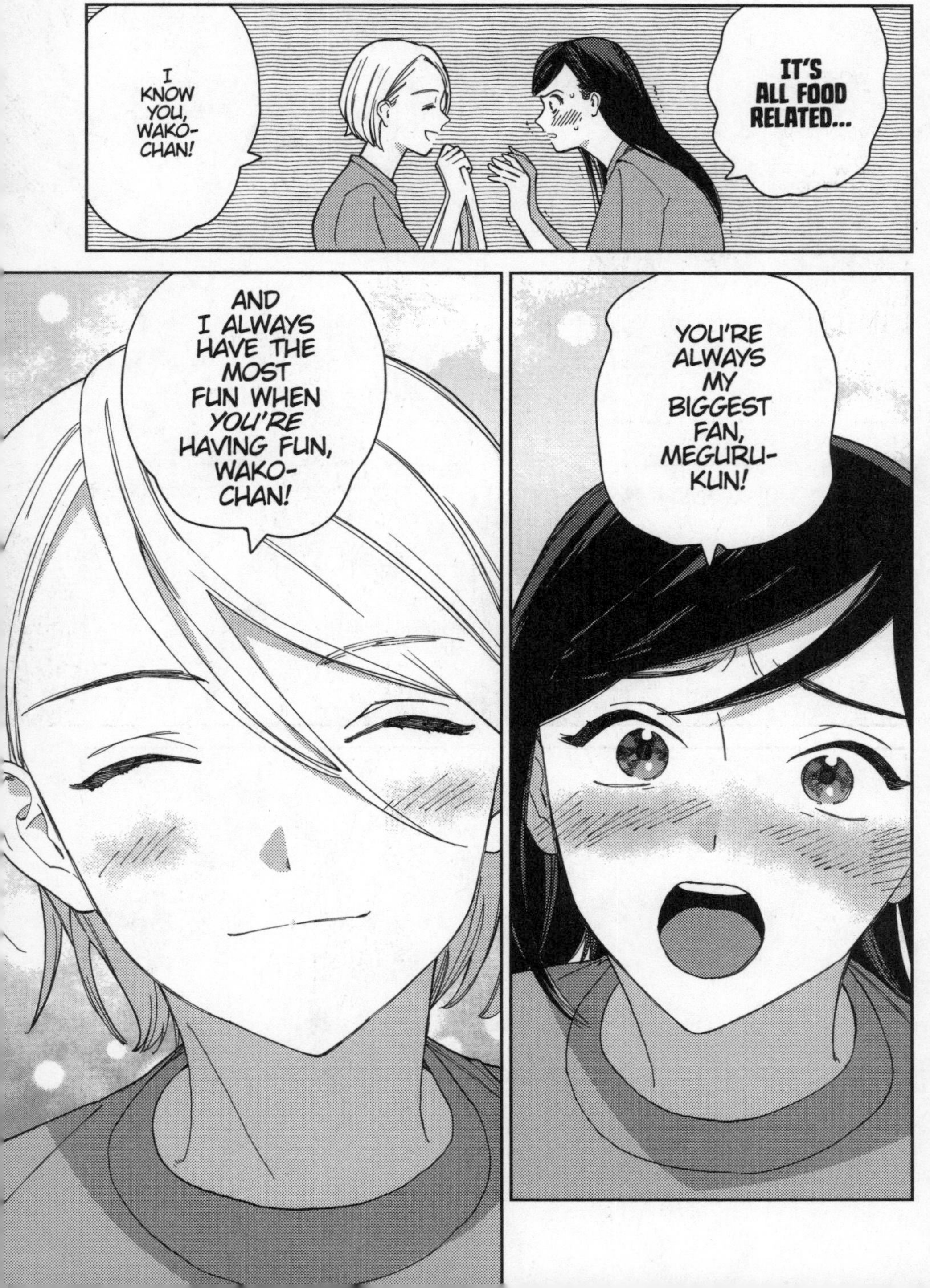
IT'S ALL FOOD RELATED...
I KNOW YOU, WAKO-CHAN!
YOU'RE ALWAYS MY BIGGEST FAN, MEGURU-KUN!
AND I ALWAYS HAVE THE MOST FUN WHEN *YOU'RE* HAVING FUN, WAKO-CHAN!

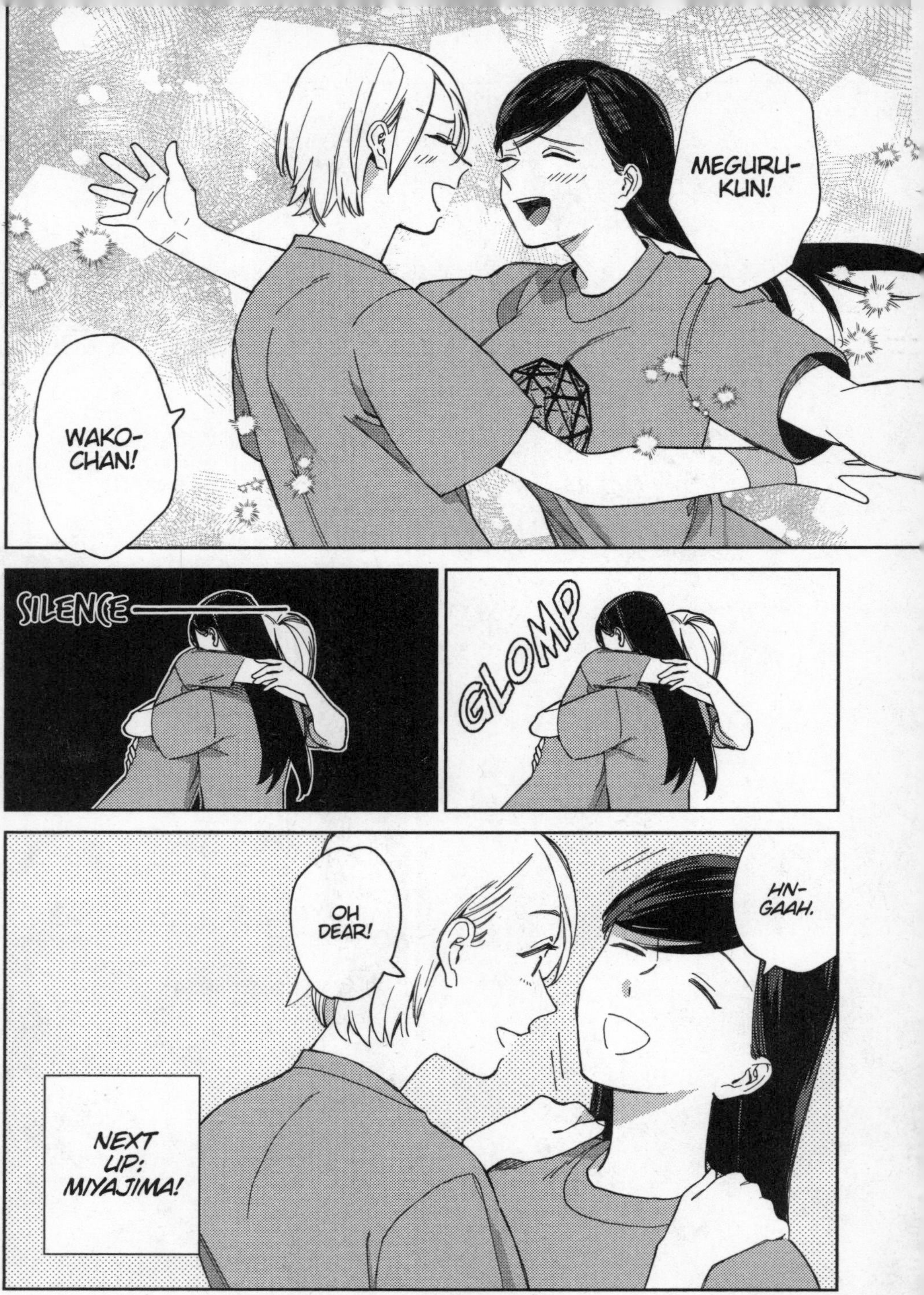
MEGURU-KUN!
WAKO-CHAN!
GLOMP
SILENCE
HN-GAAH.
OH DEAR!
NEXT UP: MIYAJIMA!

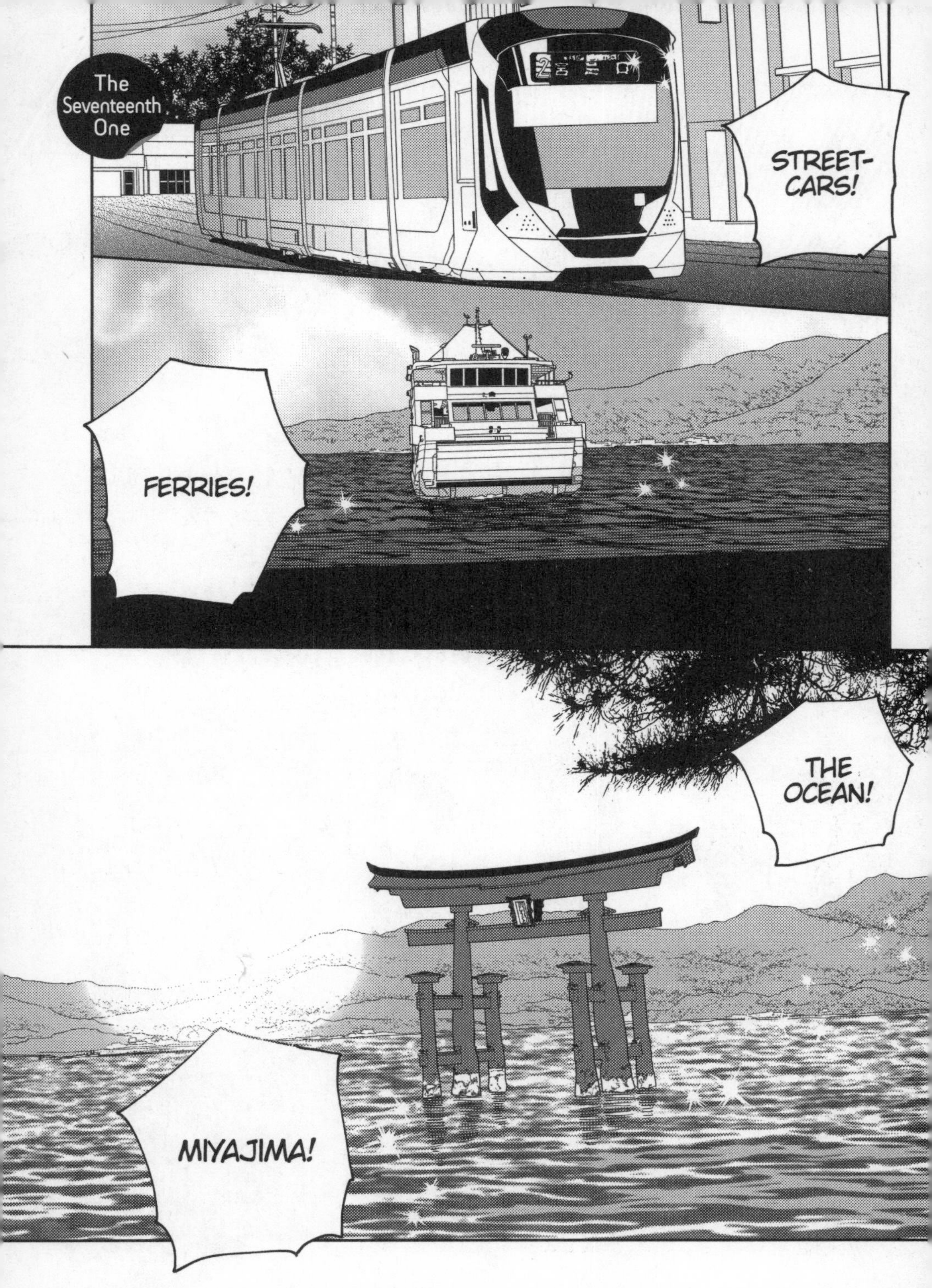
The Seventeenth One
STREET-CARS!
FERRIES!
THE OCEAN!
MIYAJIMA!

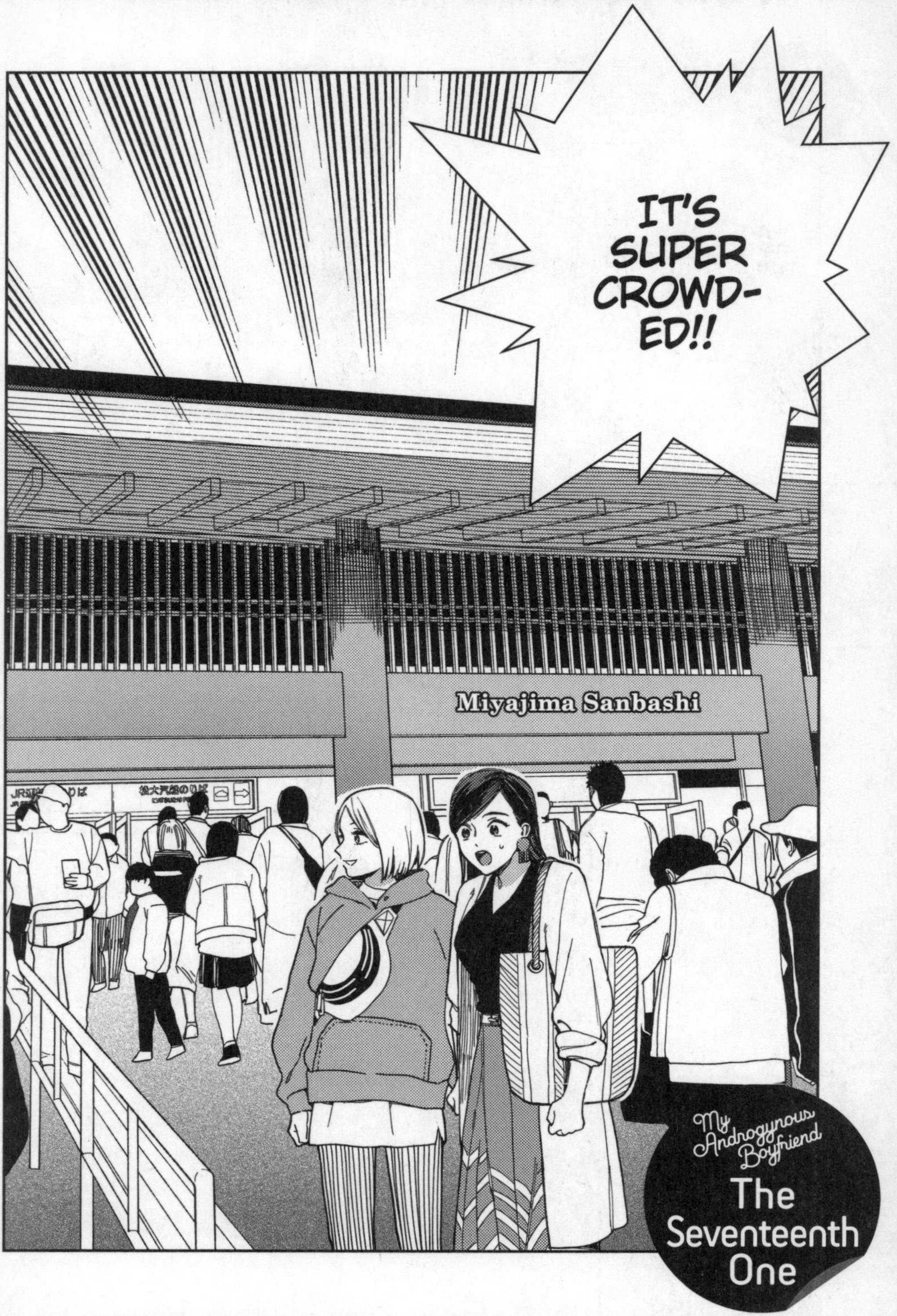
IT'S SUPER CROWDED!!
Miyajima Sanbashi
My Androgynous Boyfriend
The Seventeenth One

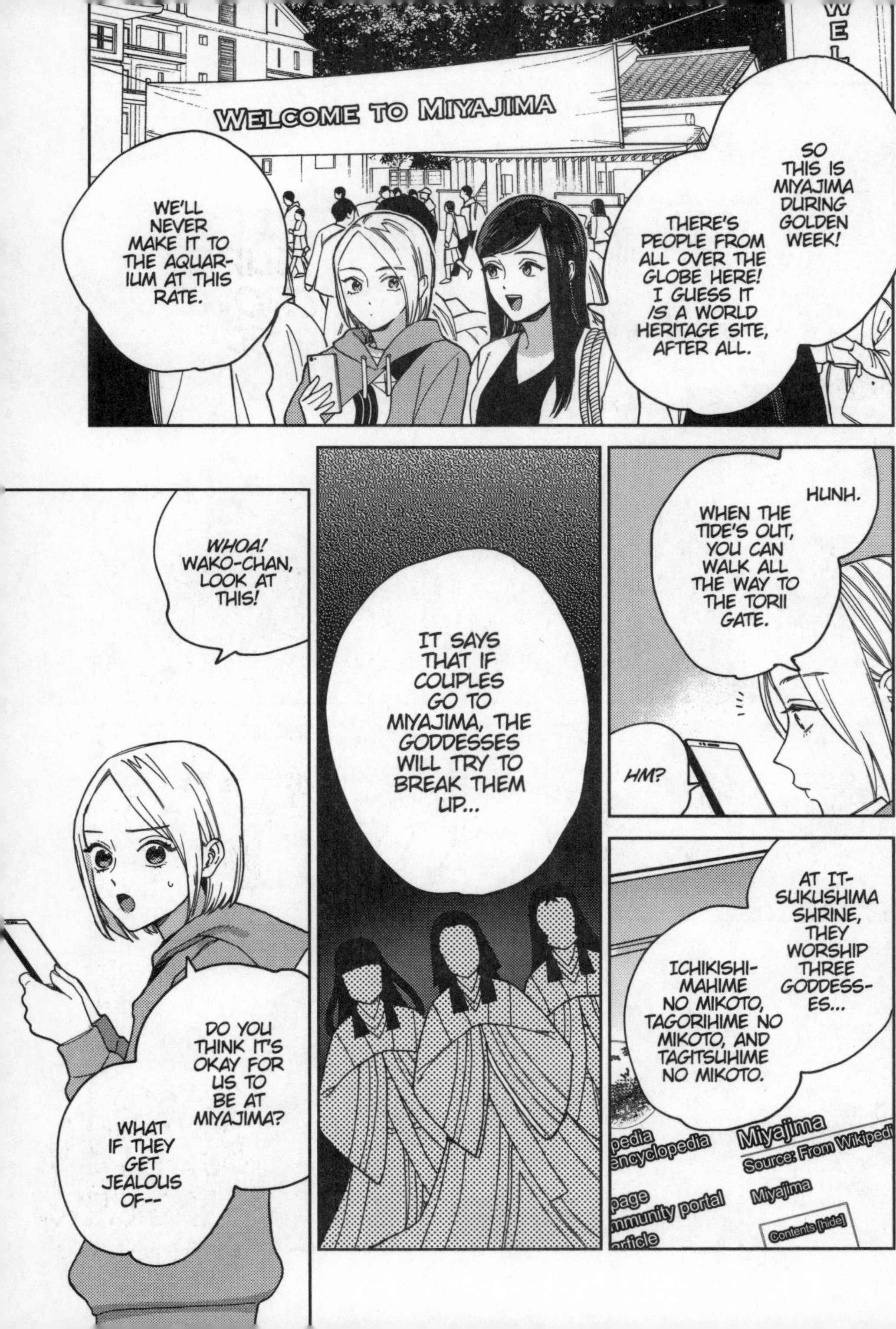
WELCOME TO MIYAJIMA
SO THIS IS MIYAJIMA DURING GOLDEN WEEK!
THERE'S PEOPLE FROM ALL OVER THE GLOBE HERE! I GUESS IT *IS* A WORLD HERITAGE SITE, AFTER ALL.
WE'LL NEVER MAKE IT TO THE AQUARIUM AT THIS RATE.
HUNH.
WHEN THE TIDE'S OUT, YOU CAN WALK ALL THE WAY TO THE TORII GATE.
HM?
AT IT-SUKUSHIMA SHRINE, THEY WORSHIP THREE GODDESS-ES...
ICHIKISHI-MAHIME NO MIKOTO, TAGORIHIME NO MIKOTO, AND TAGITSUHIME NO MIKOTO.
Miyajima
Source: From Wikipedi
pedia
encyclopedia
page
mmunity portal
article
Miyajima
Contents [hide]
IT SAYS THAT IF COUPLES GO TO MIYAJIMA, THE GODDESSES WILL TRY TO BREAK THEM UP...
WHOA! WAKO-CHAN, LOOK AT THIS!
DO YOU THINK IT'S OKAY FOR US TO BE AT MIYAJIMA?
WHAT IF THEY GET JEALOUS OF--

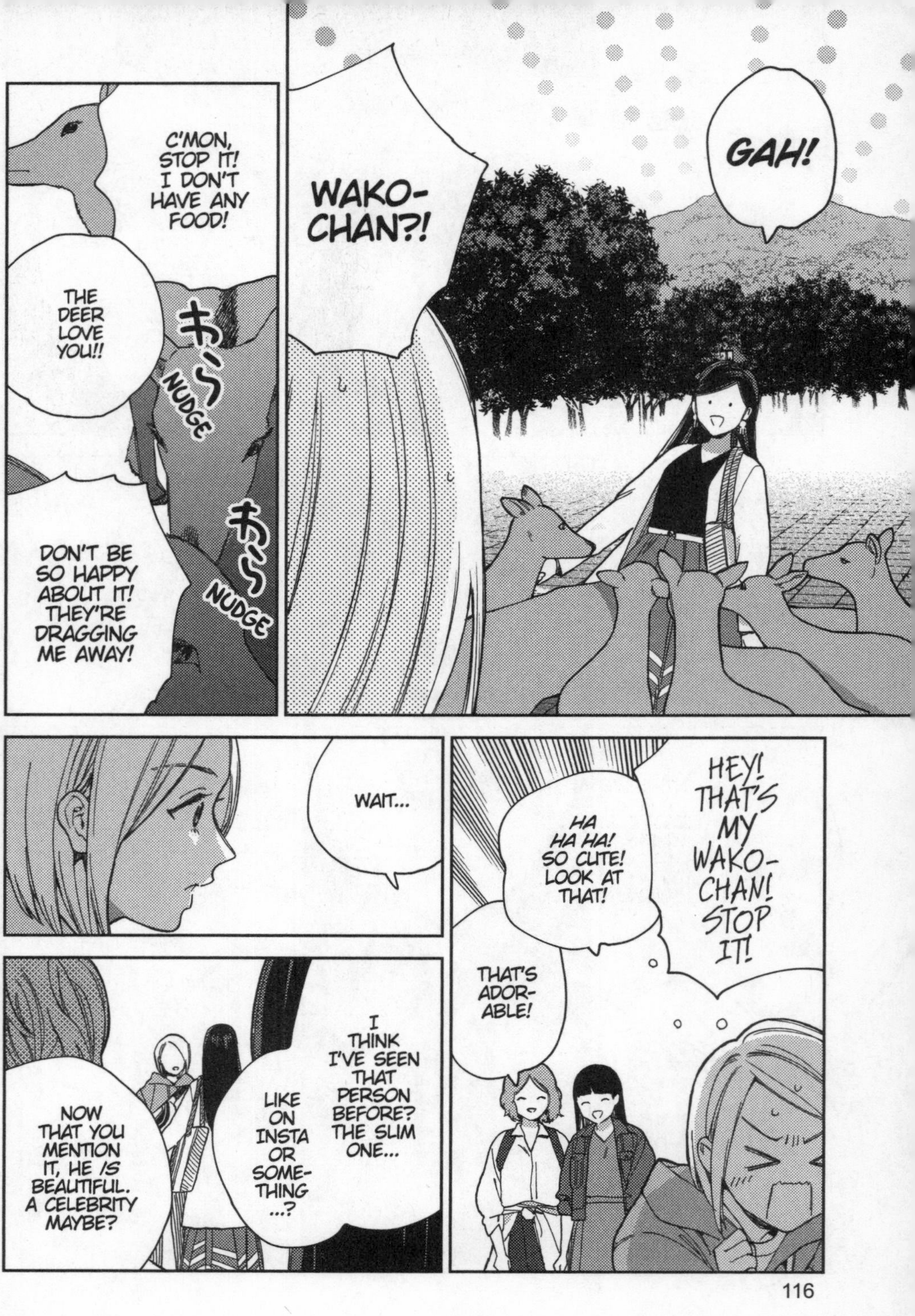
GAH!
WAKO-CHAN?!
C'MON, STOP IT! I DON'T HAVE ANY FOOD!
THE DEER LOVE YOU!!
NUDGE
NUDGE
DON'T BE SO HAPPY ABOUT IT! THEY'RE DRAGGING ME AWAY!
HEY! THAT'S MY WAKO-CHAN! STOP IT!
HA HA HA! SO CUTE! LOOK AT THAT!
THAT'S ADORABLE!
WAIT...
I THINK I'VE SEEN THAT PERSON BEFORE? THE SLIM ONE...
LIKE ON INSTA OR SOME-THING ...?
NOW THAT YOU MENTION IT, HE *IS* BEAUTIFUL. A CELEBRITY MAYBE?

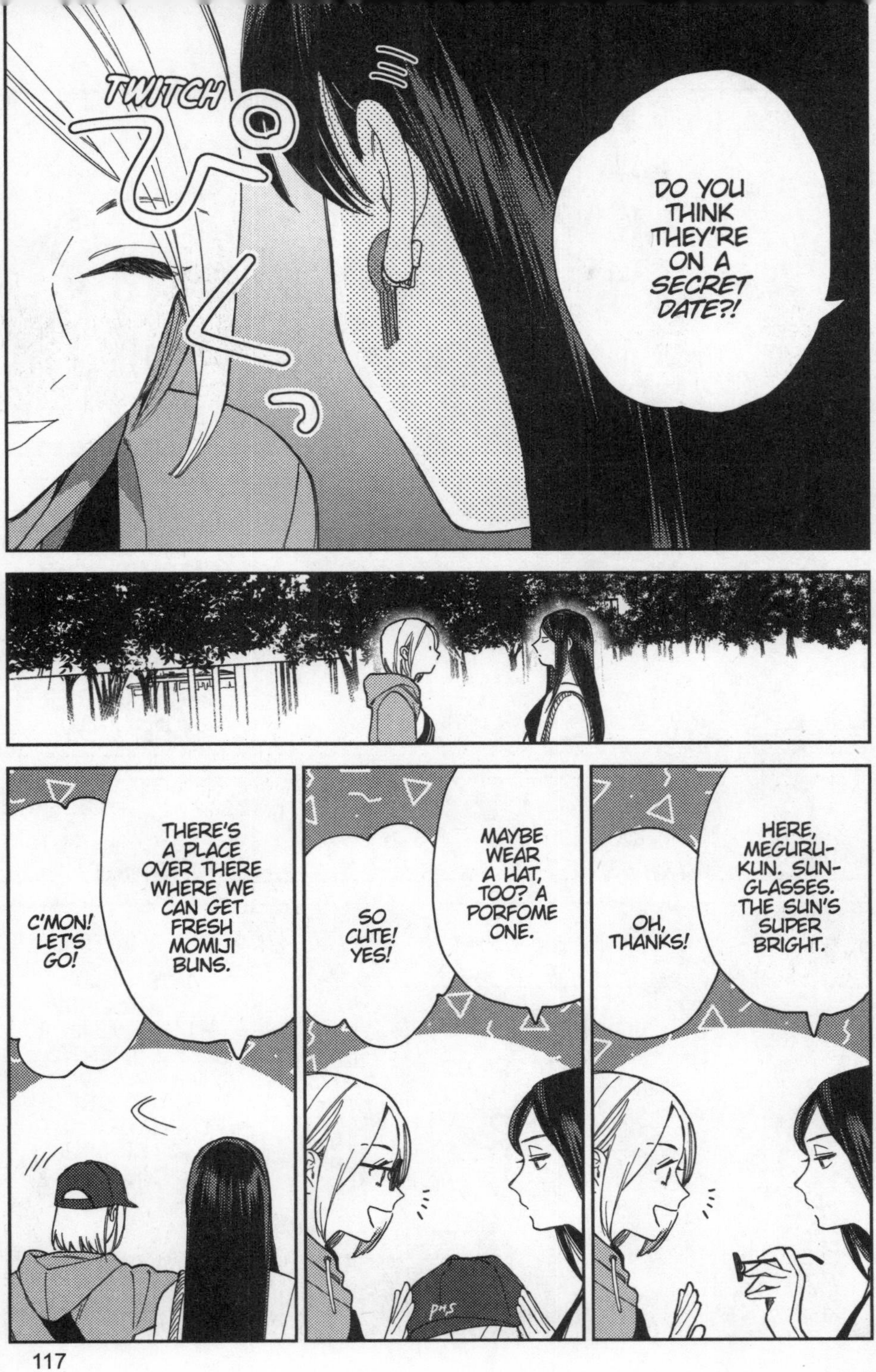
TWITCH
DO YOU THINK THEY'RE ON A SECRET DATE?!
HERE, MEGURU-KUN. SUN-GLASSES. THE SUN'S SUPER BRIGHT.
OH, THANKS!
MAYBE WEAR A HAT, TOO? A PORFOME ONE.
SO CUTE! YES!
THERE'S A PLACE OVER THERE WHERE WE CAN GET FRESH MOMIJI BUNS.
C'MON! LET'S GO!

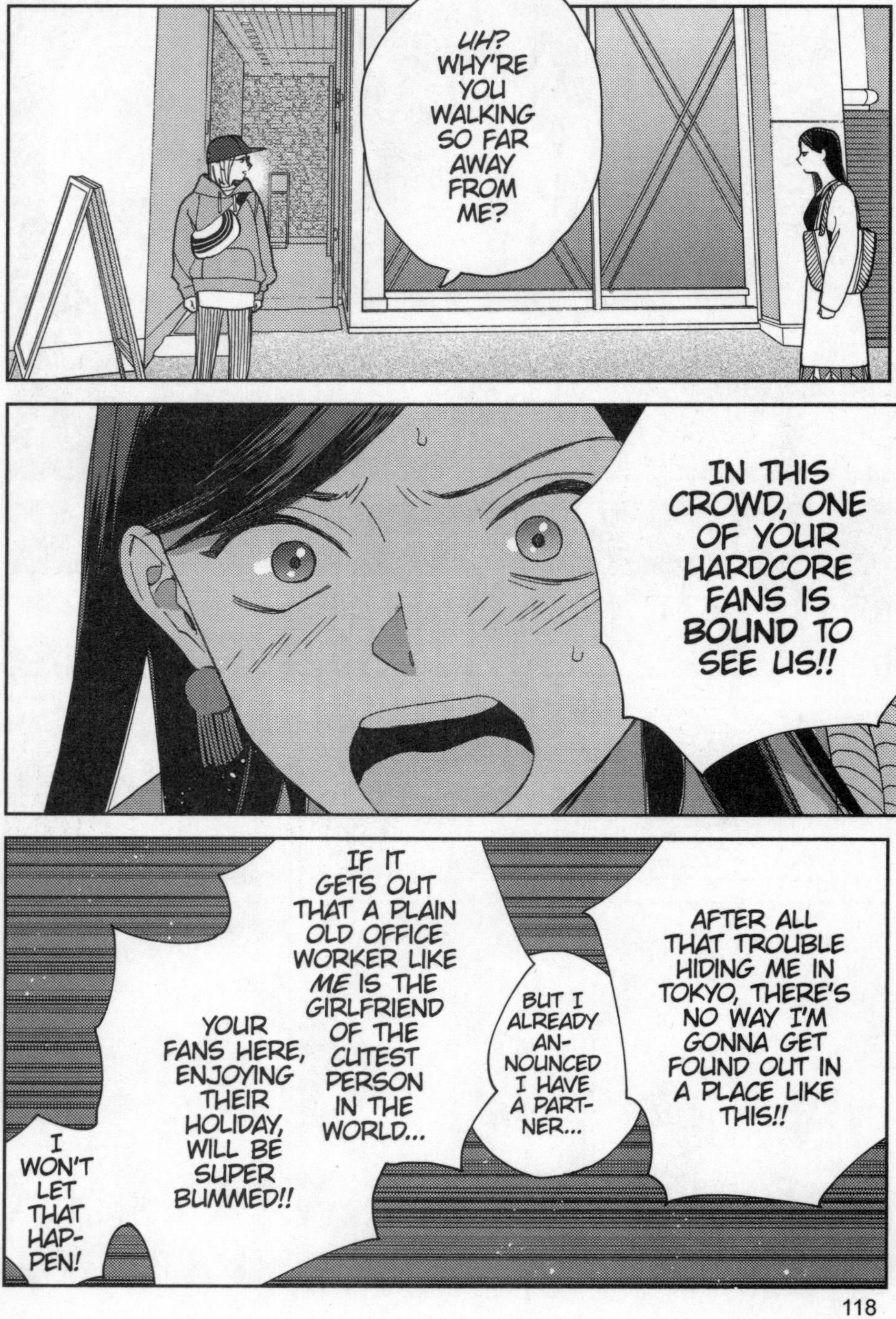
UH? WHY'RE YOU WALKING SO FAR AWAY FROM ME?
IN THIS CROWD, ONE OF YOUR HARDCORE FANS IS BOUND TO SEE US!!
AFTER ALL THAT TROUBLE HIDING ME IN TOKYO, THERE'S NO WAY I'M GONNA GET FOUND OUT IN A PLACE LIKE THIS!!
BUT I ALREADY AN-NOUNCED I HAVE A PART-NER...
IF IT GETS OUT THAT A PLAIN OLD OFFICE WORKER LIKE *ME* IS THE GIRLFRIEND OF THE CUTEST PERSON IN THE WORLD...
YOUR FANS HERE, ENJOYING THEIR HOLIDAY, WILL BE SUPER BUMMED!!
I WON'T LET THAT HAP-PEN!

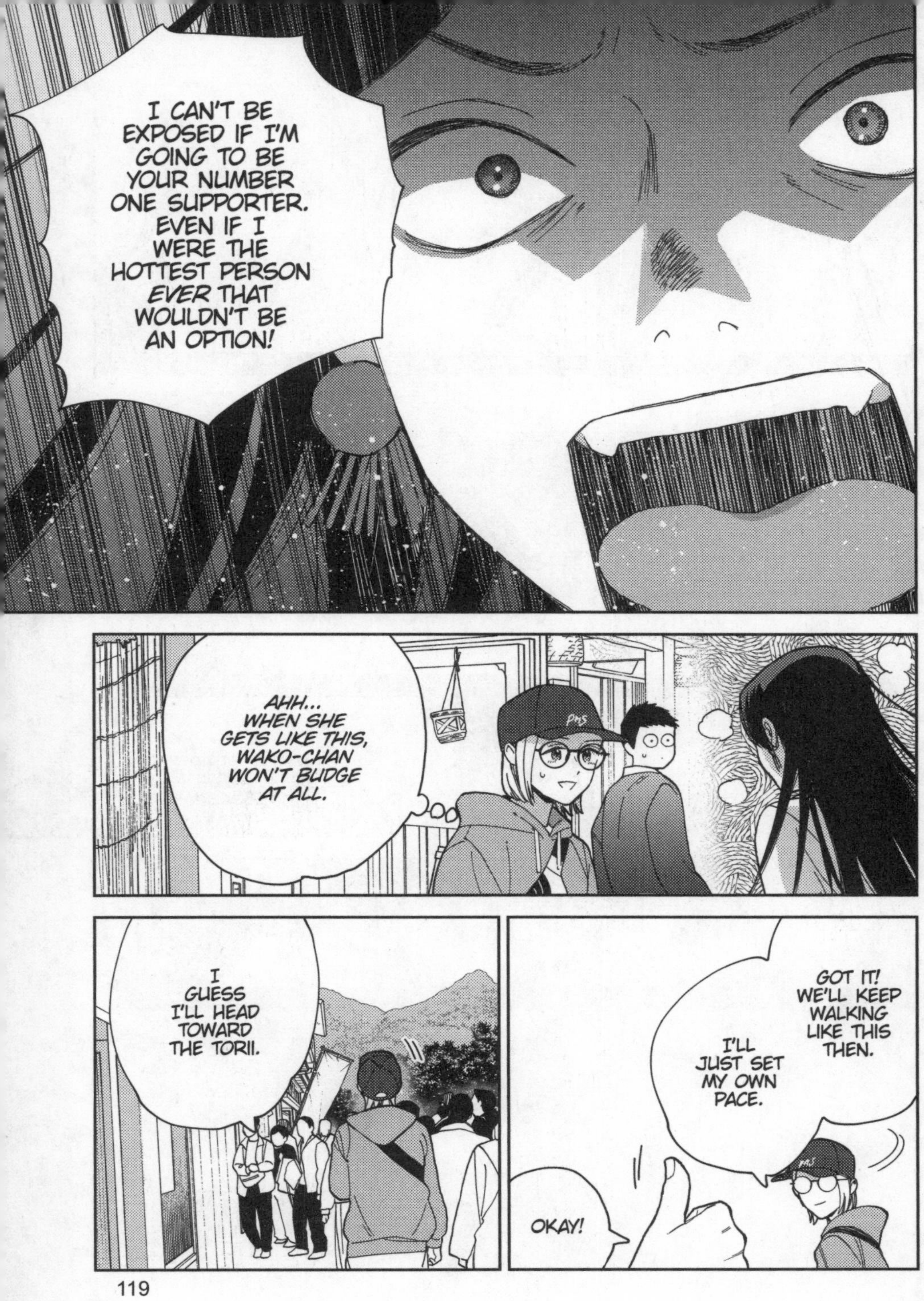
I CAN'T BE EXPOSED IF I'M GOING TO BE YOUR NUMBER ONE SUPPORTER. EVEN IF I WERE THE HOTTEST PERSON *EVER* THAT WOULDN'T BE AN OPTION!
AHH... WHEN SHE GETS LIKE THIS, WAKO-CHAN WON'T BUDGE AT ALL.
GOT IT! WE'LL KEEP WALKING LIKE THIS THEN.
I'LL JUST SET MY OWN PACE.
OKAY!
I GUESS I'LL HEAD TOWARD THE TORII.

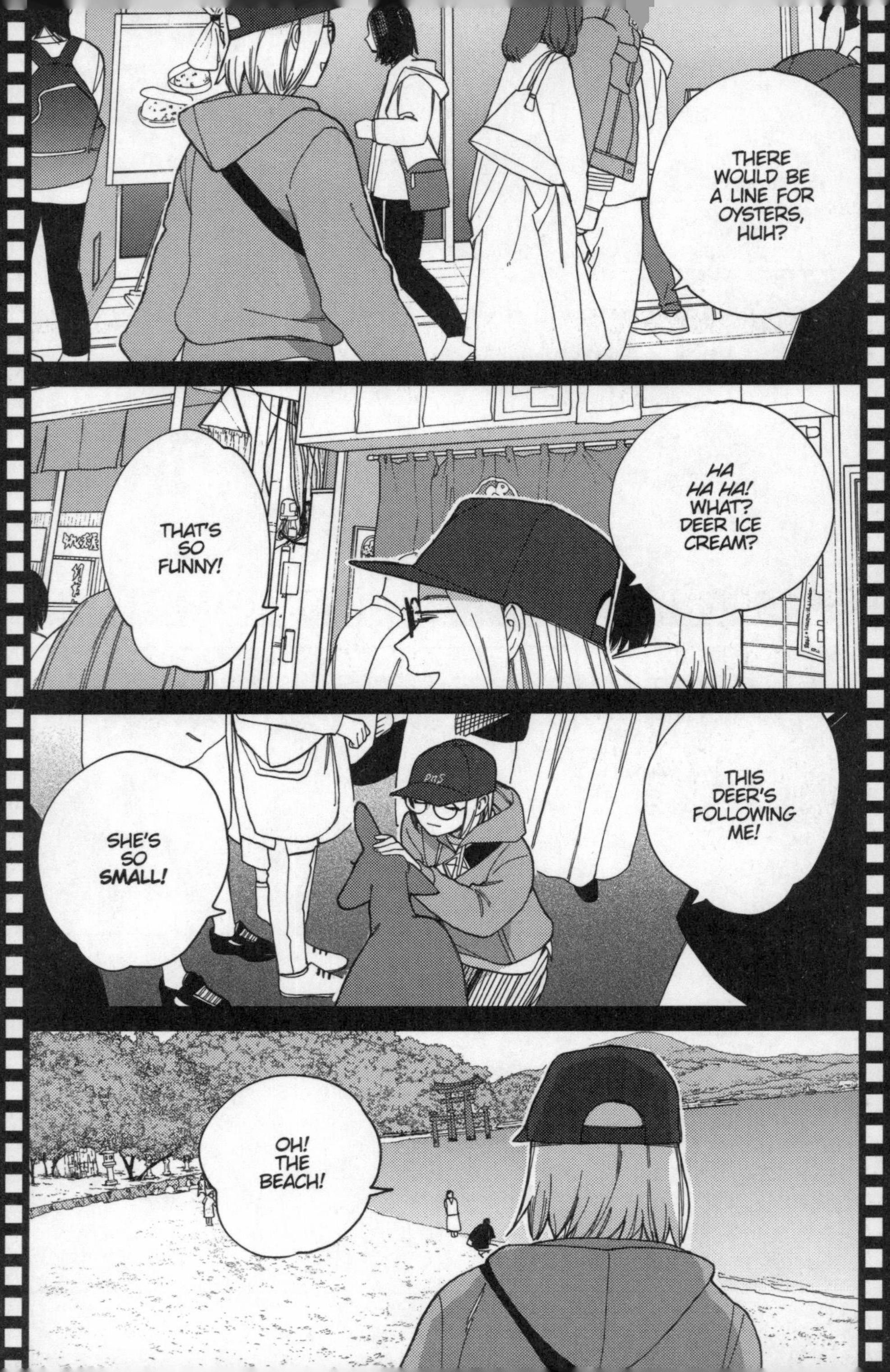
THERE WOULD BE A LINE FOR OYSTERS, HUH?
HA HA HA! WHAT? DEER ICE CREAM?
THAT'S SO FUNNY!
THIS DEER'S FOLLOWING ME!
SHE'S SO SMALL!
OH! THE BEACH!

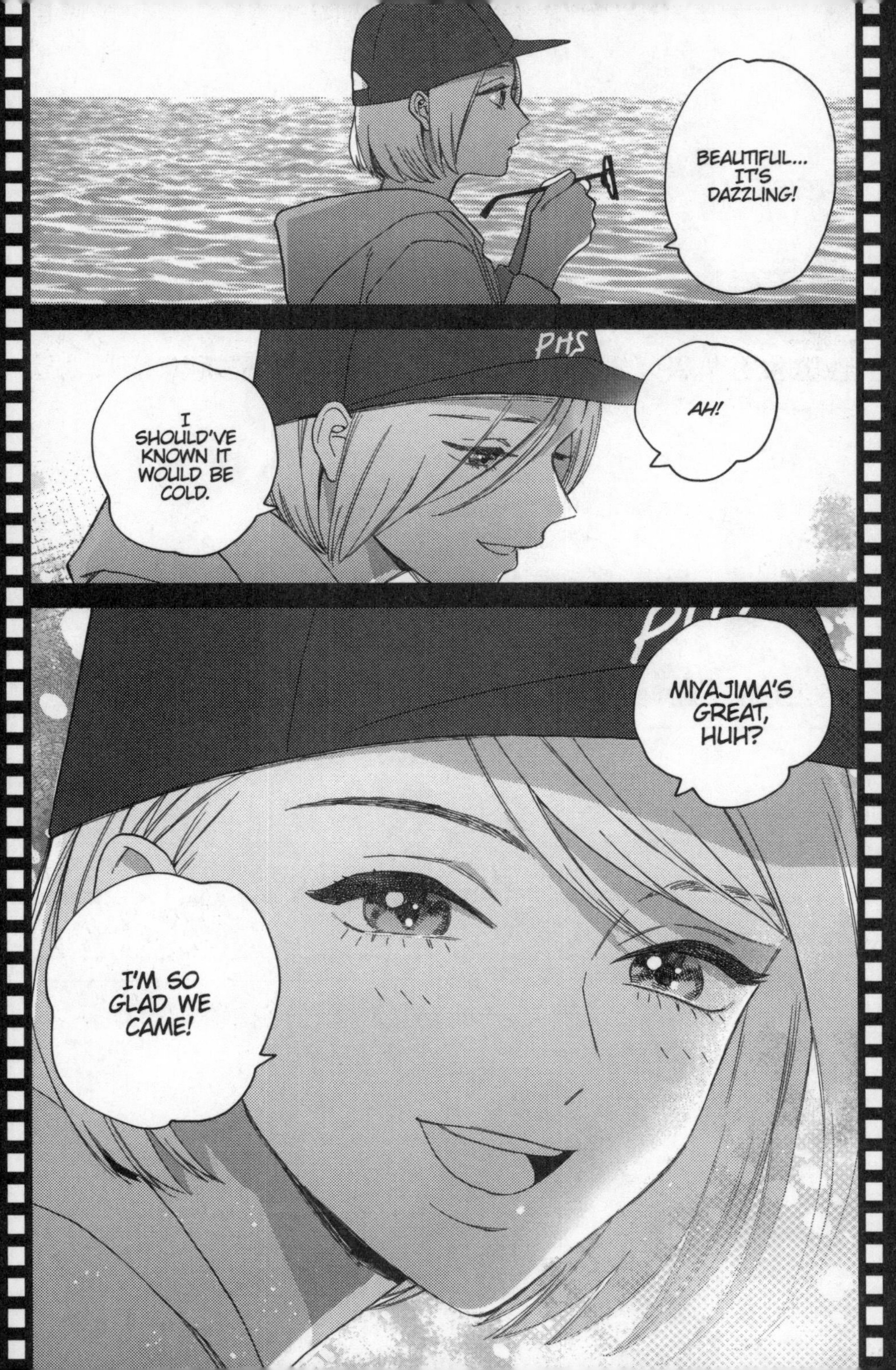
BEAUTIFUL... IT'S DAZZLING!
PHS
AH!
I SHOULD'VE KNOWN IT WOULD BE COLD.
MIYAJIMA'S GREAT, HUH?
I'M SO GLAD WE CAME!

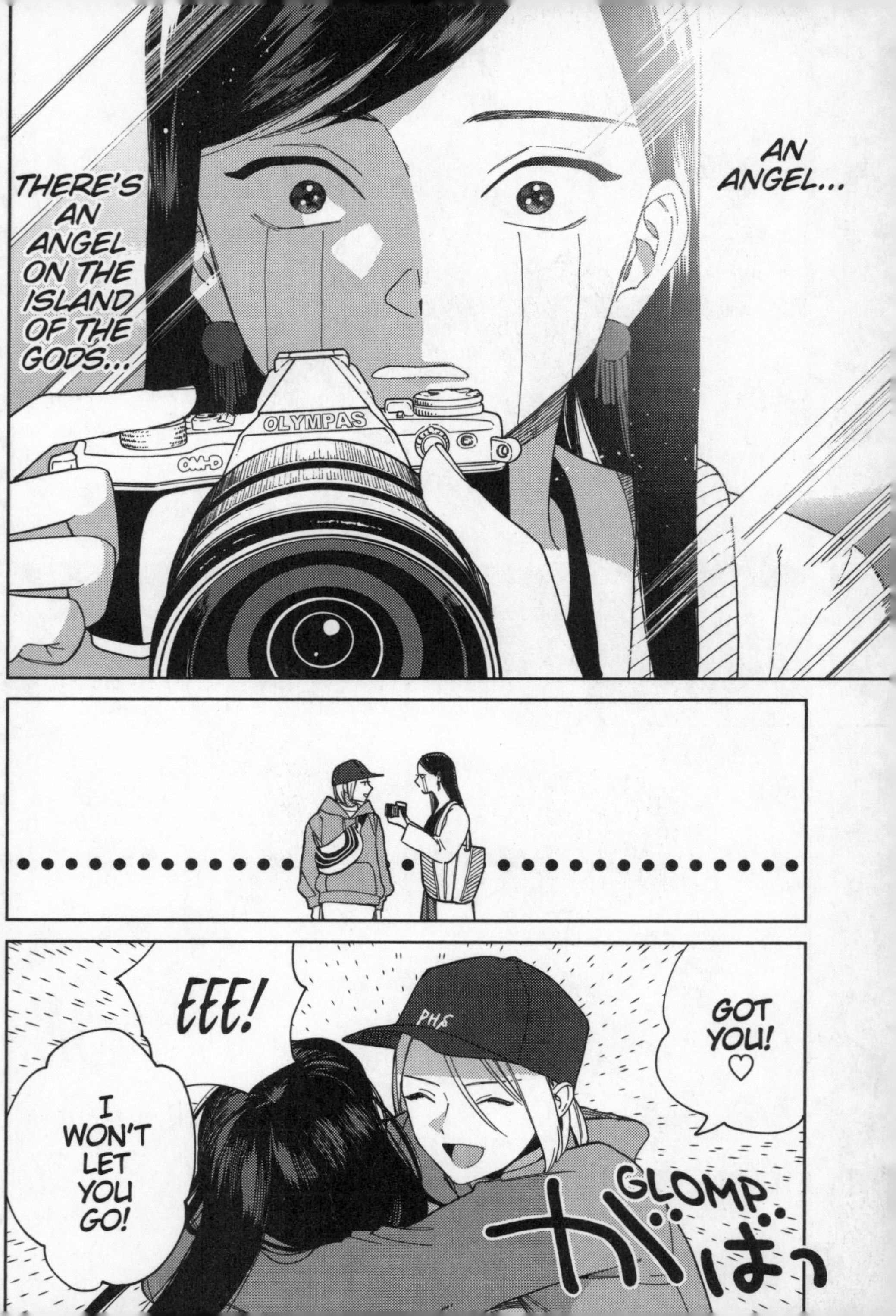
AN ANGEL...
THERE'S AN ANGEL ON THE ISLAND OF THE GODS...
OLYMPAS
GOT YOU! ♡
EEE!
I WON'T LET YOU GO!
GLOMP
がばっ

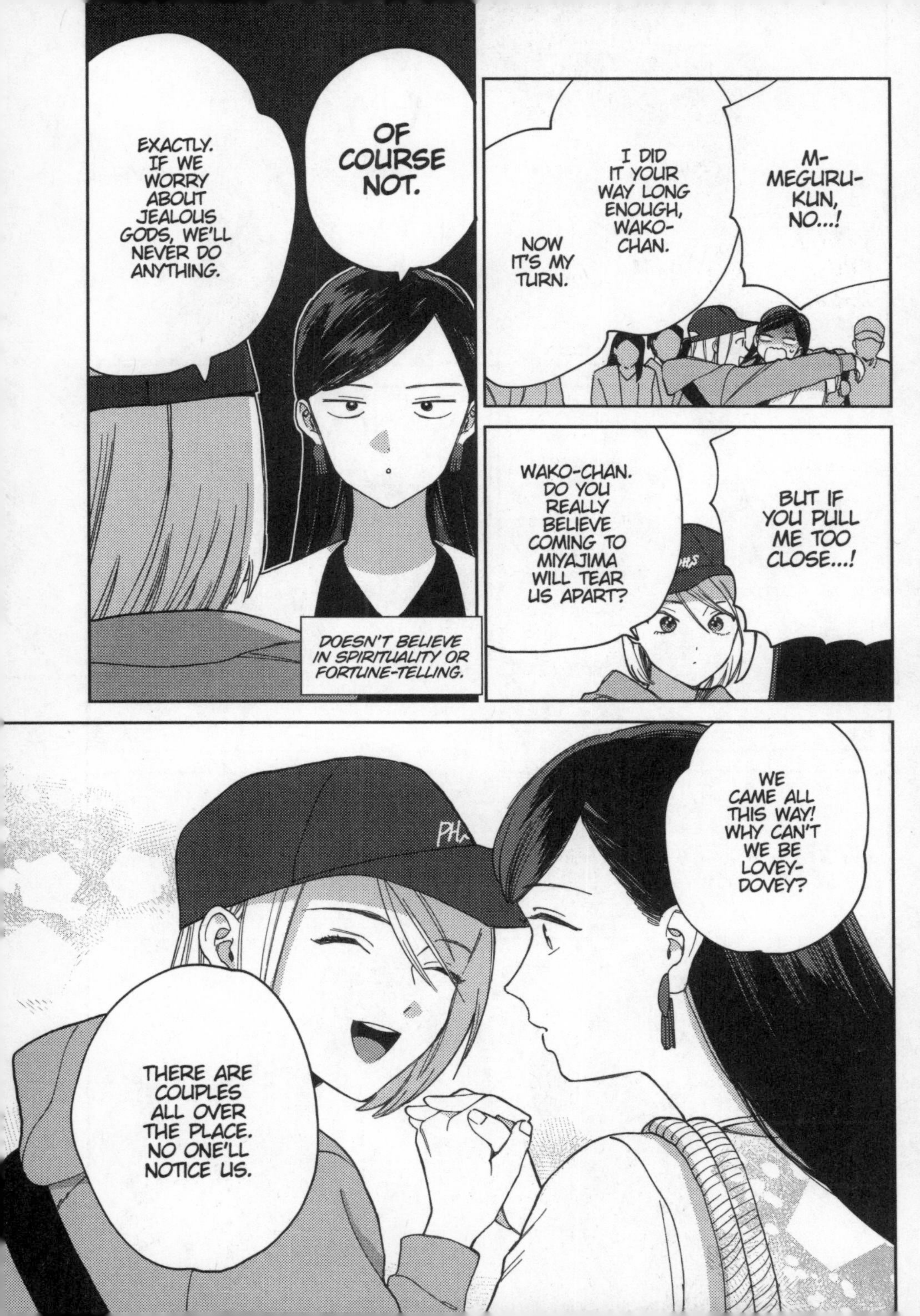
M-MEGURU-KUN, NO...!
I DID IT YOUR WAY LONG ENOUGH, WAKO-CHAN.
NOW IT'S MY TURN.
BUT IF YOU PULL ME TOO CLOSE...!
WAKO-CHAN. DO YOU REALLY BELIEVE COMING TO MIYAJIMA WILL TEAR US APART?
OF COURSE NOT.
EXACTLY. IF WE WORRY ABOUT JEALOUS GODS, WE'LL NEVER DO ANYTHING.
DOESN'T BELIEVE IN SPIRITUALITY OR FORTUNE-TELLING.
WE CAME ALL THIS WAY! WHY CAN'T WE BE LOVEY-DOVEY?
THERE ARE COUPLES ALL OVER THE PLACE. NO ONE'LL NOTICE US.

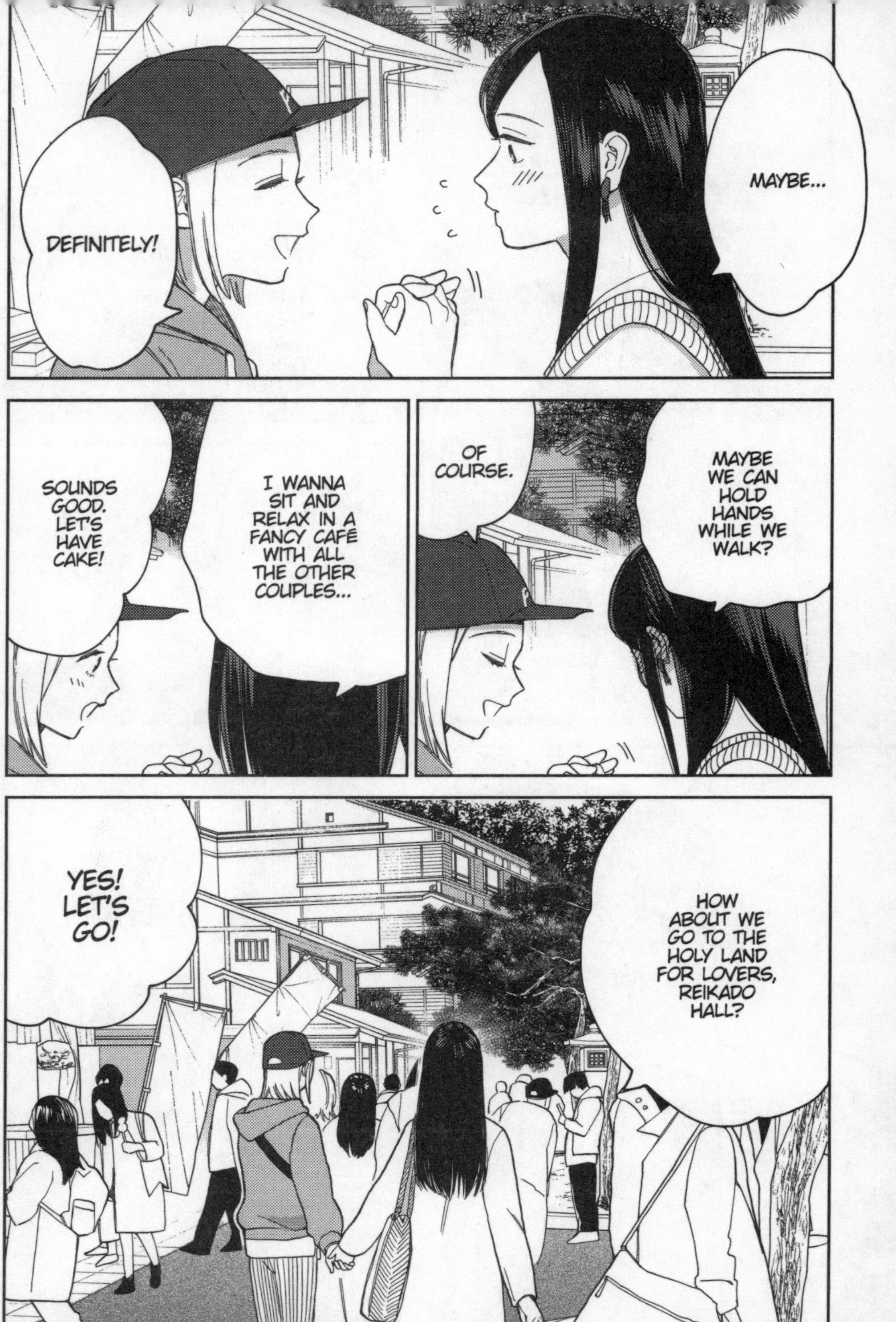
MAYBE...
DEFINITELY!
MAYBE WE CAN HOLD HANDS WHILE WE WALK?
OF COURSE.
I WANNA SIT AND RELAX IN A FANCY CAFÉ WITH ALL THE OTHER COUPLES...
SOUNDS GOOD. LET'S HAVE CAKE!
HOW ABOUT WE GO TO THE HOLY LAND FOR LOVERS, REIKADO HALL?
YES! LET'S GO!

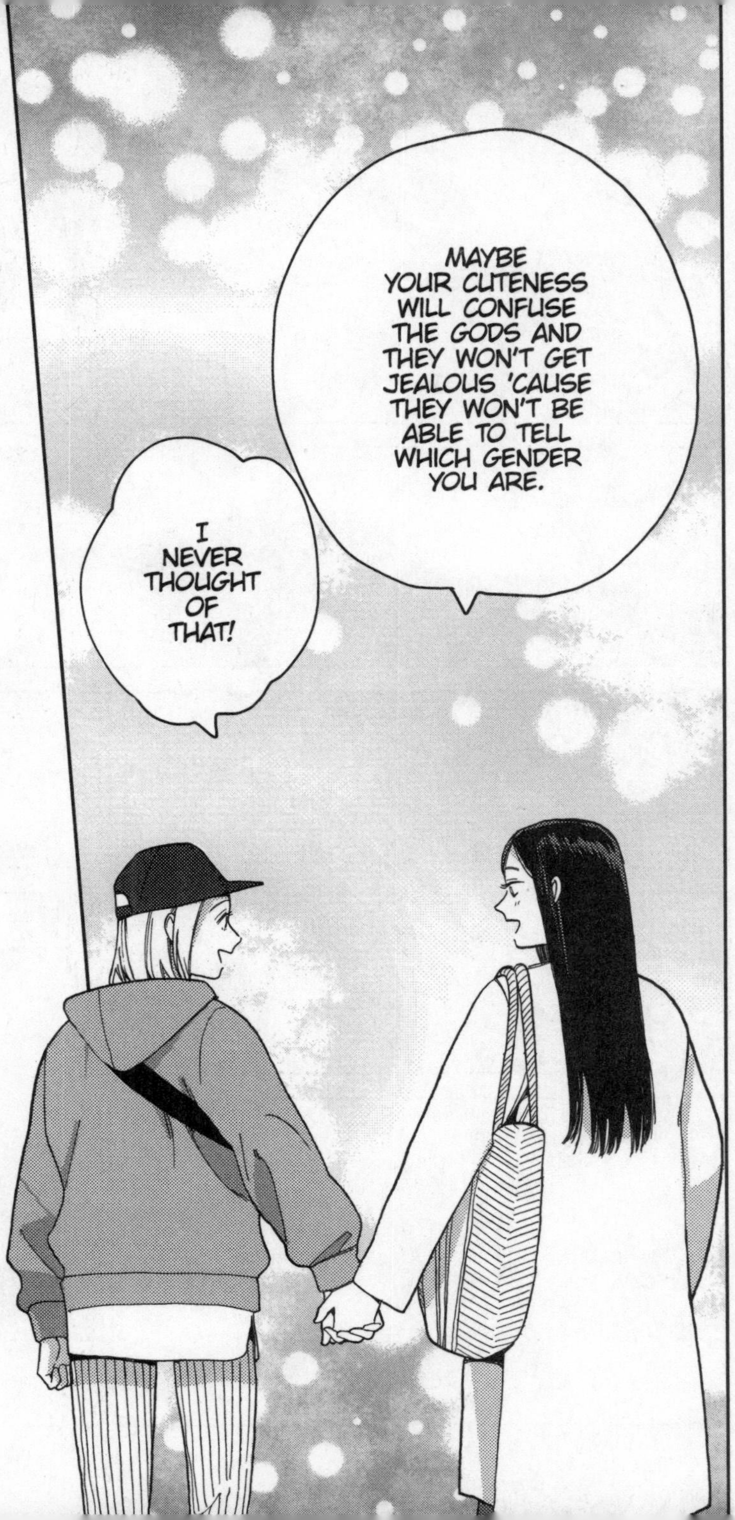
MAYBE YOUR CUTENESS WILL CONFUSE THE GODS AND THEY WON'T GET JEALOUS 'CAUSE THEY WON'T BE ABLE TO TELL WHICH GENDER YOU ARE.
I NEVER THOUGHT OF THAT!

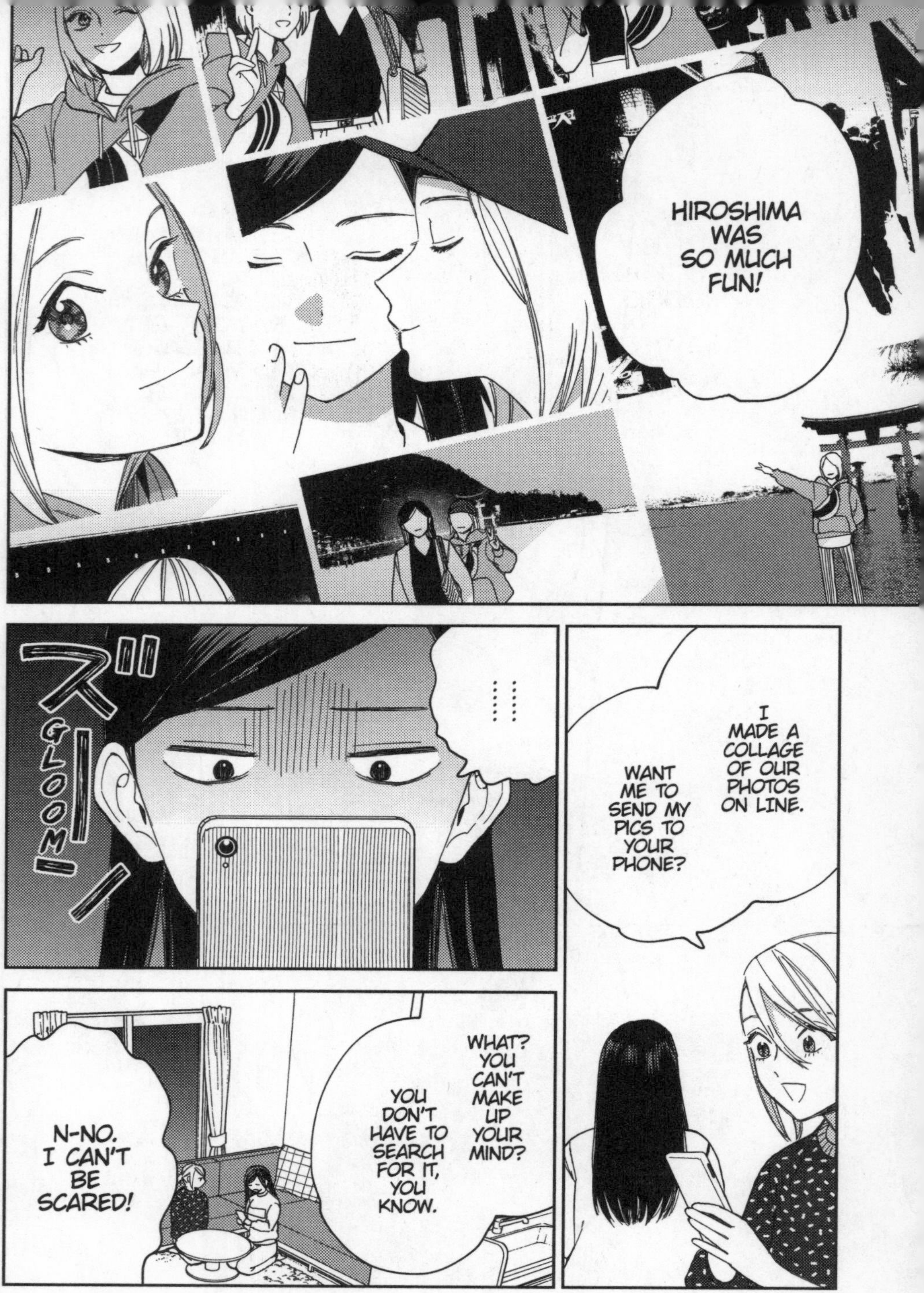
HIROSHIMA WAS SO MUCH FUN!
I MADE A COLLAGE OF OUR PHOTOS ON LINE.
WANT ME TO SEND MY PICS TO YOUR PHONE?
......
ズーン
GLOOM!
WHAT? YOU CAN'T MAKE UP YOUR MIND?
YOU DON'T HAVE TO SEARCH FOR IT, YOU KNOW.
N-NO. I CAN'T BE SCARED!

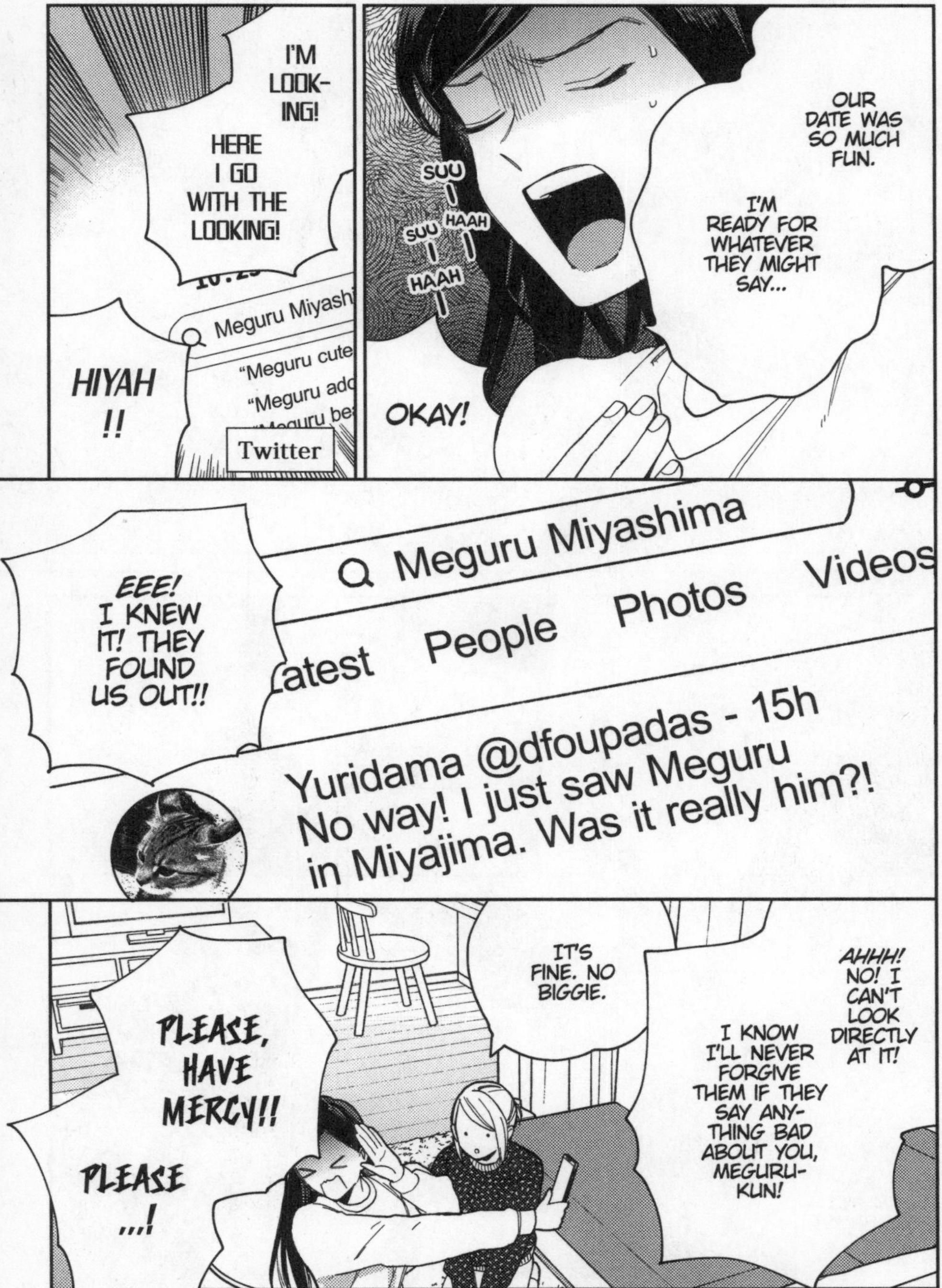
OUR DATE WAS SO MUCH FUN.
I'M READY FOR WHATEVER THEY MIGHT SAY...
SUU HAAH SUU HAAH
OKAY!
I'M LOOKING!
HERE I GO WITH THE LOOKING!
Meguru Miyashi
“Meguru cute
“Meguru ado
Twitter
HIYAH!!
Meguru Miyashima
Latest People Photos Videos
Yuridama @dfoupadas - 15h
No way! I just saw Meguru in Miyajima. Was it really him?!
EEE! I KNEW IT! THEY FOUND US OUT!!
AHHH! NO! I CAN'T LOOK DIRECTLY AT IT!
I KNOW I'LL NEVER FORGIVE THEM IF THEY SAY ANYTHING BAD ABOUT YOU, MEGURU-KUN!
IT'S FINE. NO BIGGIE.
PLEASE, HAVE MERCY!!
PLEASE ...!

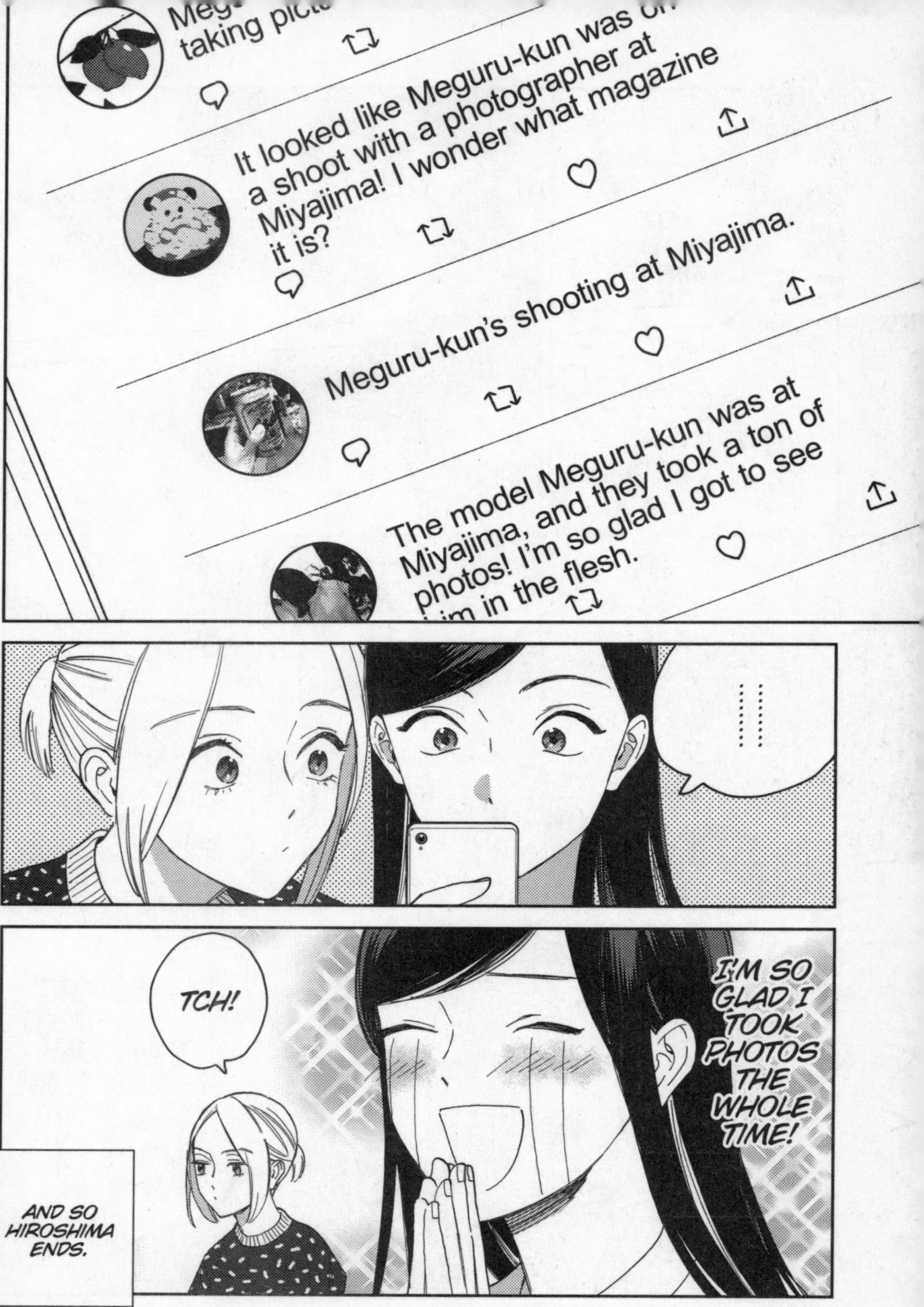
It looked like Meguru-kun was on a shoot with a photographer at Miyajima! I wonder what magazine it is?
Meguru-kun's shooting at Miyajima.
The model Meguru-kun was at Miyajima, and they took a ton of photos! I'm so glad I got to see
in the flesh.
……
I'M SO GLAD I TOOK PHOTOS THE WHOLE TIME!
TCH!
AND SO HIROSHIMA ENDS.

The Eighteenth One

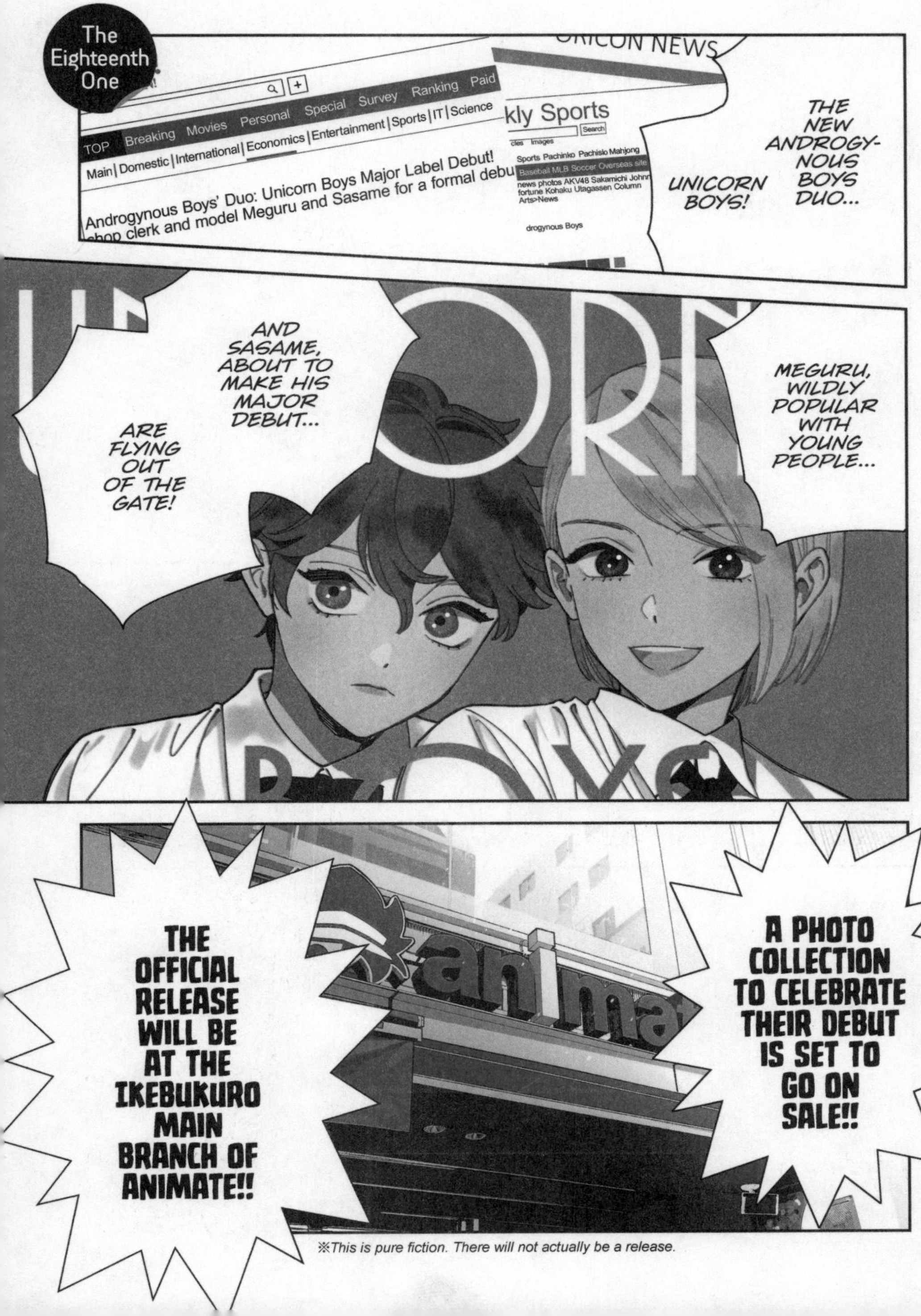
URICON NEWS
TOP Breaking Movies Personal Special Survey Ranking Paid
Main | Domestic | International | Economics | Entertainment | Sports | IT | Science
Androgynous Boys' Duo: Unicorn Boys Major Label Debut!
shop clerk and model Meguru and Sasame for a formal debu
kly Sports
Search
Sports Pachinko Pachislo Mahjong
Baseball MLB Soccer Overseas site
news photos AKV48 Sakamichi Johnn
fortune Kohaku Utagassen Column
Arts>News
drogynous Boys
THE NEW ANDROGYNOUS BOYS DUO...
UNICORN BOYS!
MEGURU, WILDLY POPULAR WITH YOUNG PEOPLE...
AND SASAME, ABOUT TO MAKE HIS MAJOR DEBUT...
ARE FLYING OUT OF THE GATE!
A PHOTO COLLECTION TO CELEBRATE THEIR DEBUT IS SET TO GO ON SALE!!
THE OFFICIAL RELEASE WILL BE AT THE IKEBUKURO MAIN BRANCH OF ANIMATE!!

※This is pure fiction. There will not actually be a release.

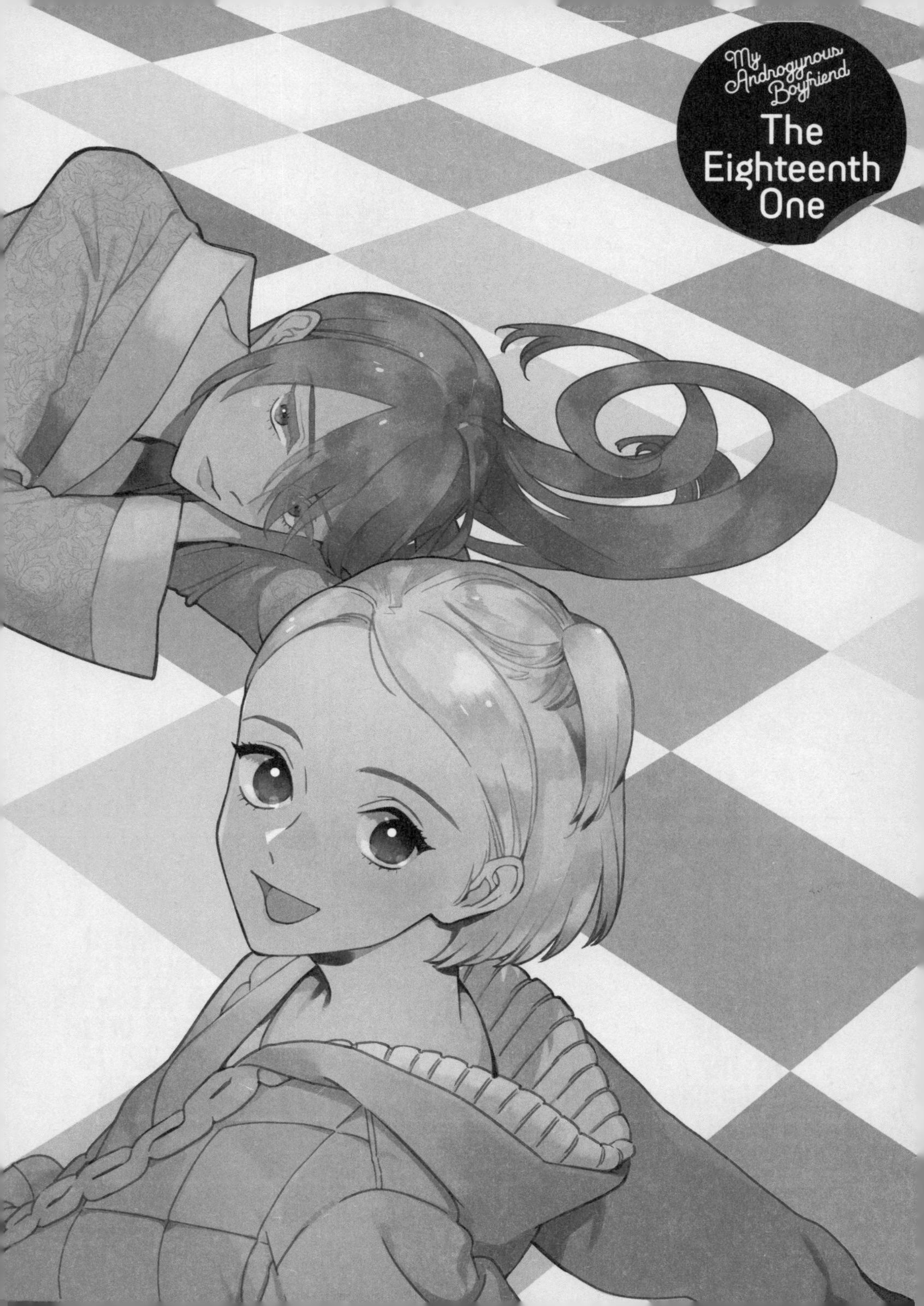
My Androgynous Boyfriend
The Eighteenth One

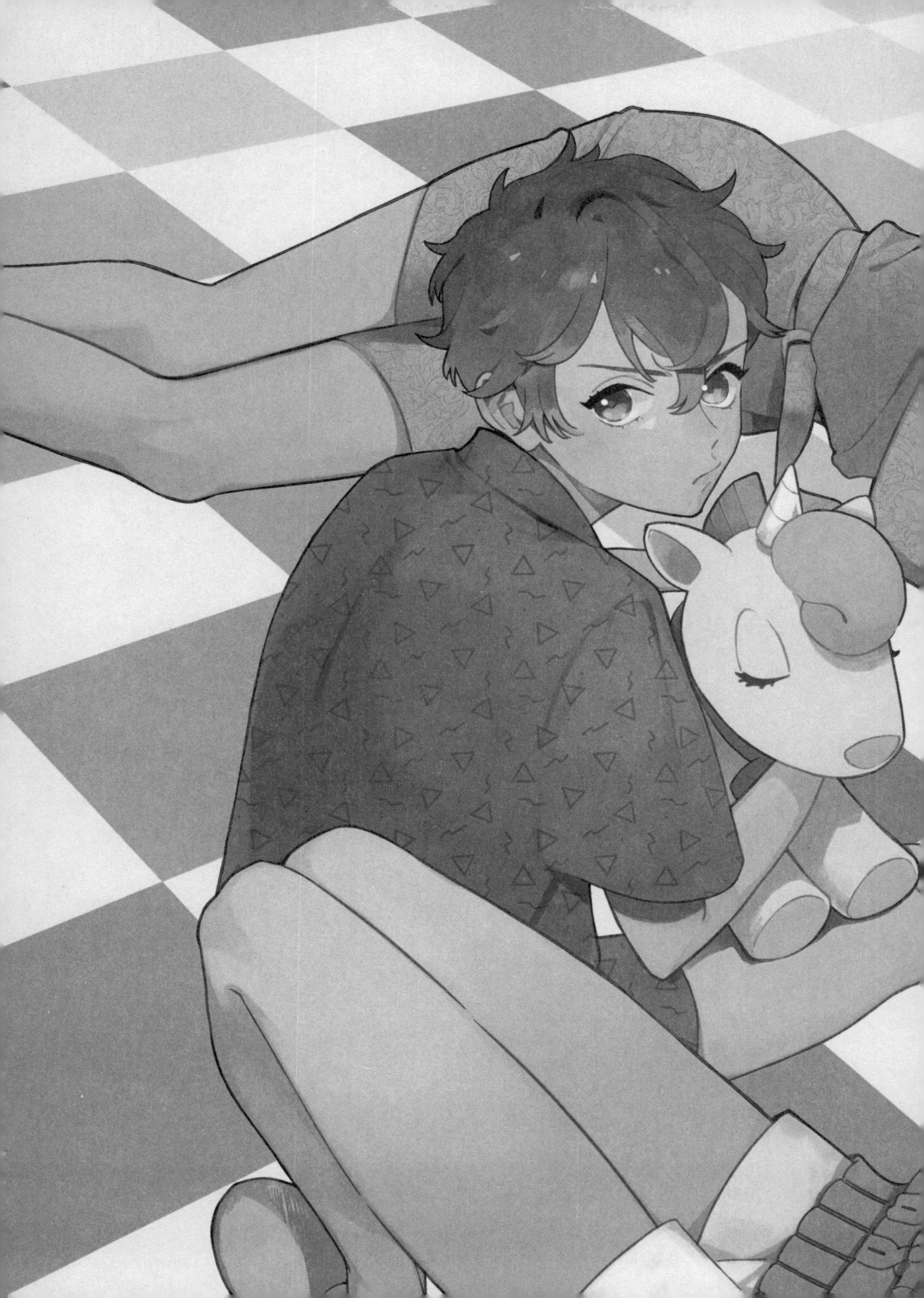

My Androgynous Boyfriend

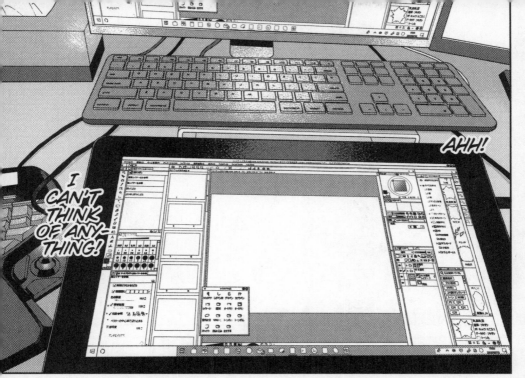

AHH!
I CAN'T THINK OF ANY-THING!
EIGHTEEN YEARS OF BEING A MANGA ARTIST. SIX MONTHS SINCE THE END OF MY LAST SERIES.
WORKING EVERY SINGLE DAY ON IDEAS FOR MY NEXT SERIES.
AS SOON AS I WAKE UP, I'M GATHERING INFORMATION, REFERENCES, RESEARCH...
I'VE SACRIFICED MY ENTIRE PERSONAL LIFE TO MANGA. SO WHY CAN'T I THINK OF ANYTHING?
AM I ALL WASHED UP?

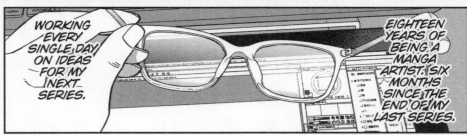

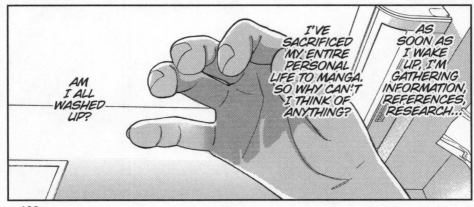

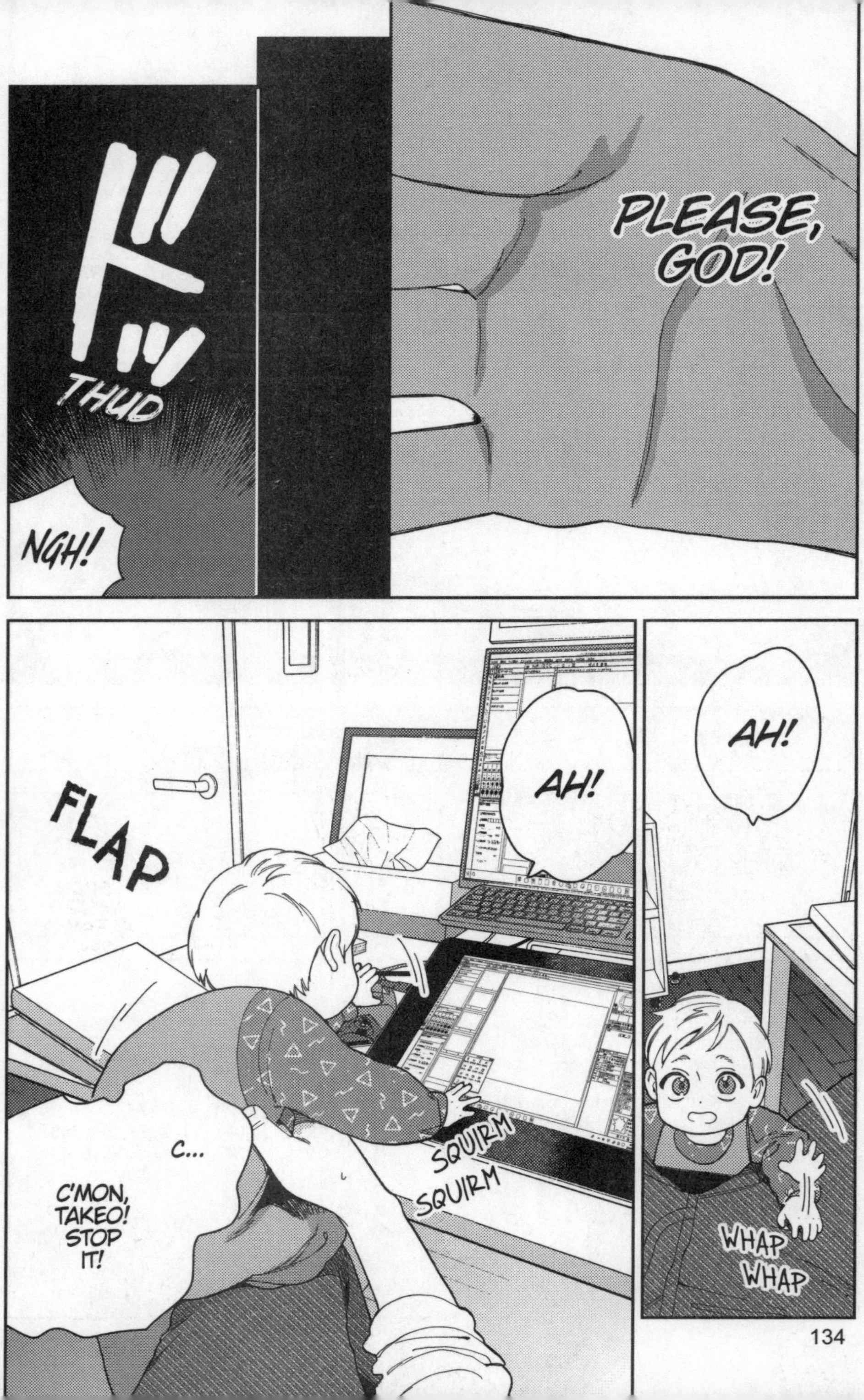
PLEASE, GOD!
ドッ
THUD
NGH!
AH!
WHAP WHAP
AH!
FLAP
SQUIRM SQUIRM
C...
C'MON, TAKEO! STOP IT!

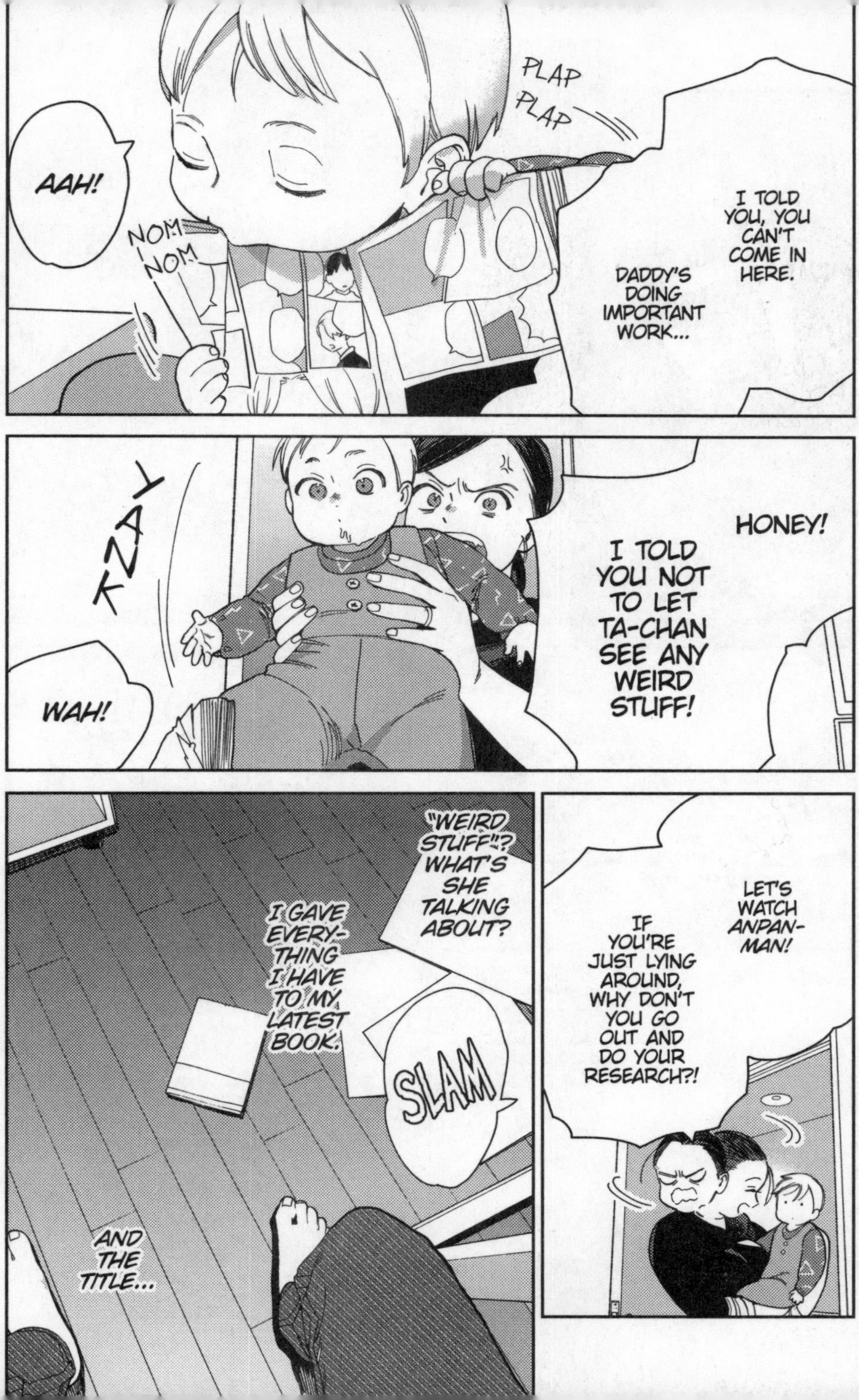
I TOLD YOU, YOU CAN'T COME IN HERE.
DADDY'S DOING IMPORTANT WORK...
PLAP PLAP
AAH!
NOM NOM
HONEY!
I TOLD YOU NOT TO LET TA-CHAN SEE ANY WEIRD STUFF!
YANK
WAH!
LET'S WATCH ANPAN-MAN!
IF YOU'RE JUST LYING AROUND, WHY DON'T YOU GO OUT AND DO YOUR RESEARCH?!
"WEIRD STUFF"? WHAT'S SHE TALKING ABOUT?
I GAVE EVERY-THING I HAVE TO MY LATEST BOOK.
SLAM
AND THE TITLE...

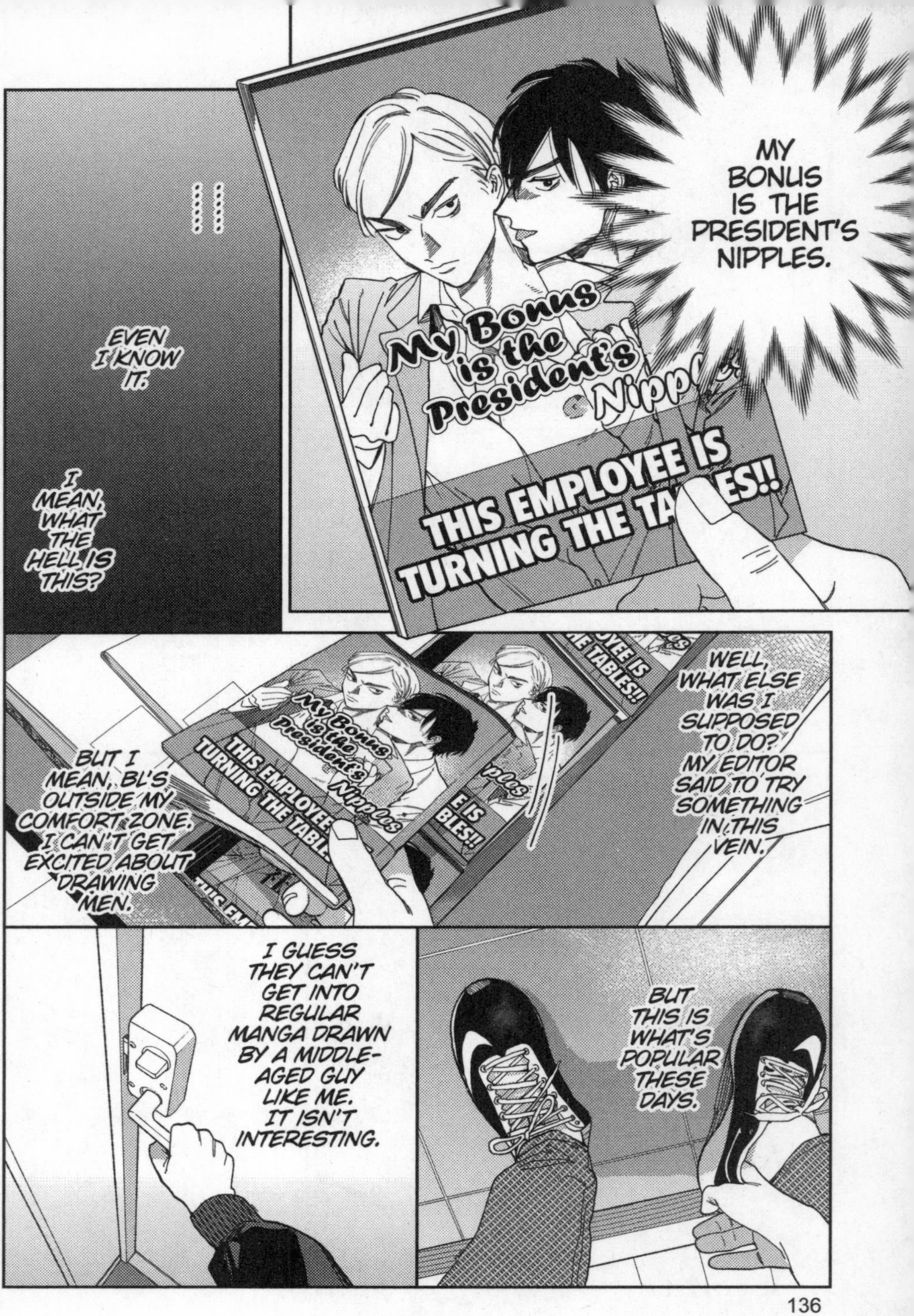
MY BONUS IS THE PRESIDENT'S NIPPLES.
My Bonus is the President's
THIS EMPLOYEE IS
……
EVEN I KNOW IT.
I MEAN, WHAT THE HELL IS THIS?
WELL, WHAT ELSE WAS I SUPPOSED TO DO? MY EDITOR SAID TO TRY SOMETHING IN THIS VEIN.
My Bonus is the President's Nipples
THIS EMPLOYEE IS TURNING THE TABLES!!
BUT I MEAN, BL'S OUTSIDE MY COMFORT ZONE. I CAN'T GET EXCITED ABOUT DRAWING MEN.
BUT THIS IS WHAT'S POPULAR THESE DAYS.
I GUESS THEY CAN'T GET INTO REGULAR MANGA DRAWN BY A MIDDLE-AGED GUY LIKE ME. IT ISN'T INTERESTING.

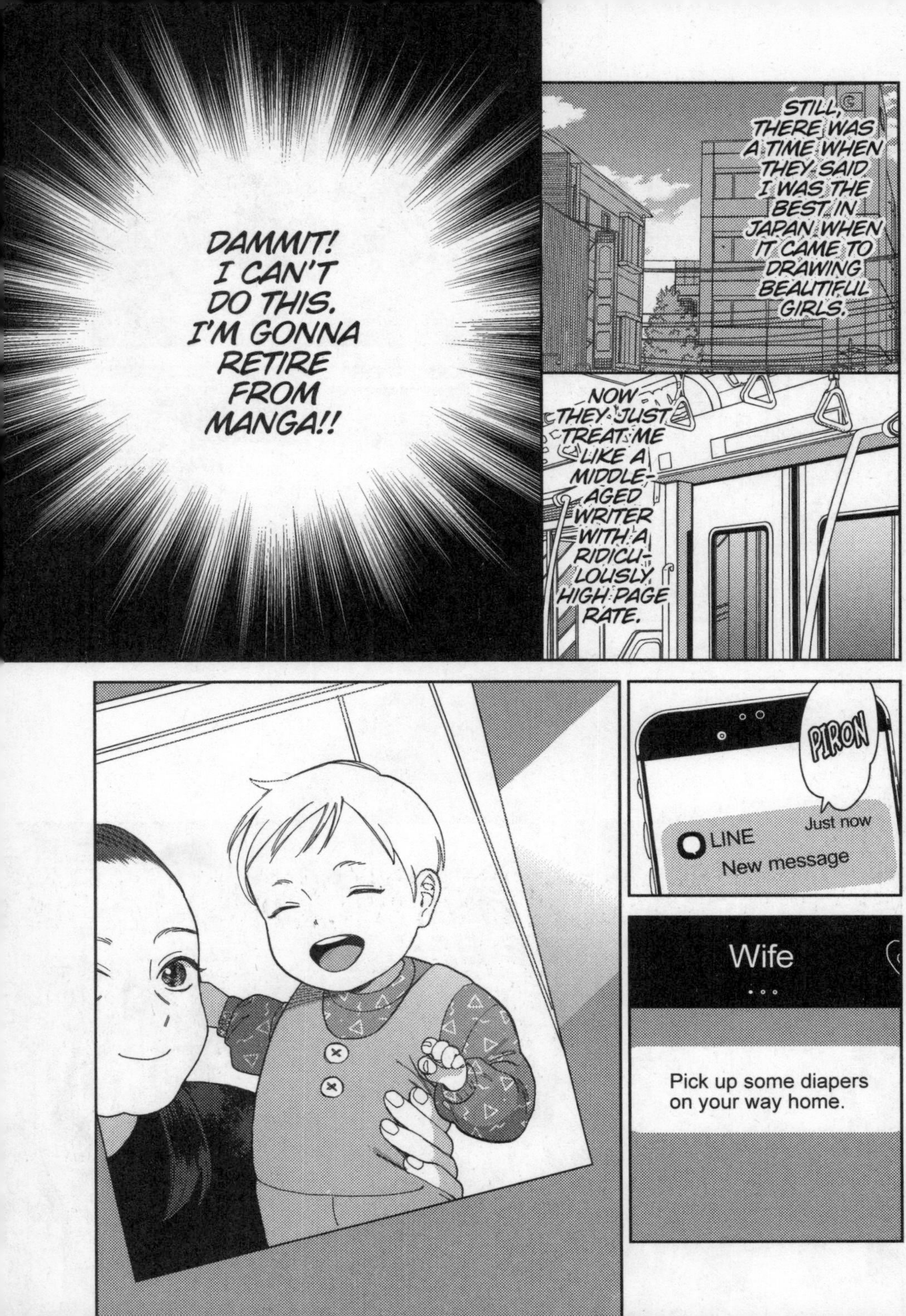
STILL, THERE WAS A TIME WHEN THEY SAID I WAS THE BEST IN JAPAN WHEN IT CAME TO DRAWING BEAUTIFUL GIRLS.
NOW THEY JUST TREAT ME LIKE A MIDDLE-AGED WRITER WITH A RIDICULOUSLY HIGH PAGE RATE.
DAMMIT! I CAN'T DO THIS. I'M GONNA RETIRE FROM MANGA!!
PIRON
Just now
LINE
New message
Wife
Pick up some diapers on your way home.

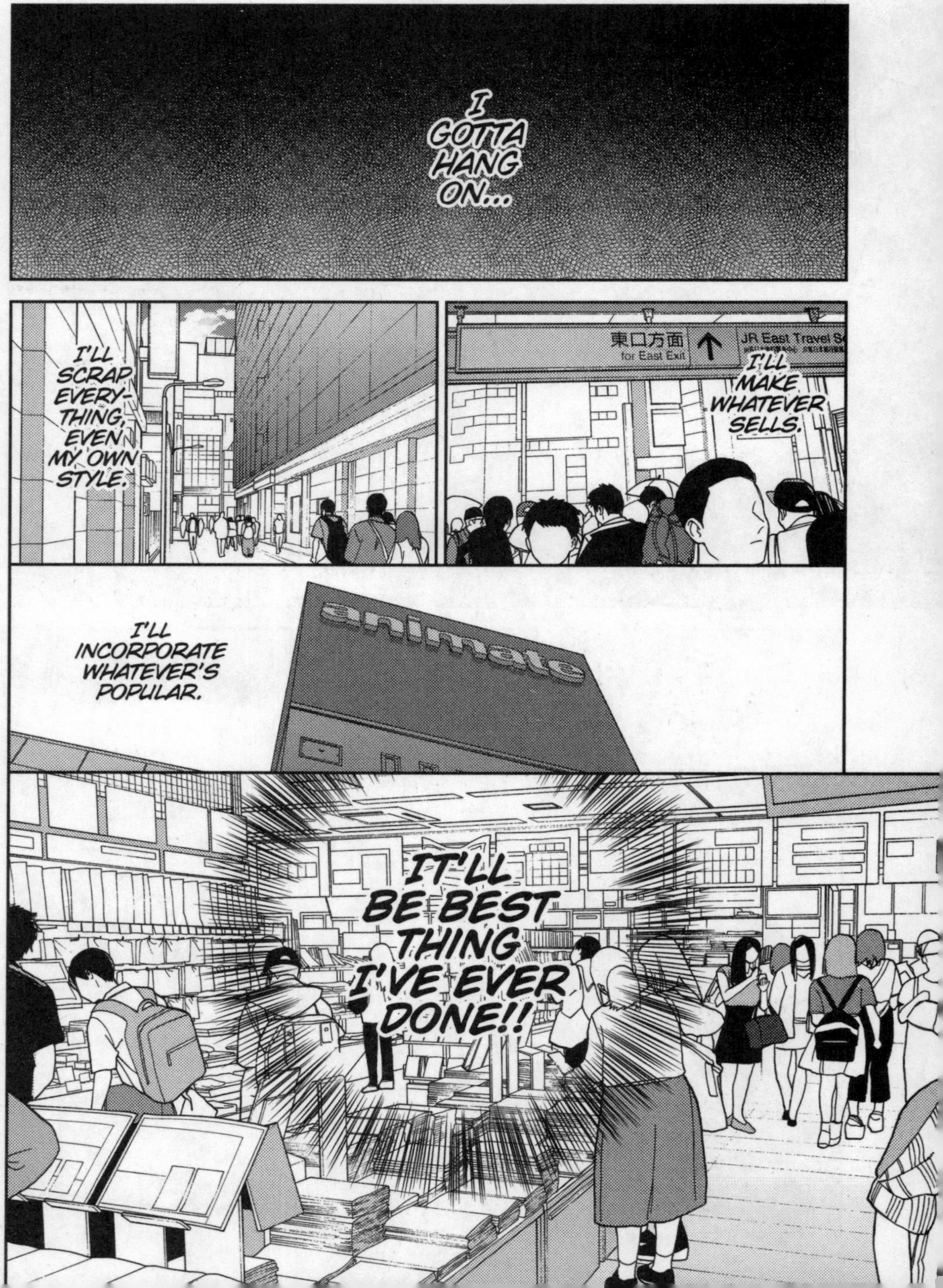
I GOTTA HANG ON...
東口方面
for East Exit
I'LL MAKE WHATEVER SELLS.
I'LL SCRAP EVERY-THING, EVEN MY OWN STYLE.
animate
I'LL INCORPORATE WHATEVER'S POPULAR.
IT'LL BE BEST THING I'VE EVER DONE!!

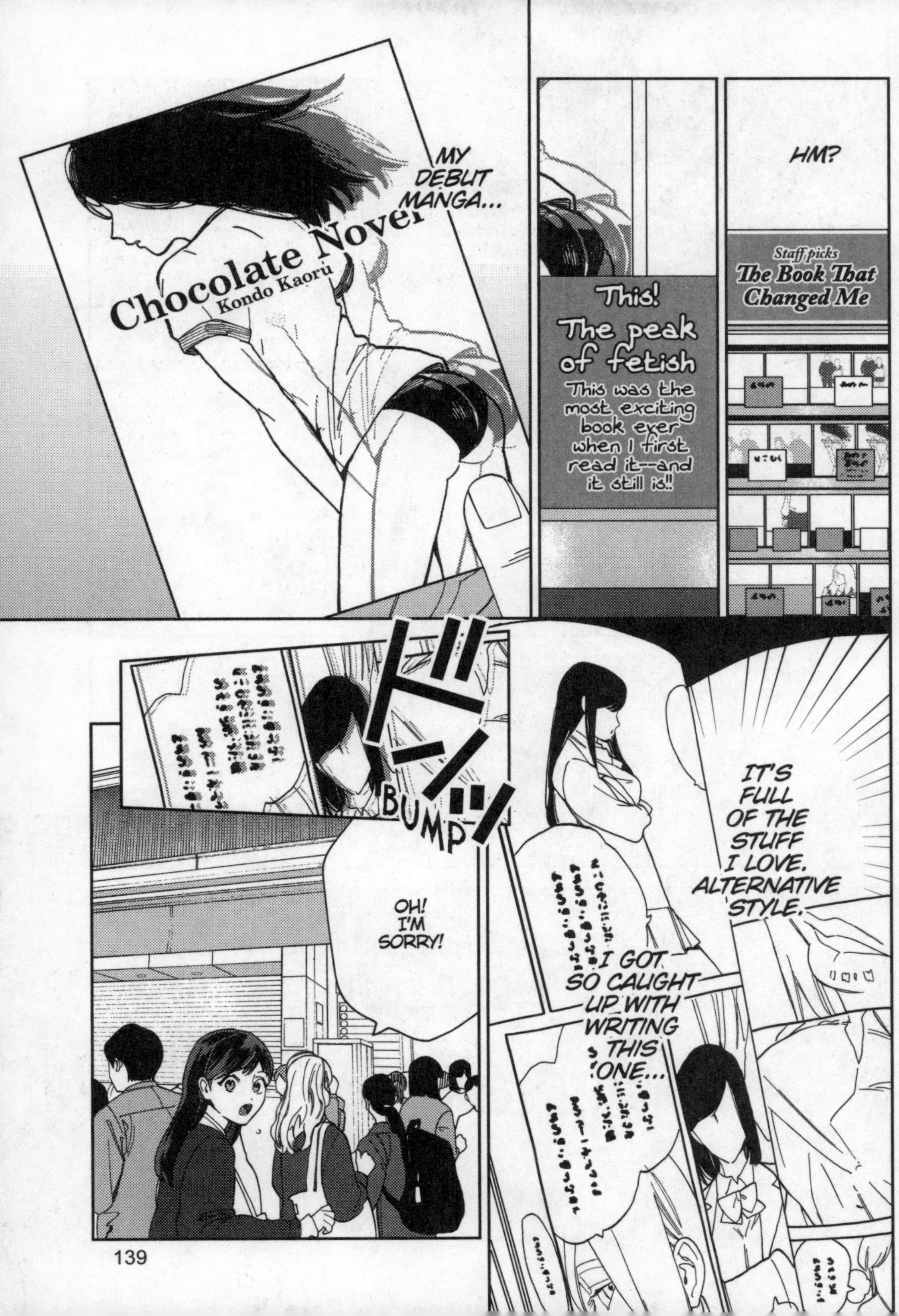
HM?
Staff picks
The Book That Changed Me
This! The peak of fetish
This was the most exciting book ever when I first read it--and it still is!!
MY DEBUT MANGA...
Chocolate Novel
Kondo Kaoru
IT'S FULL OF THE STUFF I LOVE. ALTERNATIVE STYLE.
I GOT SO CAUGHT UP WITH WRITING THIS ONE...
BUMP
OH! I'M SORRY!

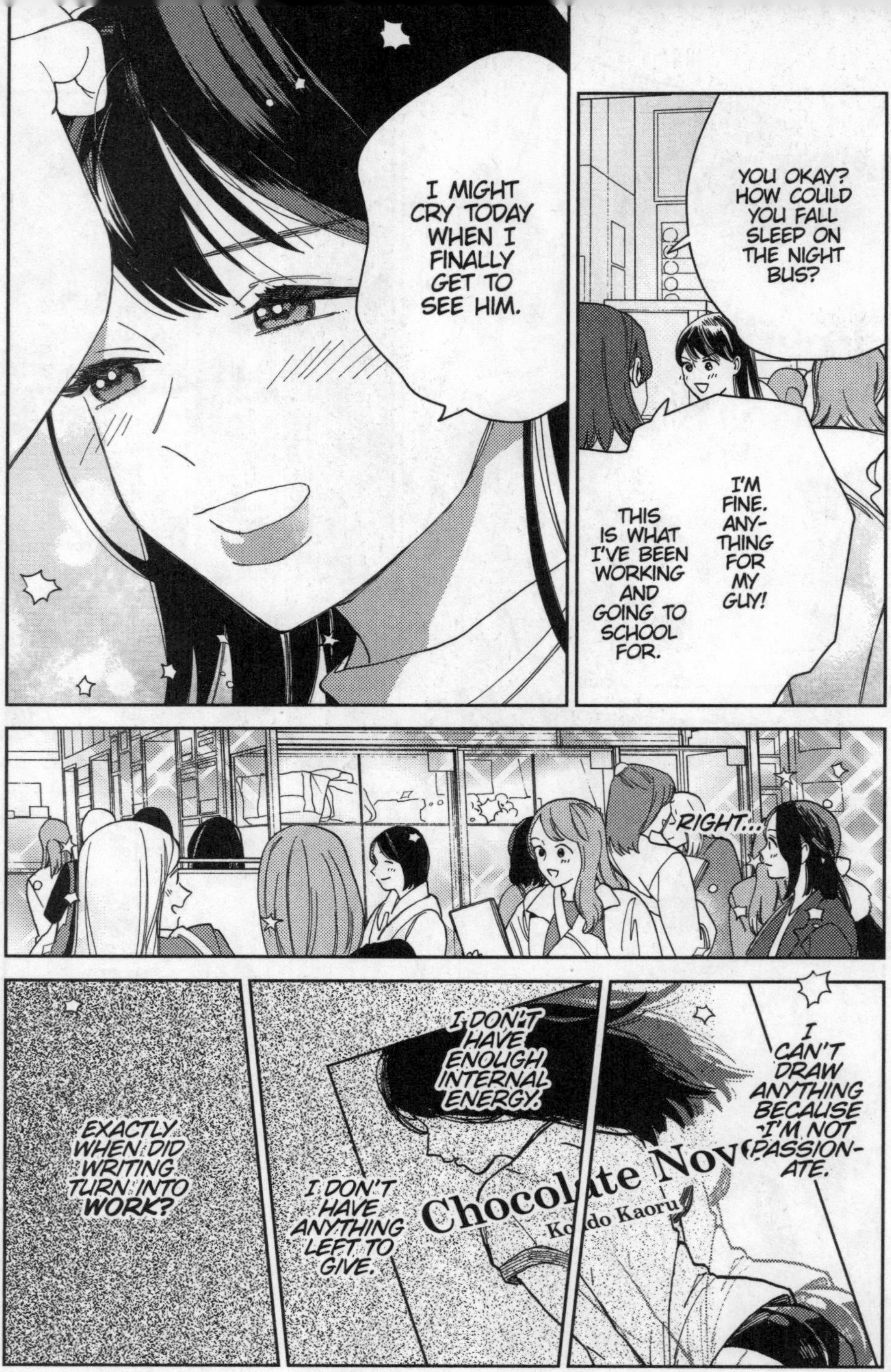
YOU OKAY? HOW COULD YOU FALL SLEEP ON THE NIGHT BUS?
I'M FINE. ANYTHING FOR MY GUY!
THIS IS WHAT I'VE BEEN WORKING AND GOING TO SCHOOL FOR.
I MIGHT CRY TODAY WHEN I FINALLY GET TO SEE HIM.
RIGHT...
I CAN'T DRAW ANYTHING BECAUSE I'M NOT PASSIONATE.
I DON'T HAVE ENOUGH INTERNAL ENERGY.
I DON'T HAVE ANYTHING LEFT TO GIVE.
EXACTLY WHEN DID WRITING TURN INTO WORK?

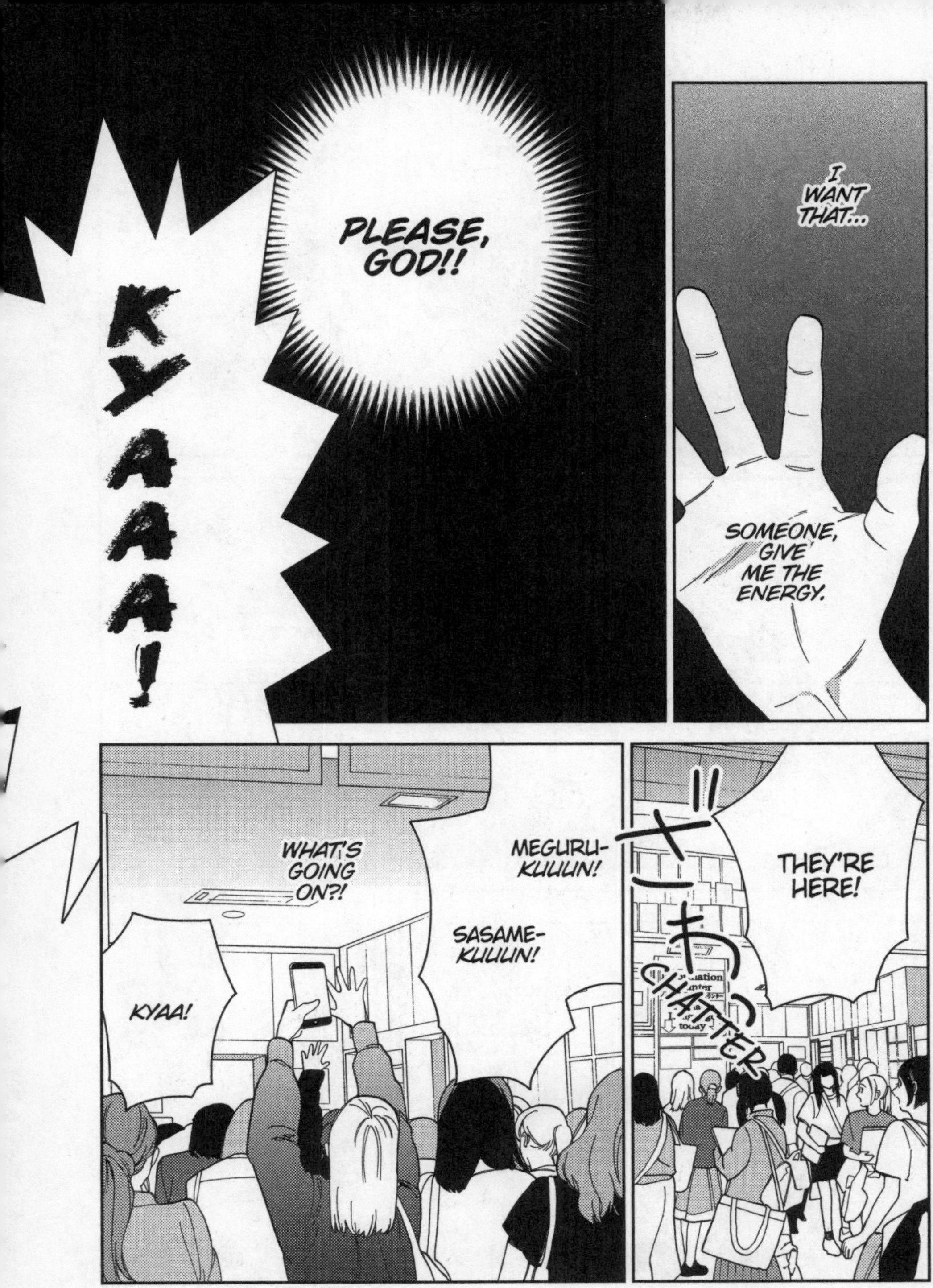
I WANT THAT...
SOMEONE, GIVE ME THE ENERGY.
PLEASE, GOD!!
KYAAAA!
THEY'RE HERE!
CHATTER
MEGURU-KUUUN!
SASAME-KUUUN!
WHAT'S GOING ON?!
KYAA!

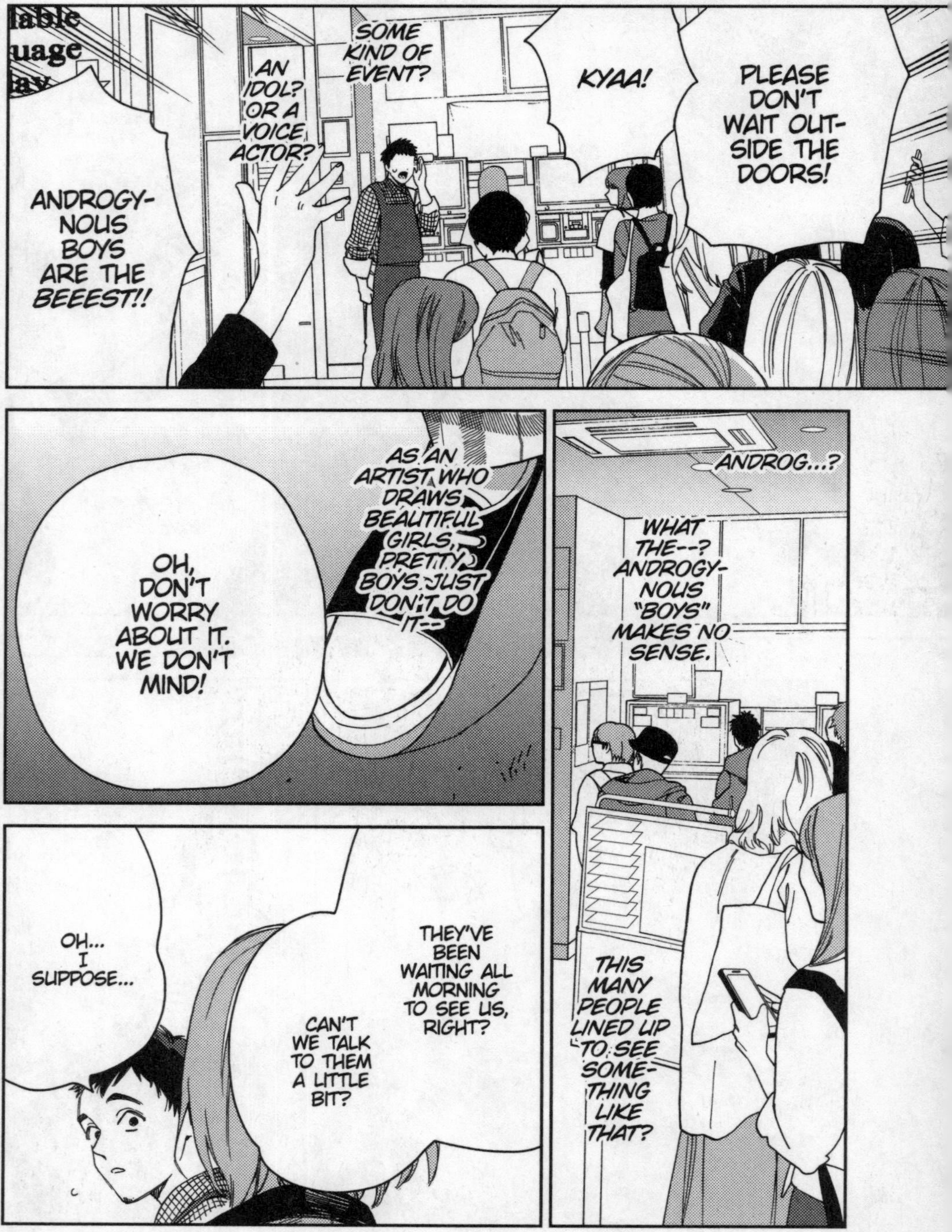
PLEASE DON'T WAIT OUTSIDE THE DOORS!
KYAA!
SOME KIND OF EVENT?
AN IDOL? OR A VOICE ACTOR?
ANDROGYNOUS BOYS ARE THE BEEEST!!
ANDROG...?
WHAT THE--? ANDROGYNOUS "BOYS" MAKES NO SENSE.
THIS MANY PEOPLE LINED UP TO SEE SOMETHING LIKE THAT?
AS AN ARTIST WHO DRAWS BEAUTIFUL GIRLS, PRETTY BOYS JUST DON'T DO IT--
OH, DON'T WORRY ABOUT IT. WE DON'T MIND!
THEY'VE BEEN WAITING ALL MORNING TO SEE US, RIGHT?
CAN'T WE TALK TO THEM A LITTLE BIT?
OH... I SUPPOSE...

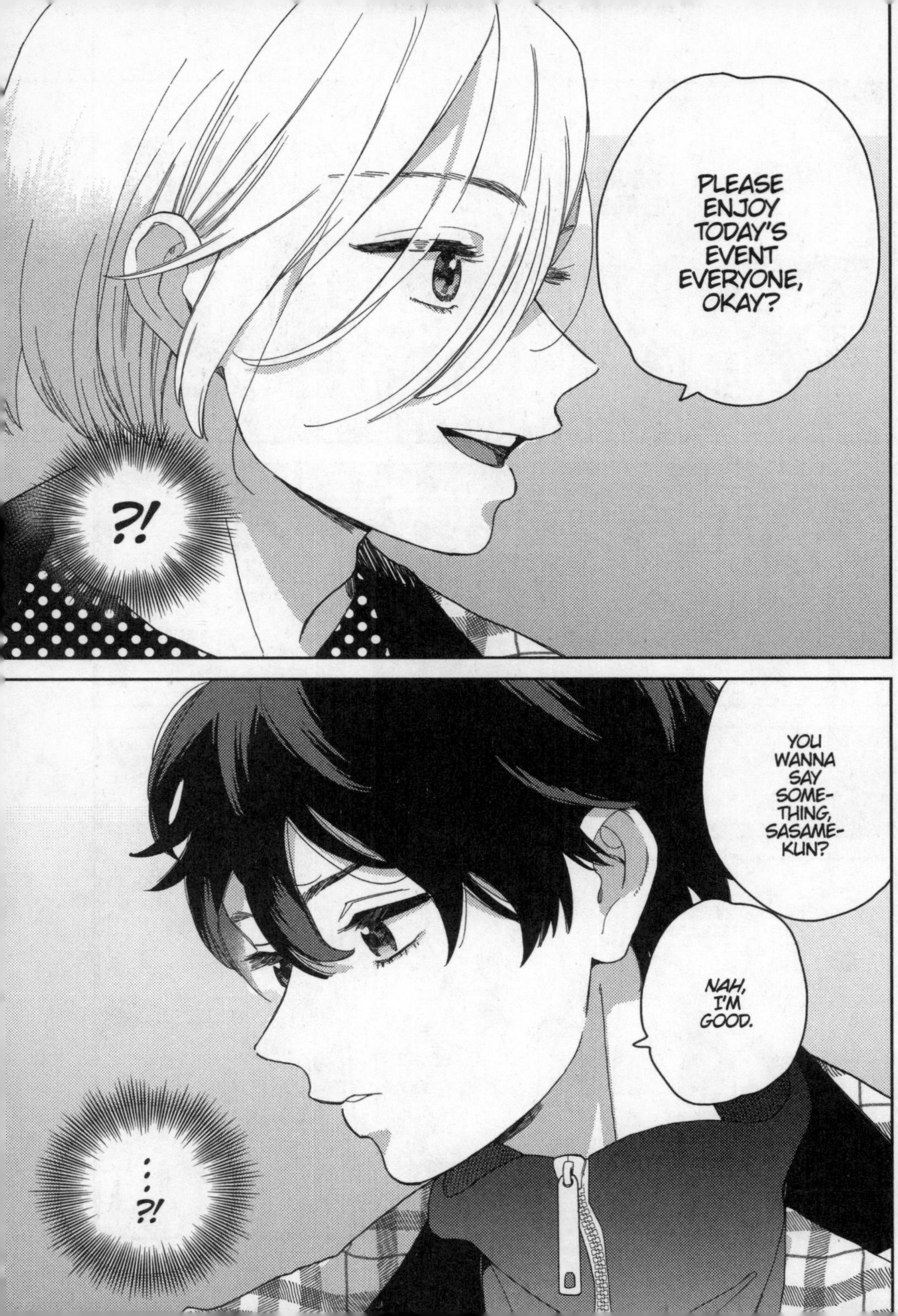
PLEASE ENJOY TODAY'S EVENT EVERYONE, OKAY?
?!
YOU WANNA SAY SOME-THING, SASAME-KUN?
NAH, I'M GOOD.
...?!

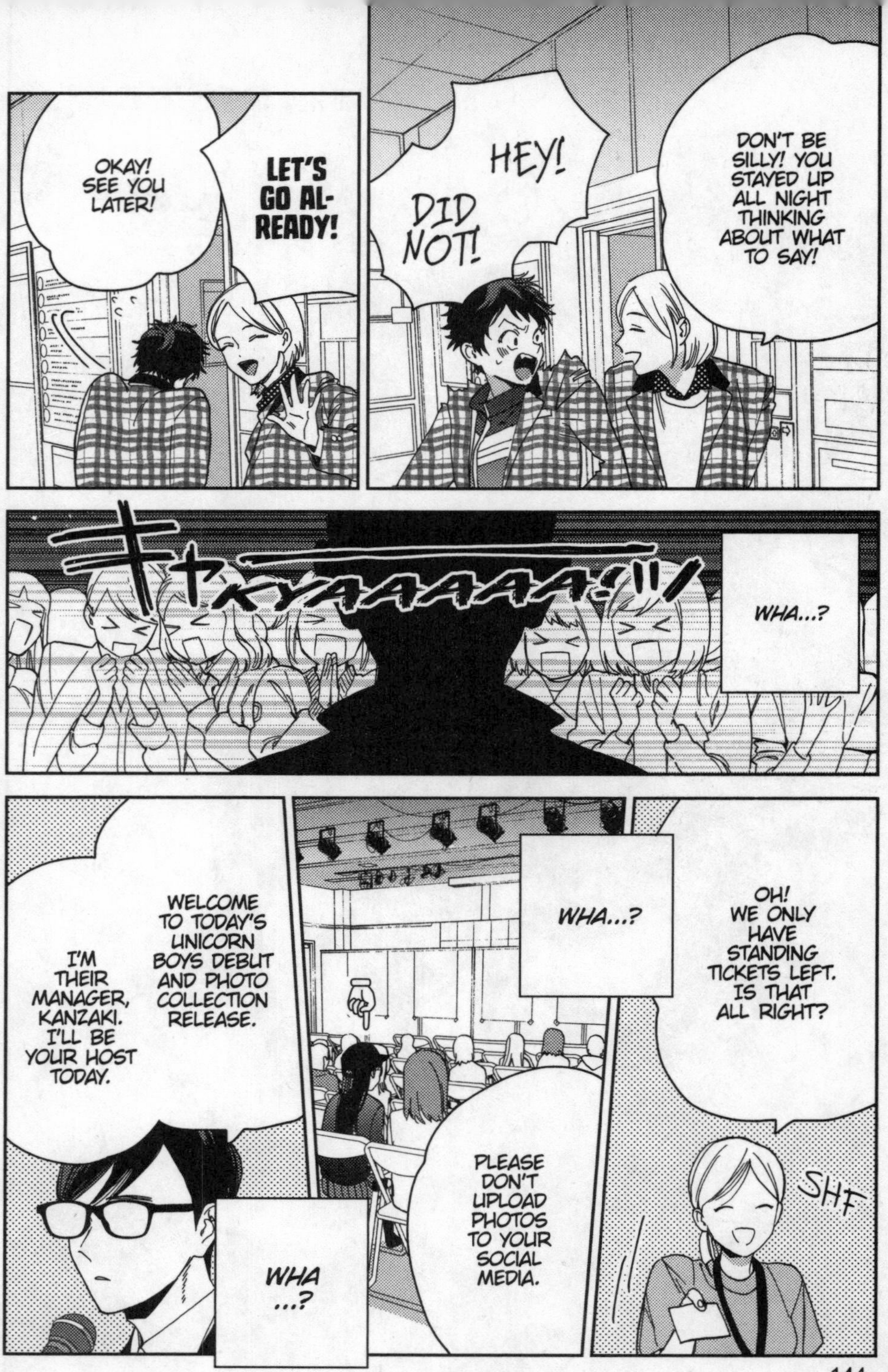
DON'T BE SILLY! YOU STAYED UP ALL NIGHT THINKING ABOUT WHAT TO SAY!
HEY!
DID NOT!
LET'S GO AL-READY!
OKAY! SEE YOU LATER!
KYAAAAAA!!
WHA...?
OH! WE ONLY HAVE STANDING TICKETS LEFT. IS THAT ALL RIGHT?
SHF
WHA...?
PLEASE DON'T UPLOAD PHOTOS TO YOUR SOCIAL MEDIA.
WELCOME TO TODAY'S UNICORN BOYS DEBUT AND PHOTO COLLECTION RELEASE.
I'M THEIR MANAGER, KANZAKI. I'LL BE YOUR HOST TODAY.
WHA ...?

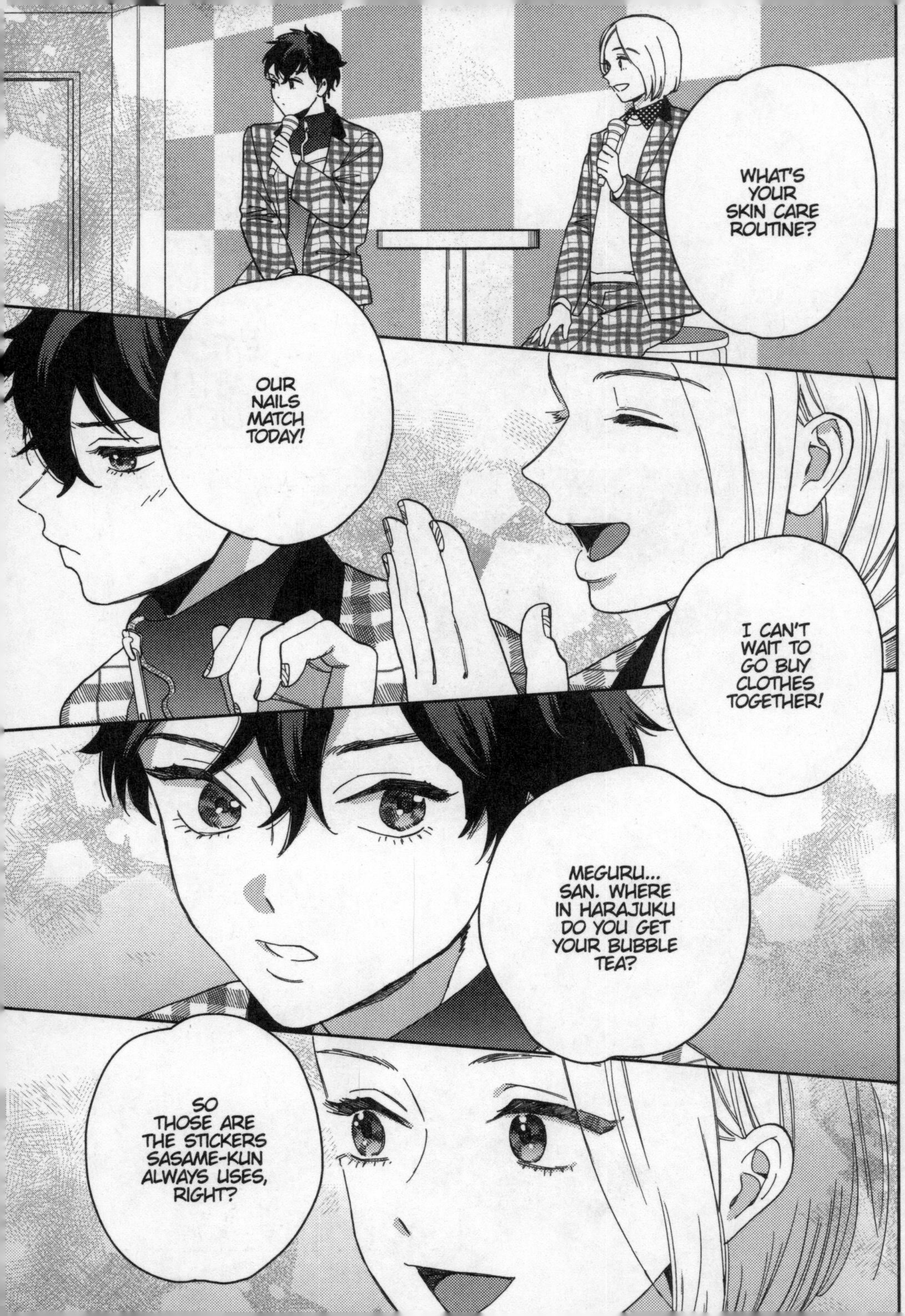
WHAT'S YOUR SKIN CARE ROUTINE?
OUR NAILS MATCH TODAY!
I CAN'T WAIT TO GO BUY CLOTHES TOGETHER!
MEGURU... SAN. WHERE IN HARAJUKU DO YOU GET YOUR BUBBLE TEA?
SO THOSE ARE THE STICKERS SASAME-KUN ALWAYS USES, RIGHT?

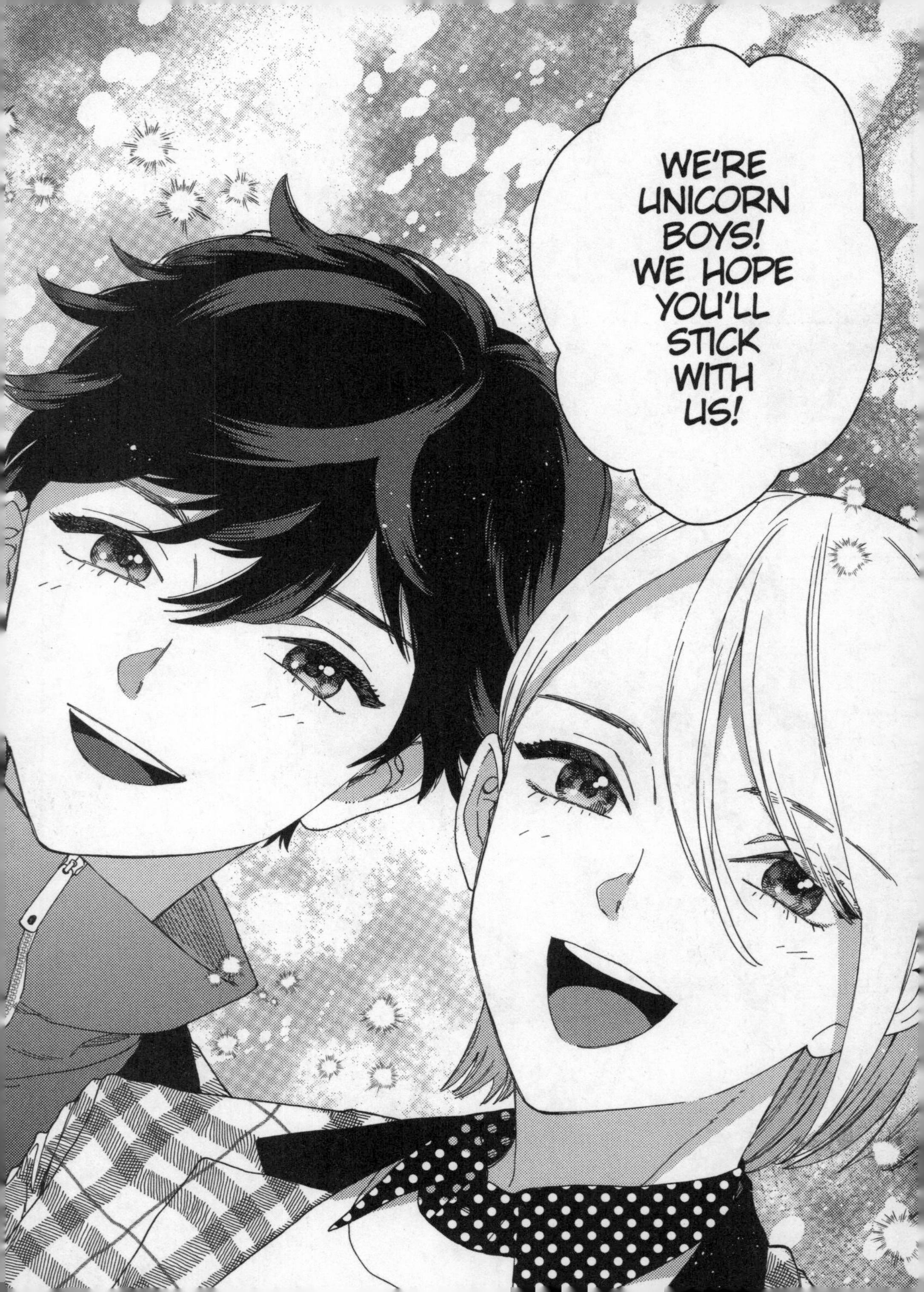
WE'RE UNICORN BOYS! WE HOPE YOU'LL STICK WITH US!

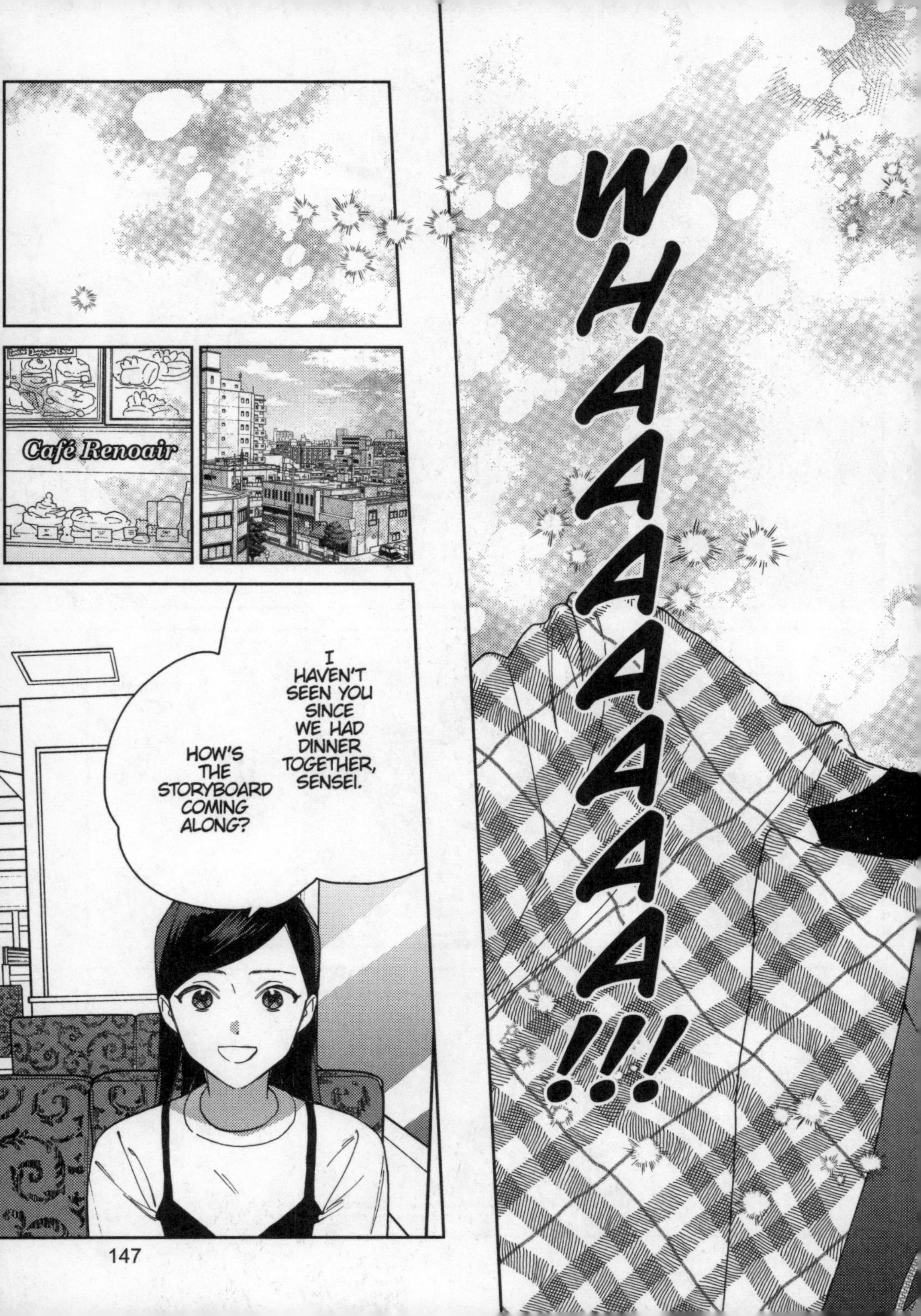
WHAAAAAAA!!!
Café Renoair
I HAVEN'T SEEN YOU SINCE WE HAD DINNER TOGETHER, SENSEI.
HOW'S THE STORYBOARD COMING ALONG?

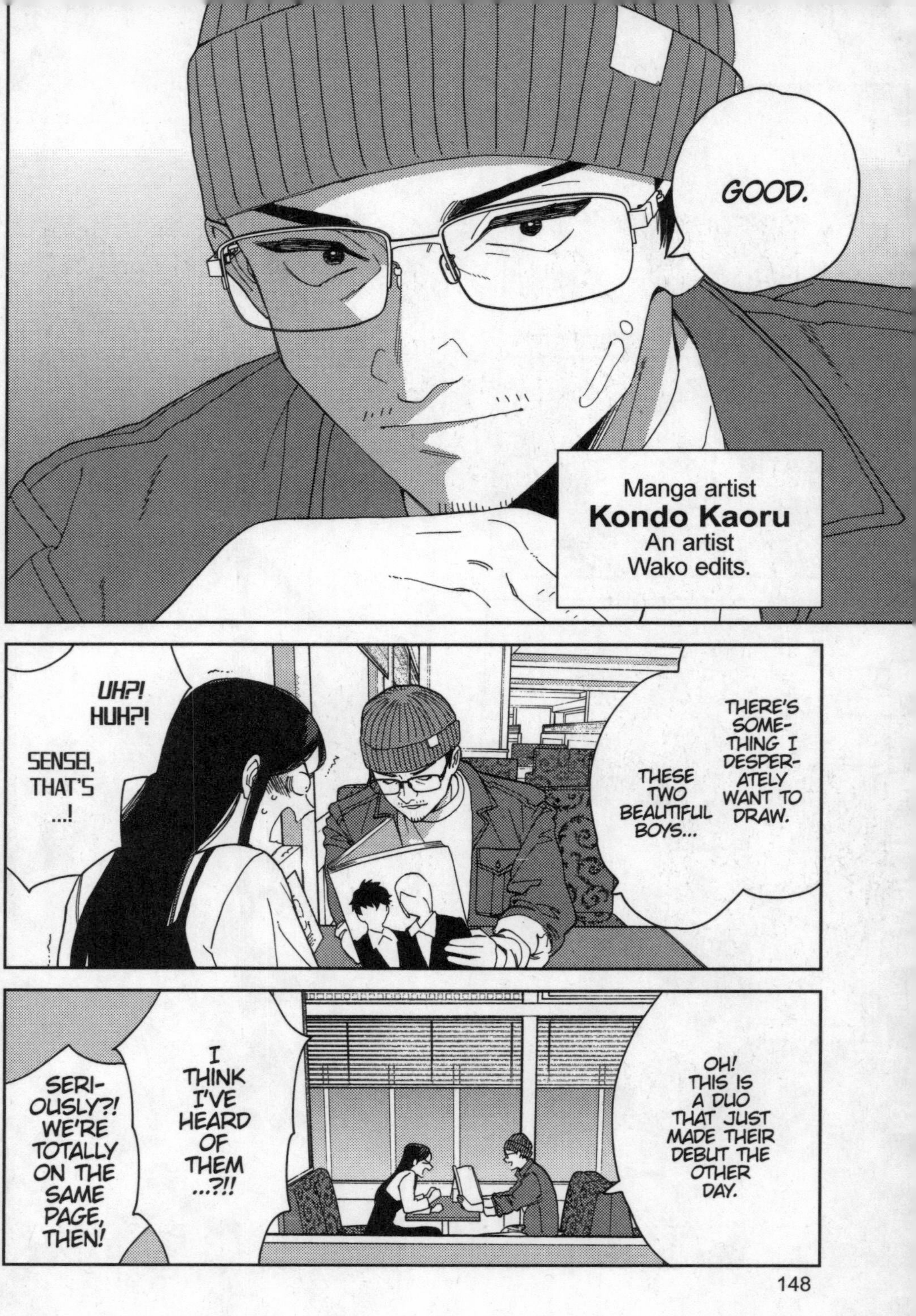
GOOD.
Manga artist
Kondo Kaoru
An artist
Wako edits.
THERE'S SOMETHING I DESPERATELY WANT TO DRAW.
THESE TWO BEAUTIFUL BOYS...
UH?! HUH?!
SENSEI, THAT'S ...!
OH! THIS IS A DUO THAT JUST MADE THEIR DEBUT THE OTHER DAY.
I THINK I'VE HEARD OF THEM ...?!!
SERIOUSLY?! WE'RE TOTALLY ON THE SAME PAGE, THEN!

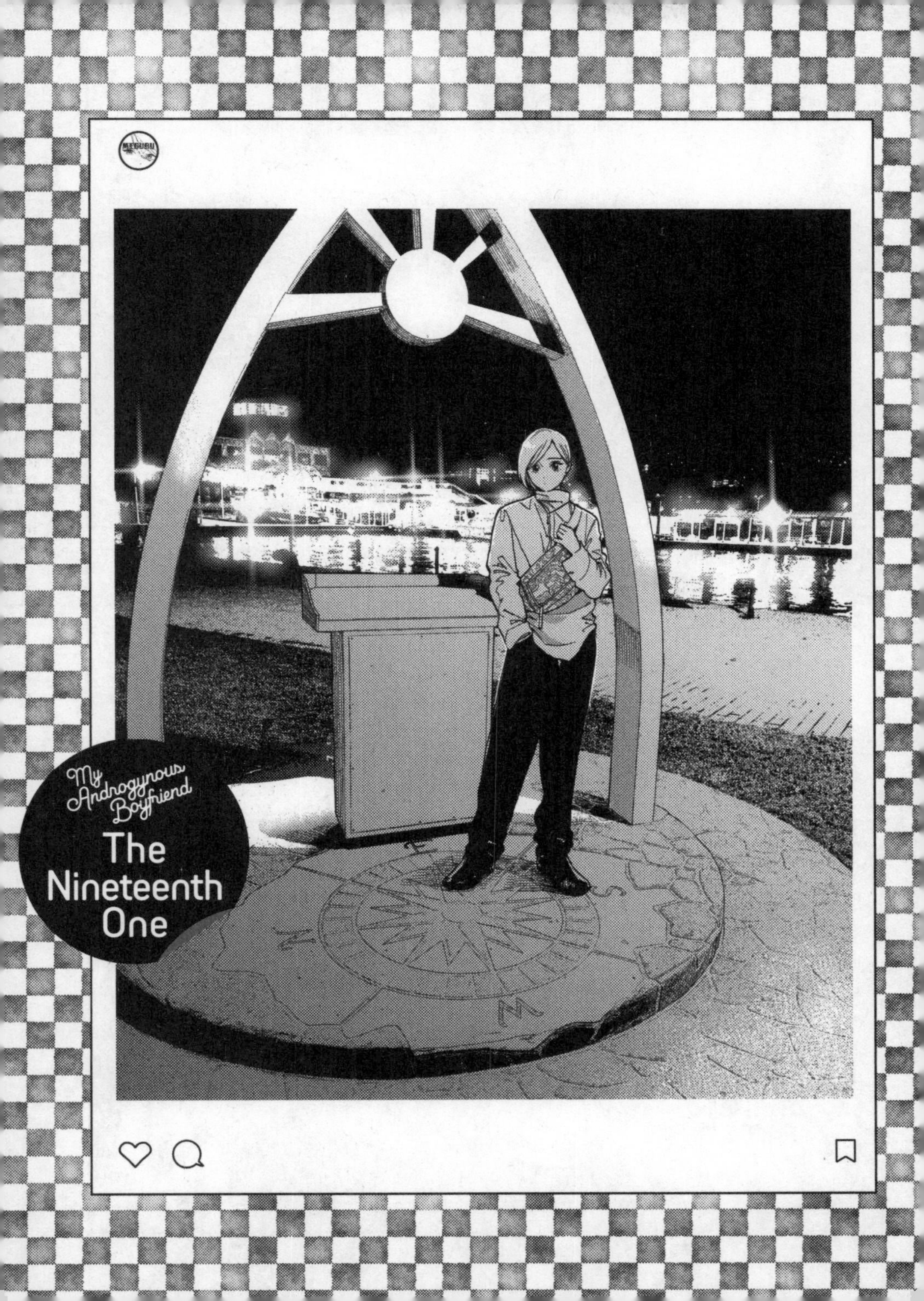
My Androgynous Boyfriend
The Nineteenth One

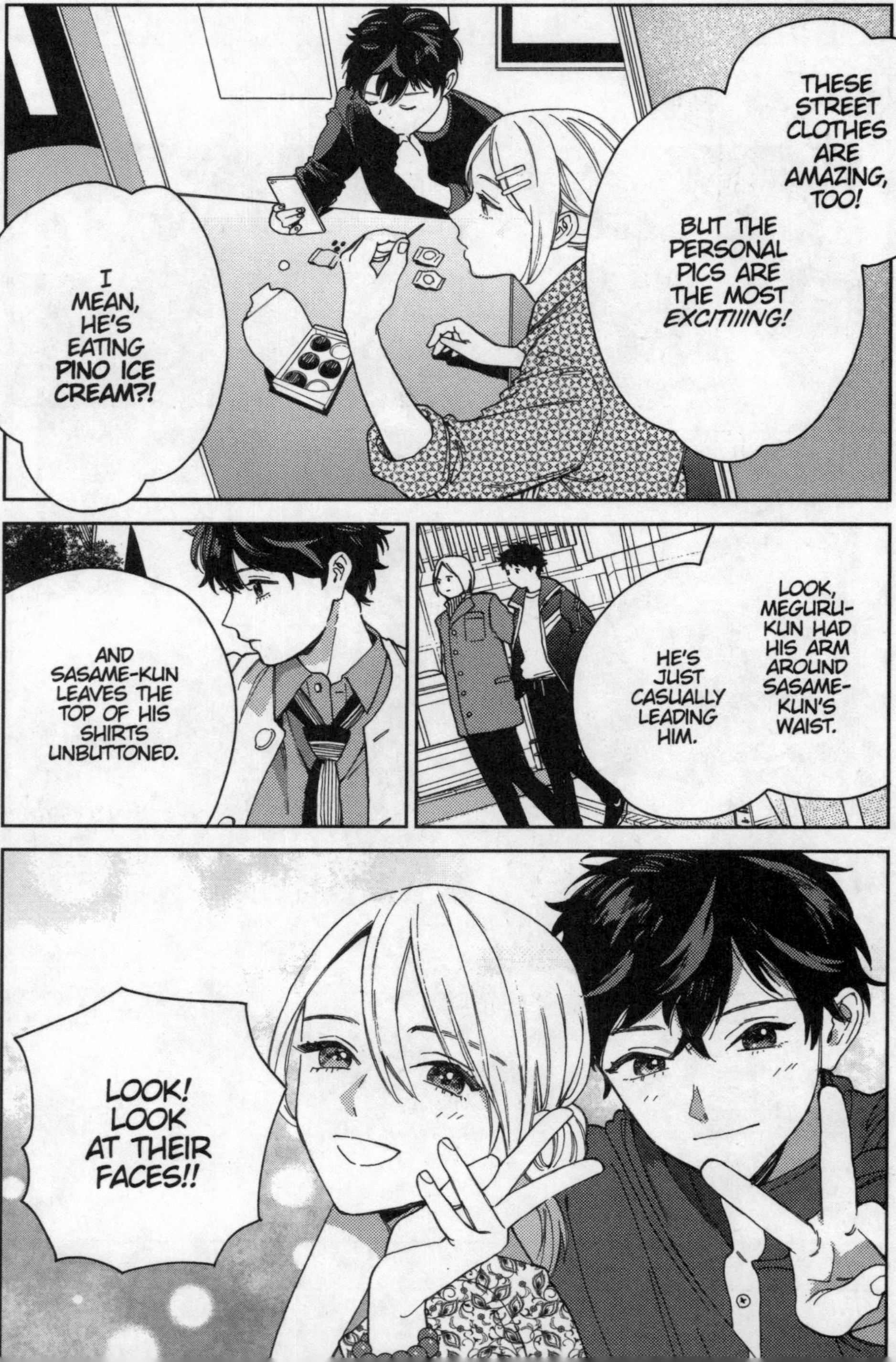
THESE STREET CLOTHES ARE AMAZING, TOO! BUT THE PERSONAL PICS ARE THE MOST *EXCITIIING!*
I MEAN, HE'S EATING PINO ICE CREAM?!
LOOK, MEGURU-KUN HAD HIS ARM AROUND SASAME-KUN'S WAIST. HE'S JUST CASUALLY LEADING HIM.
AND SASAME-KUN LEAVES THE TOP OF HIS SHIRTS UNBUTTONED.
LOOK! LOOK AT THEIR FACES!!

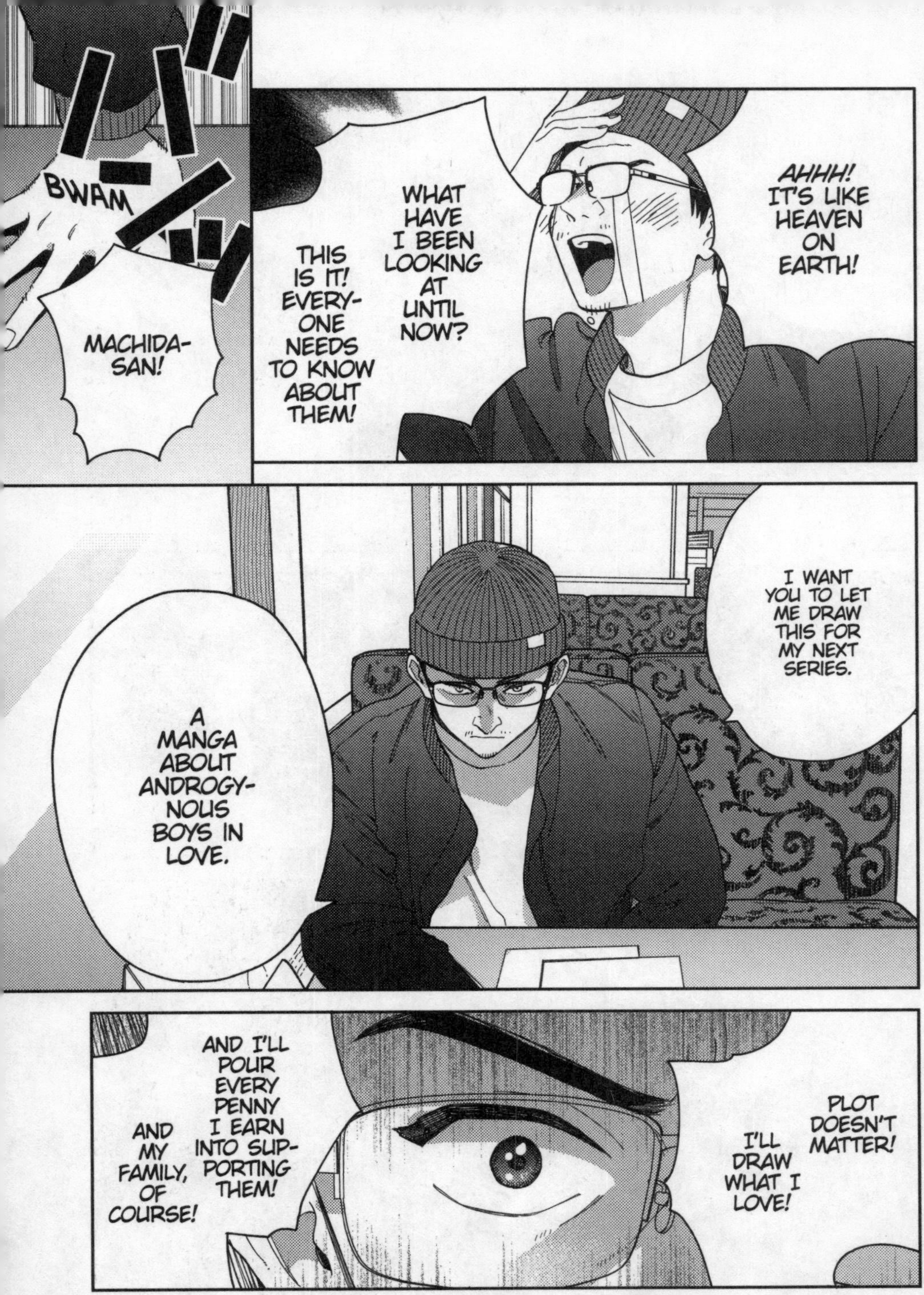
AHHH! IT'S LIKE HEAVEN ON EARTH!
WHAT HAVE I BEEN LOOKING AT UNTIL NOW?
THIS IS IT! EVERY-ONE NEEDS TO KNOW ABOUT THEM!
BWAM
MACHIDA-SAN!
I WANT YOU TO LET ME DRAW THIS FOR MY NEXT SERIES.
A MANGA ABOUT ANDROGY-NOUS BOYS IN LOVE.
PLOT DOESN'T MATTER!
I'LL DRAW WHAT I LOVE!
AND I'LL POUR EVERY PENNY I EARN INTO SUP-PORTING THEM!
AND MY FAMILY, OF COURSE!

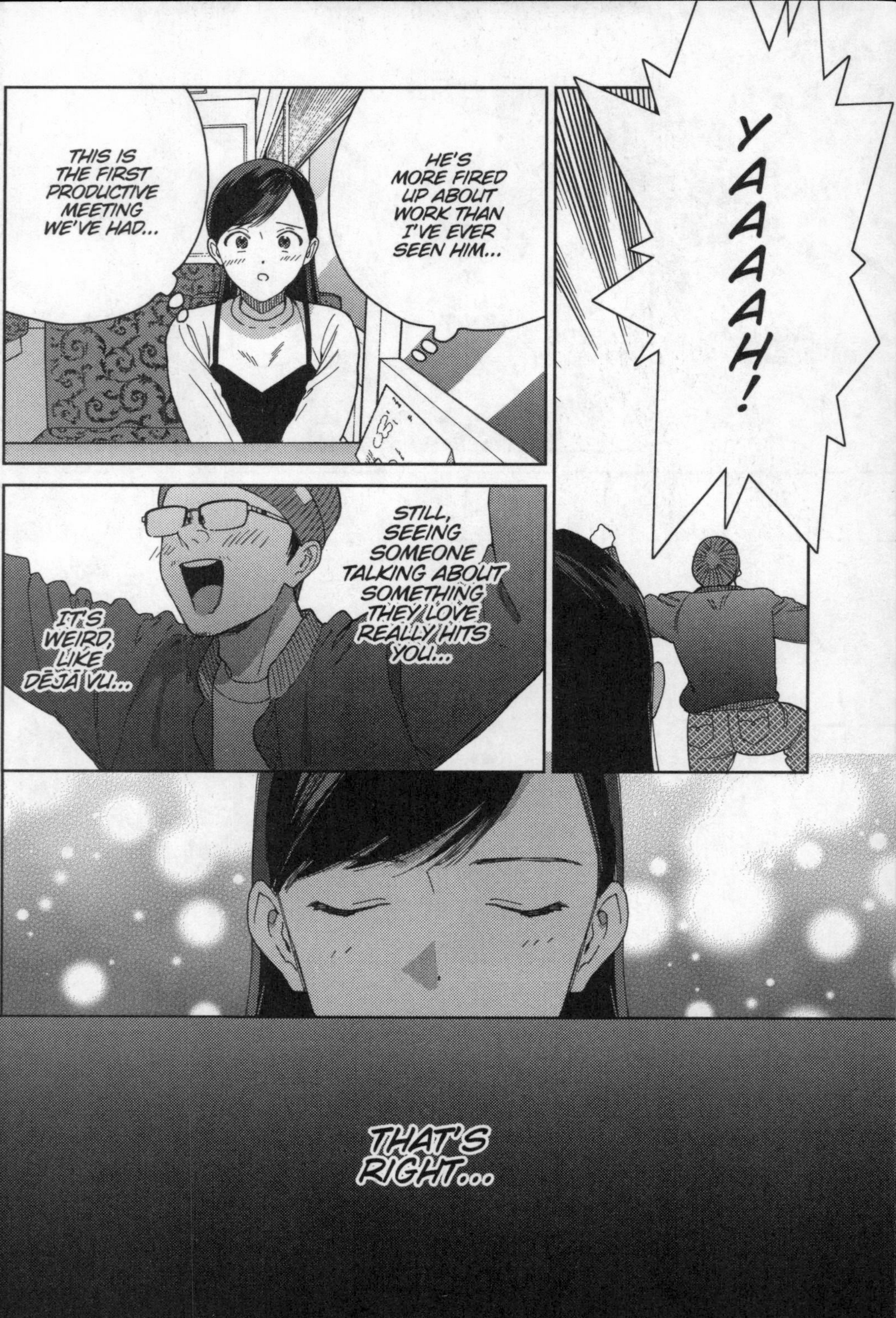
YAAAAAH!
HE'S MORE FIRED UP ABOUT WORK THAN I'VE EVER SEEN HIM...
THIS IS THE FIRST PRODUCTIVE MEETING WE'VE HAD...
STILL, SEEING SOMEONE TALKING ABOUT SOMETHING THEY LOVE REALLY HITS YOU...
IT'S WEIRD, LIKE DÉJÀ VU...
THAT'S RIGHT...

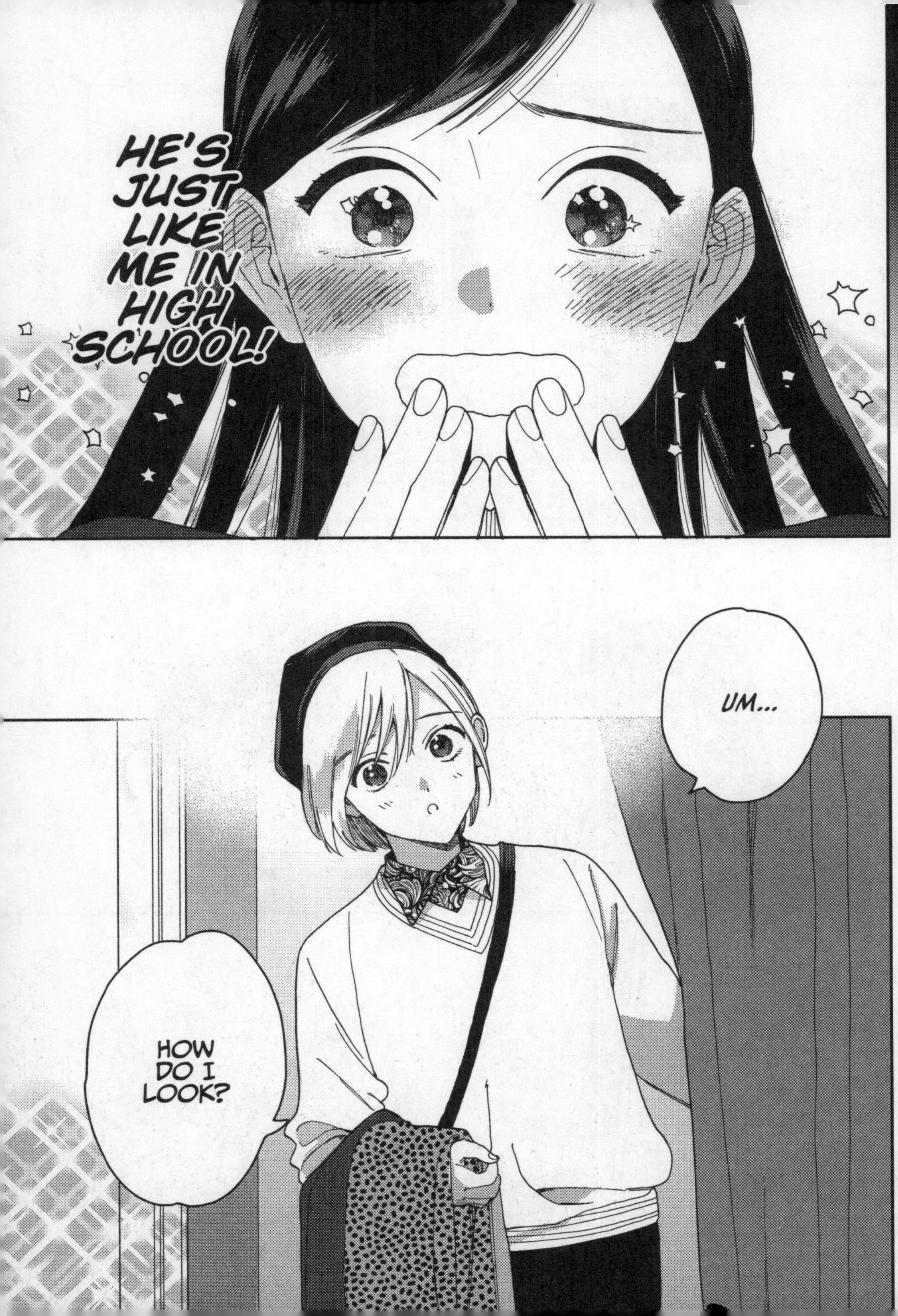
HE'S JUST LIKE ME IN HIGH SCHOOL!
UM...
HOW DO I LOOK?

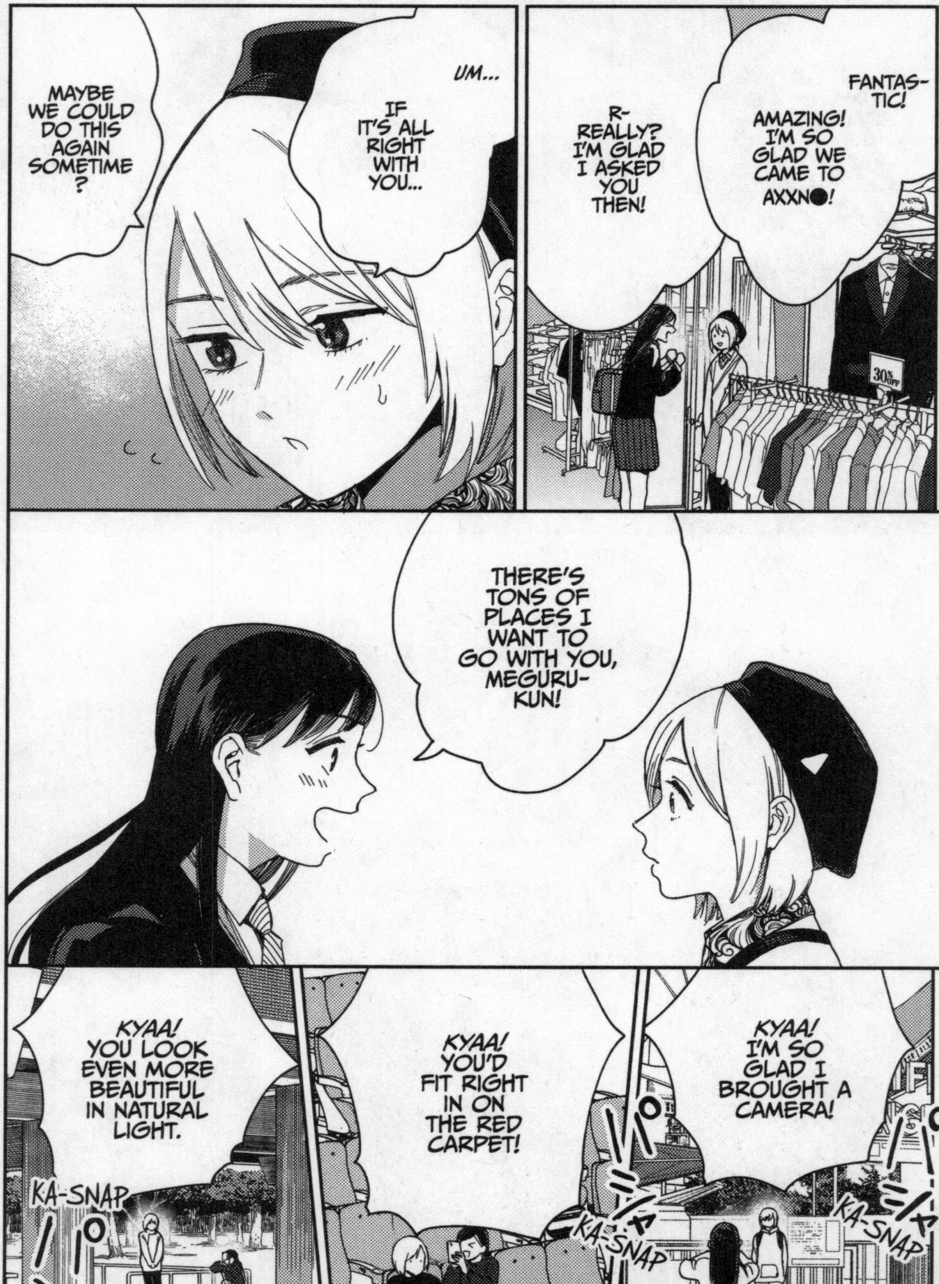
FANTAS-TIC!
AMAZING! I'M SO GLAD WE CAME TO AXXN●!
R-REALLY? I'M GLAD I ASKED YOU THEN!
UM...
IF IT'S ALL RIGHT WITH YOU...
MAYBE WE COULD DO THIS AGAIN SOMETIME?
THERE'S TONS OF PLACES I WANT TO GO WITH YOU, MEGURU-KUN!
KYAA! I'M SO GLAD I BROUGHT A CAMERA!
KA-SNAP
KA-SNAP
KYAA! YOU'D FIT RIGHT IN ON THE RED CARPET!
KYAA! YOU LOOK EVEN MORE BEAUTIFUL IN NATURAL LIGHT.
KA-SNAP

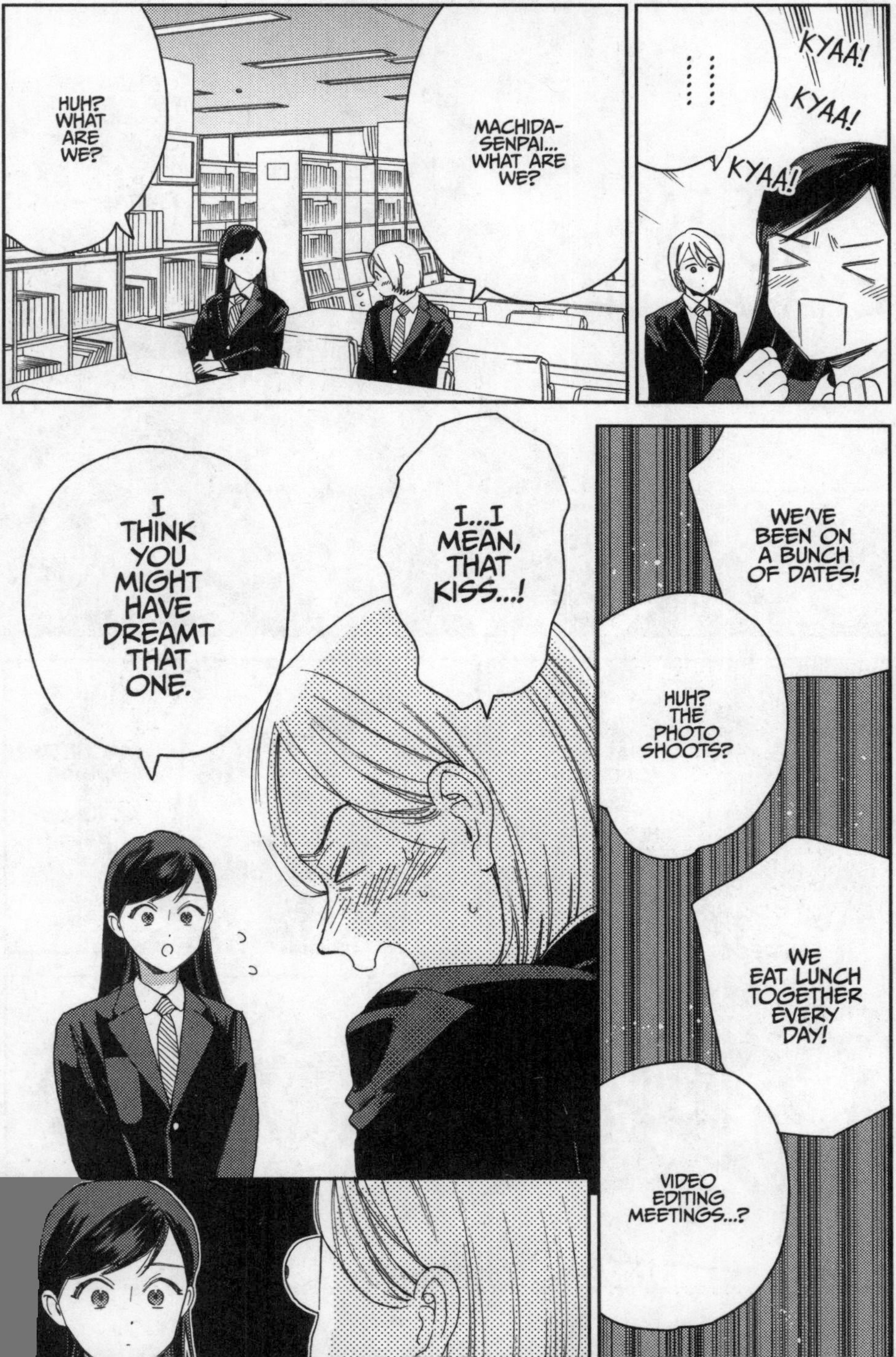
KYAA!
KYAA!
KYAA!
......
MACHIDA-SENPAI... WHAT ARE WE?
HUH? WHAT ARE WE?
WE'VE BEEN ON A BUNCH OF DATES!
HUH? THE PHOTO SHOOTS?
WE EAT LUNCH TOGETHER EVERY DAY!
VIDEO EDITING MEETINGS...?
I...I MEAN, THAT KISS...!
I THINK YOU MIGHT HAVE DREAMT THAT ONE.

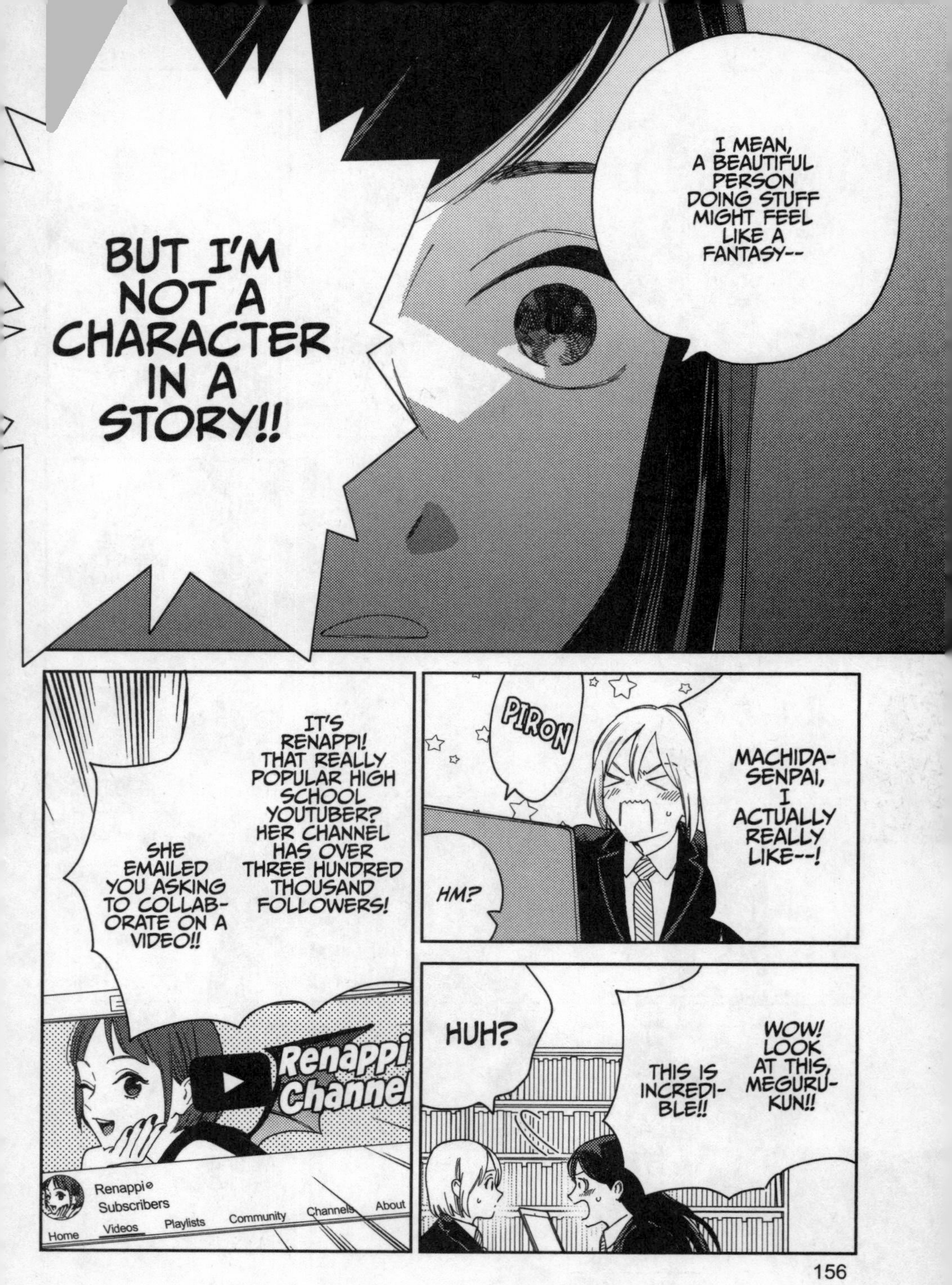
I MEAN, A BEAUTIFUL PERSON DOING STUFF MIGHT FEEL LIKE A FANTASY--
BUT I'M NOT A CHARACTER IN A STORY!!
MACHIDA-SENPAI, I ACTUALLY REALLY LIKE--!
PIRON
HM?
WOW! LOOK AT THIS, MEGURU-KUN!!
THIS IS INCREDIBLE!!
HUH?
IT'S RENAPPI! THAT REALLY POPULAR HIGH SCHOOL YOUTUBER? HER CHANNEL HAS OVER THREE HUNDRED THOUSAND FOLLOWERS!
SHE EMAILED YOU ASKING TO COLLABORATE ON A VIDEO!!
Renappi Channel
Renappi
Subscribers
Home Videos Playlists Community Channels About

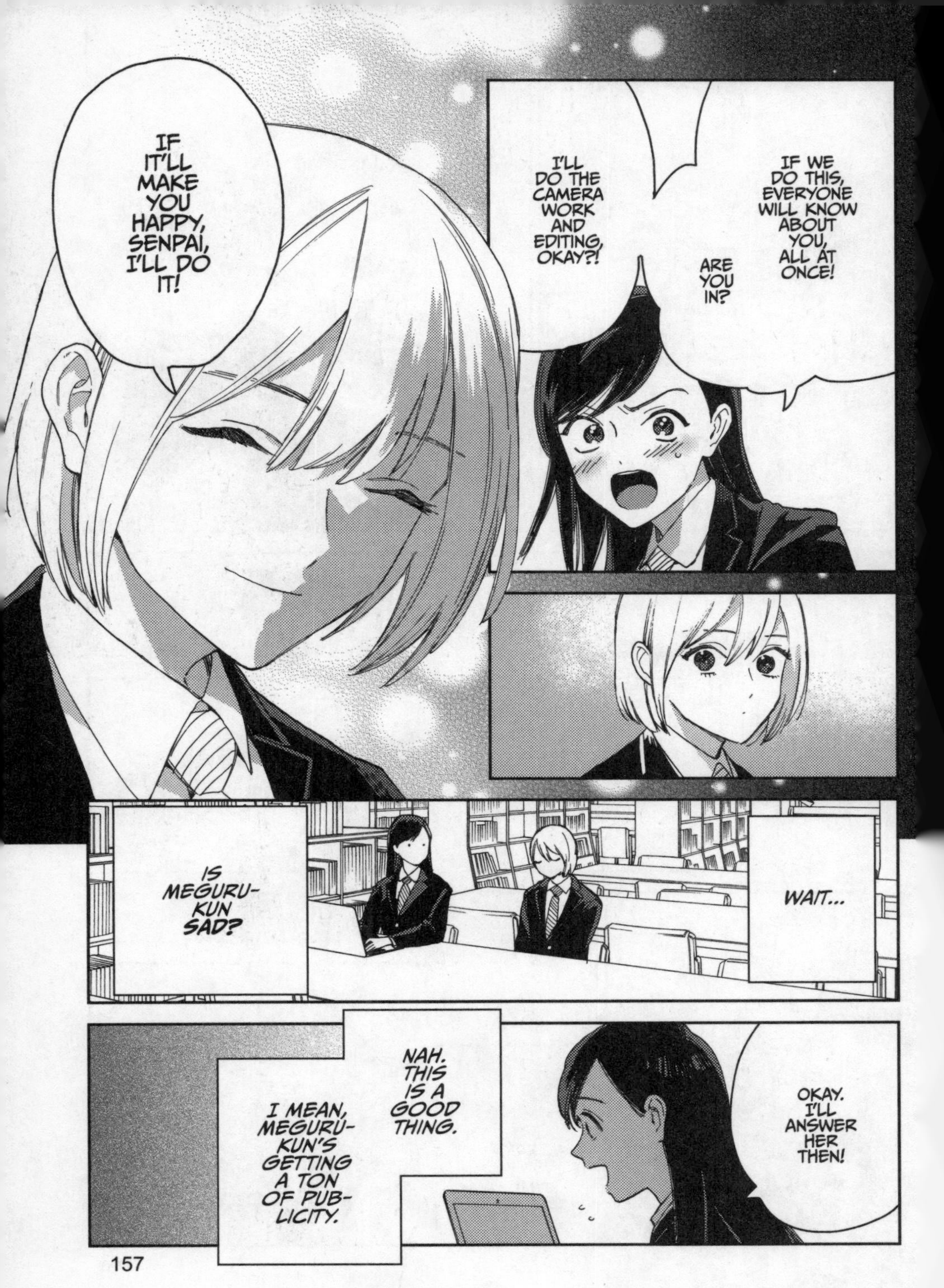
IF WE DO THIS, EVERYONE WILL KNOW ABOUT YOU, ALL AT ONCE!
ARE YOU IN?
I'LL DO THE CAMERA WORK AND EDITING, OKAY?!
IF IT'LL MAKE YOU HAPPY, SENPAI, I'LL DO IT!
WAIT...
IS MEGURU-KUN SAD?
OKAY. I'LL ANSWER HER THEN!
NAH. THIS IS A GOOD THING.
I MEAN, MEGURU-KUN'S GETTING A TON OF PUBLICITY.

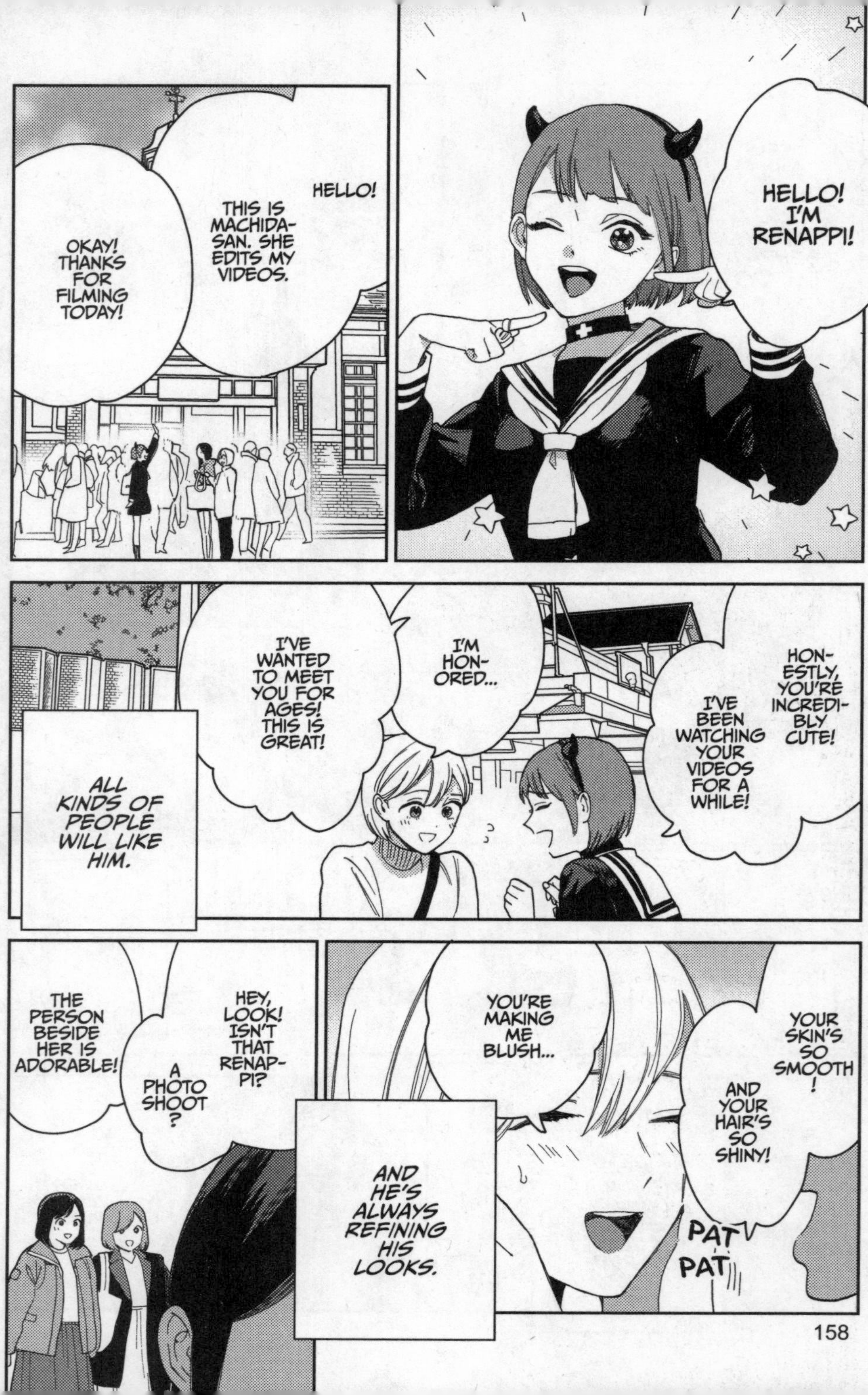
HELLO! I'M RENAPPI!
HELLO!
THIS IS MACHIDA-SAN. SHE EDITS MY VIDEOS.
OKAY! THANKS FOR FILMING TODAY!
HON-ESTLY, YOU'RE INCREDI-BLY CUTE!
I'VE BEEN WATCHING YOUR VIDEOS FOR A WHILE!
I'M HON-ORED...
I'VE WANTED TO MEET YOU FOR AGES! THIS IS GREAT!
ALL KINDS OF PEOPLE WILL LIKE HIM.
YOUR SKIN'S SO SMOOTH!
AND YOUR HAIR'S SO SHINY!
YOU'RE MAKING ME BLUSH...
PAT PAT
AND HE'S ALWAYS REFINING HIS LOOKS.
HEY, LOOK! ISN'T THAT RENAP-PI?
THE PERSON BESIDE HER IS ADORABLE!
A PHOTO SHOOT?

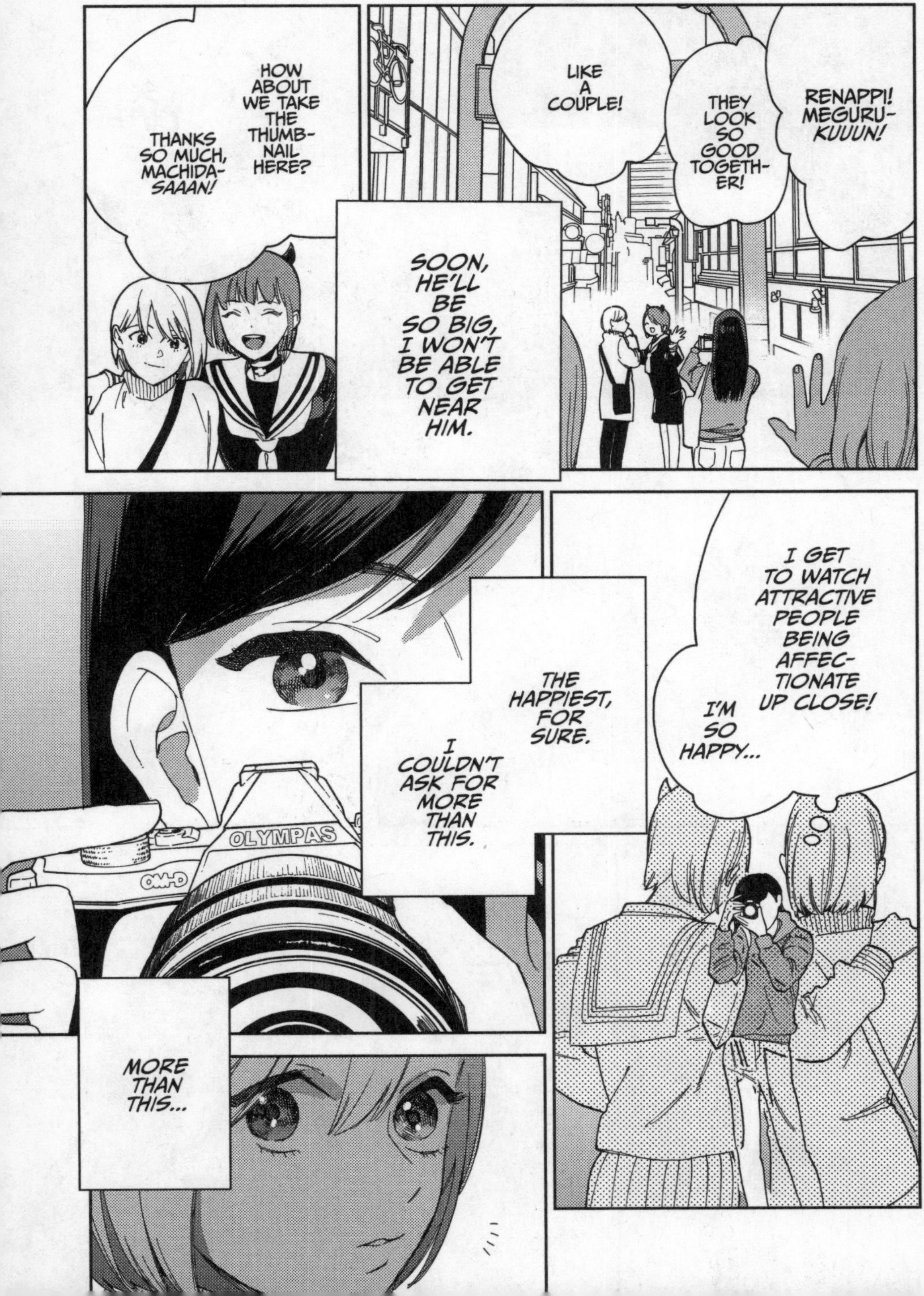
RENAPPI! MEGURU-KUUUN!
THEY LOOK SO GOOD TOGETH-ER!
LIKE A COUPLE!
SOON, HE'LL BE SO BIG, I WON'T BE ABLE TO GET NEAR HIM.
HOW ABOUT WE TAKE THE THUMB-NAIL HERE?
THANKS SO MUCH, MACHIDA-SAAAN!
I GET TO WATCH ATTRACTIVE PEOPLE BEING AFFEC-TIONATE UP CLOSE!
I'M SO HAPPY...
THE HAPPIEST, FOR SURE.
I COULDN'T ASK FOR MORE THAN THIS.
OLYMPAS
OM-D
MORE THAN THIS...

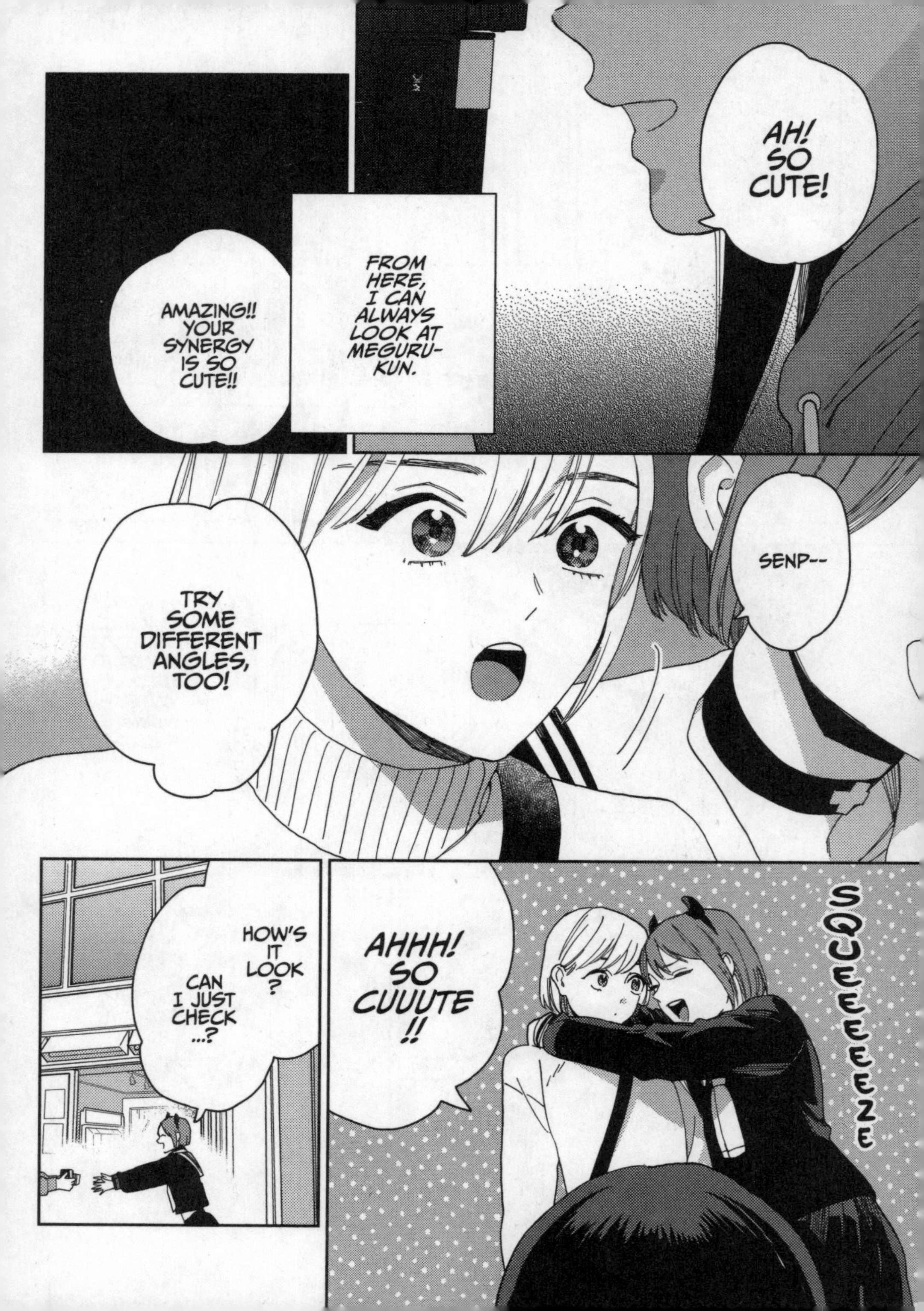
AH! SO CUTE!
FROM HERE, I CAN ALWAYS LOOK AT MEGURU-KUN.
AMAZING!! YOUR SYNERGY IS SO CUTE!!
SENP--
TRY SOME DIFFERENT ANGLES, TOO!
SQUEEEEEZE
AHHH! SO CUUUTE!!
HOW'S IT LOOK?
CAN I JUST CHECK...?

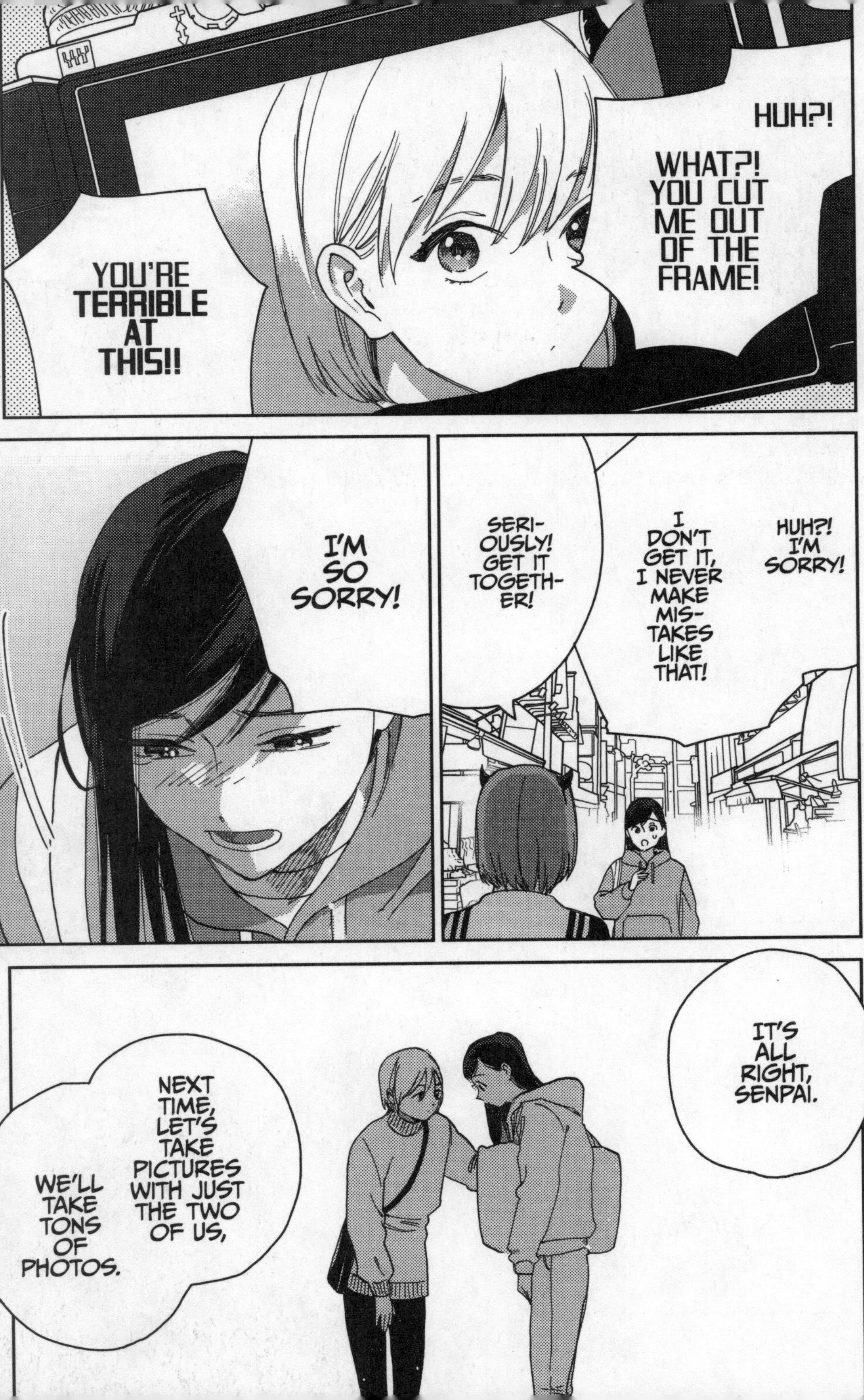
HUH?!
WHAT?! YOU CUT ME OUT OF THE FRAME!
YOU'RE TERRIBLE AT THIS!!
HUH?! I'M SORRY!
I DON'T GET IT, I NEVER MAKE MISTAKES LIKE THAT!
SERIOUSLY! GET IT TOGETHER!
I'M SO SORRY!
IT'S ALL RIGHT, SENPAI.
NEXT TIME, LET'S TAKE PICTURES WITH JUST THE TWO OF US,
WE'LL TAKE TONS OF PHOTOS.

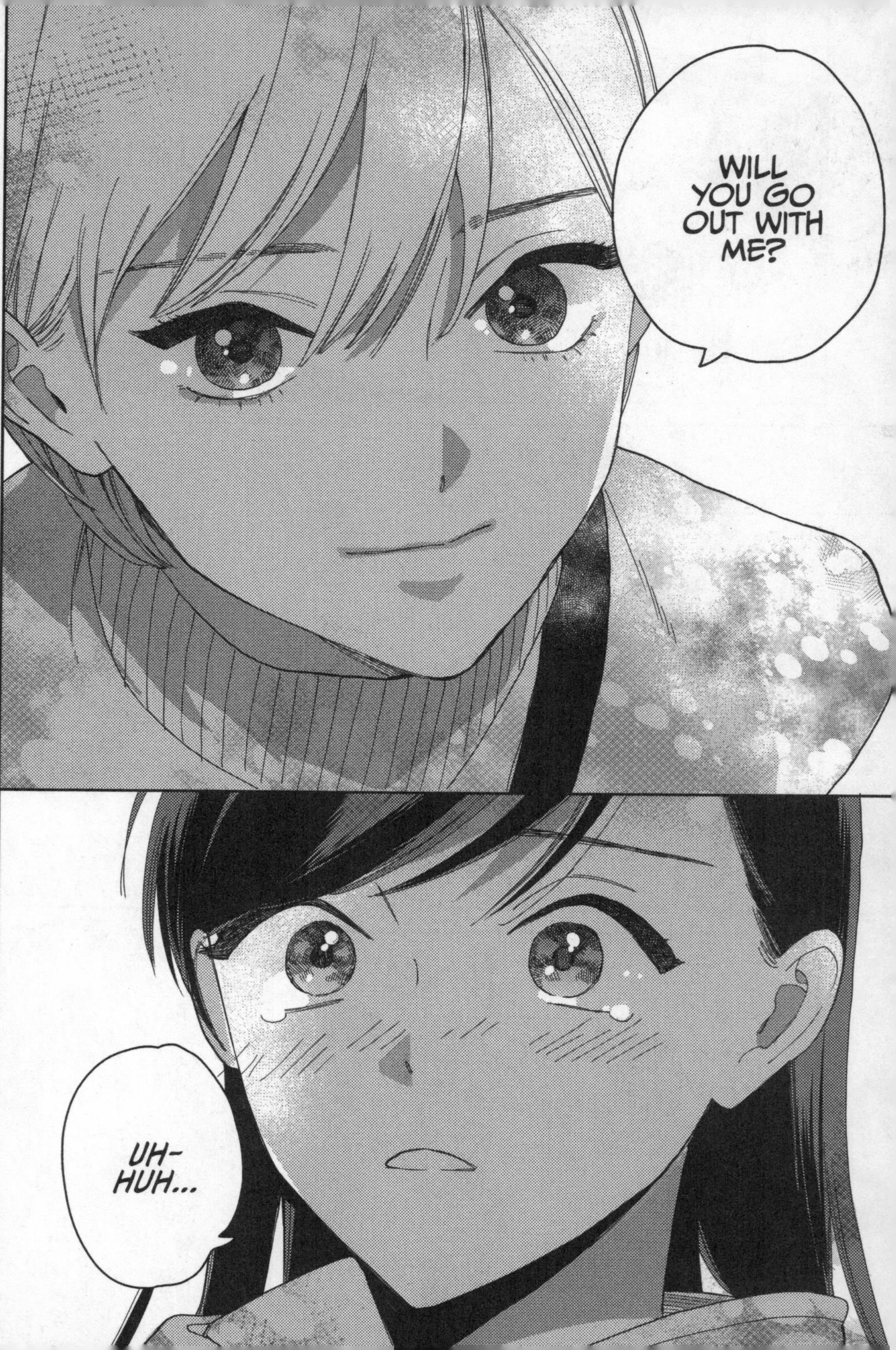
WILL YOU GO OUT WITH ME?
UH-HUH...

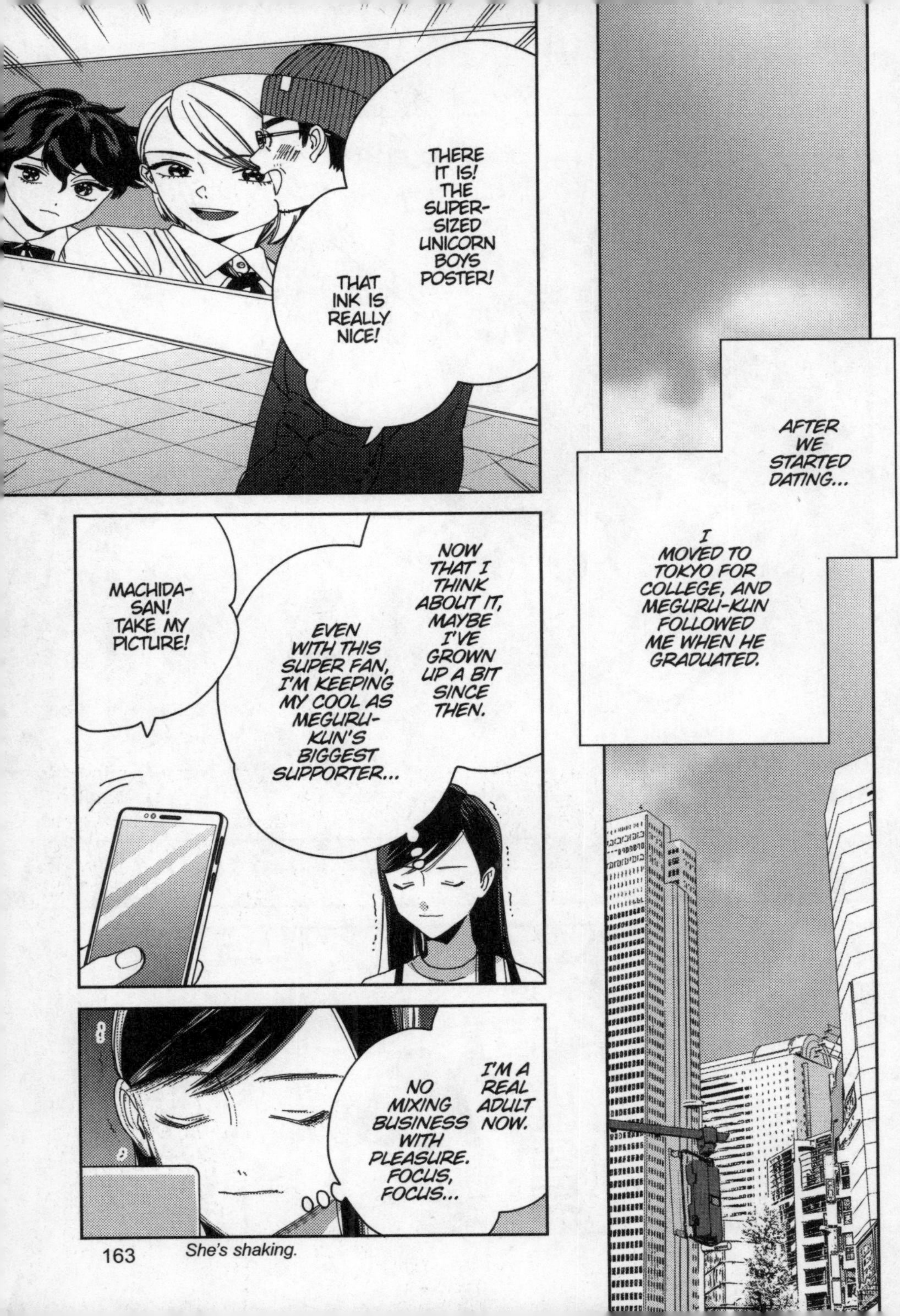
AFTER WE STARTED DATING...
I MOVED TO TOKYO FOR COLLEGE, AND MEGURU-KUN FOLLOWED ME WHEN HE GRADUATED.
THERE IT IS! THE SUPER-SIZED UNICORN BOYS POSTER!
THAT INK IS REALLY NICE!
NOW THAT I THINK ABOUT IT, MAYBE I'VE GROWN UP A BIT SINCE THEN.
EVEN WITH THIS SUPER FAN, I'M KEEPING MY COOL AS MEGURU-KUN'S BIGGEST SUPPORTER...
MACHIDA-SAN! TAKE MY PICTURE!
I'M A REAL ADULT NOW.
NO MIXING BUSINESS WITH PLEASURE. FOCUS, FOCUS...

She's shaking.

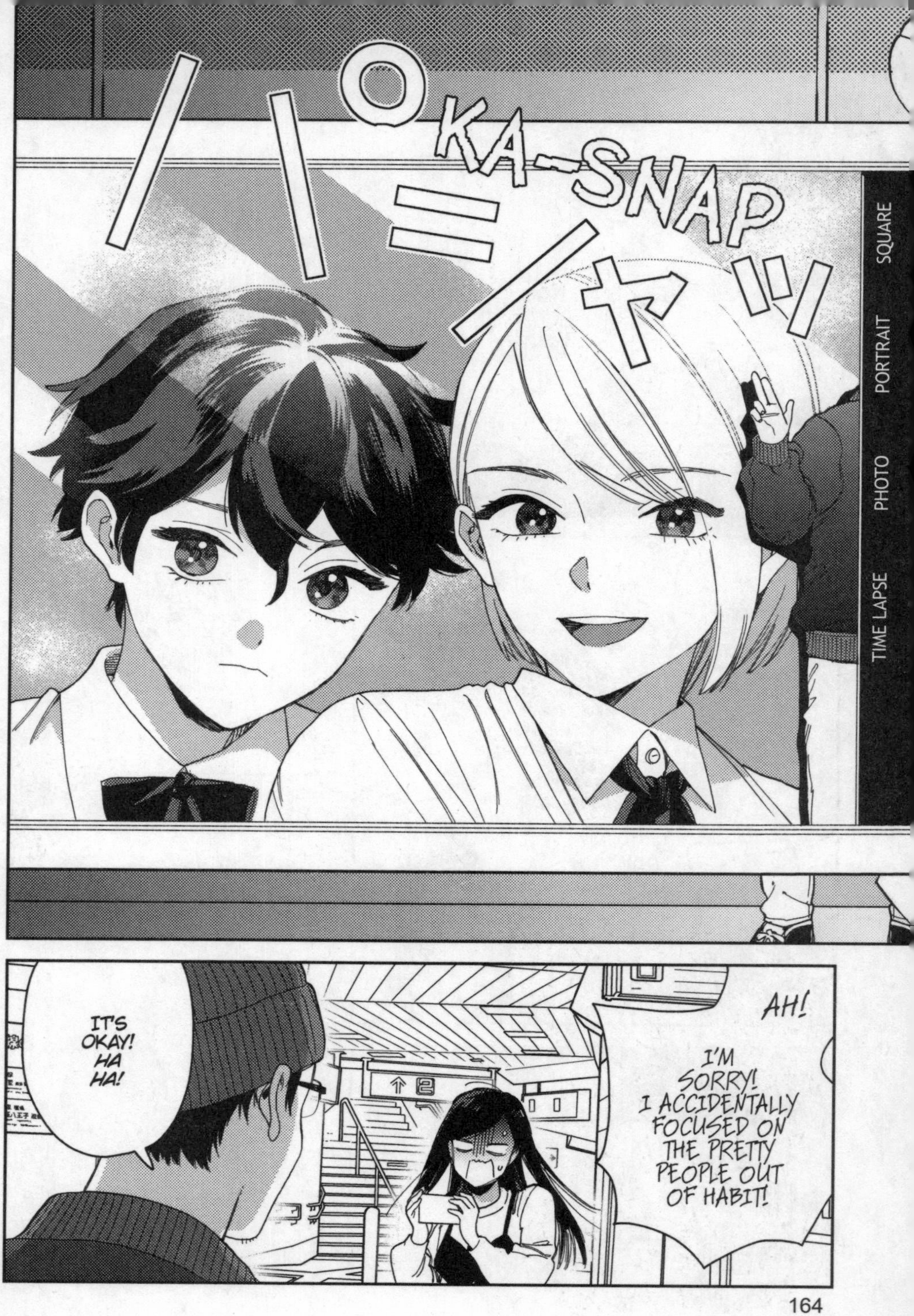
KA-SNAP
TIME LAPSE
PHOTO
PORTRAIT
SQUARE
AH!
I'M SORRY! I ACCIDENTALLY FOCUSED ON THE PRETTY PEOPLE OUT OF HABIT!
IT'S OKAY! HA HA!

The Twentieth One

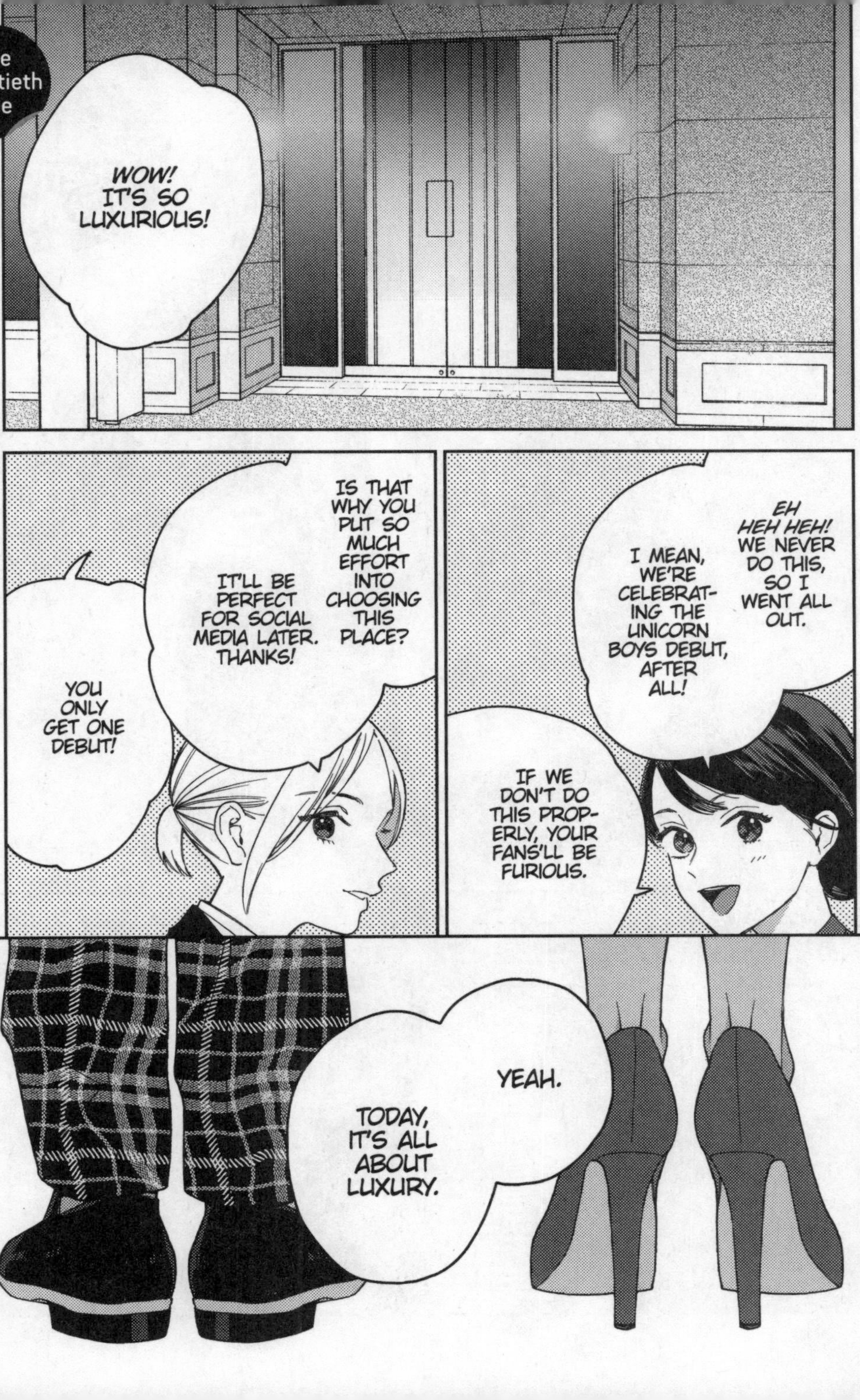
WOW! IT'S SO LUXURIOUS!
EH HEH HEH! WE NEVER DO THIS, SO I WENT ALL OUT.
I MEAN, WE'RE CELEBRATING THE UNICORN BOYS DEBUT, AFTER ALL!
IF WE DON'T DO THIS PROPERLY, YOUR FANS'LL BE FURIOUS.
IS THAT WHY YOU PUT SO MUCH EFFORT INTO CHOOSING THIS PLACE?
IT'LL BE PERFECT FOR SOCIAL MEDIA LATER. THANKS!
YOU ONLY GET ONE DEBUT!
YEAH. TODAY, IT'S ALL ABOUT LUXURY.

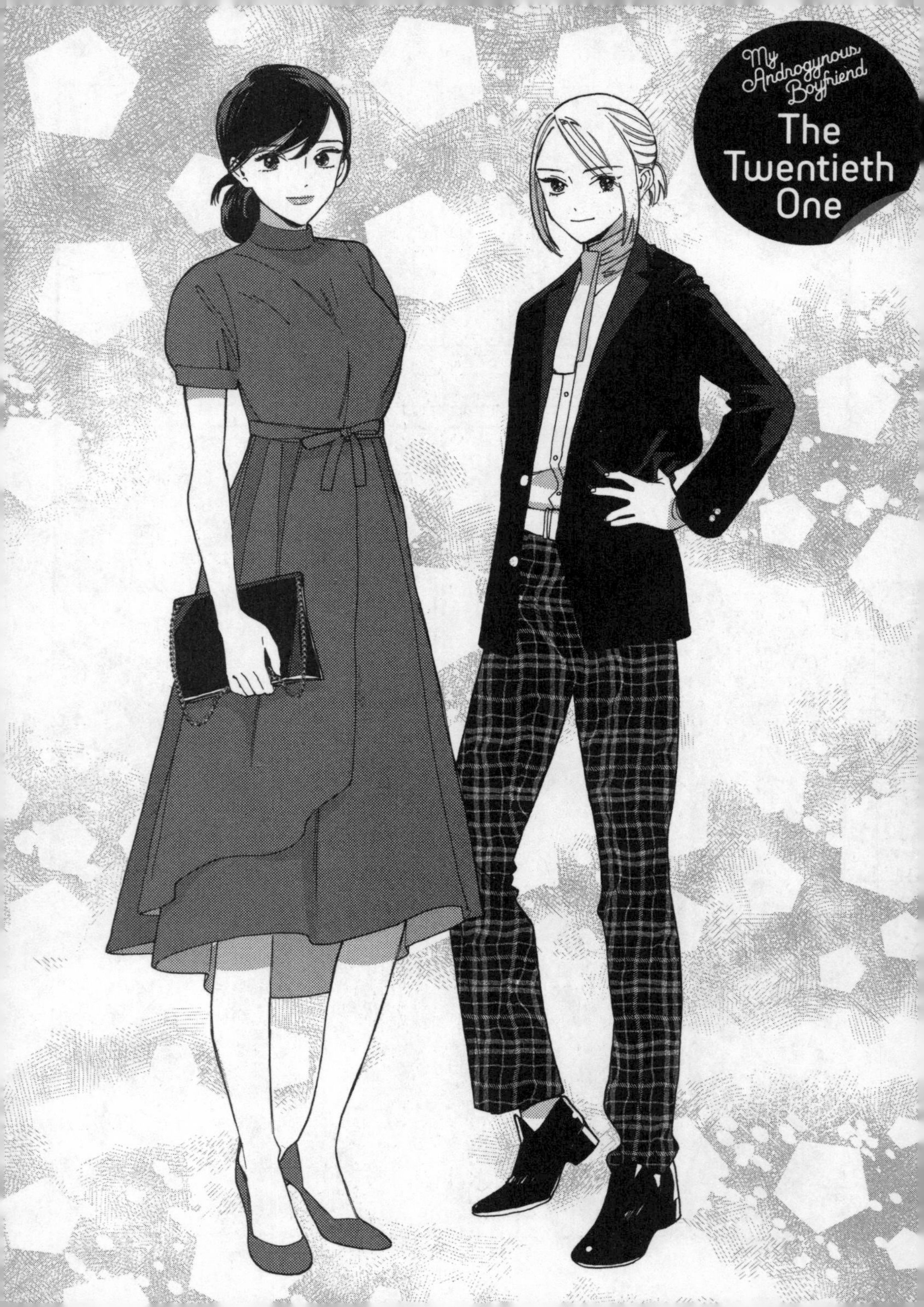
My Androgynous Boyfriend
The Twentieth One

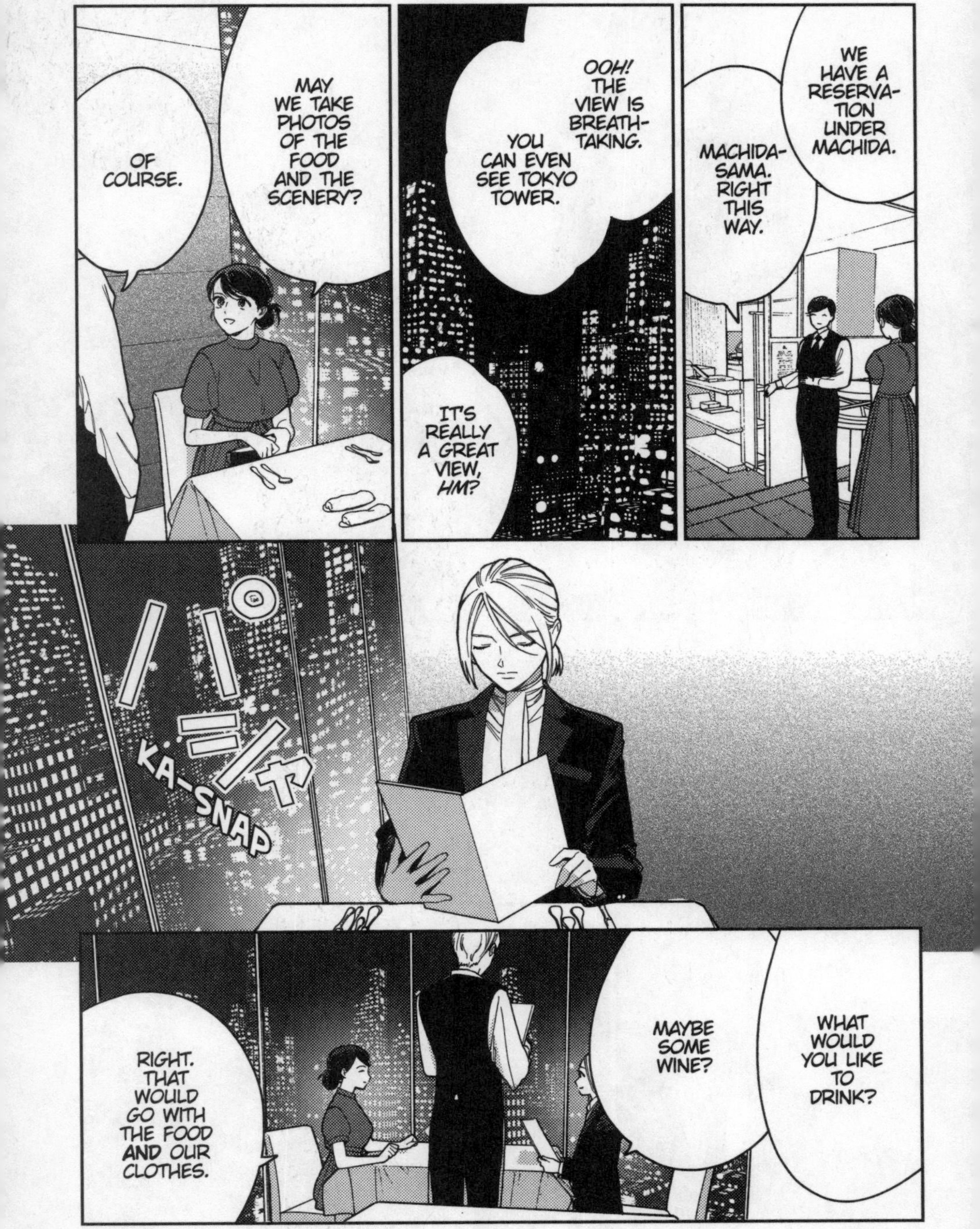
WE HAVE A RESERVATION UNDER MACHIDA.
MACHIDA-SAMA. RIGHT THIS WAY.
OOH! THE VIEW IS BREATHTAKING.
YOU CAN EVEN SEE TOKYO TOWER.
IT'S REALLY A GREAT VIEW, *HM?*
MAY WE TAKE PHOTOS OF THE FOOD AND THE SCENERY?
OF COURSE.
KA-SNAP
WHAT WOULD YOU LIKE TO DRINK?
MAYBE SOME WINE?
RIGHT. THAT WOULD GO WITH THE FOOD AND OUR CLOTHES.

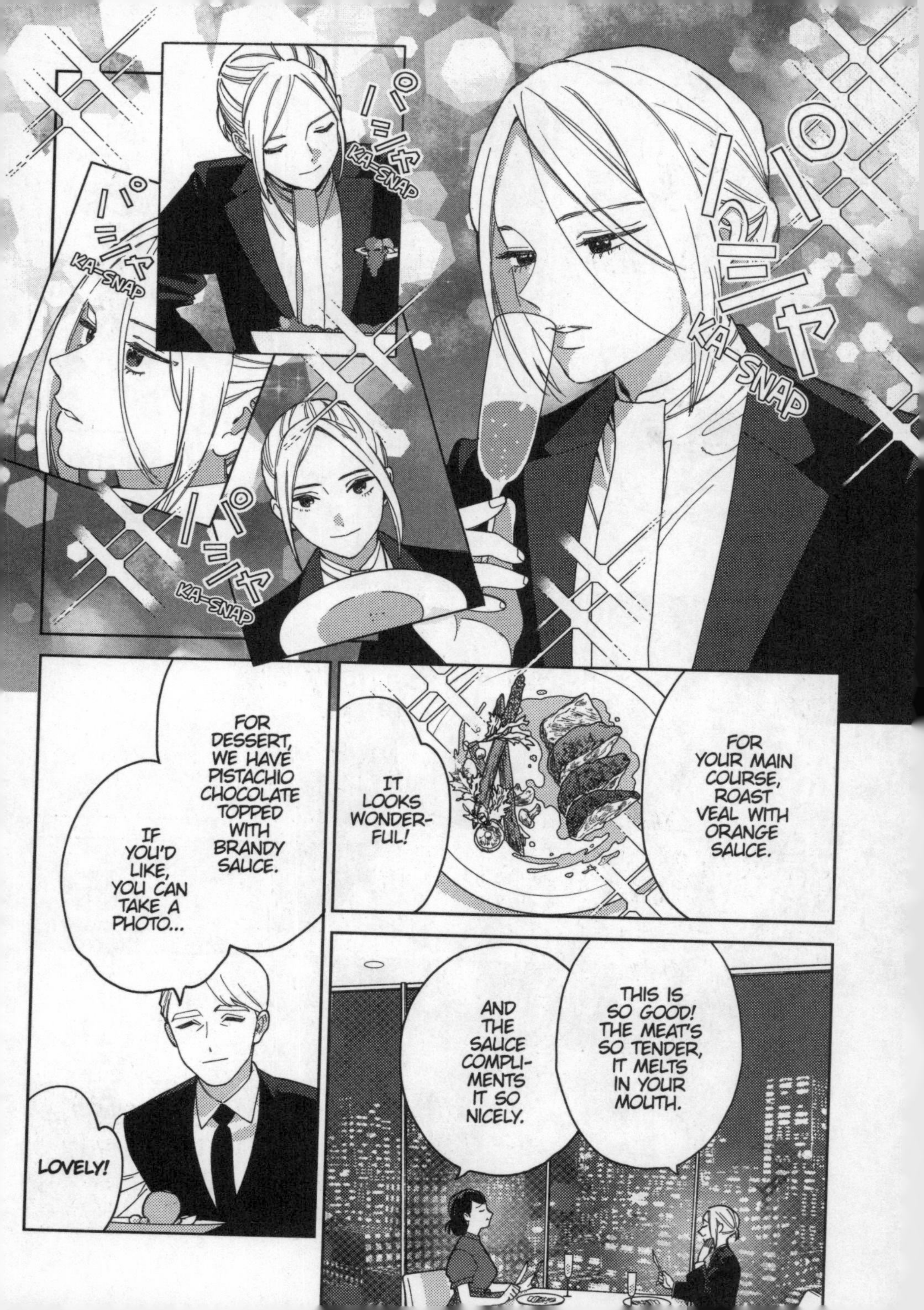
パシャ
KA-SNAP
パシャ
KA-SNAP
パシャ
KA-SNAP
パシャ
KA-SNAP
FOR YOUR MAIN COURSE, ROAST VEAL WITH ORANGE SAUCE.
IT LOOKS WONDER-FUL!
THIS IS SO GOOD! THE MEAT'S SO TENDER, IT MELTS IN YOUR MOUTH.
AND THE SAUCE COMPLI-MENTS IT SO NICELY.
FOR DESSERT, WE HAVE PISTACHIO CHOCOLATE TOPPED WITH BRANDY SAUCE.
IF YOU'D LIKE, YOU CAN TAKE A PHOTO...
LOVELY!

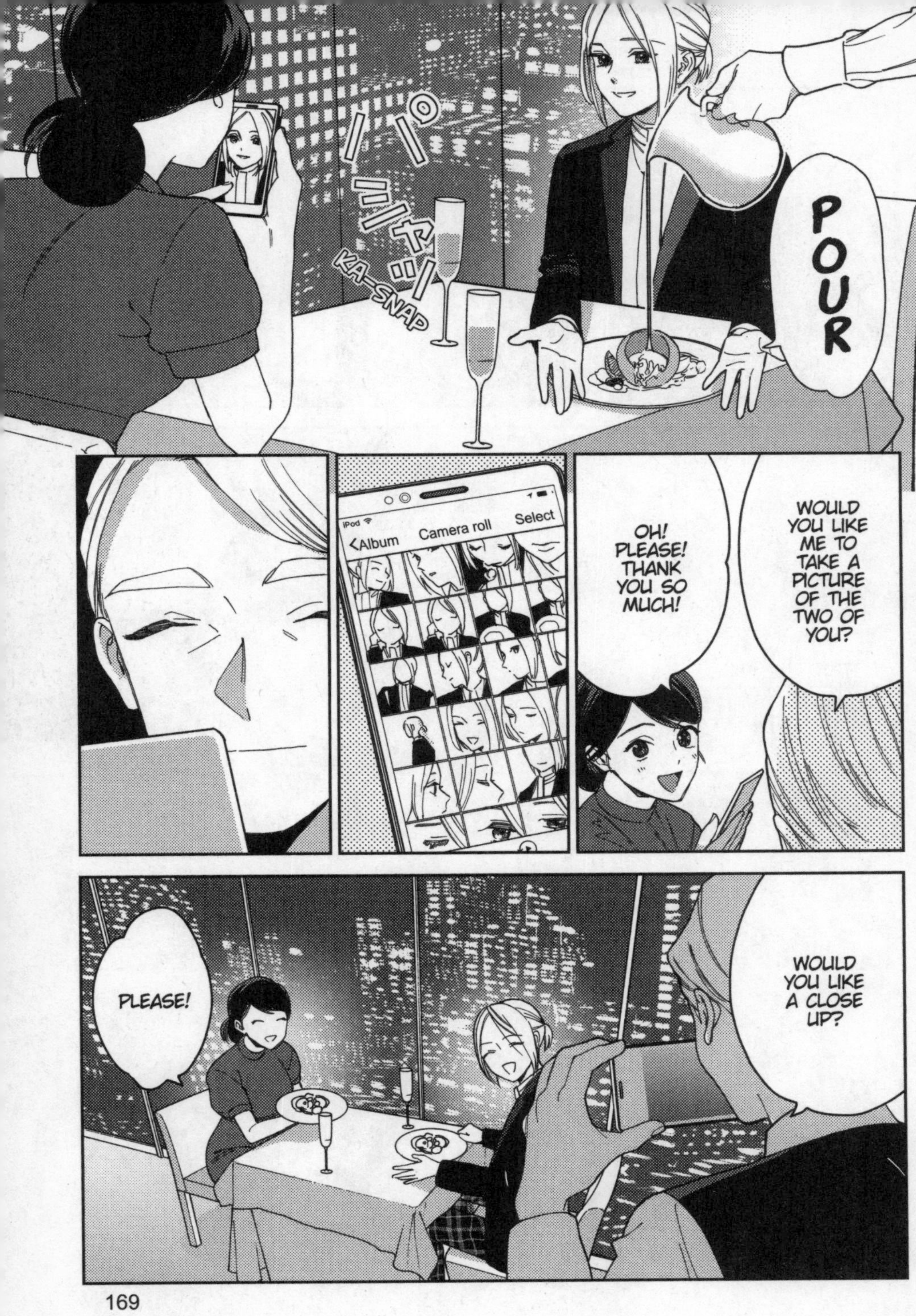
POUR
KA-SNAP
WOULD YOU LIKE ME TO TAKE A PICTURE OF THE TWO OF YOU?
OH! PLEASE! THANK YOU SO MUCH!
iPod
<Album Camera roll Select
WOULD YOU LIKE A CLOSE UP?
PLEASE!

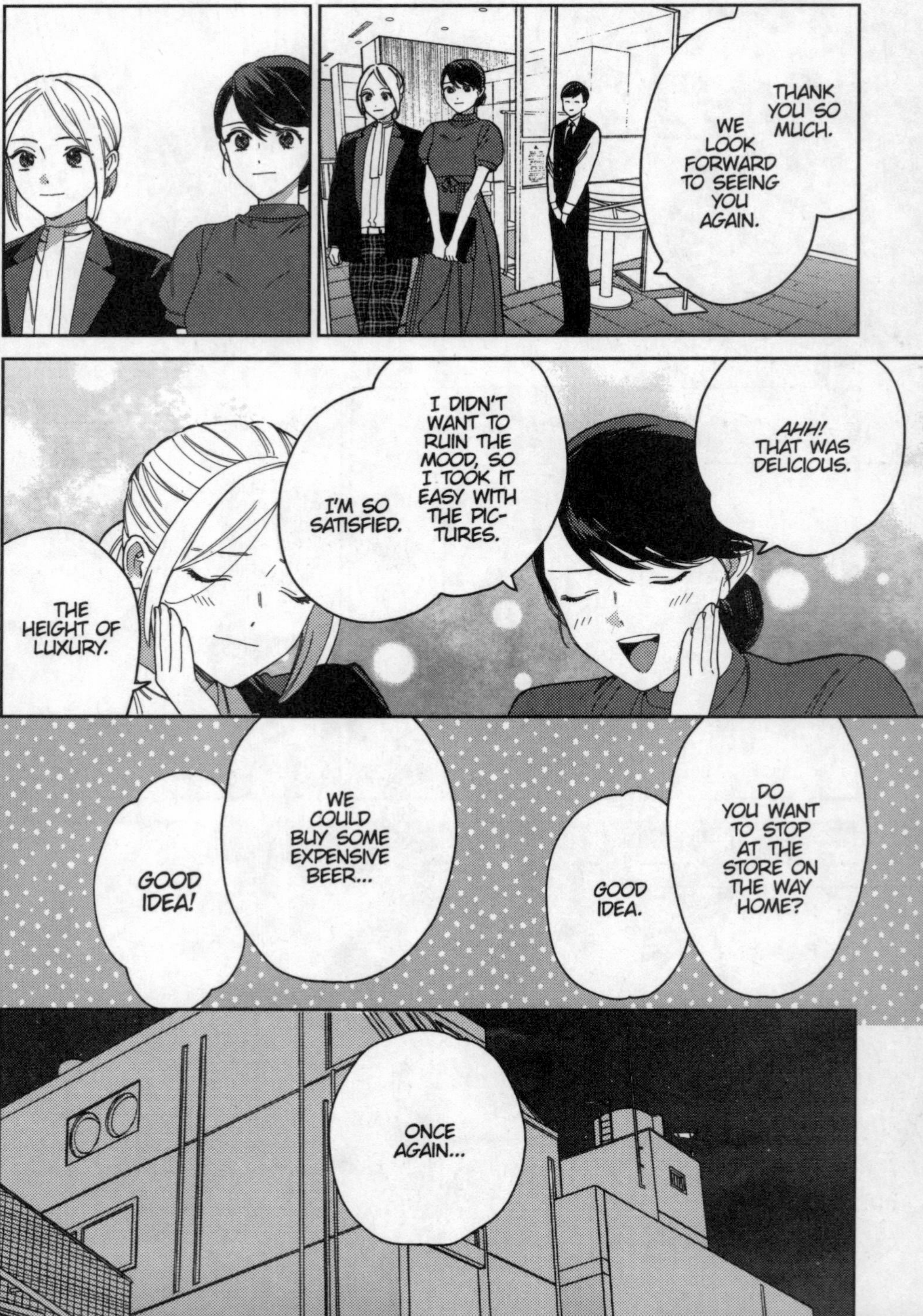
THANK YOU SO MUCH.
WE LOOK FORWARD TO SEEING YOU AGAIN.
AHH! THAT WAS DELICIOUS.
I DIDN'T WANT TO RUIN THE MOOD, SO I TOOK IT EASY WITH THE PIC-TURES.
I'M SO SATISFIED.
THE HEIGHT OF LUXURY.
DO YOU WANT TO STOP AT THE STORE ON THE WAY HOME?
GOOD IDEA.
WE COULD BUY SOME EXPENSIVE BEER...
GOOD IDEA!
ONCE AGAIN...

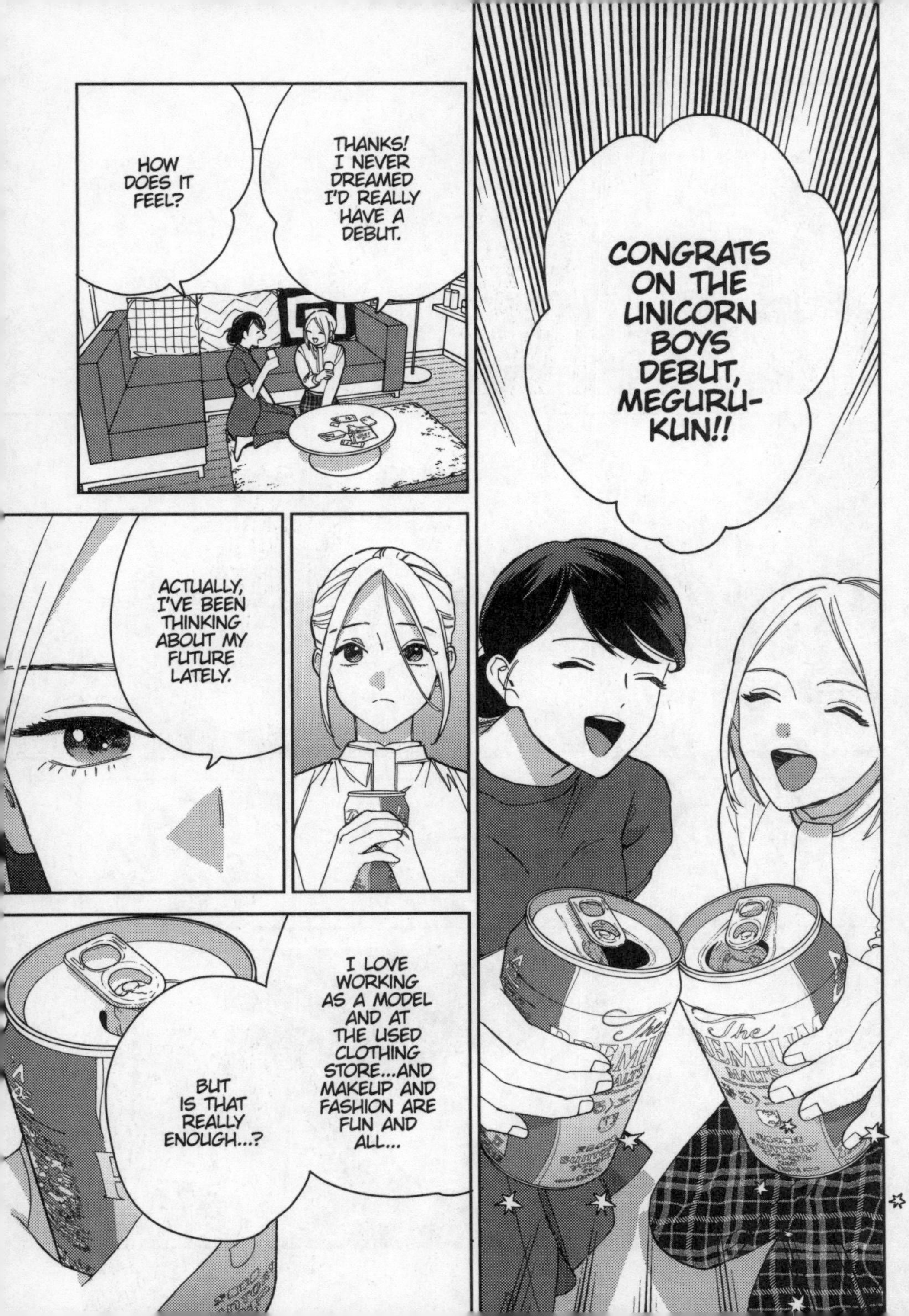
CONGRATS ON THE UNICORN BOYS DEBUT, MEGURU-KUN!!
THANKS! I NEVER DREAMED I'D REALLY HAVE A DEBUT.
HOW DOES IT FEEL?
ACTUALLY, I'VE BEEN THINKING ABOUT MY FUTURE LATELY.
I LOVE WORKING AS A MODEL AND AT THE USED CLOTHING STORE...AND MAKEUP AND FASHION ARE FUN AND ALL...
BUT IS THAT REALLY ENOUGH...?

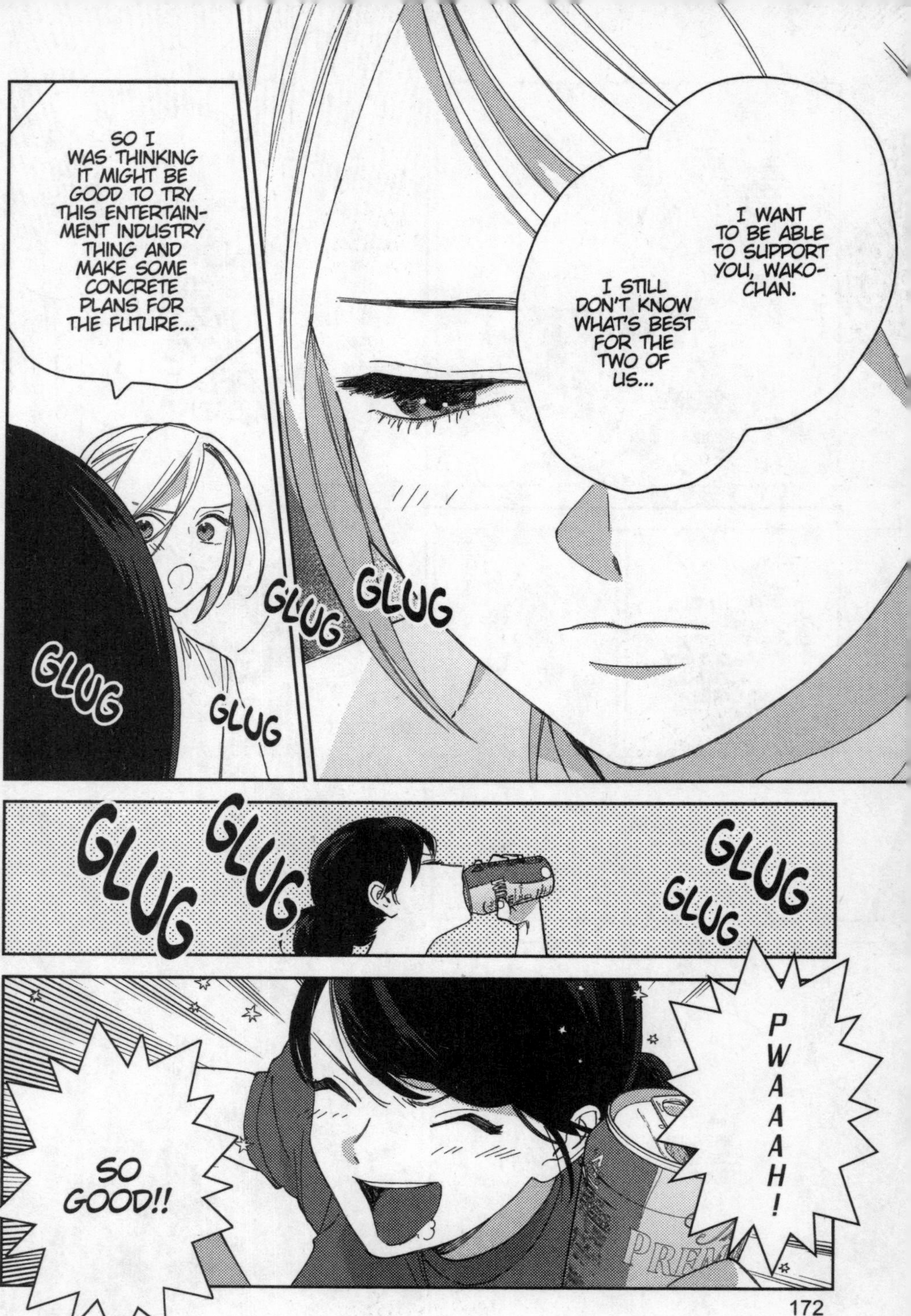
I WANT TO BE ABLE TO SUPPORT YOU, WAKO-CHAN.
I STILL DON'T KNOW WHAT'S BEST FOR THE TWO OF US...
GLUG
GLUG
SO I WAS THINKING IT MIGHT BE GOOD TO TRY THIS ENTERTAINMENT-MENT INDUSTRY THING AND MAKE SOME CONCRETE PLANS FOR THE FUTURE...
GLUG
GLUG
GLUG
GLUG
GLUG
GLUG
PWAAAH!
SO GOOD!!

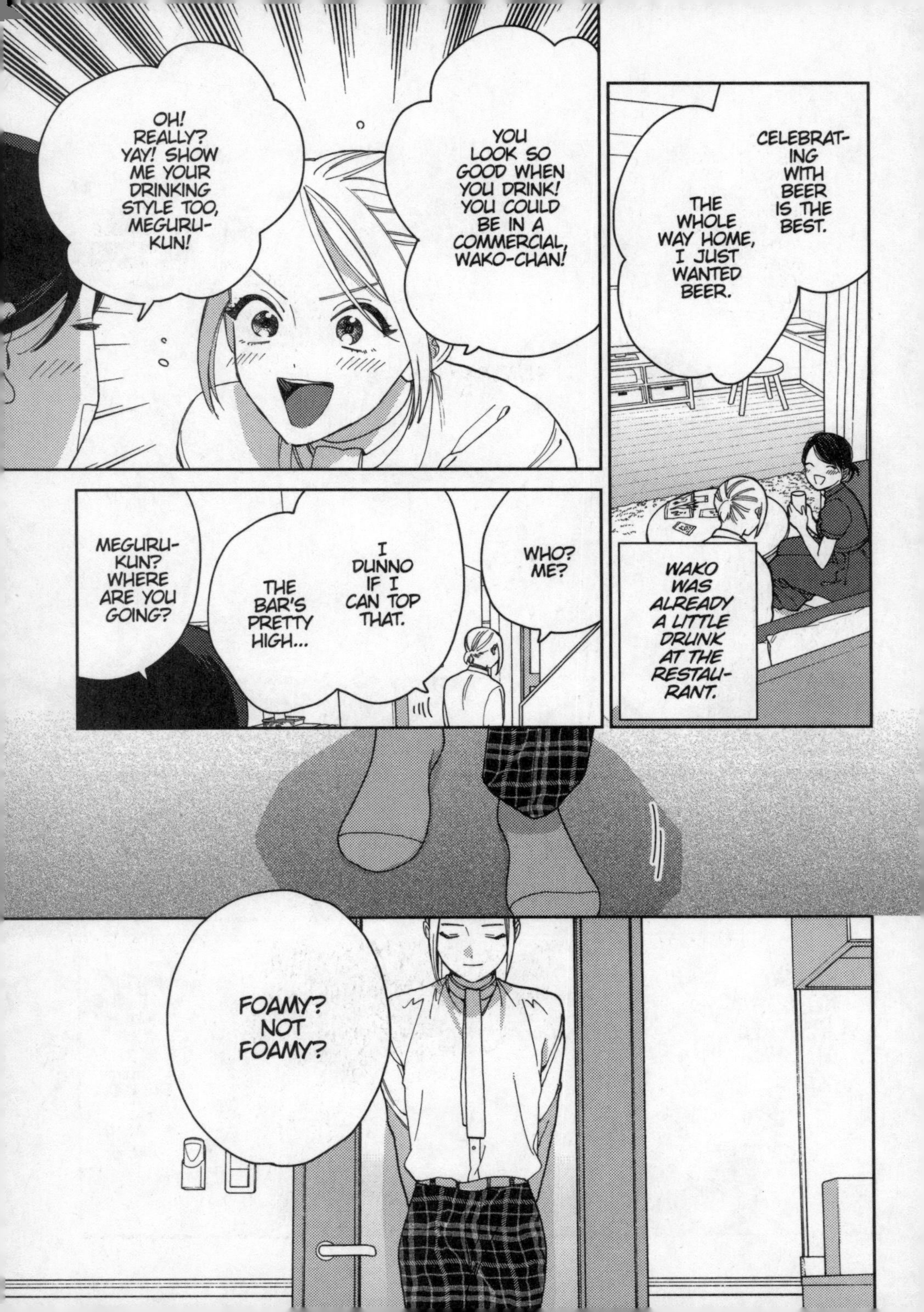
CELEBRATING WITH BEER IS THE BEST.
THE WHOLE WAY HOME, I JUST WANTED BEER.
WAKO WAS ALREADY A LITTLE DRUNK AT THE RESTAURANT.
YOU LOOK SO GOOD WHEN YOU DRINK! YOU COULD BE IN A COMMERCIAL, WAKO-CHAN!
OH! REALLY? YAY! SHOW ME YOUR DRINKING STYLE TOO, MEGURU-KUN!
WHO? ME?
I DUNNO IF I CAN TOP THAT.
THE BAR'S PRETTY HIGH...
MEGURU-KUN? WHERE ARE YOU GOING?
FOAMY? NOT FOAMY?

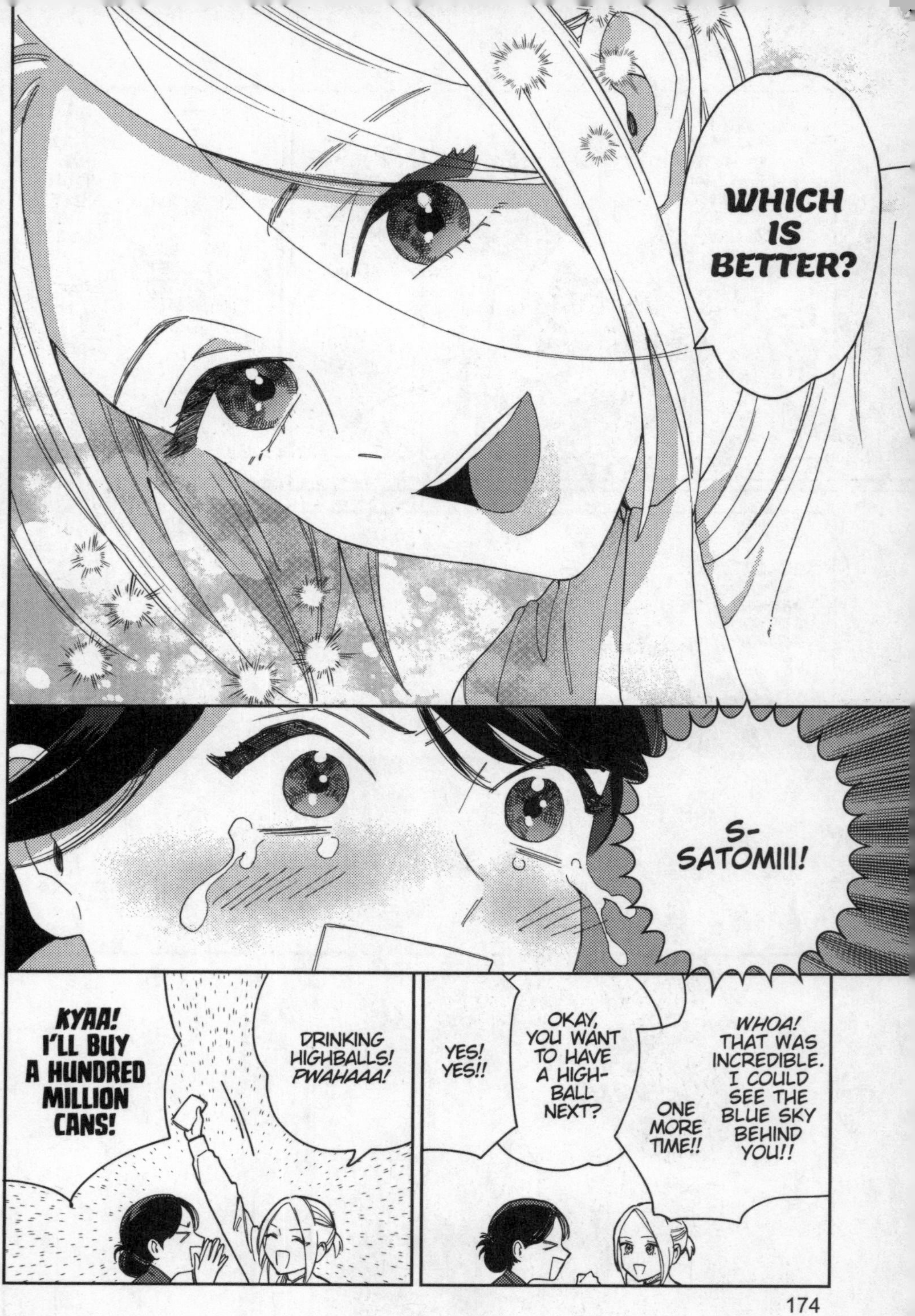
WHICH IS BETTER?
S-SATOMIII!
WHOA! THAT WAS INCREDIBLE. I COULD SEE THE BLUE SKY BEHIND YOU!!
ONE MORE TIME!!
OKAY, YOU WANT TO HAVE A HIGH-BALL NEXT?
YES! YES!!
DRINKING HIGHBALLS! *PWAHAAA!*
KYAA! I'LL BUY A HUNDRED MILLION CANS!

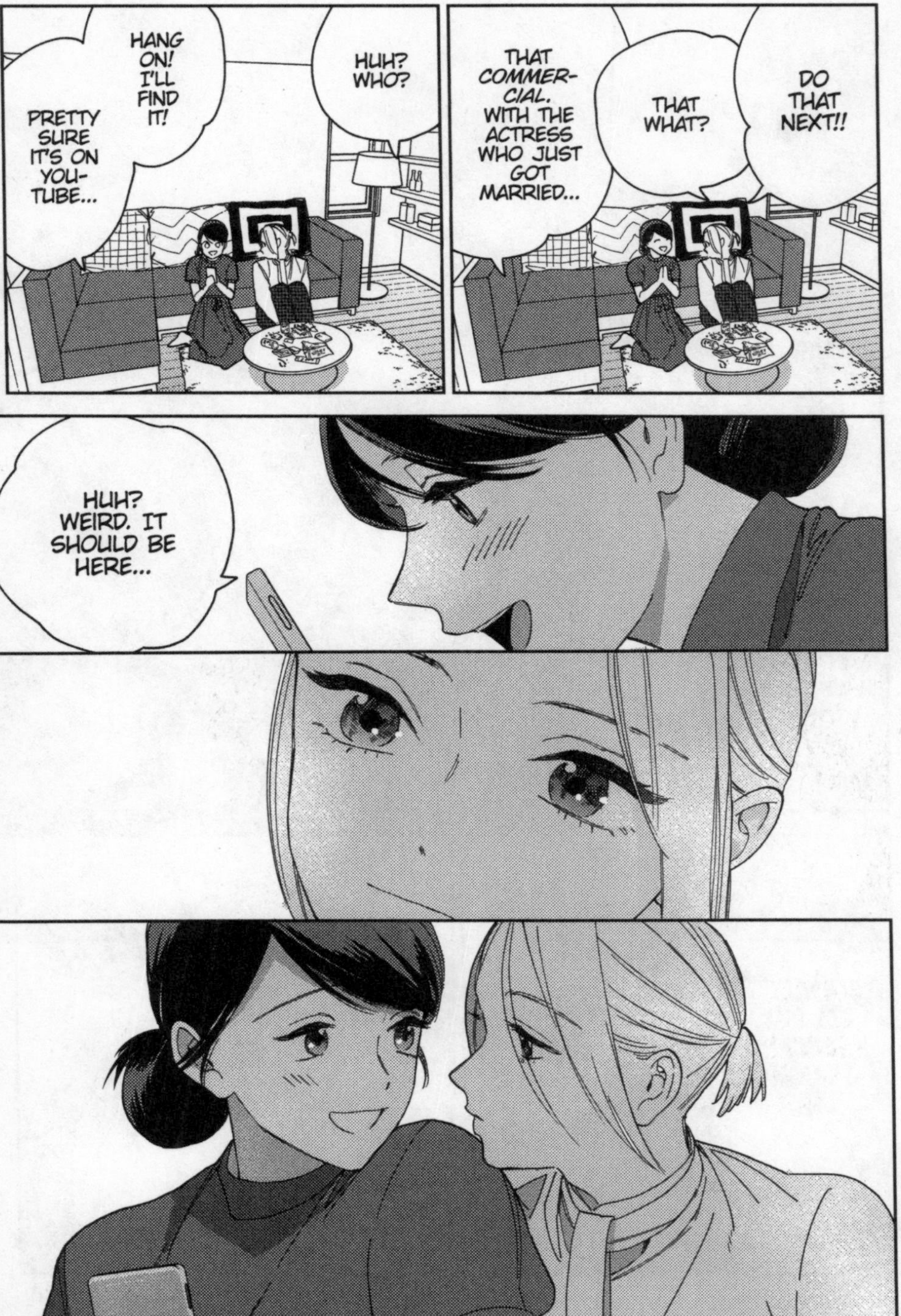
DO THAT NEXT!!
THAT WHAT?
THAT COMMERCIAL. WITH THE ACTRESS WHO JUST GOT MARRIED...
HUH? WHO?
HANG ON! I'LL FIND IT!
PRETTY SURE IT'S ON YOUTUBE...
HUH? WEIRD. IT SHOULD BE HERE...

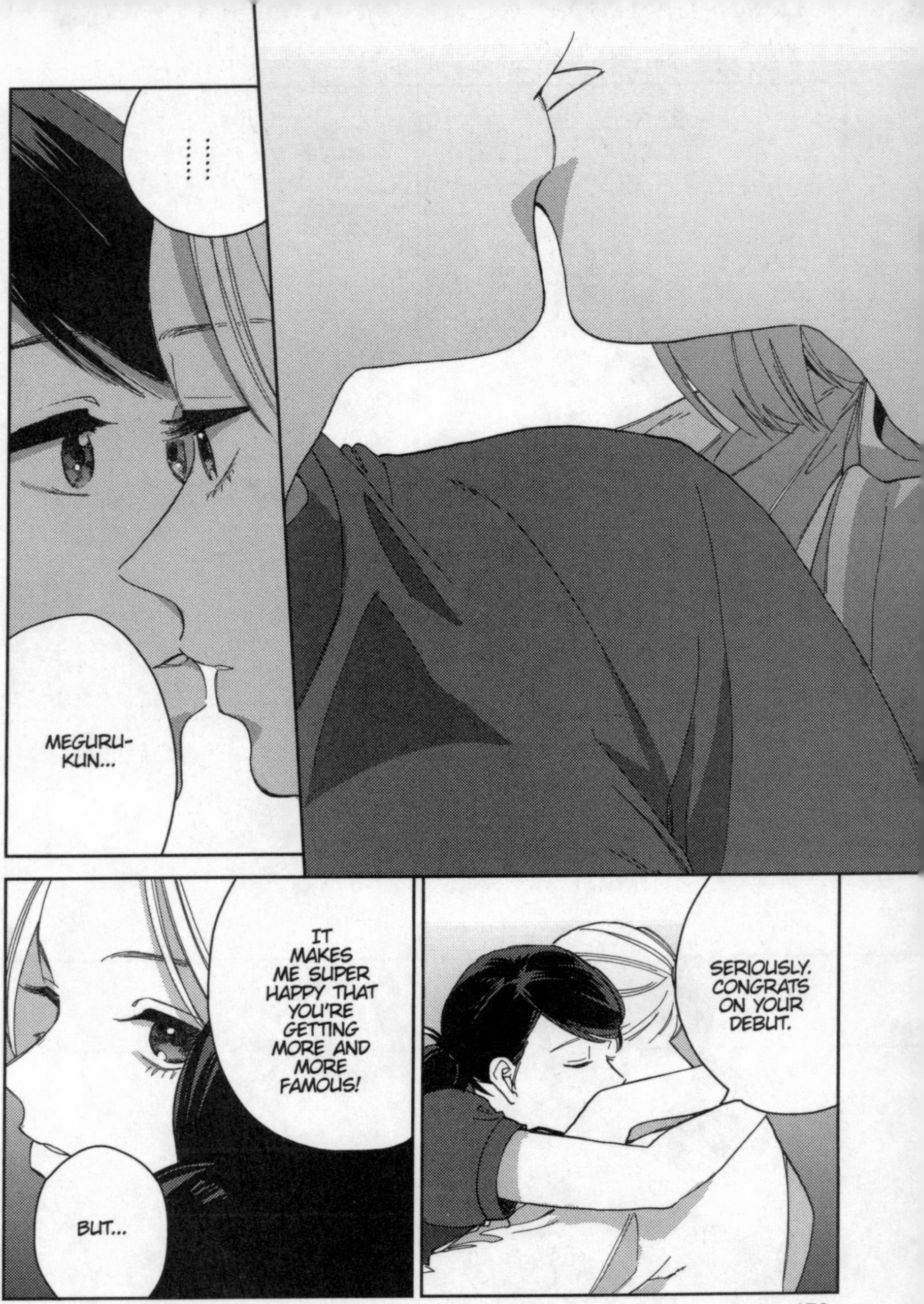
......
MEGURU-KUN...
SERIOUSLY. CONGRATS ON YOUR DEBUT.
IT MAKES ME SUPER HAPPY THAT YOU'RE GETTING MORE AND MORE FAMOUS!
BUT...

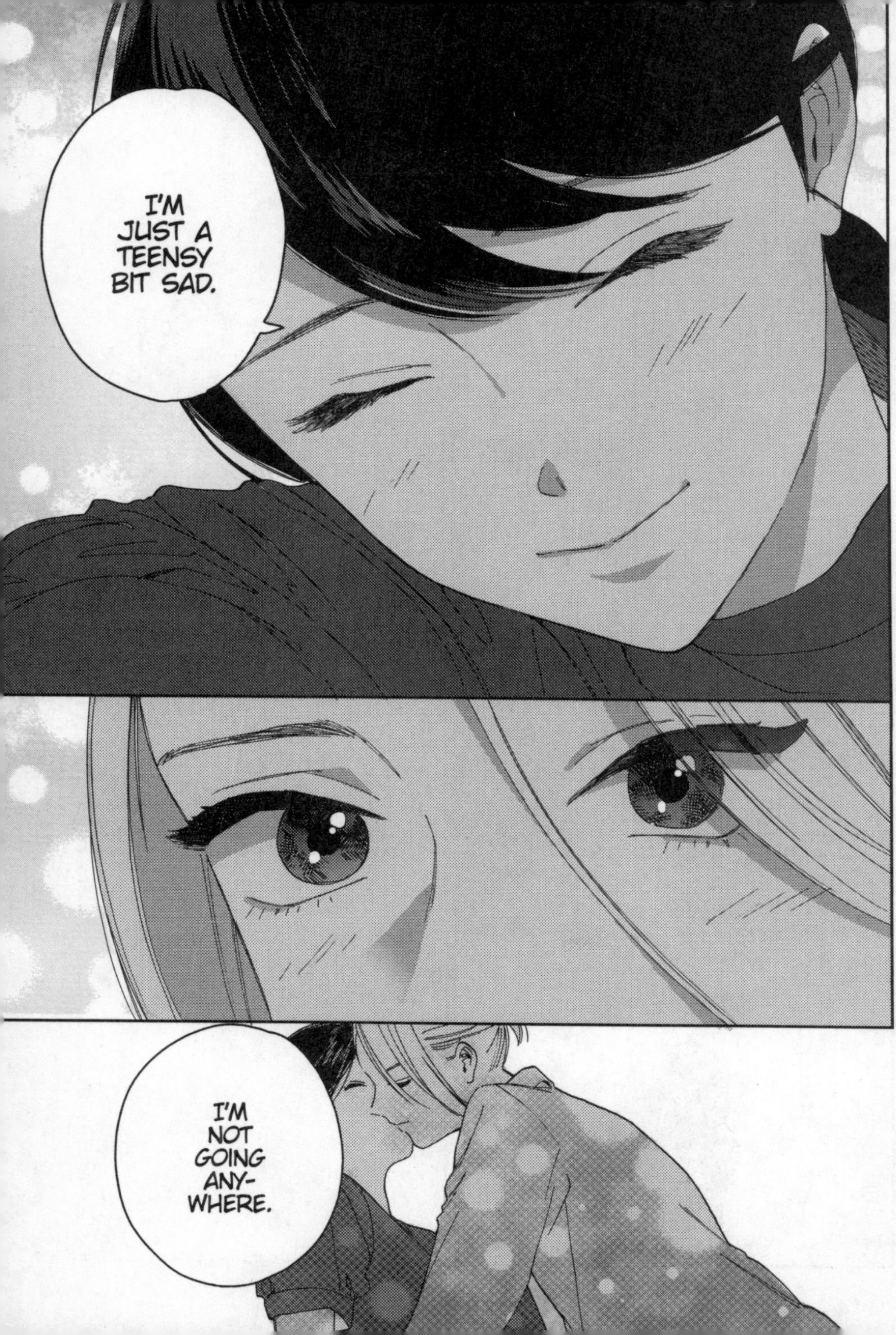
I'M JUST A TEENSY BIT SAD.
I'M NOT GOING ANY-WHERE.

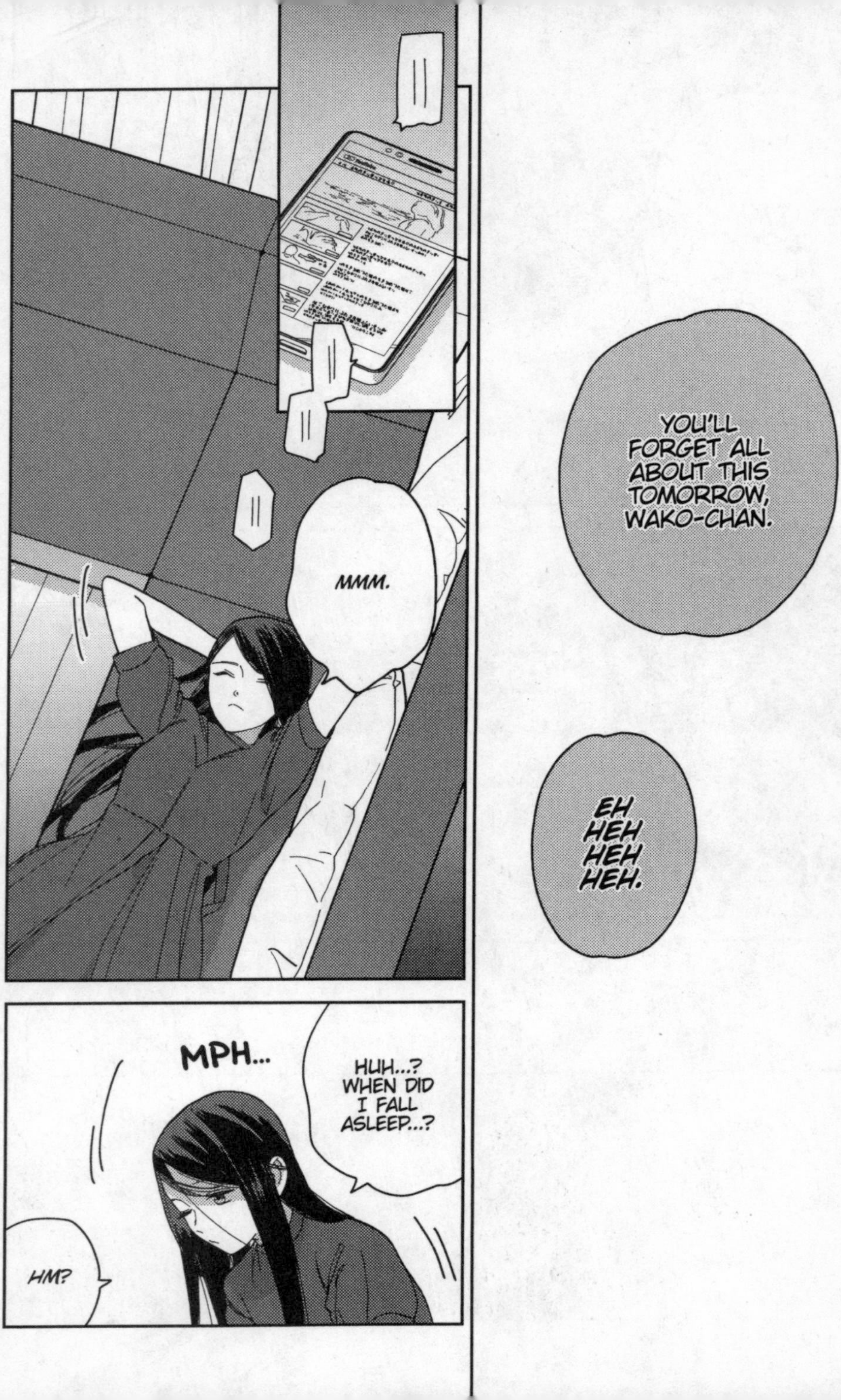
YOU'LL FORGET ALL ABOUT THIS TOMORROW, WAKO-CHAN.
EH HEH HEH HEH.
MMM.
MPH...
HUH...? WHEN DID I FALL ASLEEP...?
HM?

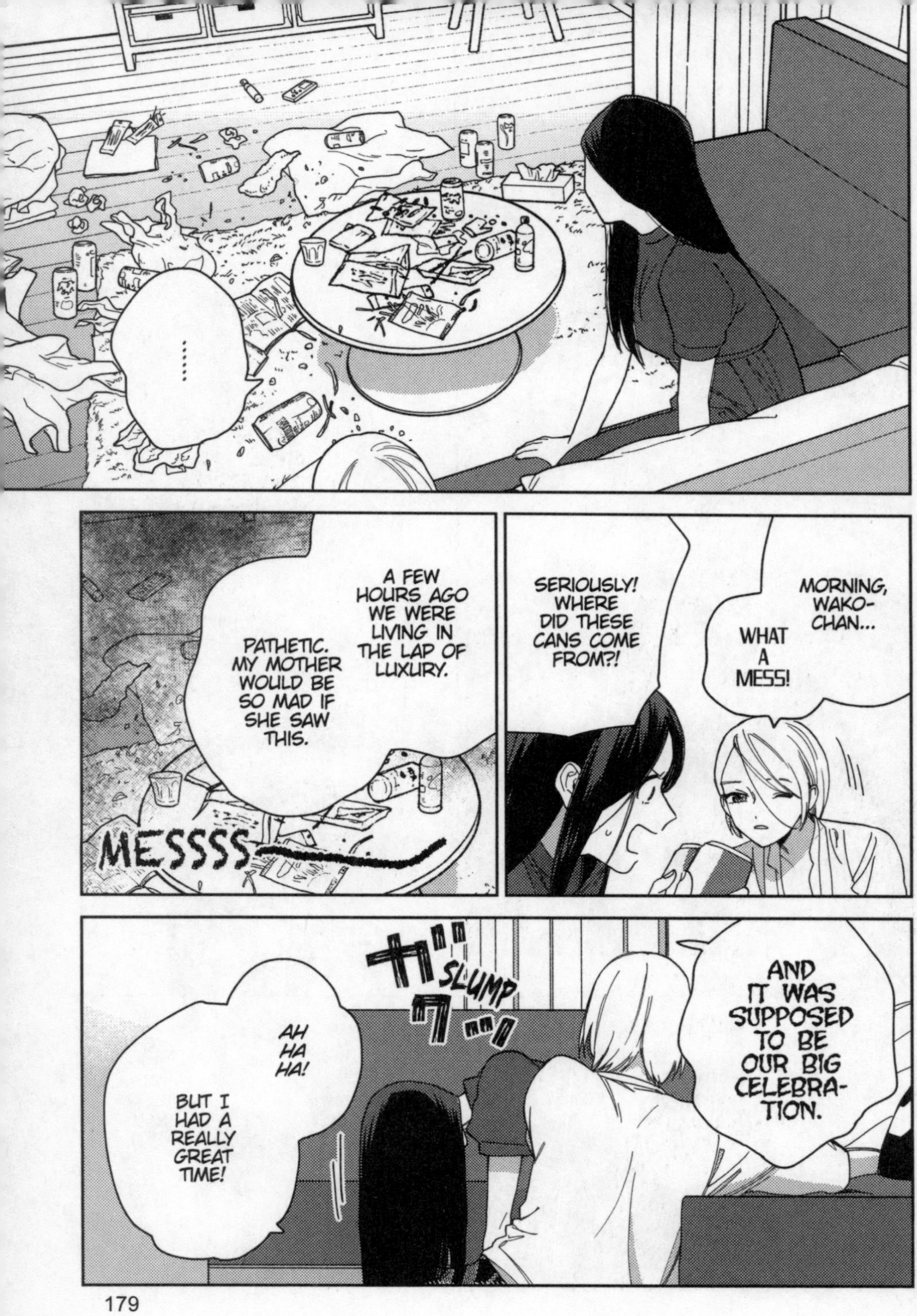
……
MORNING, WAKO-CHAN... WHAT A MESS!
SERIOUSLY! WHERE DID THESE CANS COME FROM?!
A FEW HOURS AGO WE WERE LIVING IN THE LAP OF LUXURY.
PATHETIC. MY MOTHER WOULD BE SO MAD IF SHE SAW THIS.
MESSSS—
AND IT WAS SUPPOSED TO BE OUR BIG CELEBRATION.
ガクッ
SLUMP
AH HA HA!
BUT I HAD A REALLY GREAT TIME!

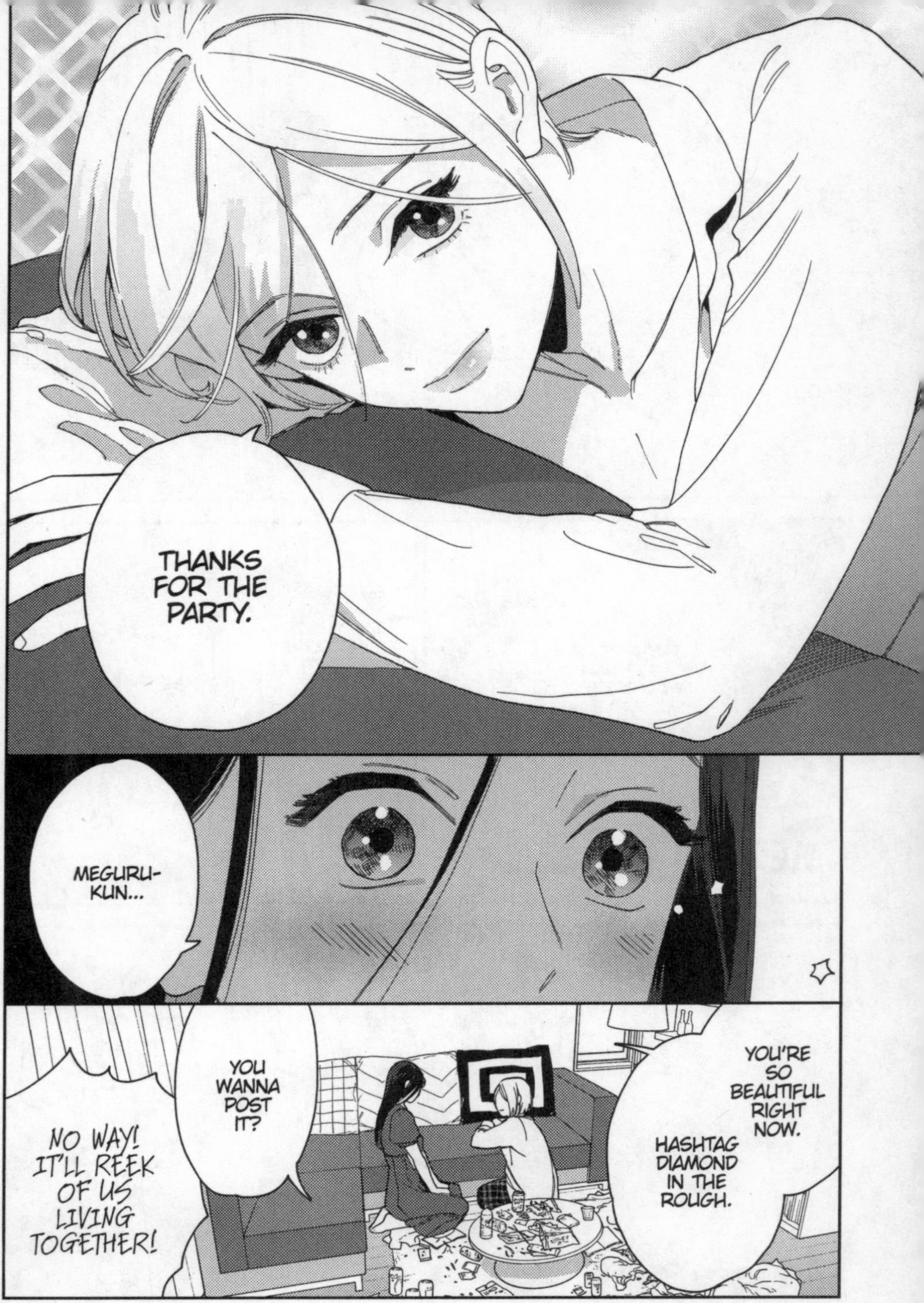
THANKS FOR THE PARTY.
MEGURU-KUN...
YOU'RE SO BEAUTIFUL RIGHT NOW.
HASHTAG DIAMOND IN THE ROUGH.
YOU WANNA POST IT?
NO WAY! IT'LL REEK OF US LIVING TOGETHER!

To be continued ...

My Androgynous Boyfriend